FROM
ANTIETAM
TO FORT FISHER

FROM ANTIETAM TO FORT FISHER

The Civil War Letters of Edward King Wightman, 1862–1865

Edited by Edward G. Longacre

RUTHERFORD • MADISON • TEANECK
FAIRLEIGH DICKINSON UNIVERSITY PRESS
LONDON AND TORONTO: ASSOCIATED UNIVERSITY PRESSES

© 1985 by Associated University Presses, Inc.

Associated University Presses
440 Forsgate Drive
Cranbury, NJ 08512

Associated University Presses
25 Sicilian Avenue
London WC1A 2QH, England

Associated University Presses
2133 Royal Windsor Drive
Unit 1
Mississauga, Ontario
Canada L5J 1K5

Library of Congress Cataloging in Publication Data

Wightman, Edward King, 1835–1865.
  From Antietam to Fort Fisher.

  Bibliography: p.
  Includes index.
  1. Wightman, Edward King, 1835–1865. 2. United
States. Army. Regiment Infantry, New York Volunteers,
9th (1861–1863)—Biography. 3. United States. Army.
Regiment Infantry, New York Volunteers, 3rd (1861–1865)—
Biography. 4. United States—History—Civil War, 1861–
1865—Personal narratives. 5. New York (State)—History
—Civil War, 1861–1865—Personal narratives.
6. Soldiers—New York (N.Y.)—Biography.
7. New York (N.Y.)—Biography. I. Longacre, Edward G.,
1946–   . II. Title.
E523.5.9TH.W53 1985   973.7'447   83-49343
ISBN 0-8386-3210-6

Printed in the United States of America

for Ann and Katie

CONTENTS

Preface   9

Prologue: Off to the Wars   23

1 Antietam   25

2 Pleasant Valley and Loudoun County   55

3 Falmouth and Fredericksburg   78

4 Newport News and Suffolk   112

5 Charleston   145

6 Bermuda Hundred and Cold Harbor   168

7 Petersburg   190

8 Fort Fisher   217

   Epilogue: A Father's Journey   230

   Notes   247

   Index   285

PREFACE

We suffer from no lack of Civil War letters, diaries, or memoirs. Of the countless first-person accounts that are extant, many hundreds have found their way
into print. During the centennial years of 1961–65 it sometimes seemed that a
book of letters or an article based on a journal or reminiscence rolled off the
presses daily. Unfortunately, of this great wealth of literature few works were
the product of well-educated soldiers with a background in professional writing.

A notable exception is the following collection of correspondence by a
young New Yorker, Edward King Wightman. His education—acquired at
what is now the City University of New York, where he received a B.A. in
1854 and a master's degree three years later—and his writing skill, honed
during a prewar career in journalism, enabled him to compose a war chronicle
that is remarkably articulate, graphic, and witty. Furthermore, the variety of
his service gave his letters great range of coverage and local color. As a private
in the Ninth New York Volunteer Infantry, and later as a noncommissioned
officer in the Third New York Volunteers, he saw action from September 1862
to January 1865 in southwestern Maryland; northern, middle, and southeastern
Virginia; and along the coasts of North and South Carolina.

Edward Wightman's writing talent and his insight into human nature allowed him to depict life in camp, on the march, and in battle with great depth
and perception. A conscientious soldier, never far from the firing line, he
convincingly portrayed the thoughts and fears of men called on to kill or be
killed. Moreover, as an avid student of history, strategy, and tactics, he studded
his letters with pithy observations on the men who commanded and the campaigns they conducted. He accomplished all of this in a vivid, graceful style
replete with metaphor, literary and Biblical allusion, and a degree of humor
missing from the personal narratives of most Civil War participants. He kept
his light touch even under the most trying circumstances—during grueling
marches, while eating wretched food, or sleeping outdoors on a frigid, rainy
night. And his ability to describe coolly even the most violent and dangerous

9

Edward King Wightman, ca. 1861 *(Photograph courtesy of Mrs. Edith Wightman Kreitler)*

moments in a soldier's life is further testimony to what his superiors recognized: that he was a courageous fighter, whose devotion to duty exacted the ultimate toll. On 15 January 1865 he was killed leading an assault across a parapet of Fort Fisher, North Carolina. His death prevented him from gaining a well-deserved promotion; his commission as lieutenant, though signed by the governor of New York the previous month, failed to reach him in time.

Edward Wightman was born in Middlebury, Connecticut, on 27 April 1835 the fourth child and third son of Stillman King Wightman (1803–99) and Clarissa Butler Wightman (1805–97). His family was of old English stock and possessed a strong religious heritage: tradition holds that he was named for Edward Wightman of Burton-upon-Trent, in 1612 the last English Baptist to be burned at the stake as a heretic during the reign of James I. The latter-day Edward's father was a Yale graduate, a two-term state senator from Connecticut, and a former speaker of the Connecticut Assembly. In 1843 Stillman Wightman relinquished a bright political future by moving his family to New York City and opening a private law practice. His career in the law was long and distinguished; some time before his death he was regarded as the oldest practicing attorney in Manhattan.

The rest of the Wightman clan (minus one daughter who died in early childhood) included Edward's elder brothers, Fred (1829–1911), their father's law partner, and James (1833–1919), a New York architect; his younger brother, Charles (1837–1934), for fifty-five years a Baptist minister on Long Island; and Edward's younger sisters, Mary (1836–1901) and Ellen Augusta (1841–99). Of the Wightman children, only Fred and Jim were married at the time of the Civil War; their wives, Abigail Hartley Wightman (1836–1912) and Lillie Hunter Wightman (?–1868), respectively, also comprised the audience for whom Ed-

Stillman King Wightman, ca. 1880 (*Photograph courtesy of Mrs. Edith Wightman Kreitler*)

Frederick Butler Wightman, 1856 *(Photograph courtesy of Mrs. Edith Wightman Kreitler)*

ward wrote. Other relatives, family friends, and college classmates swelled the
ranks of his wartime correspondents. Occasionally one wonders how Edward
had time to keep so many people informed and still tend to the demands of
soldiering. Being structured and methodical, he did find time, though he often
resorted to expedients such as sending a single letter to the family via Fred—
who was asked to censor the more earthy and sanguinary missives before the
womenfolk saw them.

Many of the qualities that marked Edward Wightman in uniform were already manifest during his college years. From sixteen to twenty-two he studied
at the New York Free Academy, where teachers and fellow students regarded
him as a singular youth. One of his classmates noted that "he was beloved and

admired as a warm-hearted, indomitable, shy, and eccentric student—distinguished for a rare humor and roguery; for consummate skill in drawing, wherein he was an irresistibly grotesque caricaturist; for enviable prowess as a gymnist [*sic*], and a ring-leader in out-of-door sports; for a signal unselfishness of disposition; and for that true nobility in friendship which is the mark of a fine nature. His chief and controlling fault was an over-modesty, which often took the form of self-distrustfulness." Looking back after Edward's death, another classmate agreed: "he was always so retired and reticent in his ways that much of his earnestness and worth was concealed from the observation of others. Nevertheless, his whole after-career was marked by the same quiet, unflinching thoroughness and truthfulness that made him a *man*. . . ."

From such descriptions, we know that he was a powerfully built young man. He stood one inch shy of six feet tall, weighed about 170 pounds, and sported a stocky build, broad shoulders, and a square jaw which during the war was fringed with long side-whiskers and a neatly combed beard. At college he was known for a feat of strength and agility "which probably no other member of the Institution could have performed"; draping a rope from the tower of one of the tallest buildings on campus, he ascended and descended the whole distance several times before an open-mouthed crowd.

After completing post-degree studies at the Free Academy, he became, successively, a physician's apprentice (a field he soon abandoned), a hardware clerk, a teacher, and a bookkeeper. During much of this time, he was also a frequent contributor to New York newspapers. His initial experience in publishing demonstrated what an associate called "an enlarged compass and depth of thought" and brought him employment with a number of trade papers in Manhattan. His longest affiliation was with the *Shoe and Leather Reporter*, an influential journal that also maintained offices in Philadelphia and Boston. Several of his *Reporter* articles were so well-researched and so relevant to the international scene that they were also carried in German, British, and French journals. Reprints of one article, which featured economic statistics never before collected, were ordered by the United States Home Department, the forerunner of the Department of the Interior.

It was while he labored for the *Reporter* that civil conflict broke out. Thousands of New Yorkers succumbed to war fever, enlisting in the ranks of the Union. Though wishing to join them, Edward resisted the urge to leave his job and his family. He did not know, however, how long he could hold back. As his employers noted: "he informed us that while nothing else on his part was likely to sunder his connection with the *Shoe and Leather Reporter*, he should feel it his duty, in case of a deficiency of men, to enlist in the service of the country."

That time came in August 1862, sixteen months after hostile cannon in Charleston harbor had precipitated war. A crisis had developed when Major General George B. McClellan's offensive against the Confederate capital at Richmond bogged down in defeat and frustration along the Virginia peninsula,

Colonel Rush C. Hawkins *(standing second from left)* and Officers and Men of "Hawkins's Zouaves" *(Photograph courtesy of the National Archives)*

spreading gloom throughout the North. Robert E. Lee's Army of Northern Virginia now poised to invade hitherto inviolate Union territory, while foreign nations moved ever closer to intervening on behalf of the Confederacy. Seeking to reassert the federal government's commitment to winning the war, President Abraham Lincoln called for the enlistment of 300,000 additional volunteers and an equal number of militiamen. He gave each state a recruitment quota; that of New York, the most populous state, was the highest. In quick time state and local officials organized rallies, parades, and other gatherings to support the war and attract enlistees. New regiments sprang into existence, while recruiters from veteran outfits stumped New York City, seeking new blood to replace combat losses.

Edward Wightman could wait no longer. Assured of employment upon his return from service, he took leave from his job and signed the muster rolls. Instead of throwing in with a new and unproven unit, he chose a three-year enlistment with one of the city's most popular and experienced regiments, the Ninth New York (more familiarly known as "Hawkins's Zouaves," after its dashing young commander, Colonel Rush C. Hawkins). Its men wore uniforms then much in vogue: short blue jackets trimmed with red lace, baggy red pants, red fezzes, and gaiters—attire patterned after that of French colonial forces serving in Algeria. But looking natty was not Edward's primary concern. As he told his family a few days later, he had cast his lot with the Ninth "because its reputation for courage, based on actual test, assures me against being disgraced . . . [and] because the class of men comprising it is much better than the average." On the first count, at least, he was correct: the regiment had distinguished itself during operations in North Carolina as a part of Major General Ambrose E. Burnside's command, the forerunner of the Ninth Army Corps. As to its "class of men," however, there could be two widely divergent opinions. On occasion Edward would describe his new comrades as frisky, spirited, and energetic, but basically decent and honest. At other times he would write disgustedly of their tendency to loot, steal, drink, brawl, curse, and defy authority.

For the next seven months, Edward's story was the story of the field service of Hawkins's Zouaves. Joining the regiment in upper Maryland during McClellan's attempt to halt Lee's incursion, he observed the closing scenes of the Antietam campaign. Three days before he reported at regimental headquarters, the Ninth New York was bloodied in battle outside the village of Sharpsburg during the deadliest single day's fighting of the war. There followed a two-month period of rest and recuperation, during which the new recruit settled comfortably into the ranks of Company B.

By November 1862 the Zouaves's erstwhile corps leader, Burnside, had replaced McClellan in army command. Under the bewhiskered New Englander, the Army of the Potomac moved on Fredericksburg, Virginia, where Lee's outnumbered but aggressive veterans lay in wait. On December 13, west and south of that colonial-era village, the Union troops took part in one of the most disastrous offensives in military history. Bringing up the rear during an assault against well-fortified positions on high ground, the Ninth New York suffered heavily. In his first combat experience, Private Wightman bore himself coolly amid a murderous storm of musketry and cannon fire. Miraculously, he escaped unhurt.

In February 1863 the Ninth New York, with a part of the Ninth Corps, was transferred to garrison duty in southeastern Virginia. For the next three months the regiment participated in a spasmodic, confused, and ultimately fruitless campaign to threaten Richmond from Suffolk and Portsmouth.

By May most of Hawkins's Zouaves had returned to New York, their two-year term of service concluded. Edward and other recruits who had joined the outfit after 1861 were shifted into a regiment with a longer service term to complete their enlistments. They were received into the Third New York, an outfit destined to remain in existence through the remainder of the conflict. The former Zouaves doffed their baggy pants and fezzes and donned the dark blue wool tunic, light blue kersey pants, French-style kepi, and standard-issue brogans that constituted the uniform of the majority of Union infantrymen.

Initially Private Wightman found it difficult to adjust to a regiment he considered inferior to his original unit. His displeasure did not abate during an ill-considered offensive below Richmond in which the Third New York participated in June and July 1863. In August the regiment was sent south aboard transports to become part of Major General Quincy A. Gillmore's Tenth Corps before Charleston. The campaign to capture South Carolina's largest city, already several months old, dragged on interminably. The siege troops were themselves besieged by lowland illnesses such as malaria and dysentery and by forced labor under a tropical sun. In the face of Charlestonians' resistance, the Union high command conceded defeat early in 1864. They shipped most of Gillmore's people, the Third New York included, to the main fighting front in Virginia.

This time the regiment became a part of the Army of the James, a command assigned the task of capturing Richmond, under Major General Benjamin F. Butler. In May and June now-Corporal Wightman and his comrades served in another failed campaign south of the enemy capital. First, they were thrashed by smaller Confederate forces above Bermuda Hundred, a peninsula formed by the James and Appomattox Rivers, inside which the luckless Federals were trapped like the contents of "a bottle, strongly corked." Next, many of Butler's troops, under his senior subordinate, Major General William Farrar ("Baldy") Smith, were sent by water and land to join the Army of the Potomac at a hamlet known as Cold Harbor, ten miles northeast of Richmond. There on June 1 and 3 the combined armies were decimated in a series of assaults against formidable defenses that resembled Fredericksburg for desperate heroism and ultimate futility. Fortunately for Edward Wightman, the Third New York, bringing up Smith's rear, reached the battlefield after most of the carnage had ceased.

The Army of the James then assembled outside Petersburg, the rail center twenty-odd miles below Richmond, by which the capital and Lee's army received most of their supplies and ordnance. In this sector most of Butler's troops were fated to spend the next ten months, baking under the sun, choked by dust, drenched with rain, and bedeviled by sniper fire and artillery barrages. If ever conditions were ripe to break a man, destroying his devotion to duty through stress and hardship, they were present here. But the newly promoted Sergeant Wightman refused to cave in under the strain. To his family he wrote optimistically of the situation, and he looked for a dramatic end to the tactical stalemate.

One beckoned on July 30, when coal miners-turned-soldiers detonated a gunpowder-filled shaft they had dug beneath a Rebel salient east of Petersburg. The resulting explosion tore a gaping hole in the enemy line and killed many defenders. But although plans had been made to exploit a breakthrough, every attack that followed the blast failed through mass confusion and a lack of coordination. White and black troops of the Army of the Potomac fled upon the arrival of Confederate infantry and artillery reinforcements; supporting troops such as the Third New York tried in vain to stem the rout.

The run of ill fortune plaguing the Union forces did not die, but neither did Edward's enthusiasm or his determination to see things out. A late September assault by the Army of the James against defenses on Richmond's doorstep resulted in the seizing of heavily manned Fort Harrison. A follow-up offensive, however, was beaten back just short of Fort Gilmer, key to the capital's works.

As the blue tide receded from Fort Gilmer, Edward displayed his anger and defiance for all to see. Observing the enemy's retreat, the fort's defenders shouted taunts and jeers at the men of Brigadier General Robert S. Foster's Second Division, Tenth Corps. Stung by this derision, Edward left a place of safety and walked, slowly and deliberately, to an exposed point on the forward line, heedless of the minié balls and shells whistling around him. Then he calmly turned about and marched, unscathed, to his regiment's new position in the rear.

This impulsive display hinted that he would not survive the war. Two months after Fort Gilmer, he enthusiastically participated in an amphibious expedition down the Atlantic coast to Wilmington, North Carolina. The objective was Fort Fisher, a heavy earthwork commanding the entrance to the last open Confederate seaport. An assault on Christmas Day 1864 failed wretchedly, largely as a result of Ben Butler's faintheartedness and tactical blundering. But a second expedition in January under an abler commander carried the "Confederate Gibraltar"—at a cost of some thirteen hundred Union casualties, one of whom was Edward Wightman.

His peers and superiors mourned his loss with sincere emotion. So too, of course, did his family, once they learned of his death from New York newspapers. Without hesitating, his father set out alone for North Carolina to recover his body and bring it north. On 11 February 1865 the remains of Edward King Wightman were committed to the earth in the presence of relatives and friends from the town of his birth, barely nine months after he had celebrated his twenty-ninth birthday.

In his letters, Edward revealed a great deal about himself—his hopes, fears, dreams, and the factors that impelled him to trade a comfortable life and a bright future for the arduous and dangerous life of a soldier. While displaying a devotion to the cause of Union, he also demonstrated a tolerance of the privations and hardships of service. He treated soldiering as an occasionally disagreeable duty, but one that, if properly discharged, brought the greatest personal satisfaction. He was, from first to last, a hard-war man, committed to a swift and successful prosecution of the conflict by all honorable means. Even so, he neither hated nor maligned his enemy, whom he refused to view as a soulless personification of evil. He had compassion, too, for civilians, Southern as well as Northern, caught in the maelstrom of war, and he scorned to loot or pillage, even on order. Reflecting his family's political leanings, he considered himself a Democrat, but he supported the Republican administration responsible for carrying on the conflict. In fact, he seemed apolitical, praising those national leaders whom he felt worthy, regardless of party affilation, and deprecating all whom he considered lax, indecisive, or incompetent. He was especially hard on army officers: many of them he thought overly concerned with protecting their own skins or with gaining political influence. This helps to explain why he so often refused a commission, preferring to remain in the ranks where he felt able to make a greater contribution to the service.

Some of his attitudes were very much the product of his times. Like many native Americans, he was sometimes derisive toward immigrants in the army, especially Germans and Irishmen, to whom he ascribed stereotypical characteristics. To some extent he was also prejudiced against blacks, occasionally portraying them as buffoons or overgrown children. At other times, however, he decried their treatment at the hands of whites and protected them from physical and verbal abuse. He admired black men in uniform: although he criticized their performance at the Petersburg mine disaster, he praised the valor they displayed at other points in that campaign, especially during their breakthrough of Confederate defenses northeast of the "Cockade City" on 15 June 1864.

Well informed on strategy, tactics, and the intricacies of civil-military relations, Edward viewed people and events from a broader and deeper perspective than the average enlisted man. Although he sometimes told his family that they knew as much about military movements as he did, he seems to have kept his thumb on the pulse of the army with remarkable deftness. In part this stemmed from his occasional clerkship duties at company, regimental, and garrison headquarters, where he was privy to fact and rumor emanating from the uppermost levels of command. And in part this was owing to his constant desire to know what he and his comrades were doing, where they were headed, how they were getting on, and—as far as could be determined—what the future held for them.

In brief, he represented the best type of American volunteer—brave, intelligent, resourceful, dutiful, and patriotic. And he was a good enough writer and an honest enough man to let these qualities show without appearing egotistical or self-promotive.

In preparing Edward Wightman's correspondence for publication, the editor has striven to preserve its integrity as a historical source. He has excised purely personal information of little interest to the general reader, redundant material (often Edward recorded the same event, in nearly identical language, for more than one correspondent), and passages that cannot be deciphered from the original text, parts of which have faded or been torn. All deletions are indicated by ellipses. Wightman's occasional lapses in spelling and capitalization remain intact. The only major changes involve additional paragraphing and the standardization of his eccentric use of the comma, his single stylistic failing. Left untouched are several pet expressions that may at first confound but which in time become meaningful. One example is the curious adjective "bedoozling," which apparently indicated the ultimate: any person, place, or thing that astonished or delighted. Other expressions in his letters may strike readers as anachronistic: the term "go-cart," which he applied to army vehicles, and "sock it to 'em," a shout of glee and encouragement. Brackets within the text denote brief editorial insertions, including the names of people and places Edward only partially identified. Longer editorial commentary has been placed in notes grouped at the rear of the text.

Throughout his work the editor has enjoyed the kind cooperation of Mrs. Edith Wightman Kreitler and her husband, R. David Kreitler, of Radnor, Pennsylvania. Mrs. Kreitler, the great-niece of Sergeant Wightman, extended permission to publish the letters as well as the memoir of Stillman King Wightman, a longer version of which originally appeared in *American Heritage* (and which has been edited in the same fashion as Edward's correspondence). Mrs. Kreitler also provided valuable information about her ancestor and his family prior to and during the Civil War. The entire project was made possible by the efforts of her brother, the late Dr. Henry Booth Wightman, to decipher, transcribe, and preserve the original letters.

Several historians and librarians assisted in compiling the annotated information, including Marie Ashley, the historian of Cromwell, Connecticut; Nancy Robbins, of the Thomas S. Power Library, Offutt Air Force Base, Nebraska; Russ Pritchard, curator of the War Library and Museum, National Commandery, Military Order of the Loyal Legion of the United States, in Philadelphia; Barbara Dunlap, Chief, Archives and Special Collections, Library of the City College of the City University of New York; and Linda M. Matthews, reference archivist at the Robert W. Woodruff Library for Advanced Studies, Emory University, Atlanta (where both a typescript and a microfilm copy of 135 of Sergeant Wightman's letters repose). For assistance in reproducing the photographs, maps, and engravings used as illustrations, I thank Henry M. Narducci, Jr., and Bob Hoffert. Finally, acknowledgment is paid to *American Heritage* and to the other magazines and journals in which Wightman letters have appeared: *Civil War History,* The *Lincoln Herald,* The *Maryland Historical Magazine,* The *South Carolina Historical Magazine, American History Illustrated,* and *Manuscripts.*

FROM
ANTIETAM
TO FORT FISHER

PROLOGUE
Off to the Wars

[Writing to the distaff side of his family, then vacationing at the Wightman summer home in Connecticut, Edward detailed his reasons for going to war. And in a brief note to brother Fred in New York eleven days later, he demonstrated that he fully understood the consequences of his decision.]

New York, Sept. 1st, 1862

Dear Mother and Sisters:

I can no longer delay the task of communicating to you news which I fear you may regard as painful—a consideration which has hitherto deterred me from giving it.

At the outbreak of the war my first impulse was to join the army, but a thousand obstacles interposed, not the least of which, aside from all family ties, were business engagements from which I could not honorably retire. . . . I therefore worked on, not at all satisfied with my position but nevertheless amused with the idea that although debarred from the field as a soldier I was able through the press to exert an influence favorable to the Government. I knew, too, that there were men enough out of employment who considered it a privilege to enter the army because they had no other means of support.

But from the first I have been determined to step forward if others should pause. They have paused, and I have accordingly entered the ranks—not rashly nor with the spirit of adventure, but with a cool head and under a strong sense of duty. No action of my life has been so well considered and so deliberately taken.

My decision is, of course, irrevocable. I was sworn into the service of the United States on Saturday last [August 30] as a private in the 9th Regiment, N.Y. Volunteers (Hawkins Zouaves), now located at Fredericksburg, Va.,[1] in the Corps of General Burnside. This regiment was selected, 1st because it will take me at once where I can be useful; 2nd because its reputation for courage, based on actual test,[2] assures me against being disgraced; 3rd because the class of men comprising it is much better than the average.

I could have raised a company with little exertion with machinery at my disposal and backed by married men whose assistance would have been tendered for the asking; but the days of the past month have been too much crowded with odds and ends of unfinished business that I have had no time for the study of military tactics even if I could have prevailed upon myself to break a rule by incurring obligations for unpaid favors.

It is not only desirable that our family should have a representative in the army, but where we are so well able to furnish one, it would be beyond endurance disgraceful . . . for young men [to be] living peacefully and selfishly at home, while the land is rent by faction and threatened with ruin by violence. I have no hesitation in assuming to myself the right to go, for I believe myself better able to endure fatigue than any of the others, and moreover I have given so little attention to the cultivation of social relations that I have few ties to sever and my absence will scarcely be observed. No one depends upon me for support. My life has been the sedentary life of a student.

At present I can not write further. All my time is occupied, for I leave New York for Fredericksburg on Wednesday of this week, or at the latest on Friday. I shall, of course, try and run up and see you at Middletown, exactly when I can not tell. Don't let my movements, however, interfere in the least with yours, and, above all, don't write back any reproachful or melancholy letters. My course is marked out, and nothing mortal can alter it.

Whatever may be your reflections do not conceive the idea that I am acting in haste to repent in leisure. I am both too old and have too much to sacrifice to take such a step merely from love of change.

In haste,
Ed K. W.

Washington Friday Morn.
Sept. 12, 1862

Dear Fred:

I propose to give you occasional and truthful sketches of my experiences and impressions. They will come to you very irregularly and in crude condition. They are intended, however, only for your own eye, or if *you* choose, for the satisfaction of the male portion of the family. The women would be too much shocked at what is coming. I shall write more generally to them.

Please keep the notes I send you, for it is possible I may want to make use of them some day. They will constitute the only record of facts I can preserve.

In haste,
Ed K. W.

1
ANTIETAM

[On the morning of 10 September 1862 Private Wightman, in company with numerous other enlistees and the veterans who had recruited them, started from New York en route to the front, via Washington, D.C. The trip was slow and tiresome, but he stood the trial without complaint. Not even the rowdiness of his new comrades bothered him. As he wrote his father and brothers, his introduction to army life proved "rough, but no more disagreeable than I expected to find it."

After leaving the capital, the party went afoot and by wagon through southern Maryland, seeking their regiment. Along the way they encountered the flotsam and jetsam of the bloodiest day of the war. On the seventeenth as Wightman and friends passed through Frederick, Maryland, McClellan's troops attacked Lee's outside Sharpsburg, some fifteen miles to the west. In a series of uncoordinated assaults along Antietam Creek, the Federals menaced the enemy left flank and center before nearly collapsing the right, or southern, flank. Opposite Lee's right the Ninth New York Zouaves gave a powerful account of themselves at heavy cost. For a time they seemed to carry the day, but last-minute reinforcements enabled the Rebels to salvage a tactical draw. Earlier, McClellan had boasted of his ability to crush his foe if Lee remained in Maryland long enough to accept battle. He had failed to reckon with Southern pluck and tenacity.

Even so, Antietam was a strategic success for the Army of the Potomac; on the eighteenth and nineteenth Lee led his battered ranks south, his invasion at a close. When Wightman's group finally joined Hawkins's Zouaves on the twentieth, the Federals were resting and refitting, seemingly content to let their enemy return to Virginia without further molestation. Scrutinizing Confederate prisoners, Edward thought he saw why: he wrote admiringly of their fitness and fighting trim as well as of their dedication to principle ("the struggle for independence seems to have molded their features into inflexible severity and determination").

Settling into his place in the ranks, he also painted his family a picture of daily routine, touching on such diverse items as army sutlers (civilian merchants licensed to sell to the troops—often at exorbitant prices), rations, clothing, medical care, soldierly cleanliness—or lack of same—and some remarkable regimental mascots.]

> R. R. Cars Baltimore Washington
> written in the midst of a Babel of
> confusion—Take it as it is for I
> have no time to read over and correct
> —Ed
> [12 September 1862]

Dear Bro:[1]

You saw us leave the dock at N. York for Perth Amboy [South Amboy, New Jersey]. The distance was greater than I suspected but the trip was so pleasant down the bay and through the Kills[2] that I found no cause to grumble.

You observed the rough material of our recruits. We had no sooner steamed out into the North River than the characteristics of "the boys" began to manifest themselves. Every vessel that passed was saluted with a "hip-hip"—the men swinging their red fezes (caps) frantically in the air by the blue tassels and yelling at such a rate that their voices might have been heard for miles over the smooth water. The steamers screamed at us as they passed, the sailing vessels dipped their flags—male passengers shouted—ladies waved handkchfs [sic] and on shore every cow boy and old woman exerted his and her pipe to the utmost to cheer us.

The ZouZous,[3] however, as they expressed it, soon got a "belly full of glory" and turned their attention to other sources of amusement. It was found that Terry Brady of Co. I[4] could dance break-downs and that another fellow could "whistle as well as any man that ever cocked a lip"! Accordingly breakdowns became the order of the day, and for two hours shoe leather flew around in a way that opened the eyes of the Massachusetts men as beautifully as the Fulton [Street] Market fishmongers open oysters. Besides our squad there were on board parts of the Brooklyn 14th, New York 37th, and Mass. 10th.[5]

The other regiments were at length so overcome by the never tiring performances of the IXth that they couldn't forebear cheering. In return the 9th cheered everybody and everything. Everybody proposed that everybody else should drink out of everybody's canteen and smoke everybody's segars. A conglomerate scene followed, of course, and the fraternization became complete.

Somewhere between 8 and 9 o'clock we reached Amboy and entered the [railroad] cars for Philadelphia. We at once unslung knapsacks and whipped off our haversacks and began to attack the rations—[the] Government or rather the R. R. Co. had put no lights in the cars, so we had to feel around in the dark and eat as best we could. It was here, my boy, that I first called into requisition your patent table apparatus,[6] and let me acknowledge, at the risk of being thought stupid, that until daylight I did not know the edge of my knife from the back. My rations consisted of a fat piece of ham with a strangely perplexing bone it it (A Zou-Zou here interrupts to present me with a chunk of musk mellon) and about a loaf of bakers bread. The ham was pretty salt[y].

At this stage of the proceeding it was discovered that Terry Brady (who sat opposite me winking and blinking over his canteen) could sing as well as dance shindies [shindigs]. He accordingly struck up after stating [in] prelude that this was "never so fun . . . except when he was drunk." The rest of the 9th joined in a roaring chorus with tearing vigor till the car was like Pandemonium. One song followed another till pure throat weariness put an end to the exercises.

Meanwhile the train labored along at the rate of about 5 miles an hour, to all appearances stopping at every little way station. At about 11½ P.M. a man opposite me in the middle of the car was seized with "an all-gone-ness at the pit of his stomach," and I was awakened from a slight slumber by a disagreeable splashing sound. Fifteen minutes later a drunken soldier created an excitement at one of the stations by throwing a small child over his shoulder and nearly killing it by the fall.

Shortly after 12 P.M. I was awakened by loud shouts of "Yah! Yah!" and looking out of the window saw nearly all our Zou-Zous seated on the rail fence that lined the road, bobbing and flobbing their noses into water-melon rinds like gormandizing madmen. It seems that we had been stopped an hour to wait for another train and "the boys" had improved the opportunity by foraging. For a whole mile around they scoured the fields, gathering melons, peaches, and "splendid termattoes," their red caps visible in the moonlight in almost every direction. The quantity of spoils collected was something enormous. Hearing a curious noise on the roof of the carriage, I went outside to examine into the matter and to stretch my limbs, where I found Terry Brady with two or three of his companions trying to force a beanpole about 12 feet long down the ventilator.

The train started while the 9th were still engaged in their field labors and caused some pretty fleet running. After recounting their exploits, the Zou-Zous were content to rest awhile; but they were thir[s]ty and when they had exhausted the water keg, they began to bother me out of my snooze every five minutes for water, I being absolutely the only man of the party who carried water instead of some villainous mixture of toddy.

At about 4 A.M. when I had seriously begun to sleep, a violent slap on the back opened my eyes to the fact that we were in Philadelphia [actually, in Camden, New Jersey, oposite the city]. We formed, crossed the river [the Delaware] on the ferry boat in the dark, marched up to the refreshment rooms of the Central Committee,[7] and were treated, while standing at table with our knapsacks on, to cold ham, bread and butter, tomatoes and beets: whereupon our men felt so frisky that they issued forth and plagued a poor "bummer" who was quietly sleeping on a stoop over the way, but the Leut. soon appeared and we were marched a mile to the Phil. and Balt. R.R. Depot. At this point the 9th, while waiting 3 or 4 hours for the cars, got up a lively game of ball, the Massachusetts men who had felt severely the effects of the water-melon looking on with gloomy and discontented countenances.

The trip from Phil. to Baltimore was much like any other R.R. travelling and was happily finished at about 2½ P.M. [September 11] when we arrived in the latter dirty city. We were heartily welcome[d] by big nigs and little nigs of a wholesome black or sickly molasses color who stood in front of their dilapidated dwellings showing their ivories and rolling their eyes to the best possible advantage.

A part of the N.Y. 3rd Artillery, "Germans,"[8] were crowded in with us and by their perverse silence tended to check the superabundant hilarity of the 9th. My dinner of ham and bread was taken at about 12 A.M. and topped off with a red faced pear given me by a good natured Dutchman [i.e., German] near. Half an hour after arriving in Baltimore, we were invited into the Rooms of the Relief Association[9] and asked to partake of ham, bread and cheese and coffee (covered with a coat of dust shaken from the roof).

At 5 P.M. we left for Washington. As soon as the train ran out of the City, signs of military occupation became more frequent. The roads were carefully guarded, and whole hillsides were whitened with tents or their summits crowned with batteries. The soldiers turned out as our trains rushed along and cheered or presented arms. As darkness came the irrepressible Terry Brady commenced singing and soon had us all in a hubbub.

At 8½ P.M. of Thursday, September 11 we reached the capital in the midst of a drizzling rain and after waiting awhile for rations finally went to bed at 10½ P.M. without them. Our bed was the floor of the barracks near the capitol, and our room was equally servicable [sic] to about 200 others who lay around "thick as autumnal leaves in Valumbrosa."[10] At present (daylight of the 12th) I am seated in an old car writing, having arisen at 4 A.M. Crowds of soldiers are around, washing themselves in mud puddles. Our regiment is 17 miles out, and we march this morning. Privates know nothing of general movements. I can find out nothing of the position of the army. . . .

Let me stop to go to grub. This has been written in half a dozen different places, travelling and resting, but you will probably be able to decipher [it]. Don't expect me to write too often.

Your[s] tr.
Ed. K. Wightman

Washington Sept. 12, 1862

Dear Father and Brothers:

Let me thank you in form for all past favors and especially for your exertions to get me comfortably placed in the army. Your "commission of Major General" was certainly apropos, although I did not wish to acknowledge it. If I should live to see better times, I trust to be able to repay you.

My experience thus far has been rough but no more disagreeable than I expected to find it—indeed not so much so—I expect to see much of human weakness and of vice and much else that is brave and noble. I shall never regret the step I have taken, whatever may be the consequences.

Great activity is looked for in the army here, and I shall perhaps be unable to write to you as often as you would like, but do not infer from my silence that an accident has happened. If you were here to witness some of the inconveniences of writing, you would at once give proper importance to the above.

Truly yours,
Ed K. Wightman

Washington Friday Sept. 12, 1862

Dear Bro:

The note mailed this morning was hurridly [sic] finished in consequence of the receipt of marching orders which were subsequently recalled. Last night I slept like a top, although it required at first much time to nurse myself into forgetfulness; for the room was densely packed with men who lay stretched in radiating circles around the posts supporting the [barracks] roof and elsewhere were tumbled promiscuously together like fish in a basket. I unrolled my rubber blanket on the floor and, wrapping myself in the govt. blanket to keep off the rain that came dripping through the roof, made a pillow of my knapsack and, propping the top of my head against the wall to keep muddy boots from under my nose, shut my eyes and tried to think myself comfortable, as a philosopher should. But two noisy Irishmen got quarrelling about some ridiculous trifle and kept up a yelling until we rose in a body and expelled them. Our Zou-Zou (Newfoundland) dog joined in the demonstration and had a pretty strong voice in the matter.

I was up *as usual* at about 4 A.M. After waiting for rations till about 10 o'clock, I procured a steak with great difficulty at a neighboring restaurant. The delay was caused by a crowd, for Washington is overrun with new troops from the North. Two long trains came in this morning bringing regiments from New York: one of them was the "Monitors,"[11] including Charley's friend, "Old Cooper" [Captain George W. Cooper] whom I saw and shook by the hand (A Zou-Zou has just kicked over my inkstand while searching for his canteen).

The barracks are crammed—two regiments are quartered out of doors. We have now more than 300,000 troops defending Washington, and reinforcements are continually streaming in. McClellan is endeavoring to cut off the advance of the rebels and no one here seems to doubt of his success. No fears are entertained for the safety of Washington.

P.M. We have been joined by some of our regiment from the hospitals, and the above was cut short to attend to the wants of a poor fellow who lies beside me shivering with the ague; he caught it at Acquia [Aquia] Creek.[12] Leut. [James H.] Fleming visited our quarters about 10 o'clock and announced that our march would not be commenced until tomorrow.

After feeding my sick man, I accordingly started for a stroll over this City. The Capitol is not in my eyes a pretty place, although the marble buildings of the several [government] departments are in themselves admirable. The Statues in the Capitol grounds can hardly be called works of art.

Two "contrabands" [i.e., freed slaves] came up while I was looking at the collosal[sic] statue of the Father of his country, seated in the centre [sic] of the square, and I was considerably amused by their actions and sentiments. The wooly-headed boobies came along, showing their ivories (visible at the distance of half a mile), rolling their eyeballs, and gesturing in vain endeavor to imitate the attitude of the statue. Then they tried to spell out the inscription on the pedestal.

At last one of the benighted heathen pulled the front of his wool and inquired, "Mr. sojer, who is this?" "Genl. Washington," I replied—"My," said the darkey, "He's a bustin' ole feller, ain't he? He's bin [in] all dese wars, hain't he? Guess it's a pooty likely picture of him."

"Why, he died 60 years ago," said Wightman. "Der debble he did," responded the niggers in chorus, peeling their eyes and dropping their lower jaws. "Well, he's de greatest general ebber libbed any time in de whole world, warn't he? Ain't no men un dat size 'n dese yer days!" (You remember the size of the statue.)

"Whose dat?" continued the intelligent commentator, pointing backward. "That's the Goddess of Liberty," said Wightman thoughtfully—"Is she a buster, too? Does she lib enywhere yere abouts?"

Ah, me boy, what is fame after all? What a field is here for Cheever, Greeley, and Beecher![13] Send them along—send them along.

Friday night we bunked on the floor of the barracks as usual. The Zou-Zous, for some reason, were more frisky than usual. The 29th Ohio[14] quartered with us and two or four men, finding they had some brass pieces with them, played some really fine duets. Afterwards they made less pleasant noises. They beat a big bass drum furiously in the middle of the night. They worked the most hideous noises out of a trombone at frequent intervals till daylight broke. They got on the roof and trampled over it and yelled through the knotholes till everyone was worn out and disgusted. They mounted guard at the door where they had no business to and prevented egress and ingress. Their dog, Jack, tore the seat square out of the trousers of a Massachusetts man who incautiously walked near their sleeping place.

In fact, "Them New York fellers and their damed [sic] dog" became a byword and a reproach among the[ir] countrymen. Often as I was waked, I couldn't but laugh merrily at the disgusted countenances of the hundreds whose heads stuck up all over the room as they lay propped on their elbows to examine into each new cause of disquiet. My wakefulness was increased by the want of a government blanket, our shivering friend having monopolized three of them.

At day break we were up and washing in the thousand and one mud puddles near[by]. After that we formed in double lines from ⅛ to ¼ of a mile in length, each man with a tin cup. (I have provided myself with a sockdolijer[15] that holds a quart and a pint) and after struggling and crowding for an hour jammed our way into the grub room. This room is as long as a rope walk and contains three rough board tables running from end to end. On these tables are placed at intervals buckets of hot coffee, having much of the appearance of swill tubs, and along the edges of the tables, about a foot apart, are thick slices of bakers bread crowned with chunks of fat—very fat—salt pork, boiled. We stand in our places, dip our cups into the muddy coffee tub, take the bread and pork in our fingers (the latter is as greasy as whale blubber), and make the most of our banquet. When a man is as hungry as a bear, it is not so bad as you may imagine.

At noon on Saturday the 13th we threw our knapsacks into an ammunition wagon drawn by four donkies [sic] and started (20 in a squad) on the march for Rockville, Maryland. We had a mounted guide, and a man rode on one of the donkies to direct the team. Our route was through Georgetown. The sun was hot as the mischief and burned me as red as a lobster in less than an hour. This road was dusty and made more so by the continual passage of wagon trains and the tramp of infantry squads.

At about 3 P.M. we stopped, ate our rations, and sucked water from a muddy brook. My [canteen] filter was brought into requisition immediately, and good fellowship demanded its transference, like a pipe of peace, from hand to hand, and from mouth to mouth. You who have seen the tobacco stained mouths of our Zouaves will give me one credit for generosity. However, policy, you know—as Jack Falstaff remarked, "the lion knows instinct."[16] While we were eating, the 29th Ohio, which had started three hours before us, came up. They intended us a compliment in saying we "marched like the devil."

In half an hour we started on again, passing long trains of ambulance wagons and here and there the dead body of a horse or a donkey who had fallen in the midst of his labors and every few yards coming upon a cast shoe, a flattened canteen, parts of blankets, pieces of knapsack, etc. Occasionally a darkey would appear in a neighboring field with a basket of peaches or apples with which he goodnaturedly treated us.

At 8 o'clock P.M., some time after dark, we reached Rockville, Md., having marched during the afternoon 20 miles. I used my heavy walking shoes and beyond a *quantum sufficit* of leg weariness and a slight bruise on the left heel from the doubling in of the new leather felt no inconvenience. I considered myself justified in getting a warm supper at the tavern and then, all the barracks and tents being occupied, retired to a hay loft which we had been lucky enough to find in the dark and almost before I could close my eyes fell asleep.

The village, town, or whatever it may be is thoroughly secesh. McClellan has just moved his headquarters from about 5 miles in our rear (we passed close by them on Saturday) to Pool[e]sville.[17] We are already in the midst of the army and when on the route see encampments and breastworks on the more commanding hills.

Sunday Morning [September 4]—Our loft last night had a window in each end so that a stream of cool air coursed over us incessantly. Yet I feel no ill effects. I was buttoned up tight in my overcoat and at the first symptoms of a chill covered myself with a mountain of hay. The hay seed in my uniform this morning stuck so that it would scarcely be picked out. We rose "with the lark" and after admiring a lot of dried sheep skins strung overhead climbed down from our roost, boiled our coffee in a big pot in the tavern yard, and made a breakfast on rations.

Our regiment is in the advance and Burnside, in whose corps it is stationed, is presumed to be at Frederick.[18] At 5 P.M. today (the greater part of Sunday being given to rest), we start on a ten mile march *with knapsacks* to join it. Our team has already gone back. We heard the firing of heavy guns this morning towards the north, and it is possible an important battle has been fought.[19] We expect to march 35 or 40 miles before catching our regiment.

To my astonishment some of "our boys" manifested a disposition to go to church, but the secesh declined to admit them on the ground that the building was already crowded. This afternoon my scrubby head (I was shorn of my strength in Secesh Baltimore) will probably be seen in the midst of the congregation.

I have no time to write more. My health and spirits are first rate. Remember me to the "Phellers."

Yours truly,
Ed K. W.

After this and others have been read, please put them somewhere in a drawer where they will not get rubbed. I want to keep them for reference. As soon as I am posted so as to be able to give my address, it shall be forwarded. It may be several days yet before we join the regiment, and until we do we shall be shifting our position perpetually.

Tell father and the family to have no anxiety on my account. I shall take the best possible care of myself. I would write to mother and the girls if I knew [precisely] where they are. I have seen the [New York] Herald this morning for Saturday, or rather it has been handed me by a blushing secesh girl, and I intend to read it. Army men place but little reliance on newspaper statements of any moments, though they give almost the only information we can get—Our Major Genls. keep their mouths shut as tightly as healthy clams and leave us and even our colonels scarcely room for surmises.

E.

Frederick, Md. Monday, Sept. 15, 1862

We are still eight miles south of Frederick, but I date my note there because our present locality has no name. On Sunday afternoon we were prevented from leaving Rockville, as I wrote we intended to do, by the receipt of a telegram from Frederick stating that McClellan had gone further north [to Middletown] and that his army was already short of provisions. It threatened to send us back to Washington. But during the night affairs assumed a more favorable aspect. Long wagon trains of provisions rumbled by in the direction of Frederick.

After passing a second night (Sunday) in our hayloft, we rose before daybreak and, boiling our big pot of coffee over a fire in the stable yard, hastily swallowed our rations of crackers and salt pork, filled our haversacks heavily with extra rations and our canteens with water, and, shouldering our knapsacks, set out on a quickstep for Frederick.

After proceeding four miles or so, we overtook an ammunition train and, pitching knapsacks and haversacks into the donkey bins strapped behind the wagon, continued our journey with relieved backs and lighter spirits. The wagons, about 30 in number, are laden with heavy cases of rifle cartriges [sic] and are generally drawn by four or six donkeys each, a contraband nigger being mounted on each nigh wheel donkey and holding a single rein in his left hand (a heavy whip in his right) with which he guided the whole: the rein splits at the collar and the left offshoot is shorter than the right, so that a steady pull steers to the left and a succession of jerks, to the opposite side. The two leading mules are connected by a breastpole chained to their bridles, and the nigh one therefore leads the whole troop. The darkeys keep up an incessant yell of "Yah-ay-ay! yare yare!! yare!!" which the sleepy donkeys obey or not as suits their convenience. The country through which we passed is rolling or regularly undulating, nothing but up high hills and down again all the way. In going down the hind wheels of the wagons are always chained.

We met hundreds of stragglers in squads of from two to fifty—indeed enough to make in themselves, if consolidated, a large army. The majority of them were sick, however, or miserably worn. Their countenances are sunken and melancholy and indifferent almost to stolidity. When left to themselves they progress very slowly, cooking their own food and sleeping upon the ground. It is quite common to see two or three dozen groups, within the space of half a mile, boiling food in their tin cups over fires made with fence rails. News from the seat of war is the only thing which interests them. They are all thoroughly disgusted with the life they lead and swear that if ever they get out of the army they will commit suicide almost before entering it again. It must be remembered, though, that many of them are skulkers.

I have not yet heard a favorable opinion expressed of McDowell nor of Pope: the former is frequently called "traitor." McClellan and Burnside and Halleck all enjoy the entire confidence of the troops.[20] These sentiments are recorded as representative of the views of men from all parts of the country with whom I have conversed.

At 3 o'clock we had accomplished a distance of twenty miles and determined to encamp in a meadow by the side of a shallow stream until morning. The dust stood $\frac{1}{16}$ of an inch thick on our boots and leggins. Our first step was to bathe; the next to get supper, which we did by putting our hands in our knapsacks and pulling out our greasy pork and crackers. Then I sat down on a stump and commenced penning this epistle. It is now twilight. The donkeys have been unharnessed and are grunting, groaning, and biting and squealing over their fodder, and the benighted darkies are yelling like demons.

Tuesday, Sept. 16 The first part of last night I spent in an ammunition wagon crowded with a Zou-Zou and a nigger. But the corners of the boxes hurt me so that I got out a[t] midnight and lay on the ground. At 3½ A.M. we were up, and it was discovered that in the small hours of the morning our rascally recruits had stolen a suck[l]ing pig from a secessionist and roasted him. "Our boys" are, like most privates in the army, disgustingly unprincipled and profane. Hardly one of them hesitates at a theft. Robbing a sutler is among them counted a meritorious deed. They eat pies and drink cider *ad lib* and walk off with them in their "stummuts" without a thought of paying. They swear perpetually for the sake of swearing. To make matters worse the officers wink at the vices of the men in order to secure their favor and obtain the reputation of being good fellows.

Before sunrise we were on the march for Frederick, which was duly reached at about 9 A.M. On the way we passed the ruins of the iron bridge on the Balt. & Ohio R. R., the horns and heads of numberless cattle slaughtered by the rebels in their retreat, the odorous carcasses of dead horses, etc. etc. Here we were greeted with startling mirrors [rumors] of battles fought by Burnside, of the capture of 15,000 rebels, etc., of the death of Leut. Col. Kimball,[21] and [of] 300 rebels . . . being confined in the hospital here; and in a few minutes I shall stroll out and see them.

The city of Frederick is regularly built, chiefly of brick, and is the prettiest place I have seen since leaving New York. We are now quartered in an apple orchard where we have the privilege of eating all the fruit we want. I am under a tree chewing and writing—pausing at every other word to snap of [at] catarpillars [*sic*], of which within the last half hour I have sent at least three dozen spinning.

We hear nothing definite of the location of the 9th. It is probably 40 miles west of this point, near Harpers Ferry [Virginia]. Our squad resumes the case tomorrow. I should be very glad to hear from you but do not see how you can write at present.

In haste,
Ed. K. W.

Two miles from Boonsboro and Five
miles from the battle-field of
Wednesday/ Thursday [Friday] Sept. 19,
1862

Dear Bro:

We have just stopped by the side of a muddy brook to rest, and I seize the opportunity, while my comrades are snoozing under the trees, to resume my narrative and furnish further details of our progress. My last notes left us Tuesday forenoon in the apple orchard of a benevolent fellow named Dill, a resident of Frederick. We spent the entire day in that city and when night came slept in the barn of our host. A drizzling rain set in late in the afternoon but did not disturb us. On retiring to my pile of hay, my first proceeding was to button a "bumble" bee in my coat collar where he stayed about three minutes before he could be got out. His buzzing of course was very amusing, the more so as it was pitch dark. After being kept awake a couple of hours as usual by the scolding and swearing of the Zouaves and the barking of their dog, and after having the satisfaction of hearing the provost guard march two of them off [to] the guard house, I got to sleep.

On waking in the morning, I was pleased to find a big nest of "bumble" bees buzzing close to my left elbow. It was now discovered that there was a home cider press in the barn, which was at once put in action and our canteens filled with apple juice. We then sliced up some apples, pork, and bacon, and, borrowing a long legged fry pan, went into an adjoining lot and got up a rousing breakfast. It was still raining slightly.

Orders were now received to send our knapsacks to the Quartermaster's Department and march forward to join our corps. Our knapsacks were accordingly left in a storehouse at Frederick, and we started on. Some carried overcoats, blankets, changes of clothing, etc., strapped to their backs. I took only my rubber blanket and writing materials and Abbie's [gift] knapsack. At noon we had advanced two miles out of the city, when we were overtaken by 100 empty ambulance wagons on their way up to the battleground after the wounded. We parleyed [sic] a little and jumped aboard and travelled quickly to Middletown.

3 hours later McClellans Headquarters
5 miles from Boonsboro

Gen. McClellan and staff this moment rode within six yards of me. The Genl. seems to be in fine condition. He is much heavier—more solid and rotund than I thought—but otherwise his likenesses give a fair impression of the man. A roar of cheers followed him wherever he went. There is no fighting going on at the moment, although a terrific battle is said to have been finished last night.[22] I have had no time for enquiring. The camp is full of rumors. The papers will give you the news sooner and more complete[ly] than I can collect or forward it.

"But to return to our subjects," the discussion of which was suddenly interrupted by an order to "fall in." The ambulance wagons were a stroke of luck. It was almost the pleasantest ride I remember. The body of the wagon is set on soft springs both at the sides and ends, and the seats and their backs are nicely cushioned all round. Underneath are two kegs supposed to contain water for the wounded, of whom each wagon accommodates from two to a dozen—only two when reclining at length. The wagons are similar to those often seen opposite your office, marked "Massachusetts Hospital." The drivers (like those of the ammunition and provision wagons) are paid $25 per month for their services.

General George B. McClellan *(Photograph courtesy of the Library of Congress)*

The scenery as we rode along was glorious. The Blue Ridge was before us and rich fields of corn and grain were everywhere visible on the hill-sides. Shade trees including the oak, elm, and maple lined the road and were grouped in picturesque clumps and groves in the fields.

We alighted at Middletown, marched two miles out, and took up our quarters for the night in a barn. Before morning it rained furiously, and the pattering of the drops as they fell from the roof on my rubber blanket awoke me (a thunderstorm here obliges me to resort to my blanket again and seek the shelter of a tree). About midnight a whole brigade marched by our barn to re-inforce McClellan, whose forces are being concentrated with great rapidity.

Before sunrise I pawed my way into the open air, tumbling through the barn floor in the effort: but our rations were exhausted and we could get no break-fast. Every pump in the neighborhood had been pumped dry by our insatiable squads, and there was not even enough water to drink. So we tightened our sashes and took to the road.

The propinquity of the army was now evident by a number of signs—fences torn down, old ladies bewailing the ruin of their cabbage plants, the scarcity of food at hotels and in private houses, the frequent appearance of wounded men with their arms slung in bloody cloths or their heads swathed in bandages, the walls and windows of houses perforated with balls, tree trunks, telegraph posts and fences shattered by shells, an increase in the number of dead horses and mules, all these things told of our near approach to the scene of action.

From our barn we ascended gradually over a pleasant road (a splendid one to defend, for in addition to the ascent it was skirted on both sides by dense woods, distant but a few hundred feet) to the summit of the first Blue Ridge range. The scenes of the various contests were pointed out to us, and particu-larly the ridge where Gen. Reno fell, pierced by a ball from the piece of a sharpshooter in the wood—it is said here that he was killed through mistake by one of our own men.[23] The neighboring hills still hold the unburied bodies of the rebel dead; some of our squad went and examined them. The enemy asked permission to bury the corpses but were refused, for fear of revealing our position.

In haste,
Ed. K. W.

P.S. It's sunset. I have made a supper of coffee and crackers, and the squad[s] have gone to bed in a barn. We are pleasantly located here in a clearing where we are enclosed by tents and baggage wagons. Our troops lie in line of battle, prepared for an emergency. We are still in the dark in regard to the position of our regiment. Leut. Fleming is looking it up. Today's Phild. Enquirer [Inquirer] says that Burnside is at Harpers Ferry; if so, we too shall go there.

I had almost forgotten to mention the rebel prisoners we saw in Frederick and afterwards on the road thither. Everyone who had seen them assured me that they were a most deplorable looking set of fellows. But believe me, Wight-man, they are nothing of the sort. An impartial eye cannot but admire their tough, wirey [sic] frames, although one may smile at their unique dress. I saw several thousand rebels march through the streets of Frederick followed by an equal number of paroled Union men (who had been recently captured), and truth compels me to say that had the enemy been clad in our uniforms instead of the dust covered suits of homespun gray which enveloped them, our men might have suffered by the contrast. They are naturally more lithe and active than we, and the struggle for independence seems to have molded their features into inflexible severity and determination. There is a look of savageness in their eyes not observable in the good natured countenance of our men.

Friday, Sept. 20th—Last night McClellan and I both slept well—he in a tent on one side of the street, I in a barn nearly opposite. Our squad, having come in irregularly, and the Leut. being absent, could get no rations and had to go without breakfast. McClellan had his.

At noon we received news that our regiment was about 2½ miles distant and started to overtake it. We found only a camp of stragglers. Here we got coffee and crackers and after marching 2 miles further over the battle field of Wednesday reached the great camp of the [Army of the Potomac's] left wing, including perhaps 30,000 men, early in the evening.

The innumerable camp fires blazing here and there for miles presented to us, as we descended among them, a grand scene. Leut. Col. Kimball (killed in the late great battle by rumor) received us with a hearty welcome. I had myself placed at once in Co. B, which has the right of the line, and soon became the centre [sic] of a tea party round the camp fire. They nearly shook my arm off, stuffed me with coffee and crackers, and pumped me dry of news. Then a couple of corporals took me to their tent, where, after talking till midnight, we comfortably snoozed.

This, Saturday, morning I saw Gen. Burnside while getting water at a spring. The enemy have succeeded in crossing the Potomac, and it is expected that we shall march today to Harpers Ferry.

Now I shall be glad to hear from you all. Write as often and profusely as you please. Direct as follows:

Edward K. Wightman
Company B
9th Regiment, N. Y. Volunteers
(Hawkins Zouaves)

Thus addressed letters will come straight.

Ed

Saturday, September 21 [20]

(Private)
To the Boys—

Dear Bros: I have just missed taking part in a great battle. On Wednesday our regiment was fiercely engaged on the left and lost 250 in killed and wounded.[24] In common with the other two regiments of Hawkins[25] Brigade (the 89th and 103rd New York) they assaulted a battery posted on a hill and defended by a whole division of the enemy. The boys charged gallantly over two ridges of ploughed [sic] land up to the mouths of the guns, but their ammunition failing there, and getting no support from a second brigade appointed to act in concert with them, they were forced to fall back after holding their newly taken position fifteen minutes in the face of a withering fire.[26] Our color guards were cut down almost to a man, and Kimball, our hot headed Lieut. Colonel, finally seized the flag himself and wrapped it round him. Strange to say, he was uninjured.

On Friday afternoon I walked over the field. Our dead still lay unburied, horribly mangled and lying in every conceivable attitude. The rebels had been, for the most part, removed, but large numbers of them still lay piled in the

"Hawkins's Zouaves" in the Battle of Antietam *(Engraving courtesy of Historical Times, Inc.)*

neighboring gullies.[27] Fences were everywhere broken down, trees shattered, the ground ploughed up in furrows, and everything testified to the terrible destructiveness of the agencies employed. As the rebels were yet near, we were ordered to arm ourselves from the equipments which strewed the field. From the multitude of battered muskets laying round I selected a cartridge box, cap box, bayonet, etc. Our squad was then detailed to assist in burying the dead, and we were occupied till sunset in digging graves. Older hands performed the rest.

I am pressed for time and can write no more at present. Let neither father nor the women read this.

Ed

P. S. The enemy are now so well advanced that we do not expect another immediate engagement. We have the rumor this morning that Heinzelman[28] with 80,000 men is marching from Washington to Richmond. The impression among our soldiers is that the war is finished. They think the battle of Wednesday the greatest of the war and decisive. . . .

Burnside's Headquarters
near Harpers Ferry
Monday, Sept 22nd, 1862

Dear Bro:

I believe I have not yet told you the exact position of our regiment in the army. We are in the 9th Army Corps, 3rd Division, 1st Brigade. General

Burnside commands the corps—Col. Hawkins (just appointed) the division[29] and Col. Fairchilds [Harrison S. Fairchild] the brigade. The division consists of 12 regiments (36,000 men): the brigade of three regiments, viz: 9th, 89th, and 103rd (the last German), all of New York State. Col. Fairchilds, our acting brigadier, is of the 89th. Our senior capt. is Wm. G. Barnett of Co. B, and our adjutant is his brother [Lieutenant George A. C. Barnett].

It will be some time before the regiment recovers from the effects of the late series of battles, which extended over a period of nine days and were more exhausting from the long marches with which they were coupled. The loss in killed and wounded is now estimated as high as 277. The ammunition of the rebels was pretty well used up in the contest, and they hurled against us all sorts of missles [sic]. One of four men had his leg carried away by the head of a sledge hammer; another was wounded in the thigh with a huge "chainy alley" which he showed me, and all testify to the fact that cobblestones and railroad iron fell among them in showers.

We are at present posted among the hills of Maryland, 4 miles from the Potomac. The enemy has crossed, and McClellan is close upon his heels with an army unimpeded by luggage. Union troops have, within the past two days, been hastening across the river as fast as they could move.[30]

On Saturday night our camp was incessantly disturbed by rolling volleys of musketry, whose echoes rattled round the hills till it seemed as if the left wing were again beset on all sides, and our Colonel was several times on the point of ordering the beat of the long roll. The noise was doubtless occasioned by a stubborn stand of the enemy's rear guard. Since that time we have been perfectly quiet—even dull for lack of excitement. Early this morning there was a report that the 9th had been ordered back to Washington; but this afternoon the Company Cook (a very friendly and useful fellow) informed me that the Quartermaster's man informed him that we should remain here until McClellan had fought another battle. If sent to Washington it will probably be with the intention of moving us further south to act in concert with McClellan.

We have had rumors of the taking of Richmond by Heinzelman and by [Major General Fitz John] Porter severally, but do not know whether they may be relied on or whether the rebels have any considerable force south of that city. We are told, too, that Charleston, S.C., has surrendered.

Please send on a paper now and then, and if you can, a good newspaper map of the field of action [at Antietam]. I am as much in the dark with regard to the movements of the opposing forces as though I lived in another world, and regiment[al] officers know no more than the privates. We are only the machinery.

Our camp is fixed on the top of a hill, at the base of which, distant one eighth of a mile, flows a stream of water. It is always muddy on account of the multitude of cavalry horses continually tramping through it; the springs by which it is fed, however, are less so.

Our tents are made thus: Each man has given to him for shelter a piece of heavy canton flannel about five feet square; it has on each of three sides a row of buttons and button holes so arranged that a number of pieces may be buttoned together: and the fourth side is merely finished with a hem at the edge and small loops of rope at the corners where it is staked to the ground. This is a clumsy representation of the piece. Three men generally club together to make a tent using one piece for each side and one for the back thus: [Edward's original sketch of a tent is no longer extant.] Muskets are generally in the front and rear for props or tent poles; but just a present promptness in the field requires the substitution of stakes. These little houses are called "shelter tents." In Washington, the regiment has a set of Sibley tents, capable of accommodating eighteen persons each.[31]

Our "light marching time" has been drawn to so fine a point that "the boys" begin to grumble. The quartermasters have been forbidden transportation for meat [and] beans, and with the exception of fresh beef twice a week we are forced to live on hard crackers and coffee. Four crackers are allowed each man per meal. They are entirely sufficient and satisfactory for me, for you will remember that I am naturally abstentious; but some of the other fellows are more epicurean. We confidently expect, though, that "suthin'll bust" pretty soon.

Tuesday Morning Sept. 23, 1862. The tattoo[32] beat this morning an hour before dawn, and the brigade was ordered under arms. We formed rapidly in the dark to resist an expected attack, but none was made, and we were dismissed with an order to strike tents and prepare for a march. Two hours afterwards the order was countermanded, and we were again in *status quo.* We may leave in some unknown direction in thirty minutes and may not in a week.

Compl[imen]ts to the fam[ily].

Ed

P.S. A gust of wind blew this away from me, and it was politely returned by a greasy fingered soldier, see his mark.

PPS A careless man this moment let off his piece. The ball pierced the tent next to the one in which I am living and passed through the thigh of a man not 12 feet distant. He is lying on his stomach biting his fingernails. Says "whoever did it is a blame fool." E.

Headquarters [of] Gen. Burnside
Near Harpers Ferry, Va. [in] Md.
Thursday, Sept. 25, 1862

Dear Bro:

Where the mischief my narrative of events ended I don't remember but believe it is complete up to Wednesday of this week. Affairs in camp are at present very much disordered. The whole number of sound men capable of duty is but 277 (I gave the same figures as representing the number of killed and wounded in the battle of Antietam: they should have been 265). Col. Hawkins is under arrest for presenting to Maj. Gen. Burnside for signature an order which the latter pronounced insulting both to the regiment and to his superior officers: it related to the cleanliness of the camp. Our adjutant, the younger Barnett, has been "honorably discharged" and left this afternoon for New York, and nearly all our captains and several lieutenants have received furloughs. One captain has resigned (rumor says to prevent disgrace).[33]

It would be inferred from this and from the conditions of the rank and file that we are destined to go into comfortable quarters and lie by inactive until recruited. The discipline of the men, however, is so complete that a corporal could command them.

On Wednesday morning we were ordered under arms at 3½ A.M. and throughout the day expected to march to some threatened point, but tattoo came and the evening parade passed without disturbance. On retiring we were instructed to breakfast and strike our tents so as to be ready to march at 5 A.M. this (Thursday) morning. Noon came and found us still here. At 1 o'clock P.M. we were ordered under arms while at dinner and in fifteen minutes our tents were struck, blankets rolled, and bayonets fixed, ready for an advance. It was said our brigade was to guard one of the fords of the Potomac. After waiting three hours in the hot sun, an orderly came up with fresh commands, and five minutes later our old ground was again white with "dog houses" as the boys call our little shelter tents. I am now, near sunset, in mine, but may at any moment be called out on "business of national importance."

News of all sorts is scarce, but horsemen appear once or twice a day with a pile of newspapers thrown across their saddles, which they sell to the soldiers at enormous prices. New York dailies are rarely to be had and never at less than ten cents each. [The] Baltimore Clipper (price one cent) brings five and the Phild. Inquirer ditto; they are both one horse concerns and contain little else than local items.

The Sutlers are an institution of which perhaps you [would] like to know more. They travel in wagons like those of New England peddlers and when the troops are in motion dispense their wares from them. But at stopping places they encl[ose] large wall tents at which they make profits which it would be difficult to over-estimate. Although their stock is generally slim and ill chosen, customers are never wanting. The two sutlers tents in our division always have their doors blocked by an eager crowd who throw away their money like water and even have to be kept back by a guard. They buy sweet crackers at twenty five cents a capful; a pint can of oysters for fifty cents; a little bottle of brandied cherries for seventy five cents; a jar of preserved peaches at $1.25; a cheese at twenty cents per lb., etc; and the dealers, always swearing they are out of change, either purchase [sell] a dollar's worth of vanities or take [give] change in sutlers tickets. As a result of these exhorbitent [sic] prices the sutlers frequently suffer by theft or by open robbery. While selling a dollars worth of cheese in front of the tent, ten dollars worth of . . . cigars walk out behind; the soldiers, almost without exception, think it an innocent amusement or rather a praiseworthy action to seize stores in this way.

This afternoon a wagon sutler who was going by while we were patiently awaiting marching orders endeavored to initiate trade by presenting the members of the Ninth with a few cheap cigars. Encouraged by his friendly demonstration, to which they ascribed a proper value, they entered his wagon and possessed themselves of nearly every article it contained and then started off his horse at a full gallop. During the smoking and eating that followed many moral sentiments found vent. The whole thing was pronounced, on reflection, to be "dam[n] mean."

Dress parade is over, and I have a pressing invitation to take tea with a couple of corporals. Inasmuch as there are some mashed potatoes and fresh meat in question, the invitation is accepted.

Prof. Lowe's[34] balloon is visible from my dog house door in a westerly direction. He is doubtless surveying the proceedings on the other side of the Potomac. Wish him luck!

Good bye for the time [being]. I must get my knitting and go to the neighbors. Love to the folks.

Yours truly,
Ed

Near Harper's Ferry
Saturday Eve. Sept. 27, 1862

(Private)

Big thing! Within my dog house *by candle light!* This afternoon we received our rations of soap and candles. The candle of the household of which I am at present a respectable member is stuck in the heel of my bayonet, the point of which is inserted in the ground—big thing!

Since I last wrote to you, our quarters have been changed. Just before dinner on Friday we were ordered to be ready to march in ten minutes. We accordingly bolted our hot soup (how the fellows yelled as [though] they were scalded!), struck our tents and shouldered them, and, forming four abreast, set out at the govt. step for an unknown destination. The entire division went with us, and as the canvass [sic] houses sunk away like melting snow the appearance of the hills changed as if by magic. Nothing was left but forests of little sticks which had been used as tent poles, empty cracker boxes, etc., etc.

We marched a few hundred yards and then sat down in the hot sun to wait for the wagon train, which took some 2½ hours to pass. At the end of that time we rose at the sound of the bugle, walked 50 paces—halted—stacked arms, and waited again. This strategy was repeated till towards evening when we resumed in earnest, trotted three or more miles over hills and through vales and across the bridge of Antietam Creek to the new camping ground [near the Antietam Iron Works]. The sight of the long line of burnished muskets in front of us, winding along the narrow path and flanked at a distance by the flashing sabres of cavalry, was both beautiful and inspiring—but the dust, whew! You never imagined anything like it.

On reaching the place destined for the new encampment, we were dismissed and in less time than it takes to write it had jerked down a quarter of a mile of rail fence for fires and were scattering over the fields in search of straw for bedding. A city of tents arose as if by enchantment. The troops are more concentrated than before.

Now for the reason why I marked this note "private." I want to give you boys the full advantage of my camp experiences: but some of them are so rough that I had much rather the "old folks" and girls should hear and see nothing of them. Remember that I find no fault myself but am perfectly content to take things as they come, but this record is made in order that you may know what to expect in the event of any of you being called into the army. One must come with the expectation and determination to rough and tumble. There are no grandmothers here to tuck one in bed o'nights.

I have told you that 277 sound men are left in the regiment. Two days ago those sound men, without exception, including your humble servant, were so weakened by diarrhea as to be unfit for service. Having taken the precaution to prepare myself for such an emergency by laying in a stock of old McClellan's infallible pills, I soon recovered; but many had to be sent to the hospital. The trouble is said to come partly from fresh unsalted meat and partly from our unhealthy positions (wait a minute, there goes tatoo [*sic*]). Ever since the battle of the 17th our diet has been soldiers coffee, Confederate crackers captured at Frederick, and occasionally beef. We are out of salt.

The weather is almost insufferably hot in the middle of the day and freezing cold at night; this, together with a dew as heavy as rain, has knocked us up. I have a rubber blanket, but many of the boys have no covering at all for the night. I am resolved that, should my knapsack be recovered, never again to part with my government blanket. Some of the men are so badly off for shoes that they removed those on the dead men killed in the late battles—indeed, at the battle of South Mountain, on Sunday, the 13th [14th] inst[ant—that is, of the present month]., our Zouaves were so famished with hunger that they fed themselves from the well filled knapsacks of the dead rebels. From personal inspection of the battlefield of Wednesday I can testify that the shoes had been taken from the feet of our Union soldiers by the enemy as far as they could reach them, and that the pockets of our men had all been turned inside out for plunder.

The sufferings of which these experiences are the index are, however, rare among the Federals and temporary. When we are encamped long enough to enable supplies to overtake us, they cease.

The old regiments received so many hard knocks during the late fighting that, as they ruefully acknowledge, they "have a bellyfull." Still, every one is surprised that McClellan does not move faster. We want to finish up everything before going into winter quarters.

An account of the doings of the Abolition Governors in convention[35] has reached us, and the men curse fearfully over it. They believe with all their hearts in McClellan and are unwilling to be slaughtered in the experiment of muddle headed politician generals.

For further news see accompanying note [following, dated September 29].

Antietam Creek Md. 7 miles
from Harpers Ferry, Va. Monday
Sept. 29, 1862

Dear Bro:

We moved to this place in common with the whole division on Friday. The movement of such a mass of troops with their equipments takes time. We started in the middle of the day and took till sunset to march three or four miles. The road was crowded with men and blocked with wagons. We were whitened with dust, which rose in such dense clouds as to blind and nearly stifle us.

On reaching the new camping ground, the tents were at once erected, straw secured from a neighboring farmer for bedding, and rails taken from the fences for fires. In fifteen minutes we had created a new city and made a new home for ourselves.

My first two tent companions, as I have told you, were two corporals, [William J.] Rogers and [George D.] Cornell: the second [two were] Jack Adaire [Private John B. Adair], a morose little Frenchified American, dirty and selfish, and a sick young Irishman who was eternally telling over his complaints as a good Catholic does his beads and who kept me awake pretty regularly by coughing. These last fellows I got rid of as soon as possible and rushed for refuge to a young German barber named Whetlaufer [Private John Wettlaufer] and his chum, Jimmy Folan [Private James H. Folan], otherwise "Cockroach," with whom I bunk at present. The barber, I regret to say, is continually away when off duty, after young pigs and vegetables—my stomach is innocent in this matter, for he is a glutton and eats all he steals. "Cockroach" is a printer, about 18 years of age like his chum and withal a humerous [sic] fellow. As I write one lies on his back beside me reading a novel and the other on his front—picking a bone. Our haversacks lie in the corners of the dog house, and the three rifles, safe from the damp, are covered with straw except where their glittering barrels here and there peep through.

Since parting with my government blanket and overcoat, I have occasionally been cold at night, for the atomosphere [sic] is chilly and the dews heavy; but last night Cockroach came in with a big double blanket which he solemnly assured us he had "found." By a strange coincidence a teamster was shortly after looking for a blanket he had lost. Cockroach said, "Anyway it was bought for the service of the United States, and as long as he lived it should be used for no other purpose." All three of us slept warm, I in the middle, the place of honor having been voluntarily assigned me.

I have not had an unpleasant word from either officers or men since leaving home. I treat all good naturedly but without familiarity, and as a consequence, although they abuse each other like pickpockets, they never insult nor interfere with me.

There is no chaplain in our regiment[36] nor in those adjoining us, and Sunday, therefore, passed without any services. The drills were omitted, however, and some leisure afforded the men. I took the opportunity to bathe in the famous Antietam Creek, muddy and cold as it is. On the road back, chancing upon a sutler's wagon and being minus my dinner, I squandered ten cents on what he termed "an elegant can of gingerbread"—It was just the nicest dinner I have had in three weeks. I lay down under a shady tree with a canteen of cold spring water by my side and chewed and swigged, while a circle of hungry Eastern troops gathered round and stared till I thought their eyes would drop out: all this made the gingerbread taste better.

Our camp is full of donkeys and horses, all branded "US" on the left shoulder. The cavalry men always ride their horses at a gallop and the darkies their mules at a trot. Darkies are as plenty [plentiful] here as bedbugs on the "Granite State" [the steamer Granite City]. The 9th has twenty of them, mostly from Virginia and North Carolina. We have little nigs (under 12 years), [named] York, Dempsey, Holland, and a half a dozen other "woolly headed cusses," as they are called, who are eminently useful in their way. In return for their services, they get food, clothing and such odd pence (rare) and bits of pie [and] cheese as the Zou-Zous choose to give them. They seem both contented and jolly. They are allowed not tents but sleep around the cook's fires covered with such blankets and old clothes as they can get.

As to the cleanliness of the soldiers, perhaps the less said the better, at present. They do as well as they can under the circumstances, but their fatigue suits (they have no change with them) are ragged and soiled and no amount of care could make them look respectable. When we get our knapsacks there will be a new order of things. I have worn but one uniform since entering the service and have but one set of underclothes with me. They are washed with an awful quantity of soap every time I take a bath, and then I have the pleasure of waiting for them to dry. The last time the operation was performed, a midday sun blistered my back. Golly! these Maryland suns fairly fry the fat out of one.

But let me cease talking of myself and enquire how you are and how Aunt Mary is. Not a line has reached me yet. Mother and the girls are presumed to be at home and Jim and Charley still engaged in Government business [in the New York state militia]. What are your prospects and what is doing in New York? How do the fishing and rowing go on . . . ? I must stop. The roll calls for dress parade. Good bye.

Ed

Antietam Creek 7 miles from
Harpers Ferry, October 1st, 1862

Dear Bro:

We expected to move today to Harpers Ferry where it is said we are to encamp for awhile and to receive our Sibley tents from Washington and our lamented knapsacks; but the order was withheld and we are still here (near sunset Wednesday eve.).

During the last two days we have been obtaining rest and feeding like kings. A train of 30 wagons came up night before last, bring[ing] rice, molasses, beans, salt, and salt horse [i.e., salted pork]. We have therefore feasted at dinner time on beef-tea and crackers or bean soup and crackers in so lordly a style that we instinctively used straw toothpicks afterwards and crawled out of our dog houses to survey the premises and the weather as though perfectly at home. Company B has had no rice and molasses yet, but it's on the *qui vive,* me boy.

There has been another change in our household. The cheerful little "Cockroach" has left us to take the position of assistant cook for the company, in which capacity he has intimated the intention to serve with honor to the country and with an eye open to your humble servant's necessities. Cockroach is quite a philosopher—thinks a great deal. As I was lying on my back last night just after roll call, the German barber on one side and the Irish printer on the other, the flickering light playing over the group from the [candle on] top of a bayonet where it was perched, "Cockroach" broke the silence by observing, "I take notice, Jeff Davis appointed Wednesday, [the] 17th of September as a day of humiliation and prayer, and while his people was a doin it, his sojers was a makin . . . [haste] towards Virginny—which shows that the 'prayer of the wicked availeth not'." Having thus delivered himself, the chunky little cockroach turned over and composed himself to sleep. He says his business now as cook is "to fat up you lean buggers for the next killen' time." These solemn jokes are very common in camp.

I think I notified you of the resignation of our adjutant. Capt. [James R.] Whiting [Jr.] (son of Judge Jas. R. Whiting of N.Y.) of the battery company [Company K] has also resigned. Rumor says he drank himself into the *delirium tremens.*

Our battery has been sent to Washington for limbers. The regimental band, one of the finest in the service, and supported by a contribution of 25¢ per month from each member (and from $400 to $500 from officers), joined us on yesterday and now makes a grand feature of our dress parade; it had been left behind as useless during the fighting season.

Saturday Morning, Oct. 4th. Our camp is still unmoved. The health and condition of the men during the past week has vastly improved. Food is now plenty and various, and the facilities for washing and bath[ing] are everything that can be desired. In addition to salted meats we now have fresh beef, beans, and desiccated [dehydrated] vegetables. Our soups are now unapproachable and their titillating effect on the palate irresistible. Ah, Wightman, would [that] you had my appetite for a season. Open air living is a grand thing when you are once used to it.

On yesterday Burnside's Corps was reviewed by the President, "honest ole Abe." At 7 A.M. we were ordered on dress parade and marched with the band a mile or so to an open field into which troops were pouring from every neighboring camp. They were [ar]ranged in seven long lines, facing the road, the cavalry being posted in the rear and on the left flank and the artillery on the right; they covered a large area of level ground and the broad smooth slope of a hill in the rear.

The President promptly appeared on horseback in citizen's costume, escorted by a troop of officers and cavalry: dressed in black with a white choker, like a parson, and holding his big mouth ajar, after the manner of a sick oyster, the amiable magistrate rode, hat in hand, through the ranks, with Burnside on his left and McClellan and a host of division and other officers in the rear. A roar of cannon and a flourish of bugles greeted their coming, and as the long serpentine line of horsemen wound its way onward, the regimental bands in succession "discoursed sweet music" and added a new charm to the scene. The sky was perfectly clear.

The Zou-Zous are great favorites with Burnside, and he checked the progress of the President to call his attention to our tattered colors. It was observed that Abe's lower jaw dropped and his eye rolled as though the great man were mentally ejaculating, "Thunder!" As he passed by, a red cap behind me (presumed to be a butcher) remarked *sub voce*, "Ain't the old bugger lean? He wouldn't pay for skinnin."

The review was quickly and happily concluded. The whole affair took but a couple of hours and afforded a striking contrast to the tedious exhibitions of New York militia. You would think the maneuvering of our soldiers wonderfully rapid. Practice makes perfect.

Forty odd recruits came in a couple of days since: they left New York a week later than I did and stopped to drill at Alexandria. On Thursday night we had a moonlight serenade by the band.

At present no more news. We may stay here for weeks or be sent away at a moment's notice. I have as yet received no letters from home.

Ed

Camp near Sharpsburgh [*sic*]
Saturday Oct. 4, 1862

Dear Bro:

Hitherto I have not attempted to picture for you our daily life in camp, because we have been constantly on the move and had no settled routine. Even yet we are far from the system prescribed for permanent encampments. Still a sketch of our habits and practices here will give you something of an idea of a soldier's life.

General Ambrose E. Burnside *(Photograph courtesy of the Library of Congress)*

At the first streak of dawn reveille beats, and we are dragged forth for roll call. In Company B twenty two men come out of "dog houses" on hands and knees and after standing erect and stretching themselves form in double line in the company street. They are all yawning. Big men and little men mix themselves up without regard to size. Some have leggins on and some have not, while other lazy boobies appear in their stocking feet, or with one trouser leg up and the other down. Some are bareheaded, some have their fezes on hindside before, and all have more or less straw in their hair. If it is cold, a part of the men wear overcoats and a part blankets.

The orderly, with a roll book in hand and [a] little darkey beside him holding a candle, says in a bedoozling sort of a way, "Front," at which the men with their hands in their pockets walk around sideways and look at him as sleepily as a cud-chewing cow at twilight. The names are called, and at the command of "Break ranks, march!" the poor fellows cease the effort to keep their eyes open and, crawling into their tents, flop down and finish their snooze.

But, having been once roused, they can't sleep and so take their towels and soap and go down to the brook for a wash and to replenish their canteen[s]. The water is muddy, of course, and blue with soap from the multitude of ablutions—but that is nothing. The first day we came here, every fish in the neighboring brooks was killed with soap. The little innocents floated by, belly up, in shoals.

Hands, face, and neck and head receive a thorough scrubbing. Then we adjourn to the Springs. However clear at first, they soon become yellow with mud. Crowds stand around them and a foot is placed in every available spot.

At sunrise the motley groups present at a distance [a] very picturesque view, the uniforms of many regiments being mingled; and as if to spice the scene with activity white horsemen and black donkey drivers are continually rushing over the hills, clattering along the rough road, and splashing through the water.

By the time we get back, breakfast is ready. The company cook calls out, "Fall in, Co. B for grub," and tin cup in hand we form in single file like the boys at the post office and are served in turn. Cook stands over three great kettles of coffee (sweetened with sugar but without milk) and measures a cupful to every man, at the same time furnishing him with four hard crackers [hardtack]. At dinner time, perhaps, he omits the coffee and gives soup and boiled meat; the latter is taken away in our fingers. We then retire to our tents to eat.

After breakfast "the doctors call" is beat, and the sick go to the medical wagon, which is fitted up as a small apothecary's shop, for advice and medicine. Some go to shirk work. The doctor examines them and, after prescribing, marks on the roll-book against their names respectively "Q" and "LD" or "D," which signifies "[Restricted to] Quarters," "Light Duty," "Duty," and the Orderly Sergeant is guided in his appointments accordingly.

At 8 A.M. the drum beats for guard mounting. The full band appears to assist in the ceremony, and the old guard is formally relieved and the new one mustered in. The proceedings somewhat resemble, in a small way, a dress parade except that the manual of arms is omitted and an inspection substituted. At present about half a dozen men are called out from each company. They serve as camp guard twenty four hours, two hours on and four off. Egress from the regiment[al] grounds is thus prevented except in one direction, which those pursue who go for water.

At 9 A.M. the recruits are taken out for two hours drill.[37] The physical exercise is nothing to me as I am the only pupil in Company B and previous practice at the gymnasium enables me to tire out my instructor almost without effort. Each company breaks in its own recruits.

At noon we dine luxuriously and then "sit awhile," or rather doze in the straw. At 2 P.M. the recruits work two hours more, after which all are busy polishing up pieces and buttons for dress parade, which occurs at sundown. Then we are all in high heels and good behavior. Everything is done with a will and as by machinery. Those who drooped in the sun an hour before are now apparently fresh and over charged with motive power. The full band strikes up, and the Zouaves march into the field with a splendid tread—so firm and elastic and in such exact rhythm that you could not imagine them the drowsy loafers of early morning. A parade is a beautiful thing to look at, and ours attracts a multitude of gazes from the other regiments.

When the companies have been dismissed, their arms are inspected by the lieutenants and orderly sergeants, and the men sent to their quarters. Then follows a supper of coffee and crackers, and the Zouzous gather in groups upon the "grass" to fight their battles o'er again. Roanoke, Camden, Newport News, South Mountain, and Antietam all furnish themes on which they are never tired of discoursing. They laugh at and brag over lucky shots, they wonderingly tell of narrow escapes, and they whistle at the recollection of charges against grape and cannister [sic]. They recount who fell here and who died there and show a soldier's sorrow as they enumerate the virtues of their lost companions.

Tattoo breaks up the parties at 8 P.M. and half an hour later "taps" warns us to "douse the glim," and, retiring, we talk ourselves to sleep.

W.

Antietam Creek 7 miles from
Harpers Ferry, Monday morning
October 6th, 1862

Dear Mother and Sisters:

At about sunrise this morning, while on my way to the cook after a cup of coffee and my ration of crackers, the first communication from home, in the shape of a letter from Mary and Ell with an appendix by Fred, was handed me; its date is Sept. 30. . . . The girls write so naturally that I almost imagined them, as I read, within arm's reach where I could pinch and bother them to my hearts content. My breakfast, between reading and eating, was quite a banquet. In return let me try to amuse you by sketching an account of such features of life as may be supposed to be of interest to housekeepers.

Our chamberwork and parlor dusting are very easily accomplished. The bed of myself and two companions consists chiefly of a sprinkling of straw upon the ground. Over this I spread one half of my rubber blanket, covering myself with the other half and in the absence of my knapsack making a pillow of my cartridge box. The man on my right prefers to rest his head on a three cornered stone. When there is no prospect of a rain or of a heavy dew, I throw off cap, Jacket, leggins and boots. The bed-making is done by giving two or three hasty scrubs to the straw.

Don't suppose I have forgotten how to spring up on my elbow in the night and kick out my left foot at burglars. Not at all. I made a splendid hit at my

German friend not long since. He was foolish enough to return from guard duty at 12 A.M. (Jim's hour), and of course his close-cropped head was honored with a heavy salute the moment it looked in at the dog house. Luckily my boot was off and the barber is good natured.

Our bed now is also the dining and the reception room. It is "put to rights" by levelling the straw and thrusting all accoutrements in the corners. We dine reclining on one elbow, after the style of the ancients, generally out of a tin cup, holding a spoon in the right hand. When guests come in to chat or help devour a piece of cheese or other novelty, they are expected to lie spoon fashion or to coil themselves up ingeniously so as to make room for the greatest possible number. Sometimes they are packed as close as cobble stones.

Now for the cooking—we breakfast at sunrise, dine at noon, and sup at sundown. The meals are prepared for the whole company by a cook and his assistant, chosen by the orderly sergeant from the ranks; their service is voluntary, and they are exempt from all military duty.

At the first flush of dawn the cooks send a couple of the regiment's darkies down to the spring for water. In a jiffy the nigs return with three kettles of awfully muddy water, strung on a rail. The kettles hold from 6 to 8 gallons each: they are cylindrical, without covers, and made of sheet iron. The muddy water is soon boiled over a crackling fire built of neighboring fences, and a large tin cup full of ground coffee is then housed in each kettle. Whenever there is danger of boiling over, a little cold water is dashed into the mixture, and its effect is instantaneous. In a few minutes the kettles are lifted off with a rail, and a cupful of brown sugar stirred into each. This accomplished, the cook and his assistant stand guard over the mixture and yell out at the top of their voices, "Fall in Company B for grub!" Co. B form[s] in single file, while cook measures out the coffee and his assistant the crackers.

For dinner we have boiled meat or beef tea of some kind, but the process of manufacture is so complicated that I will not venture to attempt a description. What has been said will suffice to give you a good general idea of our way of doing things in the company cooking department. But aside from this, much is done through private enterprise. An opinion prevails, for instance, that in whatever manner crackers are treated by fire, they are improved. So the boys toast, boil, or fry them. They make mixtures of meat, crackers, potatoes, and such other vegetables as they can lay hands on and call the conglomeration "lobscourse." The get flour of the sutler and make flapjacks. They fry sliced apples. In fact, there is no end to their greasy combinations. Our professional cooks are *not* the neatest men in the regiment. Picture to yourselves a couple of slippery esquimmaux [Esquimaux—i.e., Eskimos] clad in the habiliments of destitute Irishmen, and you will have a tolerable notion of them. Still, don't understand me as censuring them; their appearance never interferes with my appetite.

Our washing at present is of little consequence, as we have with us only the clothing on our backs. A ration of soap, however, is given out once a week, and every Saturday we wade into Antietam Creek and play washerwoman. Our under clothing then and there receives a thorough scrubbing. The quantity of lather and the energy of wringing would raise the eyebrows to the roots of your hair with astonishment. When the washing is done, we "go ashore" and, hanging the "pieces" on bushes or spreading them on the grass, sit patiently in the shade till they are dry. In better times, when we have our baggage, a Sunday inspection compels the men to show a clean suit on their person and another in their knapsack.

As ever affect. yours
Ed.

Antietam Creek 7 miles from
Harpers Ferry Oct. 6th, 1862

Dear Sister Ell:

At home they think you rather slack in the way of letter writing. I feel therefore very much flattered by your attention to me and think you well merit a prompt and special answer and the more so as you rose before that wakeful old lark of mine and held your confab with me before commencing that grand operation, viz: doing your hair. As I have already given to others such items of news as you would consider interesting up to the present time, I will, after gently reproaching you for ommitting [sic] to advise me of the condition of *my* cat, "Sinckhem," proceed to tell you of the jolly animals that sojourn with us Zouaves.

You will take it for granted that we always have in and around the camp more horses and donkies than you can shake a stick at, and they kick and squeal at such a rate that a conniption fit would be the least penalty you would escape with on visiting them. But I only intend to speak of the private property of the "boys."

1st. They own two horses . . . poor worn out creatures [that] were rescued by the Zou-Zous from a couple of cavalry men who were about to shoot them as useless. They are of little practical value, being kept mainly for ornamental purposes. . . . If Mason [a family friend] should take a freak to raise a regiment of abolition sunday school scholars, I will use my influence with our regiment to secure for him one of these steeds the instant he gets his commission as Colonel. If he really wants to be Quixotic, he'll never have a better chance.

2d. They have a variety of dogs. Two weeks ago we could boast a cat also. A Mrs. Quinn, the wife of a man in Company C and who followed him everywhere, had a gray and white cat named "Queen" which was remarkably intelligent. "Queen," she would say, "I bid you give Michael his supper": whereupon Queen would march off to the cook, get a piece of meat, and return with it to Michael, a brown little curly tailed dog. But alas! Mrs. Quinn was so shocked with the scenes of the late battle that she suddenly jumped into a homeward bound wagon a few days ago and, taking with her her caravan of pets, returned to New York, leaving her husband disconsolate.

We have dogs enough left, though. The most famous of them is "Old Carlo," a great, shaggy, brindled fellow, who has served his sixteen months with honor and, it is to be hoped, will finally return home bathed in glory. Carlo has the benevolence of the Newfoundland dog blended with the sturdy strength and pluck of the mastiff. He resembles both. The toothless old chap is a tremendous fighter. Woe to the unlucky canine who provokes him, for he is quick tempered and never was known to be "licked" (except by his mother when a pup) (JOKE).

Perhaps you remember my mentioning in a previous letter a black Newfoundland dog called "Jack" who accompanied the squad of recruits from New York. Well, Carlo got jealous of Jack and broke his right foreleg the other day, and it was only by the interference of half-a-dozen Zou-zous that Jack was rescued from drowning in a pond where Carlo had dragged him and was holding him under. On the same day Carlo attacked a pig in the water and broke both his forelegs. Yet the old dog in his intercourse with our men is as amiable as a lamb. The sight of a red cap, no matter where he meets it or whether he has ever seen its wearer before, makes him nearly trip himself up with tail wagging.

With the exception of Camden he has been in every battle in which the regiment has engaged. At the battle of Antietam he was wounded in the breast with a fragment of shell and skedaddled at a double quick for the hospital, where after having the wound dressed, he lounged round as if off duty and free from care. While at Newport News Carlo was bitten in the leg by another dog, and the intelligent brute joined the sick squad next morning at "doctors call" and every day thereafter until cured. The men consulted the doctor first, and then old Carlo, who had sat on his haunches awaiting his turn, walked up and lifted his leg for inspection. Every day he appeared regularly with a fresh bandage.

Carlo shows the greatest dignity on dress parade. He takes his position on the right of the regiment, and when the band starts down the line, old Carlo marches ahead as majestically as though girt with [the] sword of a Major General. The Ninth thinks everything of him. Besides Carlo and Jack we have other dogs, but they are only trifles.

There! I flatter myself that is sufficiently full and satisfactory in the animal way. If you want further details, say so. Say anything you choose with the largest liberty. Write as often as you can conveniently. I shall always be glad to have home pictures and to read home news. . . .

I remain truly your affect. Bro.

                                                                  Ed.

2
PLEASANT VALLEY AND LOUDOUN COUNTY

[After its violent participation at Antietam, the Ninth New York enjoyed a pleasant interlude in a valley of the same name. In the country between Virginia's Blue Ridge and Bull Run Mountains, the regiment salved its wounds while McClellan made plans to renew battle against Lee—plans never put into effect. While awaiting action, Edward learned the rigorous and exacting business of infantry service. He also visited ravaged towns such as Sharpsburg and Harpers Ferry, ruminated on Christianity's role in wartime, condemned his army's propensity to burn and pillage, chronicled some unseemly intraregimental rivalries, and depicted the suffering of soldiers confined to field hospitals.

Already critical of the material available in the officer corps, he toyed with the notion of seeking a commission, before rejecting it decisively. From a secure niche among the rank and file, he condemned McClellan's indecisiveness, predicted his demise, and saw Ambrose Burnside replace him once the War Department lost faith in "Little Mac." Though echoing the prevailing opinion that Burnside was a good man, Edward was nevertheless wary of the army's future under a general who had repeatedly advised Washington of his unwillingness to command so many troops.]

> Camp among the Blue Ridge
> Mountains Md (2 miles from Sandy Hook)
> Wednesday, 8th Oct. 1862

Dear Bro:

My last note to you, I believe, brought matters up to Saturday last. Mary asks about the observance of Sunday and the manner in which the duties of the chaplains are discharged. There is no Sunday in camp. I have seen no religious services among the soldiers and know of no chaplain in our brigade. The chaplain of the Ninth went home to get a commission and is now a captain in some new regiment.

Clergymen meet with so many obstacles in the army that few of them have the pluck to stand up and fight unflinchingly against them. A minister and a soldier are antipodes in sentiment. The one preaches "election" and the other fatalism. The minister prides himself upon the clearness and eloquence with which he *elucidates* his principles, and the soldier is equally careful to show by his *actions* that he risks everything on his. Theoretical Christianity alone will never find rest in the camp. Men of action always despise simple declaimers. A white cravat might preach and pray itself into a decline in the presence of a regiment and yet produce no other result than a satirical jeer or a cry of "hypocrite."

But let a real earnest *practical* Christian come into the army—one who will pray *with* the men and not *at* them, who identifies his interests with theirs and treats them with the air of a brother who loves them with all his heart rather than as a superior officer who has corrected them of sin by court martial and condescendingly promises to use his influence with the commander-in-chief for a reprieve—a chaplain who is a living exponent of the principles of the Bible . . . such a one would be respectfully and gladly received. But foot soldiers cannot endure the criticism of the citizens on horseback, whether they wear white or black cravats.

The hardest characters among us occasionally show religious superstition. I well remember that when our squad of recruits were about to march from Frederick, leaving our knapsacks behind, Terry Brady and two or three other "roughs" refused to go till they had secured their prayer books, and the whole party was consequently kept waiting. I have heard these same men, who ridicule the psalm singing of pig stealing Connecticut men, eulogize with great feeling the Christian virtues of a plain hard working chaplain just as they would the sympathy of their own Colonel or the genius of McClellan. Our regiment at present uses Sunday merely as a day of rest. We are rarely near a church and cannot hear preaching if we would.

On last Sunday I visited the hospital where some of our wounded are lying; all but about forty of these crippled have been sent home on furlough, and many of them will probably remain there until the regiment is mustered out in May. Those who stayed behind were too seriously hurt to be transported. Immediately after breakfast, Corporal Rogers of Company B and I procured a pass (if not lost I will enclose it as a curiosity) which was signed by the orderly sergt. and Lieut. of the Company, by the acting Col. Kimball, and by Col. Fairchild, acting Brigadier, and having provided ourselves with a few delicacies for the sick, set out on our walk of four miles. Rogers' shoes, which nothing but one of the waxed-ends from Abbie's knapsack had held together for a week past, were so far gone that the Zouave quickstep played upon them with a noise like the sound of milk clappers. We were stopped by a picket guard at the bridge over Antietam Creek, but the pass saved us from arrest and the guard house. A little further on we stopped at a cool spring covered by a little stone hut (a very common institution in Maryland) to fill our canteens. The road was pleasant, there were but few stragglers out, and the air was cool.

A walk of three miles carried us by the late battlefield into the village of Sharpsburgh, quite a nice place boasting two hotels. Everything here showed the mark of Burnside's cannon: liberty poles shattered, houses riddled, stone walls breached, and pavements torn up. The small wooden hotel and tavern where we took dinner (for we were determined not to waste so rare an opportunity of sitting on chairs at a table) was perforated like a honeycomb with Union balls. The parlor especially had been ill used. One window sash had been smashed clean out, and the plaster of the ceiling and walls had been ploughed and broken up in a mighty thoughtless harum-scarum style.

When Rogers and I tumbled into the room, we found the black eyes of half-a-dozen billious [sic], long-haired Southerners fixed upon us. There were no seats vacant, so we called for extra chairs. Our Southern brethren eyed our red fezes and spit tobacco-juice in profound silence for about five minutes. Then one of them observed, with a gesture round the room, "You men did this yer!" To which Rogers, surveying the premesis [sic] with the air of a mechanic who had done a nice job, simply responded, "Yas-as!"

Some of the guests bore the character of Union Marylanders travelling; but one of them, who told a number of impossible stories about the romantic habits and tremendous feats of Burnside, was evidently one of the farmers whose log house and roughly cultivated fields form chief items in the scenes of Maryland. At the announcement of dinner the two N.Y. Zouaves took the right of the line and made a "double quick" charge on the edibles in a style that left their competitors ignominiously in the rear. Roast beef, bread, vegetables, apple sauce, and pies melted away like snow in Indian summer. . . .

Leaving the dinner party entangled in a labyrinth of amazement, we loosened our belts five holes each and complacently continued our journey through the town. We were stopped once and our papers examined by the provost guard. After crossing a second bridge over the Antietam and walking a mile beyond, we suddenly came upon the hospital. It consisted of about 20 tents arranged in two lines and surrounded by trenches to ensure them against dampness. As a protection against the heat of the sun they had also double roofs, the upper one of which is termed a "fly." The tents were rectangular in shape, and each contained eight thick straw matresses [sic] and as many patients: the latter were severally grunting, groaning, reading newspapers, and chewing tobacco, and one or two wounded in the arm had crawled outside in their drawers and taken their seats in the sunshine on an empty cracker box.

The countenances of the sick, of course, presented a variety of expression[s]. Some appeared to have been opened by bullets merely to let out a superabundance of good nature and to make a vent for the egress of their philosophy; but others habitually wore an expression of pain and depression. Nurses, male and female, were in attendance; they appeared to me to be both rough and untrained. The air of the tents was almost insufferably close and tainted, though the facilities for ventilation were all that could be desired. The boys (about 40 of the 9th) received our offerings, together with two or three dozen N.Y. Heralds handed us for them at Sharpsburg with favor.

When we had started on our return (for we were required to be back at sunset for dress parade), we saw by the roadside one of our regiment, almost skeleton in appearance, who, although still afflicted with fever and so weak he could scarcely rise without assistance, had left the hospital to join his comrades in the field. He said he was "Sim Hubbard from Connecticut."[1] We carried his rifle and accoutrements to camp and sent him back to the hospital. He gave a sickly laugh at his helplessness and promised to do as much for us sometimes.

Shortly afterward Leut. Col. Kimball, accompanied by wagons containing our full band and the little nigger "York," went by on their way to serenade our poor fellows. Once we stopped on the road for water at a deserted house around which four gray kittens were playing, and once for apples. Just as the sun slipped down behind the western hills, the summons for evening parade greeted our ears, and, rushing up, we were just in time to respond to our names; but I was unlucky enough in my hurry to dash my canteen against a cup of coffee which Whetlaufer had placed in the dog house for me and so lost half my supper.

Monday was a general loafing day. I neither have nor can I borrow military or other books at present.[2] Our spare time is generally spent in scrubbing up equipments. Rifles are anatomized, screw drivers, emery paper, buckskin, oil, etc, brought into requisition and a mass [detail] got up on short notice comparable with house cleaning. Daubs of rust and dust get on your nose, and your hands become coal-colored when there is no water to wash [with]. In such circumstances one feels as if he had been dipped in cobwebs. However, no one thinks of complaining of such trifles here. I mention them partly for your amusement and partly for my own, for I don't often indulge in such criticisms.

On Tuesday morning [October 7] we were ordered to be ready to march at 7 o'clock. By eleven A.M. the whole division was in motion under direction of Col. Hawkins, who is released from arrest and has formally assumed his new command.[3] The job in hand was to march between two or three miles over the Elk Ridge (marked Maryland Heights in the newspaper maps) and establish a new encampment. The Ninth had had the right of the line, and I, being in Co. B and a pretty tall fellow, headed the column.

The impression among those who have never seen an army on the march is that soldiers march in exact line and in step as when on parade. Not at all—At the route step every man bobs along to suit himself, straddling or mincing, as seems best to him, but he is not to lose his relative position and must be able to spring into place and maneuvre [sic] at a moment's warning. We generally travel four abreast with rifles at a right-shoulder shift; but the mountain roads were so narrow that we could only advance in double file and the ascent and descent so steep that we skinned our noses going up and walked on our backs coming down. Golly! didn't we grunt! Je-ru-salem, didn't we sweat!

But when after an hour of heavy dragging work we had labored to the summit and the glorious little valley between Elk Ridge and South Mountain burst upon our gaze, green with verdure, dotted with villages, and looking so deliciously cool with its groves of waving shade trees and winding streams of dark water, the boys exhausted the little stock of breath they had carefully husbanded in a loud shout. The colonel allowed us to stack arms, unsling haversacks, and kindle fires for boiling coffee. On the march the cooking apparatus is placed in wagons and kept too far in the rear to be come-at-able, and each man must therefore depend upon his own tin cup for boiling, upon his canteen for water, and for a mixture of ground coffee and sugar upon his previous experience and foresight.

After resting two hours we commenced the descent. The struggles for water at every brook we passed were wonderfully earnest. In the midst of one of the streams, rather broader and deeper than the rest, the tired horse of "Old Gunpowder" Kimball laid down with him, treating us to a hearty laugh at his expense. The animal wouldn't get up and the Colonel had to wade ashore. "Did you see my agility?" said he with a sheepish grin. "Agility," replied one of the boys, "we don't call it that in the country."

But I have already strung out this narrative too long. Shortly after the above incident we halted, the pioneers[4] cut down a couple of lengths of rail fence for our entrance into the field, and we pitched our tents therein. We are two miles from Sandy Hook, Md and four from Harpers Ferry, Va., between the South Mountain Range and Elk Ridge, which at this point are about a quarter of a mile apart at their bases. Israel's creek runs between, and aside from it we have an abundance of nice water from a clear spring.

As ever yours tr.
Ed.

Near Sandy Hook, Md. Oct. 9, '62

Dear Bro. Fred:

Your note of Sept. 25th, accompanied by family letters and newspaper clippings, came to hand on Wednesday night (8th inst.) The map is especially valuable. Thank Abbie for her letter and remembrance. She will not, of course, imagine [it] an intentional slight if I do not reply to her individually. When I address you, she will consider that the firm of Wightman and Hartl[e]y is addressed.

The note of introduction to Col. Hawkins[5] came with the rest. It is ra-a-ther strong for a bashful man, but I shall doubtless use it at the proper moment. The omission to enclose it at first I did not notice because I preferred to do without it; but since you have taken so much pains on my account, I shall try to use it to the best advantage. I am very reluctant to connect myself with the medical department. Nothing is to be learned in camp hospitals, and the work is disgusting beyond expression. I would attempt nothing beyond rendering assistance in field surgery.

My military instruction thus far amounts to nothing. My "Hardee"[6] was necessarily left behind in my knapsack; it will arrive in a couple of days. The knapsacks of the old men [i.e., the veterans] have already come up from Washington. The other recruits have been drilled regularly as I have written you, about four hours per day when not on the march; but they are both awkward and slow, and the clumsy ones keep back the rest. They are not allowed to mix with the old men. For myself, being alone in the company, I made more rapid progress and after four lessons in the manual and marching was allowed to appear on dress parade. They give themselves no further trouble about me, though, and I must depend on observation and books for the rest.

In haste,
Ed

Camp in the mountains 2 miles
from Sandy Hook, Md.
Thursday, Oct. 9, 1862

Dear Father:

I had the whole family [in photographs] in my doghouse last night—all but the placid, kind cap'n who, I suspect, is bringing up the rear and will appear in due time. The mail came in just as "taps" was sounding for the extinguishment of lights. I got a fresh ½ candle and, throwing myself upon the straw, soon had you all around me without being crowded for accommodations—father, mother, Fred, Abbie, Jim, Mary, Ell: and Charles supposed to be tramping along behind. The perusal of my packet was completed at the moment the last bit of candle was consumed.

I am glad to hear of the happy conclusion of your summer trip and hope its effect upon [the health of] mother and the girls may be better than temporary. . . . Some of the girls, indeed all of them, seem to imagine that I have an intense longing after sweetmeats and tarts and that my health must be giving away. On the contrary, I find that plain Government fare agrees with me remarkably well. Indeed, I am satisfied that it is best for me to restrict myself to it as far as possible. My appetite is almost voracious, and my health and strength are much improved since leaving New York.

As to exposing myself carelessly in battle, the probability that our regiment will engage in one soon is so small that it will seem almost superfluous at present to allude to it. You may rest assured, however, that I shall not under any circumstances attempt Quixotism [sic]. The simple discharge of my duty is all I aim at. . . .

It is raining. Perhaps the ommission [sic] of parade will enable me to send a few words to mother.

Respectfy. I am Yr. Affect. Son
Ed. K. Wightman

Camp near Sandy Hook, Md.
Thursday, Oct. 9th, 1862

Dear Mother:

Never think it "almost needless" to write. Whether you have news to tell or not, your letters will be equally acceptable. I have no idea, though, to tempt you to do anything that will limit your time for exercise. Perhaps this, though, applies more directly to Mary: I remember her old confining habit of solitary letter writing. Don't let her or Ell make their correspondence with me an excuse for staying in-doors. They should be shut out on the front stoop for an airing every day, like old Dr. Owen. Tell them I have my eye open for a trace of husbands for them. Do they fancy Terry Brady or "Cockroach," or are those gentlemen not sufficiently refined? Perhaps they may take a fancy to some other fellows I shall come across and describe. If so, let them only notify me, and they will have an agent ready made.

Are you and Mary getting strong again? And are you regular enough in your habits, and do you take exercise enough in the open air to *earn* health? I saw myself in a glass [mirror] today for the first time since leaving New York. Having eschewed the useless practice of shaving, I was not surprised to find my head with its short crop of hair all round, resembling a thistle bird. I am brown, too, as a berry. Probably five or six layers of skin have been successfully burned off my face. I have not counted them but nevertheless have a very distinct remembrance of the blisters and soreness.

The shower is past and we shall have a parade after all. I must put this in the letter bag and polish my piece.

Your aff. son,
Ed.

Pleasant Valley, Md. 2 miles from
Sandy Hook, Md. Tuesday, Oct. 12 [14] 1862

Dear Bro:

As our officers persist in saying that we are encamped in Pleasant Valley, I place it at the head of my letter, though your map represents it as being on the other side of Elk Ridge.

If I am not mistaken my narrative is complete up to Wednesday of last week. Since that time I have been one way and another so bedoozled that I was perfectly content to let the world wag along while I spent my spare time snoozing on the straw, lazily opening an eye now and then just to keep posted on the order of events and to frighten off the flies. Besides, I have recently been promoted to the lofty position of company clerk, a place that gives me no glory and plenty of work: for the orderly is a sickly fellow and can do no writing to speak of. I have access, however, to the company books and, of course, all the opportunity I could wish to become acquainted with the forms of documents. I have also secured a copy of the "Army Regulations" so that I shall not trouble you to purchase [it]. My "Hardee" will doubtless come to hand in a day or two.

I made a personal complaint to Col. Kimball this morning of the inconveniences of sleeping without a blanket and doing duty in wind and rain without an overcoat. He was about sending out a wagon train and immediately ordered up the knapsacks of four squads from Frederick. We expect them tomorrow night. I shall then draw upon the Quartermaster for two suits of underclothing: they will be the first things I have drawn since leaving home. At Washington I bought a heavy loose blue shirt, which has since done good service. My heavy marching shoes are worn habitually.

"But to return to our subject." On Wednesday of last week we struck tents and re-pitched them in order and by rule. This time six men buttoned their "pocket handkerchiefs" together, two on each side and one at each end, the inmates sleeping across in a row. The occupants of "ours" are a little fussy fellow, (a trifle like you) me boy, named [Private Robert M.] Buckmaster, Whetlaufer, the German barber whom I have before described, and a lanky booby—named Wightman, whose boots are eternally punching through one side of the tent to get soaked with night dew, while his head is bursting out the other side: these three form one department separated from the other only by a pole. On the other side of the pole are [Private William W.] Travis, a quiet good looking fellow with a light moustache [sic] and imperial, formerly a farmer and milk cart driver successively; and [Private] John Smith, a tall, tough, perverse, conceited "Hinglishman." Another man, [Private William H.] Bailey, belongs in the 2nd Department or apartment, but he has always been absent on safeguard duty, i.e., protecting a house in the neighborhood.

Buckmaster is the assistant cook who was displaced to make room for "Cockroach." A small farmer from New York state, he was seduced by ambition of military fame to join the army and after a year's hard labor and much scheming succeeded in being made a corporal, but was soon reduced for neglect of duty, and his health has ever since been on the decline. I sketched his lugubrious countenance and scrubby head the other day with [such] conscientious faithfulness and exactness of detail that a portrait painter in the company pronounced the work "a gem" and fell into ecstasy over it. He then circulated the paper among the dog houses, and as its minute excellencies were revealed by candlelight, waves of laughter pealed out upon the air with shocking vigor. Buckmaster is one of those who is always straining to be popular and never can be, and I begin to think it was pretty mean in me to have him ridiculed. He has since been taken to the hospital.

Travis is quiet and harmless and the butt of Smith. He is remarkable for nothing except for having a very sore great toe which he is always squeezing and making faces at when off duty and for having borrowed a pair of socks from one Wightman. Smith was intended by nature for a mule, but was probably fashioned into an Englishman for want of sufficient material to make the animal complete. Whenever I have a little spare time, I stir him up on some English theme, and the way in which he gets mixed and muddled up in his excitement . . . would make a horse laugh. He always furnished an hour's amusement after the labors of the day before we get to sleep. John has been a soldier for 15 years, a part of which was served in the Crimean War.

"But to return to our subject." Our tents had scarcely been re-pitched when a change in the weather (pre-indicated on Monday by a flight of geese to the South) occurred. The temperature fell rapidly, the sky became overcast, and we were soon beset with a cold drizzling rain which continued at intervals through Thursday, Friday, Saturday, Sunday, and Monday. Early in the forenoon we had company drills and in the afternoon a battalion drill with knapsacks.

By the bye, I forgot to mention that those of the Regiment who left their knapsacks at Washington received them the latter part of last week—about Friday. The rejoicing thereat was unexampled. At the same time quartermaster's stores were distributed, and the happiness of the "boys" was complete: for previously they were ragged and many of them barefoot or almost shoeless. If the 9th had been marched into New York as captured rebels in their old worn fatigue suits, before their knapsacks came, there would never had been an end to disparaging comments and to predictions of a sudden collapse of the Confederacy for want of supplies.[7]

"But to return to our subject." Where was I? At the battalion drill. We started out at about 1½ P.M. on Tuesday [the fourteenth] at the route step, with knapsacks (luckily I had none), for Brownville [Brownsville], less than two miles distant. "Amid the point proposed" we stacked arms, went to the houses near for water, and were fortunate enough to secure in addition a few apples. When half-a-mile had been passed on the way back, I happened to notice while "at rest" that my next neighbor, lazy [Private] Sam Osborne, had no pack on his back. When told of the fact, he was thoroughly astounded and walked back as sneakingly as a plucked fowl.

A little further on we were led into a field and put through a course of sprints at the double quick that could have made your tongue loll and your eyes goggle. We were formed in line of battle and rushed up hill and down over stones, stumps, and ploughed ground, formed into hollow squares in half a dozen different ways (some of them peculiar to the regiment), and wheeled and halted "to the top of our bent." We got back only in time to prepare for parade. Kimball informed us that we are to see active service again in a few days and says the knapsack drills will be continued.

Our destination is unknown. Burnside has assumed command of the 2nd and 12th Army Corps, and the 9th is now under the orders of Gen. Wilcox [Brigadier General Orlando B. Willcox].[8] The generally received opinion is that we are to go to Harpers Ferry, then by rail to Washington, thence by steamer to North or South Carolina. A second party believe we are to advance with McClellan's left wing into Virginia. In one case a warm climate of considerable ease seem[s] before us; in the other, plenty of rough work.

Wednesday, Oct. 15th. Today is much like yesterday, only more pleasant. In the morning a dozen or so of recruits came in direct from New York. The[y] say affairs there wear their usual aspect. I am glad to observe in yesterday's

Herald that drafting has again been deferred till the 10th of November⁹. . . . We had the knapsack drill again this afternoon and the usual evening parade, but there is nothing of importance to note.

You will see how disconnected all this is. It is scribbled in snatches at odd moments. Don't expect to hear from me so often hereafter—not half so often. I have not the time to write and there is no need of doing so. You are now familiar with the general current of my life and can see how little there is in it to excite uneasiness or alarm. If you do not hear from me (on account of the inconvenience of writing or of the irregularity of the mails) for two or three weeks at a time, be assured I am well: for if injured I will write to you immediately.

Our company now numbers about 90 men in and out of the hospital, and the making of payrolls, discipline [disciplinary action] lists, keeping the books, etc., together with drills, will consume all my time. Distributions of mails are made at Headquarters, Washington, for the army twice a week, on Wednesday[s] and Saturdays. When our corps is on the march, it will be difficult to receive letters at all. The boys have been without them a month or more at some periods. I think daily newspapers must be stopped on account of their bulk or to furnish reading matter for the hospitals. If any newspapers have been sent me, they have been stopped before reaching me. Weeklies come through, however. Many of the Regiment get the [New York] Sunday Mercury regularly. . . .

Many sutlers are hovering round in expectation of the arrival of the Paymaster, but we must meet him elsewhere. Four months pay is due the 9th.

In haste,
Ed.

Pleasant Valley, Md.
Friday eve. Oct. 17th 1862

Dear Bro:

A grand event has occurred and I write to inform you of the particulars. Until Thursday evening I believe there was nothing worth noticing after the date of my last [letter]. Thursday evening came enveloped in a thunder storm that ripped and tore around the camp in a terrific manner, prognosticating something extraordinary. We Zou-Zous "lay low" and let it continue to prognosticate. Roll call was omitted "because of the ———" drenching rain. But at about 8½ P.M. there was a lull, and the cry of "Wightman, Wightman!" passed along the line. But Wightman couldn't be induced to come out of the straw till a Dutch sergeant yelled through a button hole, "Viteman, eer-r-res yer knapsack from Frederick."

In another instant I was rushing madly towards the end of the tent on my hands and knees: it had been buttoned up to keep out the rain but [a] stone wall itself could not have withstood such a battering rain. There followed a shock which shook the tent-poles and a sound like the tearing of stout carpet rugs.

Than [sic] I found myself in the open air making for the colonel's tent. The thunder growled, but I was after my knapsack. Those visions of warm blankets and comfortable overcoats which had made up my dreams for a month past during the chilling hours of our black foggy nights—were about to be realized. I was going after a fresh stock of pencils which had thus appeared just in time to relieve the stubby stump I have so long economized with. The eye of my mind was dwelling upon certain light gaiters for a change, upon new socks, a clean shirt, an apothecary's shop, a toothbrush, and other priceless treasures which only a soldier can appreciate.

Col. Kimball sat in front of his tent warming his hands at a blazing fire, a chilling smile sitting grimly astride his features. Beside him was a pile of knapsacks. When Terry Brady and the rest of us had come up, the Col hemmed and, bending forward, pressed the hot legs of his trousers against his shins. Then he said, "Ah—boys—ah—I'm afraid there's some,—ah—disorder here." Then he rolled his eyes over the knapsacks and smoked like blazes. "Wall, I begin to think pretty hard."

"Fetch one of 'em here," said the Colonel. His orderly brought a knapsack, and by the red glare of the fire light read the magic letters "E. W."—"Open it," continued our commander gruffly. It was opened and I saw, What do you guess? Somebody-else's overcoat and that's all, by golly! "I never was so beat in all my life." It would have made you laugh yourself fat, you bony booby, to see our fellows' countenances at that critical moment. Didn't I laugh? Course—funny, you know.

Finally we agreed to postpone further examination till morning, when I was lucky enough to find in strange knapsacks my Testament, a vial of laudanum[10] and the remnants of some adhesive straps [for bandages]. All else was irrevocably gone. The Col. offered to repair the loss as far as possible with Govt. goods, and I accordingly ordered immediately through the Lieut. [Adjutant Thomas L. Bartholomew] a blanket, overcoat, and a suit of underclothing, to be furnished as soon as red tape can get them and free of expense—I have also ordered a second suit to be charged to me through the orderly. You will recollect that our goods were stowed in a Government warehouse at Frederick and a receipt taken for them. Some time after, quartermasters were changed. When our officer went to take them away, he found all the knapsacks torn open and what remained of their contents strewn over the floor of the store-room. . . .

I remain,
Ed. K. W.

Pleasant Valley, Md.
Tuesday, Oct. 21, 1862
[No greeting]

What'n thunder makes you describe an epicurean banquet to a fellow living on crackers and coffee!!!! "That's what I want to know!" Merely for curiosity, of course. You see, it seems so funny that you should be able to furnish a motive for the waste of time involved in the elaborate painting of dainties which I cannot recognize, however skillfully they may be delineated. Now "a delicious cut of roast beef," "a fine tenderloin steak," "the rich juice which followed the knife and slice after slice was lightly spread upon the platter," "fat lima beans with glistening sides piled up together in helpless obesity," etc., are all meaningful [meaningless] expressions to me, so long is it since I have dwelled in cities where such things are common and so poor my memory (shudder). I acknowledge, however, that when the phase [sic] "mealy sweet potato" met my eye, I did spasmodically stretch out my right arm and persistently fix my gaze on space—probably the shadow of some old habit that sticks by me.

Your letters, by the bye, caught *me* at dinner, a meal which with us requires *none* of the superfluous paraphanalia [sic] and ceremony you describe. When the Sergeant called out, "Two letters for you, Wightman," I was standing in line with twenty others, tin cup in hand, patiently awaiting my share of "rations." Our dinner had been delayed an hour or so to enable the cook and his assistant to boil their underclothes in the company kettles—and the clothes needed it so badly that none of us thought of complaining. Well, I put the letters in my pocket, got half a cupful of boiled rice with a table spoonful of molasses on top, and a double handful of cracker crumbs, and, crawling into my dog-house, leaned on one elbow and ruminated. That was all. Depend upon it, sir, the simplest way is the best way. . . .

On Sunday I procured a pass and walked out to Harpers Ferry, a distance of 4 miles through a very picturesque country. I was alone and went very leisurely, stopping to admire every fine view and to shake every persimmon tree on the road. We always have a thorough inspection of arms and knapsacks on Sunday morning, so that it was late when I started, [and] at 1½ P.M. before I reached my destination. After dining at a pie cellar, the proprietor of which vainly endeavored to "cheat and defraud" me out of my change, I proceeded to examine the place.

Harpers Ferry is a little smoky town situated at the junction of the Shenandoah and Potomac rivers, which at this point present a peculiar appearance. Both are broad streams (perhaps ½ as wide as the Connecticut at Middletown) and neither seems to average more than two feet in depth. The water runs noisily over a bed of solid rock, which as far as the eye can reach in every direction raise their knobby heads in countless numbers above its surface. In the Potomac, long, low islands appear here and there, green with verdure and supporting a few scattered trees. The banks of both streams rise grandly on all sides and in whatever direction you raise your eyes heavy forest-covered mountains overtop you. You can imagine better than I can describe the splendor of such scenery in the fall. It reminds me of West Point, N.Y.

I crossed from the Maryland side on a pontoon bridge, and first struck the "sacred soil of Virginia" within a stone's throw of the engine house in which John Brown was caught.[11] The pontoon bridge is a plank road over the

Potomac, its width from 12 to 15 feet, and the planking, bound together at the ends by cross beams and ropes above and below, is supported at intervals by heavy scows which point up and down stream and are anchored at stem and stern. The bridge of the Baltimore and Ohio R.R., recently destroyed by the rebels, is close by and has been rebuilt. I should have been glad to visit various encampments on London [Loudoun], Bolivar, and Maryland Heights, but it was necessary to return in time for dress parade. I climbed Bolivar Heights, however, passing Sumner's[12] headquarters on the way, and from the summit got a view of the rivers and mountains worth going many a mile to see. To the northwest at the distance of a couple of miles, the flat surface of the table land was covered with the white tents of the army.

When returning, I found a rusty cavalry carbine in the grass by the road. I left it there. A storm overtook me before reaching camp, but I escaped without much of a ducking.

Ed. K. W.

Pleasant Valley, Md.
Oct 25th, 1862

Dear Bro:

The accompanying note of Tuesday has been detained from day to day with the intention of adding further news; but thus far nothing of moment has occurred. The drills have been rather more severe and prolonged than before, and the weather a little less pleasant; but the extra work is a good neutralizer of the cold blustering fall winds which course through our valley. My blanket and underclothing came to hand nearly a week ago, and ever since I have slept comfortably; the former is neither so heavy nor large as those issued at New York, but is yet good.

I had almost forgotten to mention the two great fires which occurred within a couple of days and utterly destroyed two magnificent doghouses of the 9th Regt. One was caused by a recruit in Co. B (the brother of Corp. Rogers [Private George W. Rogers]) who threw a lighted match in the straw; and the other by a member of the pioneer corps. There was just as much noise and fuss made in extinguishing the flames as there would be in saving a block of stone fronts in 5th Ave. It was "Ya-a-ah!" "Ah-h-h!" "Sail in, Fortys!" "Play away, Big Sevens!" etc.[13] Nearly all the Regt. turned out to take a hand in the sport.

The spring water in our brook has grown so icy cold with the advance of the season that my bathing has been brought to a rather ignominious end. The morning wash alone tries a fellow's pluck considerably.

As to our future movements, I can give but little light. Rumors are plenty among us. We shall doubtless either advance with the left wing of McClellan's army into Virginia or join one of the great coastwise expeditions.[14] One of the latest reports is that we are destined for Texas! Another makes us winter where we are. Your [low] estimate of camp stories is correct.

Thirty men have been added to our pioneer corps, and we are being drilled as

Harpers Ferry, Virginia *(Photograph courtesy of Historical Times, Inc.)*

skirmishers.[15] I believe we are on the eve of great events. McClellan cannot afford to waste the fall months. Unless he accomplishes something, the next Congress will play the deuce with him and the country. The wrangling and rascality displayed this time will be more than disgraceful.

In haste, yours truly,
Ed.

P.S. Noon. We have received marching orders and are to submit to a general inspection at 3 P.M. Each man is allotted 60 rounds of cartriges [*sic*]. Shall probably move tomorrow morning.

W.

Pleasant Valley, Md. Monday eve.
October 27th, 1862

Dear Bro:

. . . Tomorrow at 8 A.M. we march (it is said) for Berlin [Maryland] on the Potomac, 11 miles distant. Rumor further says we are to go into winter quarters there and to act as a guard to the [Baltimore & Ohio] R.R. until mustered out; this, though, is only a camp rumor, and the "wish," perhaps, "is father to the thought." We were to have moved on Sunday, but a heavy storm set in on

Saturday night, continuing through Sunday and followed by a hurricane of wind which even now rocks and threatens to throw down the tent. I have no time to write particulars, but will try to do so in another letter.

I have been interrupted once by roll call and once by having my candle extinguished by the blowing out of the end of the Kennel. Thank everybody engaged in the [recently-sent gift] box matter and particularly father. "Taps" prevents my writing direct to him. Tell him I think nothing a hardship which private soldiers can endure; that generally we have nothing to complain of and that he must not bother himself or put himself to any pecuniary inconvenience on account of imaginary troubles of mine.

In haste,
Ed.

Camp in London [Loudoun] Co. Va. about 3
miles from Berlin, Md.
Tuesday, Oct 28th, 1862

Dear Bro:

I wrote you a hasty note last night, advising you of our anticipated march this morning. Let me give more details.

On Saturday afternoon, preliminary to the proposed start on Sunday morning, the arms, accoutrements, and knapsacks of the whole regiment were carefully inspected by McClellan's chief of engineers—a long, cold, and tedious process. While inspection was going on, Burnside rode up, then Col. Hawkins (now superseded in the division command and acting only for the Brigade), then Gen. Sturgis[16] and lady on horseback, accompanied by other damsels, and finally, most contemptible and least distinguished, three newspaper reporters. Burnside stayed but a few minutes, but he performed his tremendous feat of twisting off *that hat* and holding down his head to show the ladies the forehead on top. They smiled pleasantly and bowed, and it is to be presumed they saw it; and the hero then rode away, apparently the proudest and happiest man in the army.

Now Kimball, you must know, is over anxious, in the absence of Hawkins, to sport before the public as *The* Colonel of the Zouaves—Kimball's Zouaves. So although Hawkins had ordered *no* "parade" in the brigade, his Lieut. [i.e., lieutenant colonel] sent the men into quarters as soon as inspection was done, to cast off knapsacks and prepare to astonish their visitors with a grand display. But as the music sounded and the companies came rushing forth to form on their colors, Hawkins ignominiously squelched the whole thing. Somebody was mad.

As evening came, the air felt damp and the sky became overcast. At midnight rain was falling quite heavily. Sunday was gloomy and cold. We could only lie in our tents and watch the water dripping through and listen to its pouring as it came down in endless streams. No order came to move and we were content.

Monday morning showed a continuance of the same weather, but with an increase of coldness and much wind. As the rain ceased, the wind began to blow at a terrific rate until it seemed like a hurricane. It was like a winter day.

This (Tuesday) morning was calm and pleasant. During the night the ground had frozen hard, and there was ice enough to show that if the winter season had not commenced, it is at least near. By eight o'clock the brigade had struck tents, shouldered knapsacks, and were ordered to "fall in!" The rest of the division, except two batteries, had preceeded [sic] us, and we left Pleasant Valley deserted.

Bearing the weight of knapsack, 60 rounds of ammunition, and two days rations of pork and crackers, we trudged onward to the Potomac and passed southward through Knoxville without stopping. After pausing a few moments, we crossed from the railroad to the bank of the canal running parallel and close to the river and walked on it to Berlin, a small town important as a R.R. station and the site of a bridge now destroyed; the heavy stone piers only are standing. We crossed into Virginia from Berlin on a pontoon bridge which bounced and swayed under us in a manner to knock us together and trip us now and then in a most unseamanlike style—yet we were proceeding at the route step.

At about 3 P.M. we reached our present position (on the road to Winchester), having travelled, according to my estimate, between 7 and 8 miles with trifling fatigue. After pitching a tent for 3, 3 of our companions having left us, I went three quarters of a mile for straw. Found some persimmon trees by the way and with salt pork, raw onions and crackers made a "jam up" supper.

We are encamped in a wood. The weather is moderated. Tomorrow we start again, so you see I am after all running away from your box. Well, it will save the carrying of extra weight, which on these marches tells.

Answers are due to various letters remaining in my pockets, but I have no time. Even this is scratched at short intervals of duty. Tell the family to be patient—they are many and I but one. Let nothing more in the package line be attempted until I am conferred with.

In haste,
Ed.

P.S. Send me a newspaper map of Eastern Va.

Camp near Wheatland, Va.
Saturday Eve No[vember]. 1st, 1862

Dear Bro:

. . . Unless I am at fault, my last [letter] to you was . . . sent from the neighborhood of Scottsville, Va. On Wednesday—no, on Thursday morning at 3 o'clock, we were roused, packed with knapsacks, and hurried forward to this point, a distance of about six miles, at a quick step which left the rest of the brigade puffing and blowing behind and wondering at the traveling powers of "them damed [sic] Zouaves." Here we have rested two days, washing and mending and making ourselves comfortable. There is a splendid mineral spring not 40 steps from my tent.

Early tomorrow morning (Sunday) the whole division moves again in the direction of Leesburg. I am glad to advance with the army of the Potomac and would give many a good day's rations to be present at the taking of Richmond. If the shining rifle beside me doesn't have a voice in the matter, I shall be awfully disappointed.

Ever since we have been here, my whole time till after midnight every night has been occupied with the company rolls: they are now (4 copies of them) complete, and the job is happily done. The regiment was inspected and mustered for pay on yesterday morning. The rolls are to be forwarded at once to the proper department, and it is expected that the 9th will be paid off on the 14th inst. for four mos. service. I have taken special pains to impress upon the Government that it owes E. K. W. for exactly two months.[17]

The evening of our arrival here was moonlight [moonlit], and the boys, feeling frisky, amused themselves by tossing the niggers of the regiment, great and small, in a blanket. The darkies were asserted to be getting rebellious and to need admonition. One after another they were dragged from their hiding places and sent heave[n]ward with tremendous force, kicking and yelling and showing some of the drollest commingling of legs, arms, boots, teeth, and eyes you can imagine. Their despairing yells contrasted strangely with the imperturbable, solemn "one-two-three" of their tormentors. Some of them must have gone up more than 20 feet, descending on their heads, necks, elbows, etc., only to go up again. It was confoundedly mean, but I laughed myself double at it. Some uncleanly whites were treated to the same process. Such vaulting and summer-setting one would go far to see.

Time presses and at present I can write no more. A note came to hand last night from Jim, enclosing one from the girls. I have also rec'd a tip-top note from S. K. W. [Stillman King Wightman] and only wait the coming of the box to reply. The matter is in our Quartermaster's hands and will meet with all possible attention.

This has been spattered with grease by one of my tentmates who sits close, gnawing a bone. Assure everybody that I am perfectly comfortable even without the box and really shall need no more clothing of any kind.

Ed.

Camp near Upperville, Va.
Tuesday Morn. Nov. 4, 1862

Dear Bro:

I wrote that we should march westward on Sunday. We did so, accomplishing seventeen miles with knapsacks and heavily laden haversacks. At night we encamped within two miles of Union, quite a little town with houses built, as in Maryland, of logs filled in with plaster and white washed. You will see we are aiming towards Winchester and are to cross the Blue Ridge into the Shenandoah [Valley].

In Virginia, as far as we have come, we find much easier marching than in

Maryland. The roads have been almost level and in splendid condition for traveling and the scenery, although not presenting so many sudden transformations as in the latter state, is yet sufficiently attractive. But the people of Maryland are mostly loyal: those of Va. bitter disunionists. Neither disguise their sentiments.

On Sunday we were accompanied along the route by heavy cannonading to the right.[18] On Monday morning I took my knapsack and went out on picket duty, but during the night the rebels had retreated 10 or 12 miles before our artillery and cavalry, and about noon the regiments struck tents and moved on. This time we made a knapsack march of from 12 to 15 miles, halting at about 9 P.M.

Our last days work was tedious, for other troops were ahead, and we had to go their pace. Again artillery and cavalry blocked up the roads, so that at one time we would pass over but ½ a mile distance in ½ an hour and again be urged almost into a double quick until we fairly flew along the road, up hill and down, wading brooks, and plunging through the woods as though the dogs were after us. Some of the boys were so fatigued by night that at every halt they would throw themselves back upon their knapsacks and sleep, a thoughtless act for the air was cold and a blustering wind was blowing. Luckily I was relieved from picket duty at night and enjoyed comfortable rest.

We saw Burnside twice yesterday, followed by at least a regiment of cavalry; and this morning, while washing ½ a mile from camp, I saw McClellan ride by with his escort toward the mountain.[19] Thousands of Union troops surround us, and the roads are packed with them. Some great movement is in progress. It is said that Sumner's corps has advanced over the ridge and that Sigel[20] takes part in the combination. Even while I write, the dull booming of cannon is heard from the direction of Warrenton. We expect marching orders every moment.

P.S. Today our pickets exchanged newspapers with Gen. Sigels.

Camp near Manassas Gap[21]
Wednesday Afternoon, Nov. 5

A march of 5 or 6 miles this morning brought us close to Manassas Gap. We struck tents at sunrise and started just after breakfast. The cannonading still goes on. We are probably stationed here at the base of the mountains to prevent the enemy from busting through from the Shenandoah Valley. Wounded pickets are frequently met with, and today ½ dozen captured rebels, taken only fourteen miles distant, were conducted past us. We are encamped in a wood behind the brow of a ridge in line of battle. . . .

Camp in the mountains 10 miles
from Warrenton: Saturday, Nov. 8

On Thursday we struck tents before breakfast and marched 15 miles on the way to Waterloo. But after covering the above distance, and when near the town or village of Orleans, rebel videttes [mounted pickets] suddenly appeared on the right and left.

We had been advancing cautiously though rapidly, companies B and H of the 9th Regt. being thrown forward as an advance guard. A halt was made immediately and Corporal Rogers ordered to examine the neighboring woods with six men, afterwards augmented to fourteen. I was among the first six selected. We loaded our pieces, fixed bayonets, and in double file crossed the fence, passed up round a pair of haystacks which might readily have concealed a number of the enemy, and then, deploying as skirmishers, marched by the left flank into the woods. At this point came the fun. Smashing and crashing through a dense undergrowth of shubbery [sic] and creepers, with briars and thorns tearing your hands and face, your heavy knapsack almost torn from your shoulders by every sapling it struck against, your feet tripping over stumps and blundering into holes while your eyes were peering around for secesh—it was rather a perplexing piece of business.

After going a quarter of a mile thus and seeing nothing but a wild rabbit, we emerged into the open field and saw a couple of rebel horsemen on a distant ridge, one of whom fired a shot that whistled over the heads of the men of Co. H. A secesh who was wandering over the field we captured and sent to the Colonel. Matters appearing thus serious, the whole regiment deployed as skirmishers, colors in the rear, and advanced. The rebel pickets fled, and *2,500 of Stuarts cavalry*,[22] who had reached Orleans only ½ an hour before us, skedadled [sic] in hot haste, burning the bridge over the Rappahannock to prevent pursuit.

We encamped a mile beyond Orleans, but Co. B having been detailed as Provost Guard, I was sent with another man to protect the property of the rebel widow Marshall,[23] who lives in a great white house beautifully furnished and is in every respect an F.F.V ["First Family of Virginia"]. Mrs. M. has three daughters living with her, one married. She had three sons in the rebel army, but one of them was killed in Winchester. Her butler met me in the front yard with many bows and represented his mistress as well pleased with our mission.

My first step, of course, was to examine the premises, and being hungry, my feet inclined toward the cook house, where 20 darkies were holding their orgies round a rousing fire. A squad of straggling soldiers, too, were there, whom I sent out. The Aunties there placed before me a pitcher of buttermilk and a plate of smoking hot hoe cake; but, alas, I had no sooner commenced the onslaught than the Colonel came riding up, and I had to dash round the house and soberly "present arms" with my youthful moustache [sic] dripping with milk and my innocent cheeks distended with corn bread. He grinned and seemed to think I had got to work promptly. The colonel was invited in for refreshments. After he rode away, I resumed operations with more success.

Towards evening three other men from the 10th New Hampshire came to assist us. After roll call, 8 p.m., it grew cold, and the nigs having been sent to their quarters, we took entire possession of the cook house and, making a roaring fire in the big chimney place, put our feet to it and, rolling ourselves in our blankets, lay down upon the stone floor and had a splendid nights rest. In the morning (Friday) there was ice a quarter of an inch thick in a tub outside. How would you like to wash at sunrise in spring water in such weather?

I forgot to mention a good supper of hot cakes, coffee, and ham (the coffee from the regiment, for the secesh have none). For breakfast we had hot corn cake, wheat bread, biscuit and butter, bacon and milk without stint. At about 8 A.M. we were recalled to the Regt.—but I took the precaution to stuff my haversack with hoe cake and turnover pies.

Two hours after the guard had been removed the place was sacked and property destroyed to the value of $1000. Doors [were] broken in with axes, carpets cut up for blankets, vases smashed, mirrors slivered, pianos destroyed, curtains torn, books thrown out of doors and trampled on, tubs of butter, barrels of sugar, pots of preserves carried off, and the whole place in ruin. The women locked themselves in the upper chambers until a heavy force of infantry and cavalry arrived and commenced making arrests. What do you think of such a scene? Most of our common soldiers are scarcely above brutes by nature.

In the meantime a snow-storm had set in, and we were standing in the midst of it with tents packed, awaiting orders. I found my rubber blanket a perfect protection. When we finally formed, the snow was three inches deep. A slippery, muddy walk of four miles brought us to the position we now hold, which was formerly occupied by Pope's troops, whose tent poles are still standing there. My companions and I were lucky enough to be able to pave our kennel with dry boards in addition to the usual straw.

My health is still good. Outdoor living seems to toughen me against colds. I am getting well used to the weight of my knapsack and now think little of it except on a long march. My overcoat is soon expected up in the supply train; until it comes, the rubber blanket is quite sufficient. My box is not yet received but probably will be "when the proper time comes."

My time and opportunities for writing are now, of course, very limited indeed. We are said to be on the way to Warrenton.

Ed. K. W.

Camp near Gates Mill 8 miles
from Warrenton Junction, Va.
Tuesday, Nov. 11, 1862

Dear Bro:

My narrative is complete up to Saturday, when we had encamped in this place, the bridge over the Rappahannock having been destroyed by the retreating enemy. Sunday was pleasant and would have been a "day of rest" had I not been on guard all day and throughout the abominably cold night following— four hours of sound sleep I did get, though, when relieved, by buttoning myself in a borrowed overcoat and lying on the frozen ground with my feet to the fire.

Monday we remained here quietly until sundown, when a rumor came that Longstreet[24] had cut off our supply train and was coming upon us with a heavy force. We were instantly ordered under arms, with knapsacks, and our cattle and wagons were quickly trotted to the rear. We were to leave tents standing; but fearing I might not see mine again, I had strapped two [pieces] to my knapsack (I always carry two) and was in the ranks in five minutes. We formed in line of battle and marched ¾ of a mile, when our brigade was posted in a ravine at the base of a hill to support a battery of six twenty pound Parrott guns,[25] splendidly placed above.

Darkness came but no rebels. The fog settled around and in the rear of us, and nature soon showed a frozen face. No crackers had been issued, but we had rations of ground coffee mixed with sugar in our haversacks, and fires were ere long kindled among the trees and underbrush, and a happy set of fellows were squatting round them, chattering in their red glare and watching the boiling of tin cups. The bright blaze of the myriad of fires—the slender columns of smoke ascending, intermingled with sparks—the canopy of clouds above, made luminous by the light beneath, the lively and varied attitudes of the ZouZous in their picturesque dress as they busily disappeared in or emerged from the darkness or stood or sat among the many-colored foliage, made up a scene for a painter. One cannot but admire these things, especially when seasoned with the spice of danger with which circumstances heighten their attractions.

But the cold that followed froze my rubber blanket stiff and sent me at midnight from my kennel to the bivouac fire. In the morning (Tuesday) coffee was furnished by the company cooks and a chunk of raw pork given to each man; but rumors were still rife that our crackers had been pounced upon by Stuart. . . .

The anticipated danger being past, we returned early to our old camp and re-pitched our tents there. Being on "fatigue," I had the pleasure of carrying one end of our officers tent, with its poles, in addition to my knapsack. For dinner we had nothing but coffee and for supper a little thin slice of fried bacon each. Our officers made every exertion to procure hard bread, but without success. Money was sent out from the Company fund, but nothing could be had, and we went almost supperless to bed.

Wednesday, Nov. 12. An order from Burnside, read on parade last evening, informs us that he has assumed command of the "Army of the Potomac." Our men always meet him with cheers and with a considerable enthusiasm; but there seems to be a general impression that this is no time to change field officers and that the Army of the Potomac has too great a game to play to risk anything needlessly. Burnside has done well thus far but nothing to prove himself capable of maneuvering our "Grand Army" successfully. Not one man in 500,000 can do what is required of him. Still we hope on.

The cracker question is settled for the present. Four of the best thieves in Company B went out foraging last night and stole from a passing quartermaster's wagon 4 boxes of hardbread without alarming the guard. At 12 P.M. my tentmate, the barber, awoke me to listen to the dull strokes of an axe outside and then, springing out, returned with a haversack full of crackers. A box had just been opened. My legal friend, pray how, under the circumstances, would you have argued the point? For myself, I thus reflected: I am a Government machine sadly out of working order for want of oiling. The wherewithal for repairs, also Govt. property and intended to be devoted to just such purposes, is at hand. By applying it, Govt. cannot be wronged and the machine will be righted. The thieves are great rascals, to be sure, but at the worst are blind agents of a bad master and have only succeeded in *diverting* supplies. We are all equally Govt. vessels—fire buckets if you please, which must be often filled to extinguish the flames of this rebellion. . . . This (Wednesday) morning, there are two other boxes of crackers in the Orderly's tent, which must last us three days. The company fund has bought us 100 lbs of flour from a neighboring mill, and Whetlaufer, the barber, is to make flapjacks for dinner for "our mess."

There is to be a re-organization of the Army of the Potomac. It is said the 9th is to be brigaded with other 2 yrs regt[s]., including Duryea's.[26] For the past three days we have had to answer roll call every hour under arms.

Yours tr.
Ed. K. W.

Camp near Gates Mill, 8 miles
from Warrenton, Va., Wednesday
November 12th, 1862

Dear Mother and Sisters:

You write to me so often and at such length, that it is impossible to reply to you severally, and you must therefore be content to let me group you thus together.

There is so little femininity in camps and so little relating to the occupations of women that when I write to you specially, I am always puzzled to know what will interest you. Perhaps you will scarcely believe me when I say that I have had only once since leaving New York come within speaking distance of a women [*sic*] who could make the slightest pretensions to youth and respectability. . . . In Virginia, all the old ladies we see are fiercely secession[ist] in sentiment and, to tell the truth, they have lost cabbages and chickens enough to make them so. But talk of the sharpness of New England women! If the secesh with their eager visages are not a match for them "in turning an honest penny" then tasteless pies and saltless bread at twenty five cents a piece and per loaf means nothing.

The cooking of Southern women is unworthy of the name. Their preparations are uniformly flat and tasteless and to a Northerner always seem an ignorant waste of material. I can tell you nothing of their indoor life, for I have seen and know nothing of it; but it is rare indeed that one sees here in a dwelling house or on a farm that comfortable neatness and thrift so common in

New England. White paint and clapboards, nice picket fences and pretty gardens are things which have not crossed my vision in an age. The plow seems to be the favorite and almost the only implement of husbandry among the people. Of course the fields are rough.

You ask me a number of questions concerning my wants. *I have no pressing wants.* My health is, happily, better than when I left New York and I believe daily improving. Exposure only toughens me. Once an old fashioned cold caught me, but I shook it off and now live in the open air, with neck and throat bare, with impunity. My habits are much more regular than when at home, and I therefore easily escape sickness that others will not avoid. When not on duty I retire at 8½ P.M. and in the morning rise at daybreak. My sleep is generally sound and invigorating. As to our food, it is always (except in extraordinary circumstances) plenty and nourishing. Sometimes we long for variety and for what we term "luxuries," as for instances, cheese, butter, soft bread, etc.

By the bye, you ask for suggestions from me concerning eatibles [sic] to be forwarded in my next box. Don't attempt to send another box until I tell you I am permanently posted at some railroad terminus where it will come promptly to hand. Then for edibles you may send cheese (as much as you please), German bread (schwa[r]tz brod, quite fresh when packed), German sausages (the big fellows that are eaten in slices), solid cake or gingerbread of a kind that will keep, cayenne pepper (red), any sort of sweetmeats that go well with crackers (in stout, broad mouthed bottles or tumblers), dough-nuts, any of these or in fact anything solid that will keep. Being cooks you are better judges in such matters than I.

As to my clothing, give yourselves no trouble about it. I am well enough even without the contents of the box or an overcoat, either or both of which may come to hand at any moment. You have certainly done for me everything possible and ought to rest easy, without attempt[ing] to increase obligations. I have no doubt but that small packages will come direct and securely by mail; they are often sent thus to the regiment, and I have never heard of a miscarriage. Newspapers only seem to be meddled with.

What are you doing at home? Was Fred's "wooden wedding" [fifth wedding anniversary] celebrated? Are the Girls Mary and Ell making rapid progress in the science of housekeeping? Do they and you take plenty of open air exercise? What is the latest news from Aunt Mary, and where can I write to her?

I wish you could alter the model of your letters a little. Write less about me and a great deal more of yourselves. Give me all the home news—the fluctuations of dry goods. Let me hear how Ell's studies get on, and what measures you take to assure the preservation and improvement of health. If there is anything I fear, it is that you will all break down in consequence of your irregular, careless manner of living. The danger is the more to be apprehended because none of you will open your eyes to it. (End of Lecture 1)

Write to me.

Ed

3

FALMOUTH AND
FREDERICKSBURG

[As Edward feared, General Burnside proved a disaster as an army commander. Late in November he stole a march on his enemy by leading his 120,000 troops southeastward from the Warrenton Junction vicinity toward Fredericksburg, about fifty miles above Richmond. From there he could outrace Lee's eighty thousand veterans to the Confederate capital, which he expected to take by storm or siege. Errant pontoon trains, however, forced the Federals to mark time at Falmouth, across the bridgeless Rappahannock River from Fredericksburg. By the second week in December the pontoons were on hand, but the delay had enabled Lee to occupy the lower town and positions behind it including a commanding eminence known as Marye's Heights.

The stubborn Burnside refused to alter his plans to conform to the new situation. As a result, on the thirteenth his troops were cut down in a series of futile efforts to reach the high ground. As part of Brigadier General George W. Getty's division of the Ninth Corps, the Ninth New York was at first held in reserve, behind Burnside's center. Near sundown—with the outcome of the contest long since decided—Burnside committed the division to a pointless assault against the southern spur of Marye's Heights. This put the final touches to a fiasco that claimed thirteen thousand Union casualties as against only five thousand Rebel losses.

It was Edward's baptism of battle. He was astonished by the carnage but, to his surprise, unfrightened. Afterward he made no attempt to minimize the blow Burnside had dealt the army's morale—a blow compounded by the army leader's weather-plagued effort to skirt Lee's left flank late in January 1863. This "Mud March" brought an end to the "great things" expected of the campaign.

In the aftermath of the botched offensive, Edward indicted not only Burnside but many lesser-ranking officers whose incompetence and political posturing disgusted him, and those of his comrades in the ranks who seemed more interested in looting and brawling than in soldiering. He also demonstrated his lack of faith in Burnside's successor and blasted the political officials, including Abraham Lincoln, who had engineered the change of command. For Private Wightman—as for the entire Army of the Potomac—a winter of discontent had set in.]

> Camp two miles from Bealton
> Station (on the [Orange &] Alexandria R. R.)
> Monday, Nov. 17, 1862

Dear Bro:

On Saturday morning last, reveille had scarcely awakened us when the "General"[1] sounded the order to strike tents and prepare to march. We were soon in line and on the road.

But let me give you a little incident of Thursday. You know we are brigaded with a German regiment, the 103rd N.Y.V., who in common with all their countrymen are quick tempered and almost ungovernable, nothing being more justly ranked among daily occurrences than Dutch Fights—officers and men alike partaking in them. Coming in from dress parade on Thursday evening, I found a crowd near my tent which had gathered to witness the post-mortem examination of a German just killed "by a friend." At first it was said there had been a serious duel, but it seemed afterward that the affair was merely a piece of pleasantry. Two Germans, bantering each other on their respective delinquencies in the bayonet exercise, had adjourned to a quiet part of the wood, and there, after a short trial of skill and a few passes, the foot of one had slipped over a rolling stone, and the heart of the other was pierced with cold steel. There was a regimental funeral, and the death was, of course, pronounced "accidental."

To return to the march, we had gone five or six miles when the glasses of our officers detected a rebel battery on our right. We turned from the road. Benjamin's battery of 20 lb. Parrots [sic] was brought up and placed in exactly the same position it occupied a few months ago under Pope,[2] and with friendly shell screaming over their heads, Companies B and H deployed as skirmishers and charged into the woods—pine woods that as usual played the mischief with our knapsacks.

After advancing awhile, we were ordered to halt and dress on the centre [sic]. It was here that with the practiced eye of a scout I saw the dark form of a suspicious object among the foliage not 20 yards distant and directly in front of my tentmate, [Private William H.] Bailey, who, being a tall fellow, was next to me, five paces on the right. I called to him and pointed it out but being a recruit said nothing of my suspicions. He stared, pronounced it without hesitation "a man lying on his back with his knees up and arm over his head," and, notifying the nearest corporal, advanced straight forward with his piece cocked, while two or three of us covered his *man*. He turned back rather sheepishly in a few seconds to tell us he had found "a burned log." Of course, the rest of us grinned with the air of veterans who had known better all the time.

We lay among the dry leaves a couple of hours until the rebel guns were silenced, listening to the screaming shells that circled over us and to an occasional discharge of musketry on the right where another detachment of our brigade had met the enemy at closer quarters.[3] Between 2 and 3 P.M. the bugle recalled us, and we returned to the road. Further on we saw where the wagon train of Sturgis Division (the advance) had been shelled. The ruins of a wagon load of muskets lay smoking in our path.

At sunset we encamped at Sulphur [or Warrenton] Springs, with directions to be in readiness to move at daylight. We were accordingly up at 4 A.M. on Sunday and breakfasted an hour before dawn by the light of our fires, one of which was burning in front of almost every tent. Being "on guard" today, it was my duty to march in the rear and prevent straggling. We marched by the left, with the Dutchmen ahead, and, except when at rest for three hours at noon in consequence of being blocked by a wagon train, rushed along at a dog trot all day. The road was sometimes hard, sometimes cut into deep ruts and gullies, sometimes dusty, sometimes narrow and hilly. Stragglers were plenty; from the 10th New Hampshire and 103rd New York they dropped out by tens, falling with their heavy knapsacks and refusing to be stirred. Many slept as they sat resting. Our pace was increased by a clumsy blunder of the officers, who led us seven miles out of the way by taking the wrong road.

At sunset we reached the site of our present encampment, thoroughly exhausted, though having travelled scarcely more than fifteen miles. Our tent was just fixed when I was summoned out "in full marching order" for picket duty and, shouldering my duds and rations, started afresh. It was proposed to make *me*, humble E. K. W., *acting corporal of the squad*. As the American said who was invited to kiss the great toe of the Pope, "I considered myself unworthy of so distinguished an honor."

We went a mile along the Alexandria R.R. when, finding camps extending beyond, a major of the 10th N.H. [Jesse F. Angell] who accompanied us took the responsibility of dismissing the whole brigade detachment, and we joyfully returned to quarters where hot coffee and warm dog houses awaited us. How would you like to spend Sunday so, you ease-loving rogue. . . ?

Sunday night I slept like a top, oblivious of the rains that dropped plenteously around. Monday morning was misty, and we were allowed to rest till noon, when, simultaneously with the dinner call, came the order to strike tents. Almost at the same time, I received my *long promised overcoat*, a heavy and most comfortable piece of wardrobe furniture. For two days previous I had worn the old, greasy, torn coat of slovenly [Private David] Barry, a deserting recruit.

A smart afternoon's walk of eight miles finished the days work. Our wagon train, however, failed to come up, and after a little chat we washed down a couple of dry crackers, each with a cupful of muddy water, and went to bed without candles, which, by the way, have been entirely cut off, and the supply is not expected to be immediately renewed. All writing, you see, must be done by gleaming daylight.

> Tuesday, Nov. 18th Camp near
> Stafford Court House, Va.

This morning we breakfasted at three o'clock and long before dawn were moving towards Fredericksburg in company with 60,000 men (so the camp report fixed our strength).[4] The rolling up of the darkness gradually disclosed the broad turnpike on which we were traveling crowded with lines of cavalry, artillery, and infantry, all pressing eagerly forward, the men of each arm of the service bantering the other and uttering jokes peculiar to themselves.

A light film of clouds covered the sky, the road was hard and level, and, except that a light mist was falling, it was a most desirable day for work. But the 9th was pushed off the turnpike and forced to perform the 12 miles. We have just completed by going over plowed fields and through almost impassable wood paths. Yet as I sit here on my knapsack in the doghouse at 2 P.M., after doing "fatigue duty" in addition to the march, I will not acknowledge myself tired.

We are now 7 or 8 miles from Fredericksburg, and Burnside has just ridden by to establish his headquarters there. There are now but seven companies of our regiment remaining together. Co. F is in North Carolina, Co. G doing duty as body guard to Gen. Burnside, and the battery, Co. K when last heard from, was posted on London [sic] Heights near Harpers Ferry.[5]

You have probably heard that we have been placed in Sumners Corps[6] on the right. Tomorrow I expect to see Fredericksburg and later, if I live, Richmond.

> In haste,
> Ed. K. W.

> Camp near Stafford Court House
> Va. Tuesday, Nov. 18, 1862

Dear Father:

Your letter of October 25th was duly received and would have been answered long since if I had not waited in hopes of getting the box you sent me before returning thanks. We have unluckily been on the march, however, ever since its arrival at Harpers Ferry, and in consequence I have been unable to procure it, though making every endeavor to do so. Its contents look the more desirable the further they are removed from me, and the thoughtfulness and affection which actuated you to forward them so promptly I hope are fully understood and appreciated.

A winter campaign has been opened which promises great things, and I expect from it heavy and decisive blows. We are strong, the weather is fine, and the roads are in splendid condition. With all my heart I desire that the soldiers may not be spared. For myself I freely offer any sacrifice in the crisis. Full of health and vigor, I am far better qualified than the majority of troops I see to endure hardship.

As to clothing, my new overcoat completes my supply. Give yourself no further trouble about it. No later than this morning a bet was made in my hearing that "Wightman's knapsack is the heaviest in the regiment." I have two suits of underclothing, socks, and can order from [the] Government on account a fresh uniform, shoes, or any articles of wearing apparel almost *ad lib*. If we should go into winter quarters or stop for awhile at a railroad station, the box will come.

Now about Thanksgiving. I suppose it occurs on the last Thursday of the month. I should rejoice beyond expression to be with you, but of course cannot. All the family will remember me, though, and I hereby formally commission Fred to eat my share of the dinner, sweet potatoes and all, he being though a small vessel of as yet untried depth. If there are any beets on the table, Charles may make my usual joke.

As ever, your aff. son,
Ed. K. W.

Camp on the Rappahannock River
2 miles from Falmouth opposite
Fredericksburg, Va.
Thursday, Nov. 20, 1862

Dear Bro:

I was a little too fast in locating Burnside's headquarters at Fredericksburg. Though a great Union army is in front of him ready to pounce upon it, the City is still in rebel hands.

We started yesterday forenoon, in the midst of a dense Virginia fog, for this place. Sumner's whole corps came on in three parallel lines, one occupying the turnpike, and the others marching through the fields and woods on either side. Our position was on the right. About the middle of the day, we slid down the slippery hills behind Falmouth and, drenched by the heavy rains which had already covered our rifles with rust and was dripping steadily from our peaked noses and well soaked hair, wound through the muddy valley in which the wide-spread encampment of the second corps [Major General Darius N. Couch's Second Corps] seemed to be hopelessly sinking, and, wading through a couple of brooks, crossed the town and struggled up a high hill beyond, our wet feet all the way squelching out those squizzling squeaks which under the circumstances make a fellow feel as uncomfortable as though he were walking through dust and cobwebs.

After a number of tedious delays, the site of our present camp was selected, and as fuel is scarce, our first step was to make sure of a supply. Bailey and I brought in as heavy a beam as we could stagger under, and as he was good enough to drop his end so suddenly and forcibly as to spring my knees and nearly smash my collarbone, I was fortunate enough to make a grimace that pleased the entire company. When the rain ceased, we dried our clothes at the fire, and after crackers and coffee I had as comfortable a night's rest in the shelter tent, with a rubber blanket and a coat between me and the mud, as I have had within three weeks. Some of the boys awoke this morning in three inches of water; for during the night the rain fell in torrents.

Our present marching rations are ten crackers per day, with coffee for breakfast and supper and fresh meat occasionally. Feeling rather slim on such a diet, Whetlaufer went to a neighboring house this morning and bought a half peck of meal for a quarter (25¢), so that we have stuffed ourselves with "mush" for dinner and can have "slapjacks" for supper. High living, sir, high living! I was also lucky enough to come upon a persimmon tree during a lull in the showers and get a large quantity of its lucscious [sic] fruit. Something you can't have in New York, me boy!

It still rains and still promises to do so. How strong the rebs are at Fredericksburg, or whether we shall have a battle here, I do not attempt to surmise. We can see their pickets on the other side of the river and converse with them. Yesterday one of our cavalry shot a secesh soldier who came down for water and was arrested for it. On Wednesday one of the 89th [New York Infantry] (Provost Guard) killed a New Hampshire man for sheep stealing.

Ed. K. W.

Camp near Falmouth, Va.
Sunday, Dec 7th, 1862

Dear Bro:

I write only to assure the family that I am still well and that, notwithstanding the imaginary "hardships" with which father has been pleased to surround me (and in recounting which he cannot forbear to hint that he "foresaw" what really he nor I have neither yet seen), in spite of all this I am well and hearty. But no incidents of importance have fallen under my observation since I last wrote to you, nor has anything very amusing occurred the relation of which would please the girls. Besides, as the cold of December settles round me, my cramped fingers refuse to hold the pencil and writing becomes a tedious process.

My last note left us in the midst of a misty rain two miles from Falmouth in an encampment where we had sought shelter from the elements after a rough march of 12 miles over muddy roads. Our second day and night in the new camp were much more disagreeable than the first. The clouds fairly opened their flood-gates and for 24 hours let fall upon us a steady deluge of water. In our shanty we tried to lie snug; but poor Bailey was being manfully drenched outside in the discharge of his duty as guard and occasionally thrust his dripping head in at the door with a face as long and pale and lugubrious as that of a lost spirit wandering in search of rest: the blustering wind was bursting in heavy gusts against our frail muslin walls, heaving up the pegs and threatening to bring down everything about our ears; there was no straw beneath us, and by 10 o'clock P.M. half a dozen streams were coursing across the floor.

In the midst of all this a party of recruits came in from Alexandria soaking wet, and for want of accomodations [sic] one of them was boosted in upon me and Whetlaufer. I should judge three pailfuls [sic] of water might have been wrung from the fellow by only a couple of loose twists. You cannot conceive a more miserable looking object or a being more dejeted, disgusted, and despairing. He had no overcoat and but one uniform. The best we could do for him was to recommend a change of underclothing and a snooze in the mud in his well soaked blanket, leaving his shoes, jacket, and trousers standing in a corner of our crowded "place of refuge." Next day it cleared a little, and we got boards from a barn 2 miles distant and thenceforth slept upon wood.

One morning before daylight (I forget the date, but it was a couple of days after our arrival), we were ordered under arms with 2 days rations, and as suddenly sent back to quarters. Rumor said that we were to have crossed the Rappahannock on pontoon bridges and again that we were to have escorted some gunboats up river from Port Royal,[7] protecting them against rebel sharpshooters. On the 29th [28th] of Nov. (Friday) we changed camp, moving a quarter of a mile and taking up a new position (Lieut. Col. Kimball, who knows nothing about it, intimating it is for the winter) on a pine-covered hill, where we endeavor to make ourselves as comfortable as possible.

The first day of winter found Bailey, Whetlaufer, and I enscounced [sic] in a log shanty with a board floor and a tent top. Its dimensions are about 6 ft. × 6 ft. The logs are laid one upon another five high, not gapped or notched at the ends but overlapped and secured by stout stakes without and within. The crevices (very trifling on account of the even straitness [sic] of the "Virginia pine") are stopped on the outside with clay mud. Our dog house sits perched upon and boarding over the whole. We have, in addition, drawn three new tents with which to drape the walls of this vast edifice and shut out stray currents of air. This rude hut protects us well and has already defied and grinned in the teeth of a heavy snow storm which beset us last Friday and continued through the night. We do not fear freezing in it.

But let me tell you how I celebrated Thanksgiving Day [November 27]. The usual 2 hours of batallion [sic] and brigade drill being omitted and there being no prospect of anything being done in camp, I secured a pass with the determination of visiting Falmouth and getting a good dinner, "daming [sic] the expense." A couple hours travels took me into the dirty old hole of a town, and with an appetite stimulated by exercise and a taste epicunamized [sic] by wayside imaginings I began my search for a hotel. There was none. Then for a dining saloon. *There was none.* Then for a bakers shop. After a search, two little ones were found in dirty shanties; but their doors were besieged by famishing crowds, and the shrunken loaves of bread and the doughy biscuits, for which 25 cents per loaf and 25 cents per doz. were charged respectively (and which constituted everything obtainable), were snapped up by the nearest men the moment they were handed from the oven to the street. At one place a new batch of bread was to be produced in two hours; at the other fresh biscuits in half an hour. I chose the last and, after sitting [a]while patiently, pounced upon 2 doz. flat, sour, heavy biscuits as they came steaming from the fire and, paying therefore 50 cents, emerged among the indignant soldiers without, with all the pride of success.

Now for the butter. *There was none in town. No cheese.* Nothing but a few small red apples which I purchased at three cents each. Chancing into a dry-goods store, however, where the soldiers were swarming like flies around a molasses hogshead, I espied a *barrel of root beer.* I jumped up on a board bench and, catching at an old coffee pot which lay neglected in a dark corner, ordered it filled and after paying 50 cents sat down on a barrel to my dollar and a quarter dinner of sour bread, [wishy-]washy beer, and apples with a satisfaction which words would fail to express. Thousands of people standing round me would have paid triple the amount for the treat; for a good dinner is a thing not to be sneezed at, you know, me boy, and when one's on a lark, why "darn the expense!"

Falmouth was crowded with troops and sutlers had things all their own way. Vials of sweet oil the size of Bennett's balsam bottles sold for a quarter; small papers of tobacco for a quarter; knit mittens for a dollar, and other things in proportion.

The bridge across the Rappahannock at this point had been destroyed, and we could see ½ a doz. gray back pickets, with muskets stacked, seated round a comfortable fire. On the way home I saw a large tannery in the distance and . . . started to examine it; but it proved on nearer inspection to be on the other side of the river; and a few secesh getting sight of me from the opposite bank, I thought [it] prudent to retire, the more especially as they were sneaking toward me through the bushes "as skirmishers" while an old booby on horseback squinted at me through his glass. When said booby got his focus fixed, I gratified him with a solemn wink, at which he retreated. . . .

Camp near Falmouth, Va.
Thursday, Dec. 11, 1862

Dear Bro:

Active operations have re-commenced. The campaign is reopened and we are again on the move for Richmond. For some days past we have been expecting orders, but it was not until last night that any special commands came to us. Then the cooks were instructed to prepare three days rations—a hurried inspection of the Division was made, arms and accoutrements placed in apple-pie order, and the 9th directed to be ready to start at 2 hours notice *without* knapsacks.

This morning at 5½ A.M. the ball opened. The great guns raised their sullen voices as the heralds of battle, and then rattling volleys of musketry, mingled

Confederate Pickets Across the Rappahannock River Bridge at Fredericksburg, December 1862 *(Photograph courtesy of the Library of Congress)*

with thundering explosions of heavy ordnance, sent forth their deafening echoes among the hills surrounding Fredericksburg. Burnside was throwing his pontoon bridges across the Rappahannock. Even Johnny Smith, the Crimean veteran, was astonished at the vehemence and rapidity of the shots. When the fire of the small arms ceased, the unbroken roar of great guns was like the gigantic beating of a long [drum] roll, and the loud purring of the solid shot and the musical singing of shells as they circled through the air made the grandest discord of sound I ever heard.

In a moment the men were alive with excitement. Cheer after cheer went up, and you would have been astonished to see soldiers who but a few hours before had deprecated further fighting overflowing with enthusiasm and burning to be led to the conflict. The 89th N.Y. and 8th Conn., both of our brigade,[8] were already in action, supporting a battery. The 9th handed their knapsacks over to the Quartermaster (I retained nearly everything valuable in mine) and, taking pork and crackers for 3 days, with blankets and a tent [piece] slung over the left shoulder, thus (in a loop), [a]waited the progress of events.

We are to cross the river as soon as practicable. Now (near sunset) our 3 bridges are reported as destroyed; the cannonading has been kept up with little interruption. Col. Fairchilds of the 89th is reported killed.

Sunday morning, Dec. 14th
Fredericksburg, Va.

The above note was cut short by a "fall in, Co. B" from the orderly, and we were hastily marched up a muddy hill, leaving our supper on the fire, and as the sun sunk behind the mountains, stood half up to our knees in slush awaiting the word to move on to Fredericksburg. But news soon came that the City had been taken by crossing the river in [pontoon] boats,[9] and we were dismissed to quarters.

An hour later the 9th were again roused, formed in line in the midst of darkness and a chilling fog, [and] in company with the division, headed for the nearest pontoon bridge. We marched three or four miles to reach it, though it might have been done in two, because our officers lost their way and amused themselves too much with halting and countermarching.

When we landed in Fredericksburg, it was between 8 and 9 o'clock P.M. [December 11] A dead silence reigned in the streets. We formed our line of battle on the 2nd street from the river, with which it is parallel, our left protecting the head of the bridge. A division had preceded us and were already quartered in houses in the City. We were less fortunate, being made to bivouac in the snow-covered streets, in readiness to resist an anticipated attack in the night or early morning.

I was detached on picket and took up my position upon the outskirts of the City to catch stray rebels. As I had fallen flat in the mud three times on the way[10] and as the weather was foggy and chilly, this duty was not over-pleasant. By midnight, however, I was relieved and, finding a bedstead in an alley-way, dropped upon it and, although I dared not unroll my blanket for fear of a sudden call, was soon sleeping. Two hours later the snow beneath and around had chilled me through, and I had changed my base by a masterly retreat to the company fire, where I sat and dozed till daylight.

By 9 A.M. (Friday), the rebels being plainly visible from where we lay and having threatened an assault, we formed to receive them. I was detailed with a dozen others to advance up a street (at right angles to that occupied by the regiment) to the suburbs and skirmish with the enemy's advance. Lying behind a board fence, we fired through and over it at secesh, who [to] the number of 3 or 400 had their headquarters at a brick house 600 yards distant. Once, a detachment from a New Hampshire Regiment drove them back, and we joined

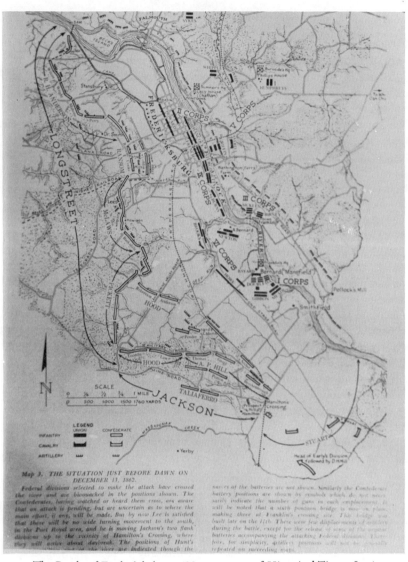

The Battle of Fredericksburg *(Map courtesy of Historical Times, Inc.)*

in the advance, but the rebs were reinforced and returned. They made some good shots. Two of our squad were wounded, one in the thigh and the other in the foot, and my scrubby head was missed only by three inches.

At noon I was relieved and got something to eat. At 8 P.M. the whole regiment, who had been hoping for *comfortable sleeping rooms* in a *house* tonight, were hustled out towards the railroad as picket guards. We were held in reserve until midnight (and allowed to sleep on the frozen ground in our overcoats), when we relieved the 4th Rhode Island, stationed on the [Richmond, Fredericksburg & Potomac] R.R. in the rear of Fredericksburg. Here we saw the rebs in force at less than 200 yards distance but were not allowed to fire. Our men were distant from each other on the track, five paces.

Shortly after daylight, we were relieved by the 10th N.H. and without time for breakfast packed off in quick time to obtain 3 days rations and prepare for an immediate assault on the enemy's works. Crackers, salt port, and ground coffee and sugar having been issued, we were marshalled on the bank of the Rappahannock behind a gentle hill and permitted to rest there until called for. Meanwhile the fight had commenced in earnest. The threat of Lee to bombard the City unless surrendered on Friday night had made the capture of his batteries necessary. The 10th N.H. skedadled [*sic*] 10 minutes after we had resigned our trust into their hands. Simultaneously, the adverse batteries opened and the cannonading grew furious. Our heaviest guns were stationed on the heights on the East side of the Rappahannock [Stafford Heights] and cast their shot and shell over our heads into the rebel works. The rebels responded from positions at least equally well chosen, back of the City.

While awaiting orders, we were amused by the bursting among us of a few of our own shells, owing either to the clumsiness of our gunners or the imperfections of our guns. Two exploded close beside me on the dock, and one of the pieces, striking a stack of muskets, glanced off and shattered the leg of a man in the 25th New Jersey, a new regiment in our Brigade. A few minutes later a dead man was borne by on a stretcher, who had been killed by a heavy fragment striking him on the head, and during the day many others were hit, and the heads of the boys kept dodging continually to avoid the scattering fragments.

Throughout the entire day our infantry were assaulting the rebel works, but apparently with little success. From a house on a hill I watched the advance of our troops in successive lines, listened to their deafening cheers as they double-quicked upon the batteries, and saw the brave hosts melt away before the terrible tempest of iron hurled against them till nothing but poor, weak remnants remained scattered in the advance, unsupported and their valor uselessly thrown away. The quick wasting of the Union troops, who disappeared suddenly as if the earth had yawned and swallowed them, was awful to gaze upon. Yet they still recklessly pounded on, cheering, and keeping up a continuous fire of musketry.

Just at sunset [5 P.M.] our brigade was ordered forward. We passed back through the city, the 9th leading, and, turning to the left in divisions [i.e., detachments], stood at once exposed to the enemy. The first division on the right (Co. B included) was met by a shell which burst close in front and scattered its fragments fairly among us. I was in the front rank and the first man on the right. Two of our men were struck, and I saw a spent ball rebound from my belt-plate. The men at first recoiled and lost position in the ranks, but soon rallied at the call of "double quick" and rushed on behind the colonel [Kimball], one man losing his head by the way.

Running down a steep bank and through a stream boiling under the shower of shot which played upon it, we climbed a hill over the bodies of dead and wounded men and cast off blankets and knapsacks and, after a moment's exposure to the play of the enemy's battery, formed under the brow of a little ridge, the shot and shell whistling and buzzing over our heads in a most confoundedly malicious manner. Our officers, who had been glad to dismount, now ordered us to lie down, and it was found that we were to support Benjamins' 20 lb. Parrott battery.[11] We did so by lying comfortably where we were and laughing at the screaming bullets until darkness put an end to the contest. Once a piece of shell tickled me on the back, and the shot coursed close above us. Our Orderly Sergeant [First Sergeant Hugo] Schmidt (now, together with Sergeant Cornell, my tent-mate), lying in the second place on my right, was wounded in the back and carried off, and the Lieut. Col. of the 4th R. Island [Joseph B. Curtis] was struck dead from his horse just behind as he led in his regiment to act in concert with us.

During the progress of these events I was often astonished but, I believe, never once frightened. What I most marvelled at was how men could walk at all, amid such a storm of missles [sic], unharmed. Yet, great as the danger was and clearly as I saw it, I found myself always philosophising [sic] and calculating chances, as though I had no further interest in the matter than a mere observer. I learned more of the characters of my companions by watching the play of their features during the short time we were under fire than I should have done during weeks of ordinary intercourse.

As twilight came on, in common with all around me, an almost overpowering sense of sleepiness seized me, and it was only by a strong effort of will I could keep awake. As soon as the firing ceased, Cornell and I tore some boards from a fence in the rear, made a bed, and enjoyed a two hour snooze, when the line of march was taken up and we were led back toward the City to bivouac[k] for the night. We slept in the open field, and early this (Sunday) morning we were led back to our old waiting place on the Rappahannock and afterwards into the City to receive further orders.

It is said that the whole 9th corps is to participate in a grand assault this afternoon, assisted by our heavy batteries. Thus far the rebs are thought to have had the best of us.

Sunday Afternoon: There has been no fighting of consequence today. Only the sharpshooters have been at work. Tomorrow, reports say, the whole 9th Army Corps are to make a grand bayonet charge, supported by the heavy batteries. The result ought not to be doubtful, but there is enough room for doubt. The *sneaks* in the army are named *Legion*, and they are shameless enough to proclaim their cowardly practices openly. When you read of the number of men engaged on our side, strike out at least one third as never having struck a blow.

Fredericksburg is merely the shell of a city. There are no people here but a few negroes and all household furniture and property of value have been carried off. The houses, of course, are occupied by the troops. Our regiment has not yet been quartered, but tonight we hope to sleep under a roof. This letter is written on a door step where I am interrupted by roll-calls, the passage of wounded men on stretchers, etc., etc.

Show as much of it as you think proper to the family.

In haste,
Ed. K. W.

P.S. We were paid off about two weeks ago, and I received two months pay, $26.00

E

Camp near Falmouth, Va.
Wednesday, December 17th, 1862

Dear Bro:

You will see by the heading of this letter that we are back again among the log houses at the old camp. My last letter, which accompanies this because I have found it impossible to mail it before, speaks of an anticipated bayonet charge of the whole 9th Army Corps upon the rebel works behind Fredericksburg on Sunday. During Saturday night, however, and Sunday, the rebel works were so improved and strengthened that they apparently became impregnable to assault. There were stone walls and redoubts rising in tiers one behind another up the long slope of the hill, protected in front by multitudes of rifle pits containing gray back sharpshooters numbered by brigades and commanded in the rear by more massive works on greater eminences wherever heavy ordnance could play with terrible effect upon the first position.

Our men would have had to advance, as on Saturday, down roads commanded by the rebel guns, form in line of battle under a pelting fire of shot and shell, and rush forward to the capture of places which it would thus have been almost impossible to retain. Had it been attempted, the slaughter must have been fearful and the attack a failure. At any time on Monday the rebs might have bombarded the City and destroyed us by [the] hundreds. I have a very distinct recollection of a single discharge of grape[12] being forwarded up an avenue through which I was anxiously gazing and hissing down into the mud around me with a vim so startling and a music so suggestive that I rose with a very awkward grace indeed and in indecent haste to retire.

Rodney [G.] Kimball, an old [college] classmate, came to see me while at dinner today (Monday). He is Capt. of the 7th Co. of the 44th [New York Infantry] Regt. (Ellsworth Avengers)—and was in the battle of Saturday and twice struck, once on the belt by a spent ball that knocked him out . . . and once on the foot: neither shot seriously injured him.

My supper was interrupted by the entrance of a man who had been popped by a sharpshooter. As no surgeon was near, I ripped up his sleeve, bandaged his arm, put [it] in a sling, and sent him on a stretcher to the nearest hospital. A Minnie [minié] ball had entered his left arm above the elbow, smashing the bone.

From various signs during the day I had become convinced that evacuation was mediated by our leader. About dusk we were sent out for picks and crowbars and iron implements of any kind fitted for battering down walls, piercing loopholes, etc. We had been under arms all day Monday and when evening came were made to lie down with haversacks, canteens, and blankets on, and rifles beside us. The streets were crowded with troops busily but silently moving back and forth. All fires were extinguished and darkness reigned everywhere.

At 10 P.M. the 9th was roused and formed and, speaking only in whispers, led toward the river. Our progress was slow but uninterrupted, but every instant we expected a torrent of shot and shell to pour in upon us. The bridge was so covered with wet sawdust or other similar material that scarcely a sound was audible in crossing, even from the hooves of horses and the heavy wheels of artillery. On reaching the opposite bank, the men looked back with a feeling of relief—the [aborted] grand bayonet charge of the 9th Army Corps had had but few charms for them.

Our course was now laid for the old camp, and we started for it at a lively quick step, so that, although a strong December wind was blowing, the perspiration st[r]eamed from me as though it were a warm evening of Spring. We had log houses and a comfortable nights rest in prospect. Camp was reached about midnight. There was little change in its appearance except that on the right successive rows of large hospital tents had been erected for the men wounded in the fight of Saturday.

Not being permitted to build fires, we got to bed as fast as possible. For the first time in a week I took off my heavy cartridge belt and box and removed my leggins and shoes. I found my ankles, from continual standing and marching, swelled out of all shape (If they were not well now, I shouldn't mention it).

Since our return we have lived much as usual. What Burnside will attempt next remains to be seen. Perhaps a flank movement will be tried. I am still in good health and spirits and full[y] equal to any emergency. The Regiment looks upon itself as remarkably fortunate in the fight, its loss having been but trifling.[13]

Send me the fullest accounts of the battle you can find. I am anxious to know what effect our unfortunate repulse will produce on the people and on the course of the administration. We are still far from Richmond, and the 1st of January draws nigh. Are all the labors of the winter campaign to be thrown away. . . ?

Yr. aff. Bro.
Ed. K. W.

Camp near Falmouth, Va.
Friday, Dec. 26th, 1862

Dear Bro:

It must now be six or eight weeks since I have heard from you. What is the matter?

In my last letter (I forwarded two by the same mail immediately after the battle of Fredericksburg) you were informed of my safety and re-settlement in the old camp, which we still continue to occupy. The account of my experiences in the rebel city were [sic] necessarily very brief and imperfect, but from it you have perhaps been able to gather a general idea of events as they occurred within the range of my vision. I can add nothing now for want of time and patience. The manual part of writing is most confoundedly tedious and slow.

Since returning but little of interest has happened. On the 16th we buried one man from the company who had long been ill with fever. It was Rosenbery [Private Thomas H. Roseberry], one of my first tentmates. I wrote to his mother last night, by the Captain's request, to communicate the tidings. . . .

We enjoyed Christmas hugely here. There were multitudes of sutlers around with everything that nobody wanted to buy. Some, though, had eatibles [sic], as for instance, butter at 75¢–$1 per lb; cheese, 50¢ or 75¢ per lb; sausages, 50¢ per lb; apples, 6 for a quarter, etc. On Wednesday I got a pass and went to Falmouth but could get nothing for a Christmas dinner but a haversack full of meal at 5¢ per lb. and 3 small papers of black pepper at 8¢ each. Next day we were lucky enough to get a bottle of pepper sauce for 40¢, which made our pork very palatable. Our dinner consisted of fresh meat boiled and spiced with pepper sauce, crackers buttered and crowned with toasted cheese sprinkled with black pepper, boiled pork cut up in pepper sauce, 2 onions in vinegar, and a pan full of warm mush. The whole was washed down with ½ a bottle of what *was called port wine*, the ½ bottle costing $1. In the evening, some of the boys having received boxes, one of them made a mess pan full of punch and was pressed by invitation to "smell the mug" and look on at the proceedings. The usual stories were told, songs sung, etc.

We were on picket again a few days ago on the bluffs opposite Fredericksburg. We were on post behind a battery during one day and night. The weather was pleasant and the night not cold so that we slept on the ground in our blankets very comfortably. We are to go out again on Sunday.

Our late defeat seems to have utterly broken up the campaign. We expect no fighting immediately. The troops seem rather proud of their bravery in the late battle—elated rather than depressed by the fight. There is no such thing as demoralization among us. Don't believe it.

Railroad matter now comes in regularly and the Q.M. (Quartermaster) tells me that boxes by express will come straight through without detention. My first box is expected up to camp on Monday.

In haste,
Ed. K. W.

[P.S.] Happy New Year!

> Headquarters 9th Regiment, New York
> Volunteers Hawkins Zouaves Near
> Falmouth, Va. Dec. 31, 1862

Dear Parents:

Your joint letter was handed me this morning, and I therefore look upon it as the last gift of the Old Year. The document is almost as suggestive of those old-fashioned family letters we used to write to grandfather many years ago: it pictures so faithfully the same comfortable scenes of home life we have always known that, as I sit here writing in my tent in the midst of Virginia, with my overcoat buttoned to the chin to keep the cold off, a little flight of the imagination transports me to the cozy sewing room where a bright fire blazes and an old gentleman with two pair of "specs" sits under the green shade of a bright gas light, industriously writing and whispering, while a matronly lady by his side gently rocks and reads. . . .

It would tickle me wonderfully to burst in among the group with a "Happy New Year"—1863! Whew, how time flies and how fast we are growing old. Verily, I shall pass 30 and be a bachelor before Richmond is taken! What a vagabond life I have led during those 30 years. Student, medical embryo, hardware clerk, teacher, bookkeeper, editor, soldier—what next? Never mind, we will take things as they come: but let me here acknowledge you as my best and most faithful and forgiving friends, to whom alone I have looked and shall continue to look for approval.

I was only joking about Richmond, though. You may have a note from me dated at the rebel capital yet. The army whose performances you laugh at can and will march there if the politicians will but condescend to furnish a general capable of leading it. Permit me to say that I think the soldiers of the Republic fight her battles better than the uniformed citizens. If the progress of the Government is blocked, it is by speculators clad in broadcloth.

You speak again of that unlucky box. Our wagon train has been delayed, and it did not therefore arrive on Monday as I wrote; but it is in as good keeping at Harpers Ferry as it will be anywhere, and more accessible. I expect it daily. . . .

A Happy New Year to the whole household and an equally happy one to the worthy Harlem branch.[14]

> I remain truly yr. afft. Son
> Edward K. Wightman

P. S. I have had and trust that in [the] future I shall have no occasion to make use of your liberal offers of pecuniary assistance.

> Camp near Falmouth, Va.
> Saturday, Jan. 3, 1863

Dear Bro:

On returning from picket this morning, I found awaiting me in camp a letter from yourself dated the 29th Dec., enclosing one from Abbie, besides letters from Charley, Jim, and Mary, all of the [same] date. The paper, envelopes, and stamps enclosed are, with those I have on hand, all sufficient for the present.

The original supply of paper you furnished me on leaving New York is still far from being exhausted.

Affairs are conducted in camp very much as usual, and there is little of importance to chronicle. We rise with the sun, answer roll call, wash in a neighboring brook, fill our canteens at the spring, breakfast on crackers, pork, and coffee, mount guard, drill as skirmishers an hour and a half, dine on pork and crackers, rest a short time, drill two hours in batallion [*sic*] movements, have dress parade at sunset and, after taking crackers and coffee for supper, answer roll-call at 8 o'clock P.M. and retire to rest. This is the regular routine, but it is, of course, occasionally varied by substitutions and interpolations. On New Years Day, for instance, the quartermaster being short of "hard tack" (crackers), issued flour instead, and we were treated to "duff" and molasses for dinner. Today we are lucky enough to dine on fresh beef soup, seasoned and thickened with onions and flour biscuit. Such are rare experiences, however.

The weather is pleasant and spring-like, with intersprinklings of cold snaps. Under its genial influence "the boys" have in a great measure recovered their health and spirits, as their innumerable dry jokes over our prospects and the present conditions of affairs and the shortcomings of our leaders, political and military, fully testify. They are the more inclined to be facetious because our loss in the late battle was so comparatively trifling. . . .

Other regiments, you know, suffered terribly.[15] There is a camp of hospital tents and ambulance wagons on our right, overburdened with cripples: heaps of unburied limbs and a large newly-filled grave yard adjoining, thickly packed with cracker-box head-boards, speak in plain terms of the numbers and suffering of the wounded. Just opposite is Prof. Lowe's balloon, "Eagle," in which one or more ascents are made daily. The gas is generated in two big travelling wagons which accompany him.[16]

As to the further movements of the Army of the Potomac, we are entirely in the dark. One rumor has it that Lee is maneuvering to meet us at Bull Run. Again, it is said that the 9th Army Corps is to be moved to Alexandria to relieve the 7th,[17] and in support of this opinion it is urged that our corps consists chiefly of two year troops whose term soon expires and who would consequently have to be withdrawn in the midst of the campaign in case of an advance. An additional consideration is that the Potomac may be closed during January, shutting off our supplies by way of Acquia Creek and necessitating a movement toward Washington. The rebs, too, may outflank us.

In fact, the men have a stomach-full of fight for the present and are willing to end it for anything that savors of rest and ease. They respect the character of Burnside, but have no faith in his ability to win victories. For myself, my conviction still is, as it has been from the start, that the state of our national finances caused by the stagnation of trade and the ruinous cost of the war, together with the threatened overthrow of an administration following the dissolution of the army in the coming spring and summer, will *force* a resort to the most desperate efforts on the part of our commanders this winter and that in the struggle the old tried troops will not be spared. The roads are in splendid condition and invite active operations. We shall see. I wish we had a patriotic leader with Napoleon's military genius.

Our regiment is now more complete than I have ever known it, Company F having joined us from North Carolina,[18] but Company G is still acting as body guard to Gen. Burnside, and a part of Company K is still at Washington with their Captain [Richard H. Morris], awaiting to receive our guns from [the] Government. (The regiment was formerly presented with 5 brass guns, 2 rifled and 3 smooth bore (12 pounders), by Gen. [John] Wool at Fortress Monroe, which are to be exchanged for new pieces.[19]) The list of our commissioned officers is as follows:

Col. R. C. Hawkins

Lieut. Col. E. A. Kimball

Maj. E[dward]. Jardine

Adj. Lieut. Thos. F. Bartholemew [Bartholomew]

Quarter Master Lieut. O. W. Parrison [Otto W. Parisen]

Co. A.
Capt. And[rew S.]. Graham
1st Lieut. Webster [actually, the position was vacant]
2nd   "   Mat Graham [vacant]

Co. C.
Capt. Victor Klingsohr
1st Lieut. F[rancis]. S. Powell
2nd   "   Jackson [Louis Jacobshon]

Co. B.
Capt. Wm. G. Barnett
1st Leut. Geo. W. [H.] Herbert
2nd   "   Ed[wi]n. Dews

Co. D.
Capt.   [Alma P. Webster]
1st Lieut. Hen. [John K.] Perley
2nd   "   Jas. B. Homer [Horner]

Co. E.
Capt. Lebaire [Adolph Libaire]
1st Lieut. Joe A. Green [Greene]
2nd Leut. Alex[ander] Vogt

Co. H.
Capt. Joe Rodriguez (resigned) [vacant]
1st Lieut. Robt. McKichney [McKechnie]
2nd   "   [Richard H.] Jackson

Co. F.
Capt. Wm. H. Hammill
1st Lieut. J. H. Perley [Matthew J. Graham]
2nd   "   J. F. [David J.] Green

Co. I.
Capt. Lance Leighe [Lawrence Leahy]
1st Lieut. James M. [H.] Fleming
2nd   "   Chas S. Glosser [vacant]

Co. G.
Capt. Chas. [W.] Childs
1st Lieut. W. H. Harison [John S. Harrison]
2nd   "   Richd. Burdett [Charles W. Glasser]

Co. K.
Capt. Rich. [H.] Morris
1st Lieut. Dowelson [John L. Donaldson]
2nd Lieut. Andrews [vacant]

Kimball, our acting Colonel, is about 50 years of age and was employed previous to the war in a newspaper office—in what capacity I do not know. He is an habitual drunkard and so testy, ignorant, and muddle headed that he is no more fit to command a regiment than an [sic] untaught school boy would be: but as a leader in a charge the boys think him "bully." He is an old friend of Hawkins and served in the Mexican War as a Captain. He rarely ventures to drill a batallion [sic] and when he does invariably gets it into a fix from which it is extricated by his inferior officers. His love of fight is so strong that he is eternally volunteering the services of the 9th for desperate enterprises.

Major Jardine, once Capt. of Co. G, is a little man of 40 [thirty-two], reported "smart," and Kimball's sworn foe. He is generally absent on detached service and acted as Colonel of the 89th N.Y. Vols. at Antietam.[20] The adjutant [sic], Bartholemew, was 1st Lieut. of Co. B when I joined it. He is about 30 [twenty-two] yrs. of age and a merchant by occupation—rather sleepy and consumptive. Lieut. Parison is a mean spirited little speculator who imposes alike upon Government and privates. His operations are disgustingly open. Of the captains all are comparatively young. Graham and Childs are bookbinders, Barnett a newsman, Klingsohr a teacher, Lebarie an actor, Rodriquez a shoemaker, Leighe a dry goods clerk, Morris a [brick]layer, and Hamill I don't know what.

The officers are as stiff and distant as those of the regular army: they scarcely ever speak to the privates even to give orders, the drilling, etc, being chiefly performed by the 1st sergeants. At parades, inspections, etc, the captains or their representatives receive their companies already formed and conduct them to the field. You may remember that after the visit of Ellsworth with his Zouaves to New York, a rival company was formed there and carefully trained there for several months.[21] Of this company the majority of our officers were members, and they are therefore very well instructed and, as the men put it, "understand their biz." The Captain of Co. B., Barnett, is especially reserved. He is a dark, average sized man with a heavy countenance ornamented with a big black moustache [sic]. The captains have been anxious to have the 9th adopted in the regular service so as to make their salaries permanent. They control Kimball and dislike Hawkins.

The privates, of course, are not such people as you or any sensible man would choose, or perhaps I should say could endure, as associates. As a mass, they are ignorant, envious, mercenary, and disgustingly immoral and profane. Being as they are here free from the restraints of civil law, they give loose rein to all their vices and make a boast of them. In our whole regiment, I know no private who will not curse and swear and but few who will not, when circumstances favor, rob and steal or, as they more euphoneously [sic] style the operations, "briz things." If they buy a pound of cheese of a sutler, a pocket-knife or a sausage is "brized" at the same time "because," say they, "the sutler overcharges like the devil and this is the only way we can balance accounts." If an "old member" loses an overcoat or a blanket, he "brizes" one from some

Lieutenant Colonel Edgar A. Kimball *(Engraving courtesy of Historical Times, Inc.)*

"green hams," quieting his conscience with the reflection that "it is used in the service of Uncle Sam."

The soldier robs hen roosts, kills sheep and pigs, and robs private homes under the plea that "secesh" has brought the country to its present unpleasant condition and made him individually endure severe hardships and should therefore be assessed. If he takes only edibles from deserted dwellings, he considers himself particularly abstemious and deserving of praise. In fact, his system of morality is regulated by supposed necessity, and the shadow of an excuse is all-sufficient to cool such blushes as would burn the cheek of an honest man under similar circumstances. I do not speak particularly of the 9th New York as regards these things but of the whole army, as far as it has come under my observation. Almost every one drinks to excess when the opportunity offers, chews and smokes incessantly, and swears habitually, "army habits," they say, "that are to be thrown aside the moment we reach home."

Of the dissentions among the soldiers the most savage come from the abuse of recruits by "old members," and they are very bitter indeed. The "old men" are "patriots who sprang forward at the first call of the Government": the recruits "bounty men" who have sold themselves to Uncle Sam. Nothing is too blunt or taunting to say to a "recruit," nor any trick too contemptible to play upon him. His only chance of securing respect is to do his duty quietly and fully and handle all assailants without gloves. My turn came two months ago, when one evening the old members, who had successively demolished the recruits, made an assault upon me in force as we were seated at a camp fire, but having previously familiarized myself with the characters and biographies of the several members of Co. B and feeling no particular delicacy in the matter, I let fly right and left with such effect that after a short and violent contest, the "boys" were dumbfounded—a dead silence reigned "for considerable minutes," and the attack was never renewed. A prompt resort to a conciliating and soothing policy clenched the nails so luckily driven, and I have been able since to boast, if not of popularity, at least of respect and friendship of manner.

My position as company clerk has been thrown up, partly because it prevented me from drilling with the regiment, partly because one of the sergeants with whom I bunked was (not to put too fine a point upon it) *crumbie* [*sic*], and partly on account of the expenses of their larder (a clerk is necessary because the 1st Sergeant [Schmidt] is German and the 2d [Cornell] illiterate).

"But to return to the subject"—soldiers may further be classed as "duty men" and "beats." A "beat" is one who plays sick, shirks guard duty, drills, roll call, etc., and is always missing in a fight. The beats of a regiment sometimes number one half.[22] It is a favorite theory with the good people at home that war is in a measure beneficial ina[s]much as it kills off rowdies and other pests of society. Don't believe it: such fellows while in the army, by living off their wits, feed from the fat of the land and in the event of a battle are either on the sick list or drop out of the ranks at the first favorable opportunity or tenderly carry away the first of the wounded, allowing their more respectable companions to advance unaided upon the enemy. These observations may furnish, in a few words, rough ideas of truths that every one who has sojourned for a while in the camps is cognizant of.

I can write nothing more at present. Twilight has come. Our picket duty the other day was, as before, on the bluffs opposite Fredericksburg, where we were posted to support a battery. The Rappahannock at that point is so narrow that our men readily conversed with the rebels on the other side, and the representatives of the adverse parties bantered each other to the hearts content. The day was warm and pleasant, but the night foggy and uncomfortably cold. A cup of water beside my head froze in a very few minutes, and in the morning our pieces were thickly covered with a white frost.

In haste I am
Ed. K. W.

P. S. Give Abbie my special thanks for her letter.

Camp near Falmouth, Va.
Thursday, January 15th, 1863

Dear Bro:

Since you last heard from me, things have gone on very much as usual, with now and then an incident to vary the monotony of camp life. A military review or a suddenly ordered inspection occasionally try our patience with their tediousness or surprise us into unwonted activity. It is no joke, after a stormy night at the end of the week, when our clothes are soiled or in the hands of a washerwoman and our pieces mottled with rust, to be required to go into the field at two hours notice in full marching order for regimental inspection.

Early last week Gen. Burnside reviewed the whole 9th Army Corps on a broad flat of table land a quarter of a mile distant, where our batalion [sic] drills are usually held. The morning was cloudy and cold. The line was formed at noon, but the General and his staff did not arrive until 2 o'clock P.M. Meanwhile regiments of infantry, troops of cavalry, trains of artillery, and ambulance wagons by the score were streaming down the roads leading to the rendezvous, so that the whole country round about seemed swarming with armed men and horses. We were early on the ground and had a fine view of the columns as they rose over the hills, wound round their base, came up out of the vales, and emerged from the woods at various points with their music and arms and banners. They poured in upon us like a torrent, and such a dash of horsemen and intermingling of commanding voices: so well ordered a confusion of movements you never dreamed of.

But the preparations were finally complete. The infantry were arrayed in two long lines in double regimental columns, with the artillery and ambulance corps stationed at the right and rear, and Burnside, followed by his staff and a multitude of attendants, rode along the front, hat in hand, bowing as the colors dipped, while the bands successively played their salutes and the muskets of the soldiers rattled as they were brought to a "present." A drizzling rain, under which we had been standing for an hour, excused us from marching in review, and the commander-in-chief had scarcely passed when we were dismissed and set out on our return.

The formality of the occasion was no sooner broken than a scene of promiscuous jollity ensued. The rain was pelting down upon us hard and fast, and a race for dry quarters and warm dinners started off every batallion [sic], company, and platoon at double quick. Cheers for Burnside were ringing everywhere. Hats were skimming in the air, witticisms flew round like hot shot, and laughter undulated over the plain like the wind over a wheat field. Yet, in the midst of all this clamor the merry thousands were maneuvering on the run, wheeling, countermarching, and facing without the slightest clashing or interference. Oh, you never saw anything of the beauty of tactics, Wightman! If you want to see them in full flower, just get a view of a hungry grand army corps rushing for grub according to Hardee. Harlem Guard, indeed!!

I think I told you that I met a couple of classmates in Fredericksburg. Since then I have chanced upon two more. There are five of us here within a circle of three miles, viz.—E. K. W., private in Hawkins Zouaves; C. B. [Lieutenant Charles B.] White, senior surgeon in the Artillery Reserve, near Burnside's headquarters; George Post (son of Dr. Alfred Post of N.Y.), Chaplain of the 15th New York Engineers; Rodney Kimball, Capt. in the 44th New York; and Eugene Douglass, private in the same regiment. A sixth, Bob [Lieutenant Robert F.] Weir by name, is superintendent of a hospital in Frederick, Md. Last Monday I started out to see White and Post. After chatting awhile with the first and partaking of a variety of "Tonics," he sent for a pair of saddle horses and, attended by an orderly, we went to hunt up Post. The minister was but three quarters of a mile distant, and we found him without trouble. He was in the back part of a double tent which had been darkened to the gloom generally considered appropriate for a study and was tugging at his hair and digesting theology. He was becomingly self-possessed and complacent, and the words fell from his lips like the purring of a water fall. He had neither "tonics" nor "fleshpots"—at least he offered none, but he showed us a big log chapel in course of erection. If the boys should see any of the members of his family, let them say that he appears to be perfectly well and to be doing well.

White now found it necessary to return to unpack some supplies just received from Acquia Creek, but he left me my horse and his orderly, and I used both to my hearts content. It would have amused you to have seen the sentinels along the road salute the mounted Zouave and the curiosity they evidently felt to know what sort of shoulder straps his overcoat covered.

On Tuesday, very much to the astonishment of Co. B, I secured another pass. Passes are difficult to get and especially at present when there are but 12 sound men in our company—capable of doing duty. They are generally given only to the old guard, and Corporal Rogers and a Sergeant had been refused the privilege of going out when I made this second application within two days—a step which in their eyes looked like brazen effrontery.

The pass was obtained, however, and after walking three miles, I dropped in upon Capt. Kimball, strangely enough, just as he was about to have dinner. If I remember rightly, we feasted on boiled ham and potatoes, bread and butter, apple sauce, rice and molasses, preserved cherries, sardines, coffee and milk, etc., etc. Kimball's regiment, formerly known as the Ellsworth Avengers, now numbers only about 250 men. Their camp is the prettiest one I have ever seen, being carefully laid out and ornamented with evergreens. Kimball is sick with a cough and disgusted with the conduct of the war and thinks of resigning and returning home.

Douglass, who enlisted under Kimball immediately after returning from a European tour of six years, is a Presbyterian minister. Since I knew him, he has grown dirty and philosophical. Nothing disturbs him. He says his health is good and things go on as well as he can expect. His tent-mate is a prodigy of a young man—learned in the Syriac and a dozen other out-of-the-way and dead languages. The two old fogies live as quietly together as clams in the same bed.

But to return to our subject—I reached home just in time to miss dress parade—a court martial offense; a terrible offense punished, by regimental order, with [a] three dollars fine and reprimand on parade. Everyone consoled with me, but I was glad of the opportunity of testing the good will of the officers. The captain, adjutant, and even cross-grained old Kimball excused me without remark, and the boys are not yet done wondering at it. I mentioned these trifling incidents only to illustrate the strictness of our discipline and to cause you to admire the good odor I have thrown around the Wightman name in this new field.

Last night we were on picket again on the Rappahannock. Two hours pacing in front of a battery, two hours patient listening to the midnight howling of the dogs in Fredericksburg, completed my quantum of duty, and although the wind blew a gale, I slept comfortably in my blanket on the quiet side (windward or leeward?) of a log.

Now for Box No. 1. It came safely to hand on the 8th of January, which I believe is S. K. W.'s birthday. I was warming my shins at the guard house fire at 10 o'clock P.M., preparatory to going on post with the third relief, when six donkies [sic] came up to the quartermasters with a wagon load of express matter. Among the boxes, undamaged and in good condition, was mine. I paid the quartermaster's charge of ten cents and sent it by Sim Hubbel to the "ranche" to await my coming. Sim Hubbel temporarily occupies the place of Whetlaufer in our "ranche" or "shebang" while the latter is detached to [General] Wilcox's headquarters. Sim is the son of Ezra Hubbel of Middletown, Conn., and has just come in from the hospital.

But to return to our subject—At 12 o'clock I threw aside my musket, got the cook house axe and, in defiance of the regulation that extinguishes lights at "taps," lit a candle and opened the box. Everything was there undisturbed—blanket, underclothes, socks, mittens, medicine, book of tactics, etc., etc. Sim woke up and looked on during the overhauling, and to increase his enjoyment I treated him to a seed cake and a lump of gingerbread. They were hard as bricks, of course, but we ate them nevertheless with considerable relish. Simeon even went [to] . . . the formality of thanking me for his share.

The blanket is a very good one, and its marking startles everybody who beholds it. I wore it on picket last night and with the addition of a strap round the waist found it made a hood and overcoat complete. Accept my thanks again for the gifts.

P. S. I have this moment subscribed to aid in erecting in General Park, if possible, a monument to the memory of our fallen Zouaves. It is to be very costly, of white marble, with the battles in which the regiment has been engaged illustrated in relief on its sides by first class artists.

In haste Yrs truly,
Ed

Bluffs opposite Fredericksburg, Va.
(Picket Station) Sunday, Jan 25th, 1863

Dear Bro:

Doubtless you expect this letter will bring news of a famous feast and of the augmented fatness of your humble servant. Alas, my dear fellow! After waiting with my mouth watering almost to salivation for the coming of fleshpots, I am ignominiously forced to acknowledge their non-arrival and my consequent inconsolable condition. The matter is that our respectable commander-in-chief, Burnside, has seen fit to poke his finger in my pie.

The trouble is this: although your second box is directed to Falmouth, it must have gone by the regular route to Acquia Creek, there to await removal by our quarter master's wagon, which goes out once a week; but our last wagon came up to camp on Saturday last [the 17th] just previous to the time when the box should have appeared at that point, and on Sunday following orders were issued for one corps to be ready to march at 7½ o'clock on Monday morning [Tuesday, the 20th], with tents and knapsacks and three days rations, to take part in a second assault on the rebel works around Fredericksburg. Sigel and Hooker and Franklin[23] were to cross the Rappahannock at and above Falmouth, while we were first to hold the front by guarding the lower fords and afterwards to go over again on a pontoon bridge and, if necessary, throw ourselves upon the enemy's center.

During Sunday [Monday] night, however, a furious storm of wind and rain arose, which continued with few intermissions till Friday evening, soaking the troops who were already in motion, muddying the roads, sticking the artillery and the ammunition and provision trains, and at length completely blocking our grand flank movement. You never heard such terrific cursing as the infantry, artillery men, and teamsters of the Army of the Potomac indulged in up to Saturday night. The advance proved a fizzle. The heavy guns sunk in every hole above the axles of the carriages, and a dozen horses and half a regiment of men [assigned] to each were not sufficient to stir them. The men, after wading almost knee-deep through the mire until exhausted, lay down at night to sleep, only to die from exposure.

Fortunately, we [the Ninth New York] remained in camp and suffered only from the water which poured into our shanties: but those of us who had dug down three or four feet into the ground "to live warmer" were either drowned out or kept busy bailing all day long. My "shebang," which in opposition of the wishes of my tent-mates I had insisted should be built above ground, was the dryest [sic] in the company, and we were scarcely inconvenienced.

During the latter part of the week the regiments of Franklins Corps passed us on their way back to their old quarters; some of them marched in good order and beyond their mud-plastered legs and disheartened countenances did not seem in bad condition; but multitudes came as stragglers—the hills and road were black with them, and they swore they were worried to death with fighting the mud. On yesterday the order to keep on hand three days cooked rations was countermanded, and it is presumed that we shall attempt nothing for a long while to come. As for the 9th, it is, as you see, on picket duty today at its old post,[24] and the morning march of a mile which brought us here was quite enough to satisfy us that knapsack travelling is at present an almost impossible feat. The roads are terribly cut up and little else than a pudding of slush. *"Sic transit gloria muddi."*[25]

But to return to our subject—box No. 2. It is still 20 miles distant and must be dragged hither in a wagon by mules. To show you the prospect of getting it soon, I will mention that of the two wagons daily sent out to fetch wood for our cook houses one is almost invariably stuck and left behind. You will see, therefore, that there must be some delay—Is the fault mine? Is it yours. . . ?

Fredericksburg lies spread out before us within a stones throw, and we have the privilege of looking at it—of hearing the church bells ring, of seeing the people repairing to their several places of worship, and of reflecting that they are praying earnestly for our discomfiture and utter annihilation. But we know that we have at least an equal number of good Christians at home with just as good voices and just as determined spirits.

There is no further news. Let me tell you an incident. A Dutch barber from the 103rd N. Y. Vols. came into our camp within 24 hours last past, to pick up such little jobs as might fall in his way. Two men in Co. I (famed for its rascality) forthwith called upon him to cut their hair and after the operation paid him a leaden half dollar and received three shillings change in U. S. stamps. The Dutchman had not been gone ten minutes with his "specie" before he discovered the cheat and returned to demand justice. Now here comes the laugh. Company I was commanded to "fall in," and the barber requested to point out the criminals, but they all had the Zou-zou cut, the only two long haired men had been shorn, and the crowd looked so much alike that Myerheer [mein herr], for the life of him, couldn't make out which was which. It was a case of tweedle-dum and tweedle-dee. According to professional habit he had seen only the tops of his customers' heads and could not recognize the[ir] countenances.

Letters from Jim and the girls have come to hand, but they are not with me, and I cannot give their dates.

From the midst of the sacred soil of Virginia, into which the Fates have transplanted and imbedded me, let my voice assure all the "White man" (and a Hunter [Jim's wife]) of continued affection and consideration.

Ed. K. W.

Camp near Falmouth, Va.
Monday Eve. Jan. 26th, 1863

Dear Chas:

My last note to you seems to have given rise in your mind, merely by its ornamental aspect, to some very serious misapprehensions. Fred says you have been so far bedoozled as to suspect me of being adjutant of the 9th. My dear boy, I am just as simple and plain a private as ever and to this moment have not given a thought to promotion in the regiment.

It may seem strange to you and when I think of it, the idea strikes me as decidedly odd: but so many other considerations have bothered me during my short five months of service that fancy remained inert and visions of glory never kept me waking. In fact, the time of service of the Zouaves is so short that from the first I had no ambition for advancement and would have made no extra exertion to secure it, being content to return as I came out, a private. But if the war is to be prolonged, I shall surely work for and take a "commission"— "The Lord willing and the wearer permit."

It is by no means certain that we recruits shall be mustered out with the old men in May, and this reflection has caused me within the last week to commence the reading of tactics in order to make myself familiar with military movements, a science, it seems, in which you believe me to be already in some degree proficient. Undeceive yourself, I am still green, though a couple of hours a day devoted to books will soon post me. As to promotion in this regiment, it has always been regular and by degrees, beginning with a corporalship. Such a thing as a leap from the ranks to an adjutancy was never heard of here, nor even from the ranks to a sergeantcy. So well defined are the rules which regulate promotion and so closely are they adhered to; so great is the out cry which follows the breaking of them and so unmeasured the envy and abuse of the rank and file sure to be aroused by the advancement of one of their companions, especially if he be a "recruit," that it is much more respectable to remain quiet and undistinguished in the crowd. Nevertheless, if I choose to attain a position, I will do it in spite of all the dead cats in Christendom, even when slung by Zouaves of the old school.

As to these fancy headings on the note paper, they came from New York, were brought on by a convalescent and sold us at two cents a sheet. Is the mystery solved? Calm your excitement, me boy, and curb your imagination.

Believe me as ever your aff. Bro.

Ed.

Camp near Falmouth, Va.
Tuesday, Jan. 27th, 1863

Dear Bro:

We are back to camp again, as you see, and not too soon, for it is once more steadily raining. Lieut. Col. Kimball left camp last evening for a furlough of 15 days. He may not return, as he is threatened with court martial for intoxication, etc. He will probably find it convenient to resign. Major Jardine is now our acting Colonel.

We hear that Hooker has succeeded Burnside in command of the army, and that Sumner has resigned in disgust.[26] Are the chuckle heads at Washington beside themselves: Will they never be done with their awkward bungling? Are the soldiers and the country to be ignorantly experimented with till the former mutiny and the people withhold supplies? The President must be crazy. From want of confidence in its leaders and *from no other reason*, the army is fearfully demoralized. The politicians forget that our soldiers are all intelligent men equally capable with themselves of distinguishing between a brave leader and a sagacious strategist.

A general growl has followed the new appointment, and fresh defeats are anticipated. The men feel that their lives are trifled with. Desertions are frequent and dissatisfaction general and without concealment. The failure of the last movement has not tended to improve the status of affairs, and the elevation of Hooker is another step in the wrong direction. Unless some happy accident of Fortune relieves us, the recall of McClellan will be an indispensable necessity. The troops already with one voice demand it, and it is to be apprehended that they will soon refuse to fight under any other man.

The rebs laugh a great deal over our late failure. Opposite Falmouth they have struck up signs on the shores of the Rappahannock, representing Burnside stuck in the mud, inquiring, "Why don't the army move?" "How about those three days rations?" etc. The rascals knew that our troops at that point were living on "mud" pudding in consequence of their detention and of the delay of the provision trains.

There is a new feature in our camp. The darkies of the officers mess have raised a hand bell. Its first tintinabulations awakened in the minds of the men a flood of associations, and for awhile it was laughable to hear the confusion of tongues shouting, "Down in front," "Hats off!" "Nigger in the pit!" "Shore in the plank!" "All aboard!" accompanied by a whistle call and other demonstrations.

Complts. to the fam.
Ed. K. W.

P. S. For gracious sake don't send any more paper and envelopes at present.

Camp near Falmouth, Va.
Jan. 29, 1863

Dear Bro Fred:

Colonel Hawkins leaves tomorrow for New York. Your letter of introduction has never been presented to him. He has always, since my advent, been acting as Brig. Genl. and away from the regiment. Besides, your letter was so confoundedly strong that I hadn't the brass to hand it to him.

You will remember that I joined the regiment without knowing of your acquaintence with the Colonel. Thinking that if I were not mustered out with it I should at least return to New York with the regiment, I gave no thought to promotion, being content to return as I came out, a private. When we crossed to Fredericksburg, I burned all my papers and your letter, which had become much soiled by carrying, with the rest.

This explanation, I am satisfied, will prevent your feeling offended by my action in the matter, and it is offered at this time in order that you may know the status of the affair and be informed of the facts without the awkwardness of an inquiry of Col. Hawkins in case you should see him. As far as Surgery is concerned, I am convinced that I could be of but little use as an assistant of our medical men.

Yrs. truly,
Ed. K. W.

Camp near Falmouth, Va.
Friday, Jan. 27th [30th], 1863

Dear Wool [Jim]:

Your perseverance [sic] in writing in the absence of direct answers certainly merits that you should be remembered whenever I can find time to write individually to the several members of the family. I am indebted to you for a great deal of news, many stamps and envelopes and things, and as being a faithful agent for the transmission of kind remembrances. In common with the last letters of the girls, yours was lost—burned, I believe on Monday last, when we were lightening our pockets and knapsacks to march against the rebs.

But the battle was "postponed on account of the weather," and as it continues to rain and a rumor reaches us that we are now under a new commander, and as the army, moreover, is not in fighting humor, it is very doubtful when and where we shall next meet the enemy. The proposal of the President to consolidate the smaller regiments by uniting two or more small ones likely is to be productive of much trouble. Some of Gen. Sickles'[27] troops have already mutinied and laid down their arms. The consolidation of the 2nd N.Y. Fire Zouaves with another N.Y. regiment[28] was only accomplished by force and then at the cost of many men who deserted at the first opportunity. Every regiment has certain peculiarities of organization and an *esprit du corps* (me comprenez vous?) which such rough usage clashes against, and dissatisfaction and resistance result. . . .

Ed. K. W.

Camp near Falmouth, Va.
Wednesday, February 4, 1863

Dear Bro:

We still shiver under the toughest kind of winter weather. The brook in which my daily ablutions are performed was this morning covered with a thick sheet of ice, although its waters run very rapidly. Two holes only were left, close at the foot of a couple of water falls, and through them I succeeded in "taking off the crust," as the men have it. Since I last wrote, we have been visited by a heavy snow storm, and two days after, my turn for guard duty having come, I spent rather a disagreeable night tramping up and down my post.

But the experiences of Saturday last (my fatigue day) were rougher still. All the wood consumed in the camp now has to be brought a distance of two miles in consequence of an order forbidding the cutting of more trees in our immediate neighborhood: for a whole forest has already been leveled here, and it is necessary that something should be left to keep off the cold winds. On Saturday morning, then, the pioneers having gone before to cut and prepare the fuel, a dozen of us mounted a pair of army wagons, each drawn by six mules guided by "intelligent contrabands," and started over the muddy snow covered roads to get up supplies for the company cook houses. You have bumped around in a lumber wagon in the Eastern States, but that was luxury as compared with jumping in and out of mud holes in an army cart in Virginia. I was unlucky enough to secure a seat and in consequence was spanked and tossed about like a darkey in a blanket till scarce[ly] a breath was left in my bruised body.

Suddenly we came to a steep hill where the road, thickly lined with bushes, took the form of a deep groove and inclined at an awful angle to a dirty stream at its foot. The mules, who had been wading to their knees in slush, here made a dive for dryer [sic] ground and, in spite of the stentorian cries of the nigger-driver who smacked his long whip and shouted, "Yah! Ya-y-y-y!" at the top of his voice, dragged us half way up the embankment and threatened to upset the whole concern. The knock-kneed nig dismounted in a passion and kicked and thrashed the leader till he was almost red in the face; but the only effect was to make them turn and rush up the other side, whisking us round in spinning time and threatening compound fractures of the tibias and humerus without number. The way in which the Zou-zous piled out of the old *cadunk* over wheels and tailboard at that instant would have jerked a laugh out of . . . [anyone].

The darkey, seeing his reputation at stake, frantically seized on rein and bridle and kicked and tugged with infernal energy. The donkeys reared and flopped their big ears and kicked and squealed, and their insane driver disappeared and reappeared from the mire with such wonderful confusion and alacrity that no one could keep trace of the order of the performances nor imagine how they would end. . . . I was rushing along on the left, laughing enough to split my side at the drollery of the affair, when my foot tripped over a stump and head-first I went, as though shot from a catapult, into a ditch, striking my shoulder against the frozen ground with all the vim of a big triphammer and slinging a pair of number 9 government shoes into the air at a summerset [sic] attitude. A little limber-legged Red-cap had the audacity to point his finger at me and raise a derisive shout. May he never chew tobacco again.

The logs had to be carried a quarter of a mile down a slippery hill and across an almost impassible stream. Being a big fellow, I was always expected to "take the butt." Our labors ceased at sunset when we had loaded ten large wagons. My shoulder aches yet—Whew-w!

On reaching home, I found that George Post had called during my absence and left two packages—one for me and one for Private Douglass of the 44th N.Y. (another classmate) with the request that I would forward the latter. My bundle contained a large piece of fruit cake, some sweet crackers, almonds, raisins, figs, dried prunes, etc., etc. Good.

Next day, Sunday, having nothing better to do, I went to see Douglass and dropped in upon his captain, Kimball. Being *unavoidably detained*, I stayed to dinner and worried down a few steaks, sardines, a little bread and butter, rice, preserved cherries, etc. Kimball expected to get a furlough and start for home on Wednesday or Thursday of this week. He will "call arn our house."

Tearing myself away at about 2½ P.M., I reached the camp of the 9th at sunset and found Box No. 2 awaiting me and Bailey and Hubbell, apparently disinterested, ready to inform me of the fact. Two minutes sufficed to tote it up from the Quartermasters, and one to burst it open with the cook house axe. A flaky pie-crust met our enraptured gaze. Three big mouths watered instantly, and thirty fingers moved instinctively and in sympathy. "Apple, I'll bet! No, by George, mince!!" were the exclamations. But picture to yourself the light of gladness which illuminated the three faces of those heroes as they plumbed the juicy depths of that glorious pie and fished out the raisins. Did we wait to take out the false top and explore the profundity beneath? Not at all. We just sat down upon our hunkies and with ecstasy-rolling eyes devoured what lay before us—all but one big piece—a quarter, which was left for the absent Whetlaufer; for to forget an absent tentmate is a capital offense among soldiers.

The pie finished, the butternuts and hickory nuts were tumbled out and the false top removed. A huge round surface, curiously punched and wholesomely browned, now presented itself in the center of the box, surrounded by a variety of vegetables and packages. Bailey and Hubbell licked their chops and said, "cake," but better discernment enabled me to yell, as I smote my thigh with satisfaction, Schwartz-brod!! and I was right. The next exclamations of my associates, as their eyes fell on the Seidlitz powder box, was "medicine," but I "said no-thing" until the removal of the cover revealed butter for the bread. The discovery of this elicited this chorus, Ah-h!

Afterwards, herbs, onions, apples, etc., were hastily taken out, and we then came suddenly upon a big lump of mould [sic], a mouldy chicken, and a mouldy piece of cheese. Did we throw them away? Not at all. The chicken was carefully skinned and the beef's tongue shaved, and both were as good and fresh as new. As for the cheese, its flavor had only been improved. Beneath lay three great Bologna sausages in a fine stage of preservation, flanked by jars of currant jelly and cranberry sauce and, well, it's no use trying to enumerate further. They were all there.

While the operation of unpacking was going on, many a man in Co. B made an "errand to Wightman's tent," and several pairs of wistful eyes looked in through the button holes. For nearly a week I have been living in clover. Cold cuts of tongue and chicken, bread and butter and jelly, apples and nuts are delicacies that do not often tickle the palate of a private—at least of Private Wightman. Mother's nut-cakes were especial favorites both with myself and the other two boobies who kept "hankerin after em" till I wished said boobies in Richmond or some other equally distant and inaccessible place.

The first night the box was in our Shebang I couldn't sleep and, feeling hungry, about midnight I quietly rose into a sitting posture. My glance fell upon the piece of mine pie reserved for Whetlaufer. It was the "witching hour," and perhaps evil spirits were abroad. At all events, I could not withstand the temptation and ate the pie and even felt complacent after it rather than remoseful. But I was so demonstrative in my enjoyment that Bailey and Hubbell awoke and called for nut-cakes, confound 'em.

The box was a success notwithstanding its detention. The bread was to all appearances as fresh and soft as when new, and the meat was none the worse for its mould. The stoutness of the box saved everything. The pepper, mustard, and onions are peculiarly valuable, as the quartermaster rarely has them. For all these things I know my thanks are due to the whole family, and the whole family will therefore accept them without measure.

The adjutant's assistant having got a furlough, I have been acting in his place as Regimental clerk for a week past.

Thursday, Feb. 5th

Another heavy snowstorm. The regiment is on picket. I am, from my position, exempt. Hooker, it is said, will shortly take us across the river. Preparations are already being made. Another failure will undo the administration.

Ed. K. W.

P. S. Change of base! The adjutant has just received an order for the *9th Army Corps to embark at Acquia Creek for Fortress Monroe* with 3 days rations. Hooker is done for. The Army of the Potomac is broken up. We are to meet the rebs on a new field. A chance for the Union yet. "E pluribus unum!!" We shall be off in a week.

Camp near Falmouth, Va.
Thursday, Feb. 5, 1863

Dear Father:

Your letter of Jan. 31st came to hand last night with its enclosure of the Express receipt. Luckily, as you see by the family letter [enclosed], the receipt is now useless, the box having already come up. It was really, as some of the men remarked, "a reg'lar Christmas box."

As to your sending one once every two weeks, that is a piece of extravagance which I hope will not be attempted. Perhaps in sketching camp pictures for the amusement of the girls and boys, I have laid on the colors too thick and given a false impression of our manner of life. We always have *sufficient* food; but sometimes we long after variety. I don't expect you to feed me at this distance and wouldn't have you attempt it. Besides, I believe we are again about to move. . . .

Abbie enquires after the health of Co. B and to know what is the matter with so many of them. Tell her that one half of the Company are in hospitals from wounds and chronic illness, and of the rest one half are thoroughbred "beats." Her jelly is fully appreciated: as to the chicken bone soup, I have no fire here . . . to carry out her directions. The herbs, however, give a fine flavor to our beef soup.

. . . Fred enquires whether the last advance of the army was not a feint to prevent the reinforcements [*sic*] of Bragg in N. Carolina.[29] No, it was in terrible earnest. There is no reason for a doubt of it. The sticking of the artillery was the only cause of failure. Hooker refused to take the infantry across unsupported. Burnside had previously maneuvered so as to cause Lee to concentrate his troops at Port Royal, two days march below.[30]

Mary's letters of Jan. 20th and 26th are recd. . . . Half a dozen letters have come from Charley, but he asks no questions.

4

NEWPORT NEWS AND SUFFOLK

[Early in February 1863 the Ninth Corps was rescued from the mud and misery of Falmouth. Under Burnside, who had returned to corps command with the rise to army leadership of Major General Joseph ("Fighting Joe") Hooker, the troops were sent to the Fort Monroe-Newport News-Portsmouth area. Noting the movement, Lee predicted an offensive against Richmond from that sector. He detached two divisions under his ranking subordinate, Lieutenant General James Longstreet, and sent them toward that same portion of southeastern Virginia.

Soon, however, the War Department decided to transfer the bulk of Burnside's command to Kentucky and Tennessee. Only Getty's division remained in the Newport News vicinity. By mid-March it had gone to neighboring Suffolk, to reinforce Major General John J. Peck's fifteen-thousand-man garrison.

In April, Longstreet moved against Suffolk along the Nansemond River in a land and naval operation that menaced the whole of Peck's force. In the end, however, "Old Pete" gave up his effort in view of the protractedness and the uncertainty of the siege and due to some Union victories against his outposts, including the April 19 surprise and capture of Fort Huger, north of Suffolk. By the first week in May, when Longstreet began his return march to Lee's main army, some 250 Federals and over nine hundred Confederates had become casualties of his stalemated campaign.

At Newport News and Suffolk, Edward saw relatively little action. Serving as clerk to the local provost marshal, he was concerned to find himself growing "fat and lazy." He recorded some unusual events during this period, including a regimental banquet that featured fried rat as the main course; the murder of Lieutenant Colonel Edgar A. Kimball of the Ninth New York by Brigadier General Michael Corcoran; the unhappy transfer of much of the Ninth to the Third New York, which occasioned widespread demoralization; and the difficulties Edward faced in trying to escape Company H of the Third for service in a more desirable outfit. He ended his account of his brief and curious

General John J. Peck *(Photograph courtesy of the Library of Congress)*

sojourn in lower Virginia by recording yet another confused campaign: Major General John A. Dix's aborted offensive against Richmond via Yorktown and White House, Virginia, in June and July 1863.]

Steamer Robert Morris on the
Potomac, Sunday Feb. 8, 1863

Dear Bro:

On Thursday night, as I have informed you, the 9th were on picket in the midst of an awful storm of rain and snow. On Friday we had received orders to hold ourselves in readiness to embark with three days rations at Acquia Creek for Fortress Monroe and, having reached our place of destination, to report to Maj. Gen. Dix[1] and await further orders.

On Saturday morning we were up and packing for a start at 3 o'clock. At about 5 A.M. the rations had been issued, and the "general" sounded for the striking of tents. A few minutes sufficed to take the muslin roofs from our shanties and buckle them under the flaps of our knapsacks. Then followed a jolly scene in the old camp. Bright fires crackled and blazed in the company streets, lighting up the laughing faces of the men grouped around them, and chattering and joking became the order of the day. The sun had not yet risen, but the sky was clear and the full moon up. The boys were drying their overcoats and oiling their pieces for travelling. Being forewarned, I had taken the precaution to make the most of the contents of my box so that nothing remained but a few onions, some Bolognas, pepper sauce, red pepper, and mustard. The former I stuffed in my haversack. The last three, rather than leave, I carried in the breast of my overcoat over the belt. The box made a snapping fire for us in front of the old ranch.

At six o'clock the line was formed and, bending under the weight of the loads, we marched over the frozen mud to the railroad depot. I lugged along, beside my rifle and equipments, sixty rounds of cartridge[s], a canteen full of water, three days rations of pork and crackers, two government blankets and one rubber one, one tent, 3 suits of under clothing besides an extra belt, blacking brush, books, etc., a pretty fair load.

At the depot we waited until 3 o'clock P.M., during which time the ground thawed, and our feet became soaked in the slush. The Zou-zous, of course, grew uneasy under such a condition of affairs and, discovering a sutler established near, went through him just to kill time. In other words, they upset his tent and appropriated his stores, which consisted of bread, apples, etc. But Maj. Jardine, commanding, stopped the fun by ordering "the assembly" to be blown, and when the men had fallen in behind their stacks, half-a-dozen of them who were caught with stolen goods in their hands were handed over to the provost marshall [sic].

When the train came in, the whole regiment was put aboard in a twinkling, and we were dancing along the rails toward the Creek. We were accomodated [sic] with reserved seats in baggage cars, said seats being our knapsacks. The men were in the best possible spirits and shouted to and at every living thing on the road: some were on the roof as outside passengers.

The country between Falmouth Station and Acquia Creek is very picturesque and beautiful, and the hills through which we plunged varied the scene continually. Acquia Creek is little else than a conglomeration of new unpainted buildings—mostly storehouses. Standing at the railroad terminus and looking down the Potomac, which at this point is very broad and at this time well covered with sailing vessels and steamers, a New Yorker easily fancies himself at Hoboken, looking across at the City and out upon the [Hudson] Bay towards the Narrows.

On leaving the cars, we formed and marched by the flank along the track to the dock. Our reception was quite distingued [distinguished], everybody turning out to catch a glimpse of us, so that we had to run the gauntlet of a crowd all the way. Some delay ensued previous to embarking and Companies B and G were at first quartered on board the old propeller [steamship] called "Planet," whose deck (half covered with coal) was so narrow that one might stand in the middle and spit over either side; but finally the steamer Robert Morris backed in and took the whole regiment.

Companies B and G occupied the upper deck and the rest below. Last night I slept very comfortably under a yawl-boat on the larboard [port] side, and tonight I propose to return to the same berth. The steamer is very slow and did not start till daylight this morning, so that we shall not probably reach the Fort until tomorrow. The trip has thus far been pleasant. The river is a splendid one, the water smooth, and the weather fine. We are now (about noon) entering Chesapeake Bay.

I forgot to mention that our fatigue party, detailed to assist in unloading the cars, helped themselves last night to half a hundred weight or so of bakers bread—such little items may seem to you worth mentioning as illustrating soldiers' habits.

Newport News
Tuesday, Feb. 10th, 1863

Early Monday morning reveille awoke me from a sound sleep, and I found we were already anchored off Fort Monroe.[2] The Fort, however, was not in sight, being hidden from view by a respectable village which has sprung up recently on the Northern side. The [Hampton] Roads were flecked with schooners and other small sailing vessels, and I counted eight small steamers filled with our troops.

At about 9 A.M. a little tug put out from shore and, passing within speaking distance of the steamers, ordered them to cross to Newport News. When we landed at the dock, we were received by the 89th [New York], who had preceded us one day; but there were no other soldiers here. Our coming took all the inhabitants by surprise. Indeed, the sutlers, disgusted with the dullness of the place, had packed up their goods and were about leaving.

The barracks here are long log houses roofed with boards. In some cases the layers of logs are placed horizontally; in others they were ranged on end. The quarters of the 9th consist of five of these buildings, two companies to each. They were last used as stables for cavalry horses, and the equine odor still lingers around the picturesque walls. I was on guard when we came in and so escaped much of the rough work; for camping and regimental property had to be borne from the boat, and afterwards the boys had to remove the manure from the floors of their dwellings and drive out the hosts of rats who had evidently fixed their minds on a permanent settlement.

The energy with which the Zou-zous hustled their freight along the dock contrasted strikingly with the tedious slowness of the Eastern men. The Red-caps did everything on a quick step or a trot and, while their slower and more plodding friends carried everything by hand, seized up and brought into service every go-cart and old wagon in the place. They made a short [stint] of labor. The bunks in the old barracks were built in the same hasty careless style. Stagings to accomodate [sic] half-a-dozen sleepers were erected on stakes about two feet from the ground, touching the walls on one side and draped round with shelter tents for curtains. Our building not being large enough to furnish basement lodgings for the two companies (B and G) assigned it, some of the boys had to build second stories among the rafters and others to make kennels under such pavillions [sic] as were raised high enough from the earth to permit it. At last all are comfortably housed.[3]

In my last letter I stated that I was appointed adjutant clerk during the absence of the clerk proper. The movement of our corps, however, cut off his furlough, and he was compelled to return to duty and I to report to my company. Since we have been at Newport News, our Major Jardine has been appointed Provost Marshall of the post and the 9th Regt. Provost Guard. The major has detailed me as his clerk. Tell the women folks that in spite of myself I have ceased to be a fighting man. My arms and equipment have been handed in and a pen given to me in their place.

My rooms consist of an office and a bedchamber. There are stoves and fires in both. They look forth upon the river, which is only distant a couple of hundred feet. The beach is of white sand and the facilities for bathing all that can be desired. Directly in front of the door and but a few hundred yards from it, the three masts of the unlucky Cumberland[4] rise from the water. The iron-clad, Galena, is anchored just beyond in plain view, and the 2nd monitor[5] is among our visitors; among the steamers flying back and forth—I notice the old "Hero" and your Harlem boat "Sylvan Grove" [Sylvan Shore].

How long we shall remain here is uncertain, but it is believed that the regiment will be employed for provost duty during the remainder of its time in service.

In haste,
Ed. K. W.

P. S. The major has just given me an assistant and a carpenter to fit up pigeon holes, tables, etc.

Newport News, Feb. 12, 1863

[To Brother Jim:]

If my former illustrated note astonished you, I am satisfied that this, which far excels the other in artistic effect, will confound you. This letter, too, as you supposed the other, indicates very rapid advancement in the military grades. After catching a glimpse of this letterhead, you are to think of me only as, "Edward K. Wightman, Esq." and "Private in Hawkins Zouaves and Acting Assistant Provost Marshall of the 9th Army Corps." Don't faint, you booby. Big thing, ain't it? No more fighting, sir, for the Zou-zous, until they return [to New York]. They are the Provost Guard of the post, and such a guard. No criminals escape them. Our guard house is always full, though the prisoners are detailed, whenever arrested, to work at unloading vessels. . . .

As to our "licking the rebels," I am as willing to do it as ever if some skillful strategist will but show me where to strike effectively. The fact of the matter is, Wool, there is entirely too much science in the conduct of the war. We want more rough and tumble, and we want, too, that the two quarrelling parties of civilians at home shall not spur and check us at one and the same time, else we shall do nothing but stand, like a horse in similar circumstances, dancing in one spot. D'ye see how 'tis? Course. You're an intelligent fellow and can see right into these things.

Tell the "president duck" [Jim's wife, Lillie] that rather than be disgracefully recalled by so distinguished a personage, I will proceed to "lick somebody." Rebs are scarce in this neighborhood, but I'll find some one to pitch into, let her be assured of that. Remember me also to her sister, who is so thoughtful of the comfort of absent friends. Ask Mary to give my regards to [Cousin] Ellen Butler next time she writes to her.

Inform Abbie that whenever she is ready to appoint me Major General, she has only to say the word, and I will accept, though "having no confidence in my capacity to handle so large an army." The office of General-in-Chief, however, has already been transferred so many times that the distinction would be no object and would confer but little honor. Besides, I wouldn't have the patience to write out such a windy defense as it has become the fashion of our Maj. Generals to prepare after their brilliant failures. No, no, unless the war is better conducted in [the] future than it has been in the past, let me continue, say I, a private—responsible for no share of the folly of our leaders. But, after all, perhaps we shall come out straight at last.

Tell Charley that he is hereby relieved of the labor of forwarding newspaper selections (until further orders), as the newsboys regularly leave a liberal supply of New York, Phila., and Baltimore papers at the office every day. His clippings and summaries have been of great use to me. As for yourself, Wool, I have to inform you that my stock of stamps is exhausted with this letter, and I shall be obliged if you will forward some more, patiently awaiting to be refunded, therefore, until next pay day, which cannot now be far distant.

Finally, give my distresses to all the phellers and oblige

Ed

Newport News, Va.
Feb. 19th, 1863

Dear Bro:

. . . . You asked to be enlightened as to the character of Maj. Jardine. He is a man of about your size, 35 years of age or so, with dark brown hair, gray sprinkled, a heavy moustache [sic], and regular features. In manner he is reserved and abrupt except when among intimate friends or when striving to make a favorable impression; then his address is agreeable and somewhat polished, though the style of his conversation is such as to make it difficult to decide by it whether he has passed more time among educated gentlemen or half-breed "roughs." He has so little faith in his literary ability that he leaves his correspondence to be conducted by me.

His antecedents I know nothing about. Rumor says he has "lived by his wits" and that he was formerly a gambler.[6] His quickness and knowledge of human nature, displayed in the tact with which he takes advantage of the weakness of those with whom he deals, give color to the supposition. As an executive officer, he is very good indeed. He came out as a captain and since holding the rank of Major has several times been appointed by Hawkins to act temporarily as Colonel of Regiments in the Brigade. At Antietam he was distinguished as the commander of the 89th N.Y. He is a thorough military man and when the term of service of the Regiment expires will probably be transferred to the regular army. He appears at present to enjoy the confidence of both Gen. Getty and Gen. Wilcox, who are close by in the first house on our left, Getty the commander of the Post and Wilcox of the Corps.[7]

Newport News, as I have told you, is such a crude jumble of log barracks that, looking out of the office windows upon the water as it rolls in upon the sandy beach, I can scarcely imagine myself elsewhere than at Rope Ferry.[8] The illusion becomes complete when I stand on the shore and look either to the right or left. The house (one story), once used as a sutlers place, has a ground plan like this:

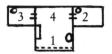

No. 1 is the office. The square place in the back corner is my table, upon which you are to imagine a set of pigeon holes. . . . A window cut in the side of the wall admits light by day, and a pair of kerosene lamps (furnished freely by a groveling sutler) enable me to work at night. The circle nearly opposite represents a little patent wood stove, which is kept in fuel by the 60 odd prisoners now in the Guard House. The dotted line across the room is a railing to keep off anxious visitors. Cross legged carpet chairs and benches are distributed here and there for the use of such of our officers as like to lounge here. The front door has a window on each side. The back door, with a clock over it, opens into an unoccupied room (No. 4) between Major Jardine's (No. 2) and my own (No. 3).

In the sleeping rooms, the doors and stoves are disposed as marked. The windows are in the ends. In my bed chamber I have improvised a wardrobe, [a] set of shelves, and a table. The table, a fancy round top similar to that of the merry knights of yore, consists of the top of a big hogshead mounted on three legs, and the whole is draped in the red blanket of the Major's orderly, giving it quite a gay aspect. The Major wants one like it, but no more hogsheads are to be had, and I won't take the hint.

Now for the rations. I draw rations from the company as heretofore, only my meals are brought to me by the guard. Military etiquette, of course, excludes privates from the officers tables; but the Major invited me to "eat anything I can lay hands on in the establishment," and the barrels of oysters and apples and sweet potatoes in the "unoccupied" room, No. 4, suffer accordingly. If we stay here permanently, of which there seems now to be some doubt, I am to draw direct from the Quartermaster, and a black cook, to be provided by the Major for general use, will attend to my innards. Major Jardine is so well satisfied that we shall remain here for a season that he has sent home for his wife, and she will probably be here tomorrow, where[upon] additions will be made to the accomodations [sic].

Now for my duties. At the drummers call for reveille, I rise, fold my blankets and, buttoning on my blouse, race up the sandy beach for a quarter of a mile to a fresh water pond. There the facilities for washing are unrivaled, and I indulge ad. lib. Then follows a run back against time, and a couple of whisks with the comb and as many scrubs with the blacking brush finish my toilet, and I am ready for business.

As soon as the first gleam of daylight reveals the way, a crowd of restless travelers besiege the office door—citizens, private soldiers, Lieutenants, Captains, Colonels, Quartermasters, niggers, etc., most often seeking passes by the 8 o'clock steamer for Fortress Monroe, Norfolk, Washington, New York, etc. For a couple of hours my tongue rattles like a mill clapper, and my pen wiggles like a lambs tail in fly time. Woe to the unlucky [person] . . . who has neglected to put his pass through the necessary preliminaries; for whether colonel, citizen, or nigger, he is hastily snubbed and must retire.

To increase the confusion, sutlers come in to ask permission to put up stores or to land goods, darkies to sell oysters, newsboys to sell papers, regimental quartermasters to get permits to take away express packages, abused citizens to implore that guards may be placed round their dwellings, corporals to deliver up prisoners to unload a vessel at the dock, regimental squads for passes beyond the lines after wood, etc., etc., and all the boobies stand outside the railing, touching their caps in rotation and calling me Major until I am tired of glory and would be content to lie down and be ignominiously carried out on a chip.

Then we have Division Guard mounting, and the Regimental reports, shabbily prepared by our officers, are handed in and have to be revised for reference. [Mean]while, official papers requiring answers shower in among general and special ones and make confusion worse confounded. I have no chance to retire until after "taps."

Inclosed are two or three papers taken from a pile of those returned at the dock. They will give you an idea of the elaborate system of red-tapism [sic] in vogue at this point. On one of them you will see Ed. [Edwin S.] Babcock's name inscribed as Lieut. Col. of a Jersey Regiment.[9] A poor private called three times yesterday before he could get the signature of his Colonel, Brigade Commander, and of the Provost Marshall, to pass him ten feet out of the lines to dig clams. He was bound to have them and probably succeeded finally, but his dinner must have been late.

The above will give you as good a general idea of my position and duties as the limited time at my disposal enables me to sketch.

Saturday night, Feb. 21st, '63

Did I ever thank Abbie for the calendar she sent me? It is nailed against the wall beside my table and has become a *sine qua non* of the establishment. Her aim seems always to cover the bullseye.

Within a few days I have received two letters from father, enclosing $10 in small change, one from F. B. W. [Fred] inclosing $1, and one from Jim containing a supply of letter stamps. Such a liberal shower of currency was entirely unlooked for and multiplies my obligations beyond what I had expected. The good will accompanying the remittances more than doubles their value. Letters have also arrived as follows: one from mother, dated February 17th; Jim, Feb. 10th; Chas., 10th and 18th; Mary, 10th, 16th; Ell—why bless me! I can't find hers; they must have been mislaid. . . .

Mother says, "I should think you would hardly know how to use or sleep on a bed, it is so long since you have seen one." Good joke! Long indeed! About six months and I do not see it yet. My bed is a plank with a blanket over it— good enough for a soldier's cot but not quite so luxurious as the one her innocent imagination has pictured. Beds and mattresses are not so plentiful in the army as she supposes. Every scrubby-headed fellow can't have one, and her son, Edward, is not so pre-eminently scrubby headed as to enjoy what mighty officers strive after in vain. My ambition at present goes no higher than board bedding, and let me inform you that it is quite as much the thing here as a hair mattress is in New York. Timber is so scarce that it can hardly be bought or stolen. So, you see, I am a lucky dog after all.

Almost ever since we have been here, the weather has been rainy and blustering. Tonight the wind fairly howls round our little house. Guard duty at such times, as you may suspect, [is] a trifle rough, and it is perhaps as well that I am out of it. So many drafts are made upon the regiment that each man is on duty every other day.

Last night the Zou-Zous on guard got up a grand feast, regardless of expense. Old Carlo, while nosing around during the afternoon, had caught and killed twenty huge rats. At the suggestion of a young Frenchman, they were [ar]ranged in a row on the ground and fifteen of the plumpest and juiciest selected for cooking. This part of the performance was conducted with much gravity and skill. Each carcass was raised high in the air by its caudal appendage and as it slowly revolved was subjected to the severest criticism, Old Carlo standing by, meanwhile, mouth open and tongue out, cocking his eye at it and licking his chops as though he had been defrauded of his lawful prey. Dressing was the next operation, and at this two or three butchers in the crowd proved adept. Then followed the cooking. Some of the rats were broiled and some fricassed [*sic*], so that the atmosphere teemed with savory odors. The grand finale was the feast. Every guardsman had his ration, and the expression of pleasure and of wonder on their countenances was beautiful to contemplate. "Well, I swear," said one of them, sucking his teeth and rubbing his hands on his trousers when he had done. "We're living like fighting cocks," and this seemed to be the sentiment of them all. They said the flesh tasted "like chicken, only a good deal better."

As ever Yrs. truly,
Ed. K. W.

Newport News, Va.
March 9th, 1863

Dear Bro:

The term of service of the regiment is so nearly expired, and we are here in a place so healthy and so far removed from danger that I no longer see the necessity of frequent correspondence. Besides, the current of my life is now so smooth that few incidents occur worth relating or sufficiently novel to amuse you. I have already given you a sketch of the routine of my office duties, and during the month of our stay there has been but little variation in my experience. From sunrise till tattoo, the pen is always in my hand, and I can scarcely get time to gobble down food enough to keep soul and body together (figuratively speaking). But I shall probably live through it, for a first rate pair of scales showed a weight of 168 lbs. yesterday when your humble servant stepped upon them without his overcoat. He will probably be able to eke out his existence for a few weeks longer, as the bears are said to do in winter, by living on his own fat.

There are signs of a movement, but it is yet supposed to be remote. The 5th of April [is] when, it is rumored, the 9th Army Corps will be shipped to North or South Carolina under their old commander, Burnside, who has already sent 30 odd men and his bob-tailed horse to this post. For a week past, Capt. [William H.] French of his staff has been bunking with Maj. Jardine. In our vacant room are [*sic*] a big valise marked "Burnside," and our storehouse is piled with his luggage. The latest telegraph from Washington states that the General will be here in two or three days. It is not thought that the 9th Regt. will join in the new expedition.

Outside of the office, things are pretty lively in the neighborhood. Our men are in remarkably good health and spirits and when off duty amuse themselves with various games, of which baseball is the chief. Two days ago a match came off between the 57th N.Y. and the 9th. The 57th, of course, were terribly beaten. Among the officers, horse racing has been in favor. Maj. Jardine has run his black mare in three races over the parade ground and has been beaten twice. Gen. Dix reviewed the corps not long since, and the troops made a grand display. When the salute was fired by Gilliss' battery,[10] in front of our office, all the windows were taken out to prevent a smash.

March 14th

Since writing the above, there have been considerable changes in the aspect of affairs. Col. Hawkins has returned and taken command of both the Regt. and the Brigade. He messes with Jardine, and consequently I have seen much of him. He is far from being popular with the regimental officers—is too impulsive and blunt.

Perhaps you have already heard of the moving of the 3rd Division of the 9th Army Corps to Suffolk, Va. Our regiment is included in the order and will close up the rear after seeing all the wagons and supplies safely off; it will probably move day after tomorrow. When it was found the Regt. must move, Hawkins had Jardine relieved from his duty as Provost Marshall [sic], and an order was issued by Genl. Wilcox commanding all detached men to return to their Regts., but Jardine got a little huffy and had himself reinstated and me again attached as his assistant. I demured [sic] a little at first, preferring to join the company, as a brush with Longstreet was anticipated. Besides, my work here is very confining. But later news encourages the idea that the 9th will have but a few days excursion and no fight, so I remain.

A stamp has been ordered for passes, which when it comes will save me an immense amount of time and labor. I enclose a system of passes prepared by me at the request of Major Jardine for Post use and which you see has been adopted at Headquarters for the whole corps. It works well and has made an end to the confusion which reigned previously.

The 9th is to be relieved tomorrow from Provost duty by the 57th N.Y. We have had 130 odd prisoners in the guard house since landing, some of them in irons. Among the rest was an unfortunate darkey who during his weeks incarceration must have been tried by his fellow prisoners at mock court martial at least 50 times. In accordance with the verdicts rendered, he was each time bucked and gagged. The prisoners are always finally released at the office, and it would amuse you to see the profoundly solemn and fatherly way in which I give them a parting admonition to mend their ways.

When the regiment is gone, the whole establishment will draw rations from the Corps' Quartermaster and employ its own cook.

Capt. French has left us, and Burnside has not yet come. He is expected daily.

In haste,
Ed.

P. S. Letters recd. from everybody.

Newport News, Va.
March 15, 1863

Dear Young Folks:

You are right in supposing that I am silent because very busy. But your many epistles deserve at least an occasional response. So here goes.

I am growing both fat and lazy. My adipose tissue increases in thickness at such an alarming rate that, should I have my piece and equipments suddenly restored and be required to double quick a couple of miles, I should puff like a porpoise. There now seems little room to doubt that I shall remain here in the office of the Provost Marshall [sic] General until the term of the Regiment expires, when I shall have the felicity of being transported on the wings of—no, on the deck of a smoky steamer or in some other equally distinguished manner to the home of me cuzzins.

The 9th leaves tomorrow by steamer for Suffolk, no one actually staying behind but Maj. Jardine, his orderly, [Private] Tom Stapleton, a wounded color bearer named Martin Myers [Corporal Martin Meyers], and myself. Tom Stapleton is the Prince of Orderlies—a regular Handy Andy—up to anything and running over with Irish humor. I am indebted to him [through foraging] for some of my extra weight. As for Myers, he, poor fellow, was hit at the Battle of Camden while bearing the regimental colors. The ball entered his left shoulder, shattered the upper part of the humerus and lodged beneath the shoulder blade, where it now lies imbedded. At the time of receiving the wound he had eaten nothing for twenty-four hours but, notwithstanding this and in spite of the pain he endured and of the weakness resulting from the loss of blood, the sturdy Zou-zou shouldered his blanket and, taking his piece in his right hand, marched during the night a distance of twenty five miles. I forgot to mention that he had performed thirty two miles the night before in the ranks. After reaching the hospital, exhausted as he was, the head and about two inches of the shank of the left humerus was excised [sic]—and he survived it all! His strength is so prodigious that ten powerful men required two hours to get him under the influence of ether. You would scarcely suppose his arm could be of much use to him in its present condition, but it is really a useful member.

Here is an item for Jim. I was quietly sitting at my table this morning, when who should come in for a pass but old *Kib*, otherwise McKibben, formerly a member of Sigma Xi.[11] He is assistant Adjutant General to acting Brig. Gen. Ferrero, commanding the Post,[12] and having raised a respectable apology for a moustache [sic] looks very much like a military man. Ed Babcock, too, came in the other day to obtain a pass on a furlough. . . .

Here is an item for Mary. Send along one of those *carte de visite* [card photographs], my duck, and perhaps you will get one in return; for three photographers to whom permission has been given to settle at the Post have invited me to sit for pictures.

Here is an item for Charles. Several schools of porpoises seem to be frittering away their time in front of our door for want of a teacher. Come out and get a posish [position].[13] They seem to be not quite *au fait* in the art of swimming and to live in a total ignorance of the beautiful performance known as the "cat dive." Now if a fish don't know how to swim and dive, what is he good for? (I fancy this question a sockdolager.)

Finally, there is nothing more to say, and therefore I say nothing.

E. K. W.

Newport News, March 28, 1863

Dear Bro:

More changes—not [no] troops but the 9th N.Y.V. remain at the Post. Maj. Jardine has not yet returned from his furlough. Col. Hawkins has been appointed Commander of the Post and Capt. Barnett (of Co. B) Provost Marshall [sic]. In the absence of the Corps, I act only as Barnett's clerk. Jardine left a great deal of responsibility on my shoulders, and my hands are full of work.

After the storm succeeds the calm. There is absolutely nothing to do now, and the danger is that laziness will become a disease with me. We had Maj. [R. Charlton] Mitchell of the 51st N.Y. for Provost Marshall [sic] for a few days, but as he had a desk in our office and the duties were new to him, instead of relieving me he made me extra work.

My short reign as the representative of the Corps Prov. Marshall [sic] was remarkable but for two events, viz.—the leveling of a sutler's shanty (wish I had power to haul them all down) and the arrest and imprisonment of a drunken crony of Lt. Col. K[imba]ll for using a forged pass—for although said pass was marked E. K. W., like the sticks in the garret I couldn't conscientiously claim it as my own. These two little incidents created quite a breeze, but we "still live."

"The boys" are getting a little wild since they have been left to themselves and may do some rash things before their time is out. I have yet to visit Ft. Monroe, Norfolk, Suffolk, and the Ironclads in the Roads—all of which I propose to do as soon as things become more settled.

Maj. Jardine may return here and may not. If he continues to act as Prov. Marshall [sic] of the Corps, he must go with it to the West. I shall, of course, remain with the regiment.

I am well as usual and hope to see you in less than a month.

Yrs. truly,
Ed. K. W.

Fort Nansemend [Nansemond] (near Suffolk)
April 13, 1863

Dear Bro:

I have been intending to write to you for a long time past, but I have been lazy and have had but little time. (No, that is a fib, I have only been lazy.) On the 3rd Inst. our regiment was suddenly ordered from Newport News to Camp [Fort] Hamilton, Fortress Monroe. The Provost Marshallship [sic] was, of course, thrown up, and I rejoined the company and marched with the Regiment. We went but eight or nine miles, but my knapsack has been growing in bulk and weight within a couple of weeks and . . . the days work made me so sore that the cramps have not yet left me.

We encamped in wedge tents at Fort Hamilton for just one week. On Friday afternoon last [the 10th], just at sunset, while Company B was having a game of ten pins with cannon balls and beer bottles in the company street, an order came from [for] the 9th to proceed to Suffolk immediately. The tents were struck at once, and without even waiting for rations we started, the boys singing, joking, and laughing as though they were bound for home. At the fortress we embarked on a steamer, Ju[liu]s A. Walker, and sailed for Norfolk. That night we slept under cover, and I felt no other inconvenience than that resulting from Col. Kimball, who was a little tight, stepping on me as he passed back and forth during the night.

There being no transportation at Norfolk, the steamer made her way to Portsmouth, where we found ourselves in the morning. But unfortunately the railroad bridges had been destroyed during the night, and the train which was to carry us thrown off the track. As a consequence we had to make a forced march of thirty miles in one day, reaching the camps around Suffolk about nine o'clock on Saturday night. Our arrival created quite a sensation here among the troops, officers and men alike expressing their satisfaction. Our old friends, the 103rd N.Y., had left their camp on picket duty, so we quietly took possession of their tents and went to sleep; but the "103 times" returned in the wee hours and gruffly demanded who had appropriated their quarters. They entered the tents and roughly pulled down the blankets of the sleepers, but no sooner were the red caps revealed than the Dutchmen danced around like lunatics, shouting "ere's de Zou Zous, ere's de Zou Zous." Then followed hand shaking, and Dutch canteens were sent around until many a brave fellow of the 9th found it easier to lie down than to stand up.

Meanwhile, our acting Col. Kimball (Hawkins has just come back from Washington this morning) had been shot through the neck by Gen. Cocoran [sic] and killed.[14] The troops were at the time under arms and expecting an attack any moment. Camp rules were therefore strictly enforced. Gen. Cocoran and staff attempted to pass a sentinel without the countersign, and Kimball, who happened to be near, backed the soldier. Cocoran drew his pistol and fired a shot, striking the Colonel in the throat and dropping him from his horse. But the lion-hearted old man was up again in a moment, and with his sword drawn, contemptuously calling upon Cocoran to "fire again." His carotid had been struck, however, and he fell a second time, to rise no more. Cocoran rode on, merely sending back an orderly to remove the body. He knew [it was] Kimball when he fired.

Next morning, when the facts came to [the] knowledge of the men, they cried and swore at a terrific rate, and the least favoring sign from any of their officers would have caused the fiercest kind of an attack by the regiment on the whole Corcoran legion.[15] Nor was the indignation confined to our regiment alone. Our old Brigade companions offered their hands and their aid in any movement which might be attempted. Happily, the men were restrained by our officers. The body has been embalmed, and there is talk of retaining it until we go [home].

Fort Nanesmond is a little triangular fort with a big magazine in the middle—roughly built and just big enough to crowd in all our men. It mounts half

The Suffolk Campaign *(Map courtesy of Historical Times, Inc.)*

a dozen smooth bore guns. I slept last [night] under a shelter tent inside the works.

It is reported that we are completely surrounded. We have been ordered to surrender a number of times, and the Rebels were to have overwhelmed us at seven o'clock this morning. An hour ago they advanced through the woods towards our works and drove in our pickets. Almost a whole brigade came skedadling [sic] in. Then our big guns opened up, and ever since we have been having a jolly time. All but two of the companies are in the little fort helping to work the guns. Company B and another are behind breastworks (they extend ten miles), slyly waiting the approach of the Secesh. The cannon are making a thundering uproar while I write. We have all been assigned our positions, and my piece leans against the breastworks in front of me and within arms reach as I sit here on my knapsack waiting for the "proper moment."[16] The boys say, "We are bound to sock it to them this time."

It is doubtful now when we shall get home—probably not this month. Hawkins himself does not know. Letters from the girls are received [sic], but I can not answer just now. It is reported that a box has been seen near camp, addressed to me. The shoes, I suppose. There seems to be trouble with the mail.

In haste,
Ed.

Suffolk, Va. April 15, 1863

Dear Bro:

I have detained the accompanying letter . . . because I feared after it was written [that] it might frighten the women folk unless I could append a peaceful ending. This is one. We are now believed to be safe from attack, as a large body of troops (Hooker Army) is on its way here. Twenty thousand fresh men will be here shortly, and then (probably by the 20th) we shall go home.

The first attack of the Rebs upon us [on April 13] was checked half way, owing, they said, to a misunderstanding among their officers. They advanced upon us through the wood in line of battle, with artillery, and then driving in about a brigade of our pickets at a double quick. Then our guns seem to have frightened them. Capt. Guthrie of the 9th was killed,[17] four horses were upset, and a caisson [hit] at the first shot. At that night I was assigned to the parapet and a road by which the Secesh was expected to approach. Signal fires blazed everywhere, gunboats roared incessantly on the river, and twice or thrice our pickets were attacked. Long before daylight everybody was roused, and everything was ready to give the "boobies" a warning when they came; but the boobies didn't come.

Today Capt. Morris, who had been transferred here from Fort Montgomery,[18] captured an enemy battery with 2 thirty pounders and captured 111 prisoners. Last night three of our Zou zous outflanked a rebel sharpshooter [and] lugging him out of his rifle pit, brought him in. . . .

The Regiment is to muster out in Norfolk on the 23rd if nothing happens [to prevent it]. Hawkins effected nothing at Washington.[19] All the authorities were absent. Kimball's death recalled him prematurely.

If any of you write to Jim, tell him this. The time of our arrival will be published in the paper when known

In haste,
Ed.

Camp near Suffolk, Va.
April 21, 1863

Dear Bro:

The Regiment will not go home until the 4th of May, and we are very busy just now defending the breastworks (11 miles in length) and strenghtening Fort Nansemond by casemating the guns and nailing the magazines with railroad irons—a heavy job. The rebel pickets are within rifle distance of us, and amuse themselves by firing at us unceasingly. While walking my beat on the parapet last Friday, I counted twenty odd balls fired at me from the telescopic rifle of a Secesh sharpshooter. None of them hit, but some came near enough to singe the hair off. It is a trifle annoying to march back and forth on guard while a marked shot is within easy reach, earnestly endeavoring to "fix" you. How would you like the posish?

Some of our guard were not so lucky; two were shot through the legs, and one in the back. One man in Company B was knocked down by a spent ball about the same time. Indeed, the firing became so harassing that a regiment of skirmishers was sent out, and a very pretty fight ensued. The Rebs, although driven back, rallied in force in the woods and sent our fellows home with a flea in their ear. We have already received the reinforcements I spoke of in my last, and you may expect to hear of a great battle in a few days, but the 9th will not be engaged in it. They remain in the works.

The weather has been uncomfortably warm since we arrived. Today is rainy. We have two camps: one close to the breastworks, of shelter tents, and another, of wedge tents, a quarter of a mile distant. Sometimes we sleep in one and sometimes in another. We have so little to do that I have got a set of chessmen and a board and derive considerable amusement therefrom. As a consequence the whole company has grown chess crazy. The Adjutant's clerk was formerly a member of the Brooklyn [chess] club, and I have had a number of tilts with him. [Private John W.] Knowles, too, an engineer and one of my tent chums, plays quite a rambunctious game. When we sit interested, neither rifles nor cannon disturb us.

I can't tell exactly when we shall return. No one knows. Tell Wool. He had better stay where he is and not bother about me.

Yrs truly
Ed

Camp near Suffolk, Va.
April 24, 1863

Dear Bro:

. . . The rebs still beset us. They are to be attacked this afternoon by five companies of the 9th and other troops. Companies B and G remain in the Fort to hold it. The firing of Secesh sharpshooters is now so close that sentries can no longer mount the parapet. It is no unusual thing for rifle balls to pass through our tents. Our men amuse themselves, when at leisure, by throwing nails over the heads of the Mass. and New Hampshire men encamped near us and seeing them dodge and duck. The nail makes a noise very much like a bullet. . . .

We get the news here regularly. I have seen the account of Kimball's funeral, and General Halleck was here the other day. I live well and am in fair condition.

In haste,
Ed

P.S. Just been shaved. Had a tremendous moustache [sic] taken off and feel like a new man.

Camp near Suffolk, Va.
April 28, 1863

Dear Parents,

Our camp has been so full of rumors about the return of the Regiment for the past few weeks, and they were so contradictory that I have abstained from giving them. At last something positive seems to be known, and I write accordingly. The old members of the 9th will return home on Saturday of this week or on Monday of next. The recruits, of whom, if I mistake not, I am one, will be retained and transferred in a body to the battery [Company K] of Capt Morris, one of our officers, who has received a commission in the regular artillery and now commands six rifled guns.

I am very sorry on your account for I know you expected me [to return home], and on my own, for I should be equally glad to see you. As for the service, however, I am just as content as ever to remain in it and just as well able as ever—better able—to put up with the inconveniences.

You may get any amount of verbal information concerning me from any and all the members of Co. B, if the boys choose to inquire of them. It is possible that I may prefer to be transferred to some infantry regiment. If so, I shall write again as soon as the arrangement is complete, giving directions for addressing letters, etc. I am on guard at night and have little opportunity to write.

In haste
Your affectionate son.
Edward K. Wightman

P.S. Please forward this to Jim so that he may not inconvenience himself.

Camp near Suffolk, Va.
May 2nd, 1863

Dear Mother and Sisters:

This note will introduce to you the drummer of "our" company. We all call him "Jennie" though properly he is Mr. Langbain [Private J. C. Langbein]. I have known him for a long time, and he has been good enough to promise to call and see you and leave such messages as I may wish to send. I would like very much to go to New York and introduce him in person, but father [Abraham] says "no." Jennie has been with the regiment since its organization and has seen much hard service.[20] He will probably answer pleasantly enough and without being offended any questions relating to soldiers life.

We have just delivered up our arms and equipment and ordered to be ready tomorrow morning at 3 o'clock to strike tents and march—no one knows where. But the old members will probably start for home, and the recruits will join their new battery. Jennie will tell you what disposal is made of us.

At present, in the face of the enemy, there is no chance for a furlough. Whenever the opportunity offers, however, I shall try and get home for a few days.

As ever, Your Aff son and Bro,
Ed

Camp at Suffolk, Va.
May 3rd, 1863

Dear Bro:

Before this reaches you, you will probably have interpreted the return of the 9th and have become satisfied that I am to remain in the field with[out] the privilege of returning home. Part of our regiment, numbering 462,[21] left this morning for New York. The recruits, including even those who came out three months after the [original] Zouaves were organized and have been in every engagement since, are detained to be mustered out in detail. The men think this treatment on the part of the government authorities outrageous, and nothing but the advice of Col. Hawkins and the flattery of Gen. Getty deter them from mutiny.[22] About one half of the regiment are thus forced to remain. For myself, I am content, but the "three months men," as they call themselves, are almost beside themselves.

Last night we were relieved at the Fort by the 6th Massachusetts, our arms and equipment were formally delivered up to the quartermaster, and the men assembled to hear the parting address of the Colonel. There was very much affected [effected by him]—that he had done everything in his power to take us home in a body but that he had failed and his letters [to the War Department] had been unanswered. General Dix requested the 9th to stay beyond the expiration of their time, and they declined for the reasons specified in the answer of Col. Hawkins, which has doubtless been already published. It is thought that what has happened since is to be credited to the spite of Dix.[23]

General John A. Dix *(Photograph courtesy of the Library of Congress)*

Early this morning the "old hams" prepared for the start and about 9 o'clock they were formed in line and marched to the R.R. Depot. The parting was a very sad one. Many and deep were the curses launched at the head of Gen. Dix by the parties, and many a weather-brown cheek was wet with tears of vexation and sorrow as our tattered flags were borne away to our own homes, whither we were forbidden to follow. Isn't it disgraceful that the Secretary of War should permit a regiment that has served two long years faithfully and well in the field to be broken up and sent back without arms, like a mob? Everybody is disgusted.

The time of many of the [remaining] men expires in ten or fifteen days. The three month soldiers are to be posted at General Getty's headquarters; the General promises to "treat them as if they were his own children." The three year men (150) will join Captain Morris' battery at once.[24] All are now at Getty's headquarters, about five miles from here.

I was left behind with a fatigue party of twelve to take down the tents and, as Getty's division had been fighting the rebs all day and the wagons are all employed, to bring in the wounded. I shall spend the night here at camp with the camp property. When you hear of the battle, don't trouble yourself about me; I have not been engaged in it, though I hear the firing very distinctly as I write. Secesh is said to have been driven eight miles and to be [a]waiting an attack in his rear. Our old companions, the 103rd N.Y.V., skirmished in the advance, and their colonel [Benjamin] Ringold is among the ones killed.

After our fellows had left this morning, I strolled beyond the works to the river bank and had quite a confab with a "Johnny Reb" who had laid aside his piece and crossed over in a skiff to exchange papers with our pickets. He is a very lean black-eyed fellow with long straight hair and was well clothed in a gray jacket and pants and so forth. I bantered him the best I knew how, but he took it very well. Wanted to known [sic] "why you fellows all wear your hair so darn short," and so forth. Asked whether we expected to subdue them and so forth.

Bye the bye, I saw another skirmish day before yesterday, when the 99th New York, supported by two batteries, made a sortee [sic] on some rebel earthworks about three quarters of a mile distant.[25] They did their work splendidly. I saw the whole thing from a rifle pit whence I could get a fair view by bobbing up my head amon[g]st the bullets when the rebel fire slackened; but it was like sitting in a "bumble bees" nest, and nothing but the exciting smell of gun powder would have carried me there. The 99th deployed so as to extend their line about half a mile and then crept along swiftly under fire, stooping behind every little elevation for cover and dodging from tree to bush with admirable activity and skill, the cannon meantime thundering in their rear and the enemy's rifle balls raining upon them in showers. As they neared the enemy's works, the fire grew hot and furious, and the men dropped by tens. Three times I saw the stars and stripes fall, but they were caught up again in an instant and floated out as bravely as ever.

Just as our men had reached the breast works and were about to mount them, the bugle sounded a recall, and at the same moment a brigade of rebel infantry issued from the wood to support their friends, but the column no sooner came out of cover then [sic] a Union shell dropped plump upon it, making terrible havoc. A second followed with equal effect, and a tempest of bullets from the pieces of our sharpshooters shattered the gray backs like chaf[f]. Some ran to the works as far as their legs could carry them, and some turned and fled back in dismay. Then our batteries played away in earnest. The range had been fixed, and our shot dropped like hailstones. Our men had hurrahed and yelled like demons. The 99th, of course, had to retire. The wounded were brought in on stretchers, the Zou Zous being among the first to volunteer to go out after them. The loss on our side is reported as high as one hundred fifty killed and wounded. That of the rebs must have been greater.

Noon, Monday May 4th. Whew, hot as blazes and I have just finished a long tramp undertaken for fun. At 8 o'clock A.M., the rebs having retired from in front of the works in consequence of General Getty's advance on yesterday, the 99th were again sent out to fill the position and follow them up. As there was nothing special for me to do, I went out close on their heels, avoiding the guard by the slight detour.

I walked without interruption some four or five miles, examining the rebel camp by the way and rambling far beyond our pickets. No tents marked the spot deserted by the secesh; for they had lived altogether under sheds of pine boughs. Their cast-off clothing was very sorry indeed—made of the cheapest homespun and worn to tatters. I sawed off a couple of old buttons from one of them with my jack knife for trophies and among other things brought in a Springfield musket and bayonet of the date of 1852.[26] I picked up, too, a rebel order enclosed as a curiosity . . . On returning, I perceived that everything had been removed to the new camp and so at once proceeded to join the remainder of the regiment. We are now back at Suffolk under the command of Captain Morris.

Our battery belongs to the Third Division, 9th A.C. [Army Corps], and it is under orders to report to General Burnside in the West. Anything for travel. As soon as the rebel siege shall be completely broken up, we will probably start. The enemy have already been driven several miles, and we are still in pursuit.[27] The remainder of the 9th are still without arms. We are comfortably provided with wedge tents.

As ever,
Ed

[P. S.] Address—Edward K. Wightman, Capt. Morris' Battery, Third Division, 9th A.C., near Suffolk, Va.

Fort Monroe, Va.
May 16, 1863

Dear Parents:

Since I wrote home last, the remainder of the 9th N.Y. Vols. have (in consequence of throwing down their arms and refusing to do duty) been brought to this place and are detained here, I may almost say, as prisoners. Until our arrival, the Fortress was garrisoned by the 3rd Infantry N.Y.V. but a part of the regiment have been mustered out of service, and it seems now to be settled that we of the 9th are to become consolidated with those of the 3rd who stay and are to adopt their uniform—a stiff, clumsy, outlandish dress like this.[28]

The time of service of about half of our men expires within the next three months. All are completely demoralized and desertions are frequent notwithstanding the utmost vigilance of Gen. Dix and Col. Alfred [Samuel M. Alford] (the commandant [of the 3rd New York]). Unless we are soon reorganized, those who remain will scarcely be worth the trouble of transferring. The men excuse themselves by saying that they were deceived into the belief that they were to be mustered out with the regiment en mass[e].

I received the letters yesterday from Jim and Mary. Others, to which they refer, have not come to hand. I am very glad, indeed, to hear of Jim's [commercial] success and good prospects and hope he will improve them by applying old Ben Franklin's homely apothegm, "A penny saved is a penny earned."

I suppose you are all in good health and spirits. So am I. At present I am acting as clerk in the Quartermasters Department. We have warm barracks, iron bedsteads with boards for bed cords, good rations well cooked, etc, etc, and are quite comfortable. Please address letters, until otherwise directed, to Fortress Monroe, Va.

As ever Affecty Yours
Edward K. Wightman

Fort Monroe, Va.
June 6, 1863

Dear Bro:

You are the darndest [sic] booby to pry into things I ever came across. What you have discovered concerning Maj. Jardin[e] and his intentions, though no news to me, forces me to relate an unwritten chapter of my history; for some time will probably elapse before I see you, and heaven only knows what facts, real or imaginary, you might dig up in the meantime and what inferences, right or wrong, you might found upon them.

Well, then, my first chance for a commission was by joining with a number of men, Cooper's Monitor Regiment, when the first of the 9th went home. I might, in that way, if Hawkins had not put a veto on the movement, have got a captaincy. Hawkins did veto it, but he recommended me strongly to Capt. Morris, and in the presence of some of our men stated that in case of his returning again to the field as Brigadier Genl., he should assign me a place on his staff.

After we had changed camp at Suffolk and I had returned from my reconnoitering expedition among the rebel camps, I found Morris had made my first srgt. of the battery company of the 9th Regt, comprising all the three year men, numbering over one hundred and fifty nominally but, excluding those who had skedadled [sic] with those going home, about one hundred and twenty nine. Next day I was appointed, by order of Gen. Getty, acting Lieut. and placed in command of the Battery Company—a difficult position, because the men were completely demoralized and disorganized, and the remaining two year men with whom they were encamped had already thrown down their arms and refused to do duty, setting an example, the effect of which it was impossible to neutralize.

The camp guard was instructed to permit no one to go out and the provost guard at Suffolk ordered to arrest all Zouaves wandering in the streets. The orders might as not have been given. The whole regiment could not keep our boys out of the city [of Suffolk], and the camp guard gave so little heed to instructions that the camp was almost habitually empty. Under these circumstances I endeavored to prevail upon Capt Morris to separate my company from the other two; but he hesitated until too late. Still, the battery men were always held to their duty, and their details were always complete. Two detachments of about eighty men each were continually drilling at the guns.

At this time a new cause of trouble arose. General order 108 of the War Department was issued, and from its wording everybody believed that we were going home immediately in a mass. In fact, the great source of disaffection was this—nothing definite was known concerning the ultimate disposal of us, and almost everybody had been enlisted in such a way and under such promises that they believed they were swindled by detention.

Gen. Getty wrote to Gen. Dix, requesting that we might be sent home. In reply an order came to send the two years [men] to Fort Monroe at once. Arms and rations were issued, and they were to start at 3 A.M. next day. In the night a number of three year men shouldered their knapsacks, took the rifles of the two year men from the stacks, and started, some overland and some for the railroad depot, determined to desert and smuggle themselves on to New York. Capt. Morris was not to be found. I used every effort to keep them and assured them that they would be entrapped at half a dozen different places on the route, having only the fatigue of travel for their pains. My first Sergt. had already disappeared with the [muster] roll. Previously I had advised Capt. Morris to place a double guard from the 8th Conn. around us for safety, but he had demurred. In the morning the two year men left in good order under [Sergeant] Schmidt but before reaching the depot broke into a confused mob. At daylight I had but 68 men left.

Capt. Morris followed to the Fort, leaving me in command of the camp. While at dinner, Gen. Getty ordered me to strike tents and be ready to move at five o'clock P.M. I did so. When everything was ready, Capt. Morris reappeared, but, at his request, I retained the command and took the men to Fort Monroe, stopping at Norfolk over night, Morris being with us intermittently.

On passing the gates of the fortress, the men found themselves entrapped. A strong guard of the 3rd N.Y. closed in behind them with loaded pieces and egress was prevented. Then we saw the two year men walking around among the trees with the cheapest possible expression and looking as forlorn as though each of them had been "sold." Their arms had been taken away, and they were prisoners. Of course, we were no longer duty men, [and] my brevet Lieutenancy, having not been confirmed by Seymour,[29] was overlooked. I was classed as sergt. and found my "occupation gone."

Capt. Morris started for New York on the same day (after telling me that the Zou zous, with the exception of the 40 selected for the battery, were to be consolidated with the 3rd [New York]) to recruit among the old men. He offered me a commission, which I agreed to accept. He thought it could be sent on to me, with an order to join him in four or five days at farthest. Unfortunately, he lost his valise, with all his papers, by the way. Among the latter was a copy of an order asigning him the guns of his battery. He wrote to me, and I tried to get a second copy from Dix's Adjt. Genl. He [the staff officer] promised well but never performed. He pretended to send copies to Morris, which never reached him. I bothered him half to death, for I knew that Col. Alfred of the 3rd wanted to do him [Morris] out of his men.[30]

This morning Capt. Morris came on in despair to appeal to Gen. Dix in person and to solicit the interference of Gen. Getty, who is a strong friend of his. What the result will be remains to be seen. Morris has nearly all the men he wants in New York. The battery business I have said nothing about before, because I considered its success a matter of doubt from the beginning. I thought that a hint of coming home might cause disappointment in case of failure. As to Maj. Jardine, I believe I mentioned before that I met him here.

I write thus fully at present, that you may understand my position and to caution you not to embarrass [yourself] by trying to benefit me. As soon as I can do so, I shall get to New York. My influence with old Capt. [Barnett] of Co. B (Lieut. Col. of the new regiment)[31] is quite as strong as with Jardine. If Morris misses, I shall see them both and can make my points without assistance. Your efforts, however well intentioned, may mar my plans.

> As ever
> Yrs. truly
> E. K. W.

> Fort Monroe, Va.
> June 4, 1863

Dear Kinfolk:

Within a few days I have received a number of letters from home, but business has pressed me so that I have had no time to reply. This morning I heard from mother, Jim, and Mary. Since my arrival at the Fort, the appointment of a new Quartermaster has necessitated the complete overhauling of our stock, and this, together with the preparation of monthly returns and vouchers, has kept me well employed. As we live now there is little occurring that would interest you, and it seems to me useless, therefore, to attempt to act upon Fred's suggestion of writing once a week.

I am sorry that you are all so anxious to have me go to New York; for just at present it seems impossible. The 3rd Regiment, to which I am now attached,[32] is to leave this place (probably next week, Wednesday) for Norfolk or Suffolk, and the Regimental Quartermaster will, of course, in consequence be very busy until long after that time.[33] I shall certainly improve the first opportunity to get home, but that first "opportunity" may yet be distant. Don't expect me until you see me.

Both Jim's photograph and Mary's have come to hand. Jim's I have acknowledged before—perhaps the letter miscarried. His abundant wool crop speaks for his good health . . . Jim says that Sergts. Cornell and Rogers and the younger Rogers have called to see you. Then you have probably heard all the news, for Cornell is the longest winded talker in the Regiment. Young Rogers is of hard shell Baptist [leanings]—belongs to Jas. Q[uincy]. Adams church [in New York City]. Can't say whether he is sound on the doctrines, for I have not examined him.

> In haste
> Yrs. truly
> Ed

> Camp 3rd Infty. N.Y. Vol. near
> Portsmouth, Va.
> Wednesday, June 17, 1863

Dear Bro:

I do not remember whether I have written to you since we left the Fort. The 3rd left Fort Monroe for this place just one week ago today [and] have been relieved from garrison duty by Robert's battery[34]—men who were especially enlisted for the purpose.

I will do the officers of the 3rd the justice to say that they are the most stupid set of asses I have seen since I came out. The Quartermaster was ordered to take wedge tents for 800 men, though we had only about 400, and wall tents at the rate of two for each company, besides twenty-eight wagon loads of stores. Luggage enough for a division. But the acting Quartermaster knew nothing about his business, and the Quartermaster Sergeant was afraid to assume any responsibility. So, although a clerk, I had to take a fatigue party and ship the goods on a steamer and, when after a whole forenoon of labor the boat left the dock for Norfolk, I had the felicity to discover that neither the Q.M. [n]or the Sergt. was with us, the miserable sneaks having shirked. I went to the Adjutant at once, and he gave me a detail of 100 men, 2 corporals, and 1 sergt. to remove the regimental trash from the dock to the cars. When the work was half done, the quartermaster appeared and said, "all right," and I made him miserable by reporting to him the conditions of affairs.

Arrived within a mile and a half of our destination, the cars stopped, the men landed and stacked guns, and the whole regiment, with all the officers to bully them, were disorganized into a fatigue party to transfer everything to the caravan of wagons. We then straggled to this camp of pitched tents in the midst of the swamp.

The place seems ordinarily healthy, though, but just at present the weather is hot and dry. The men are at work building a fort to keep open communications between Portsmouth and Suffolk, and it is said we shall remain here through summer. No more furloughs are granted, as I suppose[d] would be the case when we left Fort Monroe. I bunk at present in a large hospital tent—the clothing boxes—very comfortable quarters. Have received welcome notes from Jim, Mary, and Abbie.

Address Ed. K. W. 3rd Infty. N.Y. Vols.
1st Brig.—Div. 9th A.C.
Near Portsmouth, Va.[35]

[P. S.] I saw one of Getty's staff a few days since, and he informed me that Capt. Morris' enterprise has been knocked in the head. He has been swindled out of both guns and men.

What is this row about invasion of the north?[36] Is it a stroke of policy on the part of Abe to get more men without a draft or can't you poor boobies really defend yourselves? I don't believe Lee is going so far North as to expose his flank and communications to Hooker. Where is that great(?) general? Better try Greely next.[37]

I am now busy on quarterly returns.

Ed.

White House, Va.
June 28, 1863

Dear Bro:

.... On the 23rd inst. we left Camp Alford (near Portsmouth) and, taking such luggage as was absolutely necessary, embarked at Portsmouth for Yorktown. The QM sergt. were [sic] left behind with such things as could not be transported, and I accompanied the regiment, in charge of the ammunition and ordinance [sic] stores. Next day I rode into Yorktown on the spunkiest little mule you ever saw, moving sometimes forwards, sometimes backwards, sometimes sideways, sometimes advancing in complicating [sic] circles in an admirably strategic manner. The Great Mogul, however, held his position like a worthy scion of the house of Wightman, and the biting, squealing, bouncing, rearing, kicking mule didn't unhorse him. Of course it wouldn't do to be outgeneraled by a donkey at the opening of a campaign.

Yorktown is surrounded with elaborate earthworks, erected by the rebs, and worthy of the name of "Fort." The position, as you well know, is a very strong one. The buildings enclosed are few in number and are but rough specimens of carpentry. The exterior works stretch away from miles on either side and must have required immense labor in construction; many of them have been leveled with the ground. McClellan's intrenchments[38] remain and are equally intensive. I squinted at them [longer] than I otherwise should have done because blackberries were plenty in the neighborhood, and blackberries are one of my weaknesses.

About 2 o'clock in the afternoon of the 25th inst., the wagon train of our division (comprising 29 teams) started in a drizzling rain up the penninsula [sic] for White House, in company with Lieut. Phillip's battery.[39] Such roads, Jeresalem [*sic*]. I came with them, of course. Talk about lumber wagons—they are not a circumstance. We traveled that night until eleven o'clock, the mules, six of which were attached to each wagon, shaking us along over 25 miles of country and slapping and slamming us with terrific violence against everything on both sides of the way. First, we would whoop over on our beam ends, and while expecting an overthrow, Chunk, the fore wheels would go down to the axles in the mud hole, jerking and pitching him [the driver] on the backs of the wheel mules. Then the driver would shout like a madman and swing his heavy whip till the fog seemed peopled with hornets, buzz saws, and bullets, and the donkies [*sic*], goaded to desperation, would spring forward, tumble the wagon over half a dozen stumps, lock it amongst a clump of trees and then, whisking around, straddling their traces and strangling themselves in an inextricable snarl, look at the result with an air of sleepy innocence that would have made patient Job himself as rambunctious as a [s]tub tail bull at fly time (so to speak). You may think the picture exaggerated. Not a bit. We kept it up all the way through the swampy road to Williamsburg and, in fact, to the White House.[40]

Shortly after dark we passed through the principal street of Williamsburg, about ¾ of a mile in length and beautifully ornamented with heavy shade trees. I slept in the wagon that night. Next day our course lay through a fertile and well cultivated tract dotted with neat farm houses, and in the afternoon we even camped about six miles from here, with a whole army of Infantry, cavalry, and Artillery. On yesterday we came here.

Our Cavalry have already been out and torn up railroads and destroyed communications between Richmond and Petersburg, and Richmond and Fredericksburg.[41] The Rebs have 50,000 at Richmond, mostly convalescents. Dix (who is with us in person) has 30,000, and Foster[42] is about to join him with as many more. Hooker is to strike in concert with us.[43] You people further north must take care of Washington.

I hope you'll have a jolly time on the Fourth. Remember me to all the "phellers" on that occasion. Put in a few extra noisy cheers for me at the reading of the "Declaration [of Independence]" and propose among your toasts, "the success of the Republic." . . .

Ask "yer mom" how she would like to do the penninsular [*sic*] campaign in an army wagon. Tell her I saw one of the Willards [Sergeant Charles L. Willard] at Yorktown. He is a sergt in the 22nd Conn. The time of his Regt. is out, and they are awaiting transportation. He is quite well. Tell Charley I saw [Captain George W.] Cooper at Ft. Monroe, where he applied unsuccessfully for a furlough. He was trying for a major's commission. His Regt. is here, but he is still detached on engineering service.

Capt. [Charles T.] Gardner, Getty's Adj. Gen., tells me that we shall eventually be turned over to Morris and Jardine.

In haste,
Ed. K. W.

Camp 3rd Infty. N.Y. Vol.
Near Portsmouth, Va.
July 14, 1863

Dear Bro:

It is a long time since I have written home, but for the last three weeks we have been constantly on the march and only yesterday returned to this place. Even now I am so busy straightening out neglected accounts that I can snatch but a few moments from sleeping time to tell you where I am and what we have been about.

When I last wrote, we were at White House and about to advance further towards Richmond. On the 3rd inst. Gen. Getty's Division (to which the 3rd is attached) moved towards the north east of the Rebel Capital for the purpose of destroying the great railroad bridge at Hanover Junction,[44] thus hoping to cut off Gen. Lee's supplies and communications and prevent his being reinforced by [President Jefferson] Davis. You are doubtless acquainted with the main features of the expedition. Gen. Keyes[45] at the same time operated in concert in a different direction, a reserve being held at White House. I went with the wagon train, in charge of the ammunition for the regiment. My wagon (a secesh concern, although including mules and drive[r]) had been recently captured and was so heavily laden that I had to perform the journey of fifteen miles on foot. The rebel army wagons do not compare with ours either in appearance or strength. They resemble the clumsy lumber wagons of the north, and their tops are by no means rain proof.

On the 4th the sun shown [sic] down upon us with awful fierceness. As a battle was expected and as I saw no other means of burning gunpowder on our national holy day, I equipped myself with an Enfield rifle,[46] after serving out twenty extra rounds of ammunition per man, and took my position in the ranks near the colors. We marched only nine miles and with nothing to carry but haversacks and canteens—yet men dropped in their tracks from the excessive heat, and all along the sides of the road they lay panting and dying from sunstroke, their friends pouring water over their heads and endeavoring to restore animation by friction. The deaths from this cause were counted not by units, but by tens.

At about 4 P.M. we crossed the bridge spanning the Pamunkey [River] and, throwing out skirmishers, loaded and in common with the other regiments of the 1st Brigade, took up the position assigned us, to hold the roads leading from Richmond, etc., while the other troops moved on seven or eight miles further to blow up the railroad bridge. I had been so liberal with my rations during the day that when evening came I was forced to sup on blackberries and water, the [same] day you were feasting on pies, pineapples, bananas, lager, etc, according to Jim and Mary. After dark I took a couple of rails from the fence and, spreading them on the ground in a clover field, lay down in my jacket without overcoat or blanket and was put to sleep by the monotonous firing of heavy rebel guns in the distance. But, luckily, no long roll disturbed me in the night.

In the morning we were up bright and early. Our attack had failed, the rebs having been largely reinforced and [they] far overmatched us in the weight and range of their artillery.[47] We were therefore compelled to content ourselves with tearing up twelve miles of railroad track and retiring as quietly and expeditiously as possible. Previous to starting I refreshed myself with a hearty breakfast of blackberries and water and buckled my belt three holes tighter.[48] The Bridge over the Pamunkey was burned behind us to delay pursuit, and we skedalled [sic] twenty miles before encamping at King William's Court House.[49]

We travelled steadily but swiftly. I rejoined the wagons. In a couple of days we were again at White House. Our loss in killed and wounded was ten or twelve, our general, seeing his competitive weakness, refusing to permit his inferior batteries to open. The 89th and 118th N. York were the only Infantry engaged and they only as skirmishers.[50]

We rested only a day at White House and then marched down the peninsula to Yorktown, the wagons going [on] ahead. The roads had been rendered almost impassable by rains, and the terrific thunder showers which drenched us increased our troubles a thousand fold. Yet we waded along knee deep in the mire and with cascades of water leaking from every salient point, as jolly a set of fellows as you would wish to see. Headlong plunges and troubles provoked incessant laughter, and the droll performance of the mules and the embarrassment of their drivers were never failing sources of amusement to fall back upon. As for me, I first fell chunk into a mud hole up to the waist and afterwards partially washed my clothes by dropping up to my arms through a corduroy[51] bridge. At night, although wet as water could make me, I slept soundly in the wagon and awoke at daylight none the worse for wear.

At Yorktown we stopped one day and then started for Fort Monroe. The troops encamped at Great Bethel,[52] but I walked on with the wagons to Hampton and by 3 P.M. had accomplished twenty six miles—quite a rapid tramp for hot weather.

Day before yesterday we embarked on transports for Portsmouth and yesterday arrived here at our old camp. The whole number of men employed in the expedition was 62,000.[53] On returning, fully one third were bare footed and hundreds had thrown away their knapsacks, blankcets [sic] and overcoats. The Rebs had 50,000 in Richmond. Suffolk was evacuated when we started.

Getty's Division has been transferred and is now the 2nd Division of the 7th Army Corps. We are to remain here at present to work on the forts.

I have no time at present to answer Jim, Charley, and Mary individually, they must wait. Glad to hear you enjoyed yourself so much on the 4th and wish I could have been with you.

What a row these rascals are making in New York about the drafts.[54] They are plunderers and want to pillage, and demagogues who can tear down better than build up. How I would like to tackle the bullying crowd with a little grape and cannister [sic].

In haste,
Ed

Camp near Portsmouth, Va.
July 23, 1863

Dear Kinfolk:

I have just received letters from Fred, Jim, Mary, and Ell—letters which came just in time to cut short a growl at not hearing from home. There seems to have been the mischief to pay with our mails lately, but at length they are again regulated, and there will probably be no further trouble. While we were on the peninsula, we could neither send nor receive—communications were entirely cut off, and during the last two weeks past the heavy rains have swept away bridges and stopped the steamers, so that no messages could be sent.

You all seem to think that I may be in need of clothing or wholesome rations. No, it is only on the march that a soldier suffers. A permanent camp is home to him, and there he is as comfortable as [the] Government can make him. As to my particular case and position, it is looked upon by the men of the regiment with envy because my life is comparatively so easy. You are aware that I am in the Quartermaster Department, assisting to take care of the clothing and rations of the regiment. Do you think that under such circumstances I shall either go naked or starve? Not "if the count knows himself." As long as there are sweet potatoes on the table, E. K. W. can manage to reach them.

Let me tell you how I am situated. The Quartermaster has a wall tent for himself, his sergt. another, which if I felt so disposed, I could share with him. . . . The tent which I occupy, however, and where the clothing is stored, is a large hospital tent, 12 × 14 ft. on the ground. Ten dry goods boxes hold all our stock of clothes, including coats, blouses, pants, shirts, drawers, socks, caps, shoes, overcoats, etc. If I want clothes, I have only to take them and charge them to myself.

This hospital tent is open at both ends, allowing a cool draft of air to rush through. At the door facing the camp I have erected my writing desk and pidgeon [sic] holes on a box of great coats and when seated upon a chest of blank forms, with a blanket for a cushion, am about as well accomodated [sic] as I could be in a New York office. There are four wedge tents behind, to contain ordinance [sic] stores and accomodate [sic] our niggers. Diagonally opposite in a cosy [sic] corner is my bunk, built by myself during a spare half hour. Four heavy crotches are driven firmly into the ground for the bed posts, rising about two feet. Two wedge tent poles rest on these crotches, like parallel bars, connecting the head and the foot posts; and across from pole to pole are the smooth staves of a rice barrel. Half a dozen shelter tents form the bed tick and a double U.S. blanket, doubled, is my mattress. A single blanket covers me. I sleep like a mouse.

You see I am well clad and lodged. Now for the "board." The Q M Sergt, [George W.] Sherman, formerly of the 9th, Cornell (whom you have seen), the Company's clerk, and ex-sergt, the Quartermaster, and myself mess together. We have three contrbands [sic], "Lem," "Aaron," and "Johnny," to cook for and wait upon us, and the Regimental sutler gives us credit for such little extras as we may desire. We have fresh beef, fried as steaks, boiled in a stew, etc., Rice, boiled, baked, and made into fritters, pork and beans, tomatoes, potatoes, descitated [sic] vegetables, onions, beets (never was so beat), hominy, bread and butter (50¢ per lb.), and plenty of coffee and sugar, molasses, and vinegar. Our little bill at the sutlers averages only 14¢ per day per man. We have a complete set of crockery, and our table (a big empty box turned bottom up) is set on my (Hospital tent), a shelter tent being used for a cloth. Sometimes, in very pleasant weather, we dine in the open air. Does this look like starving . . . ?

In a word, we live like fighting cocks and have every reason to be satisfied with our condition. Bye the bye, I have just been (9 P.M.), by pressing invitation, eating Clams and drinking lager, previous to retiring. It's nothing. We soldiers can sleep with ten-penny nails on our stomach without even dreaming. Less than an hour ago I had a bath in a salt water creek near by. It is hoped that these trifling revelations will in some measure smooth the anxious minds of the good ladies who trouble themselves so much about my welfare. My health is very good indeed.

Now, as to the prospects of getting home. At present there is so much work to be done (two sets of quartermaster returns with vouchers, a set of quarterly returns, a set of transfer papers, besides an account of stock to be taken) that I have not the face to apply for a furlough. In fact, I believe none are granted now. My name will be among the first on the list, however, and I shall endeavor to get away at the earliest opportunity.

You know that Gen. Dix is in command at New York.[55] The 3rd is his pet regiment. Col Alford, now acting Maj. General commanding the division, has applied to have his regiment (the 3rd) sent to Governors Island [New York] to recruit and reorganize, and his officers believe his application will be successful. He is said to be backed by Dix. The 3rd is to be filled up with drafted men, and a detachment has already gone on to bring them down. You can take this for what it is worth. I do not believe in it myself.

Three or four weeks since, Col. Jardine sent to the head of the department an application for a furlough for me to come home on recruiting service for twenty days. It was not approved. A couple of weeks later he applied for my discharge, that I might go to New York to recruit for the 9th and receive a commission . . . and [this] has been forwarded to Washington. I have reason to believe it will fail.[56]

Nearly a month ago I drew up a paper addressed to Jardine, requesting the transfer of all the Zouaves (3 yr men) in the Third to his new regiment. It was signed by all the men, sent to Jardine, and by him transmitted to the War department. Gen Getty's Adj. Gen., whom I knew at Newport News, assured me a short time since that the application would be successful, but he was tight at the time and perhaps more good natured than reliable. Men enough of the 3rd to form a full company promised to go with me if I could get them away and pointed out means which they thought would be successful. Alford is so unprincipalled [sic] that he is detested by all his men, and he treated me so shabbily in the Morris affair that I have been laboring ever since to break up his regiment. The draft and nothing else has saved him. Some of his men, illegally held, have already refused to do duty and are under arrest and will undoubtedly be discharged from further service in the army of the U.S. as soon as tried by Court Martial.

As ever
Ed

P. S. We have the New York papers here and have watched the proceedings of the Fernando Wood[57] rabble with a great deal of interest. Nothing would have pleased me better than to have had a shot at the rascals. Remember me to everyone.

"Why don't the 'New York Army' move?" Why at the critical juncture should those noisy editors weaken Meade by withdrawing so many of his troops to protect New York[?][58]

5

CHARLESTON

[Charleston was the cradle of secession and scene of the war's opening shots. For these reasons many a Yankee longed for the chance to participate in the campaign aimed at capturing or levelling the city. And yet that campaign, begun in earnest in the spring of 1863, would not culminate until the city's evacuation by its Confederate defenders in February 1865. When Edward and his new regiment reached the Charleston area in early August of 1863, the corporal was optimistic about a quick, victorious campaign. Long before he left the vicinity the following April, he had begun to wonder if the siege would last forever.

At first it seemed that Battery Wagner, an isolated redoubt near the tip of Morris Island, southeast of the city, was the key to Rebel resistance. For this reason the siege commander, Major General Quincy A. Gillmore, pounded the fort and other harbor defenses with a wide array of cannon—an operation that Edward chronicled with graphic intensity. But neither conventional weapons nor incendiary shells known as "Greek Fire" could ensure a Union triumph. When overwhelmed in early September, the garrison's survivors escaped to points farther north, where they and other troops carried on their resistance with unabated energy. Meanwhile, the civilian population—despite seeing the lower half of their city reduced to rubble—held on defiantly. By late October, following a thirty-day furlough at his parents' home, Edward found events in "status quo," Gillmore and his subordinates seemingly mired in "masterful inactivity."

Cooling his heels on Folly and Black Islands, the young non-com wrote of his annoyances and frustrations. In addition to the problems of inertia, he and the other siege troops were bedeviled by flies and mosquitos, bad water, scanty rations, severe weather, lowland maladies, and seemingly incessant labor on camps and fortifications. Only a St. Patrick's Day outing among the oyster beds of South Carolina seemed to break the drudgery and boredom.]

145

Folly Island, near Charleston, S.C.
Thursday, August 6, 1863

Dear Parents:

On reaching the camp of the Regiment at this place, about three hours ago, letters were placed in my hands from you and from Jim and Mary, and it is so long since I have had the opportunity of writing that I have determined to let the Quartermaster's Department take care of itself for a time while I recount the incidents of the past few days. I would direct to Fred, as usual, did I not suppose him to be out of town and away from the family.

Your letters were very welcome indeed; for I always consider it a rare treat to hear from the "Old Folks at Home." Mother's apology for not writing oftener seems to me a little labored. She is undoubtedly growing older with the rest of us, but as to the plea of "laziness," that will never do for a lady who supervises so large a household and does so much cooking and mending and making and planning and trotting and thinking as she does. She can not properly plead a dearth of news, either. I don't care to hear news from her—only a few lines occasionally, with her autograph appended just to bring home nearer.

In the middle of the night of the 28th of July I was suddenly roused from a sound sleep by the Regimental Quartermaster, who burst into the tent with eyes wide ajar and informed me that he had orders to prepare to move at daylight with three days rations. I was up in a moment. The Q M Sergt was called and a consultation held; but the order for removal was written in so general a way that we could not make out whether we were to leave our camp temporarily or for good, taking all our stores and equipage. The Q M was content to go to bed and let things take care of themselves and his sergt very willingly followed his example; but for myself, not wishing to have all the work of starting come in a lump, I visited some of the neighboring Regiments, concluded that we were on a long jaunt, and at once, with the assistance of our darkies, set about packing up the clothing in boxes, striking and rolling up the tents, etc, so that long before daylight I had everything boxed up.

Shortly afterwards the news leaked out. It was reported that we were bound for Morrison's [Morris] Island, near Charleston, S.C. to assist in the reduction of Fort Wagner. Twenty two wagons came up to take our luggage. After they were loaded and had started, the Quartermaster directed his sergt to go to the dock at Portsmouth where we were to embark and superintend the unloading, but the sergt pleaded inability, and I was sent in his place. The wagon train was ahead out of sight, it was raining, and the distance to be traversed was between three and four miles. I growled like a thunder cloud, but there was no hope for it and, giving my knapsack and haversack in charge to one of the darkies, I set off after them and arrived in Portsmouth in time to have them all safely housed under cover, although in the contest the goods of two other regiments of the brigade were boosted out into the storm.

No men had been detailed to unload the wagons, and I had to get it done by a squad of contrabands. The steamer Adelaide, which was to take us to Charleston, had been delayed and did not come in till midnight. I slept on a bale of hay. At about 2 o'clock A.M. the Quartermaster woke me and said that the troops only would go aboard the Adelaide and that the sergt and myself were to remain for the present with the luggage. The darkey to whom I had entrusted my personal property has friends in Portsmouth and consequently lingered there until the last moment. Just as the steamer was leaving the dock, he came rushing off with the whites of his eyes rolling in a frightful manner [and] told me that while asleep on deck both knapsack and haversack had been stolen from him. I tried to get him aboard again so that he might have time to search for them on the passage, but it was too late. Afterwards the knapsack turned up nearly empty. It had been "gone through."

Through the carelessness of the darkey I thus lost my Zouave suit complete, in which I had done all my campaigning; all my underclothes; my portfolio ([from] Fred); Abbie's needle book; a host of relics picked up for the girls on half a dozen battlefields; all my papers; my gold pen and pencil case; besides books, my U.S. and rubber blankets, etc. I would rather have given $50 than lost them, but some thing similar has happened once before, and when I heard of it I laughed in spite of myself. The haversack (containing a new knife, fork, and spoon and three days grub) has not yet turned up and probably never will. Our company sergt about an hour ago triumphantly showed me a pencil case and pen he had bought off one of the men on the passage for seventy five cents. It was mine. He knows the fellow who sold it, and if I don't haul him over the coals, my daddy's not a lawyer. As to Abbie's Testament, containing my photographs of Jim and the girls, a benighted little nigger was found trying to read it on the dock. It was secured and handed to me by a friend. Fred's book of tactics and a couple of other books, together with my overcoat, belt, and belt plate and a pair of white gloves, were also left—quite a little piece of luck for which I congratulate myself. The loss of the underclothes and blankets, as you will probably infer from my last letter, I can readily remedy.

But to return to the dock at Portsmouth. On the second night of our stay at that place occurred a row. Ten men and a sergt had been left with us as a guard over the luggage, and about as many more stragglers were loafing around, perhaps fifteen out of the twenty more or less intoxicated with liquor they had bought or stolen in the city. Among them were a number of Zouaves. Now if there is any one thing the 9th Regiment agree in as a principle, it is that niggers were born to be abused, and "licking a nigger" they count the climax of a drunken spree. As luck would have it, our contraband Aaron made himself so forward, laughing at their eccentric performances, that he attracted their attention, and a couple of them, highly incensed, scaled the boxes on which he was perched and assaulted him with bayonets.

Wa[r]ned by his yells, I rushed to his rescue and, grasping the bayonets, tried to wrench them from their hands. You would have laughed to see us rolling and tumbling among the boxes, tents, barrels, and trunks; legs, arms, heads, and feet all mingling and locked together, first one on the top and then another. It was like the mingling of Shakespear[e]'s many colored spirits. But finally my hands became so cut and blistered and pricked with the sharp edges and points of the bayonets as they were twisted and wrenched about that I was forced to let go my hold. This untangled the group, and Aaron and one of the Zouaves rolled to the ground, while the others remained in my arms.

But, unluckily for the poor darkey, a dozen Zouaves below were yelling and like hungry sharks waiting to seize him. They jumped on him and kicked him till he was nearly dead, and the rascal who held the bayonet struck him a blow across the face which laid open his thick lips with a gash half an inch in breath, breaking off a couple of teeth besides. A Corporal of the 3rd, who interferred [sic], was knocked down and hit over the bridge of the nose with the bayonet. The assailants then skedalled [sic], knocking down, by the way, a herculean contraband belonging to the Lieut. Col. of the 117th N.Y. Vols, and threatening to "lick" the officer [Francis X. Meyer] himself.

I took poor Aaron to the hospital stewart [sic], and together we managed to sew up his countenance. A big dose of company whiskey was then administered, and the patient was put to bed on a box with a tent for his covering. He is now nearly well, but heaves a huge sigh whenever his drubbing is referred to. Quite natural he should.

I can't tell you half the trouble we had getting transportation and rations for the men. The Quartermaster Sergt. spent all his time in Portsmouth and Norfolk and would not attend to it himself. Only once I managed to get away to visit the Gosport Navy Yard and the city of Norfolk. You will remember that this navy yard was burned by the Government in 1861, and at the same time a number of war vessels were destroyed there.[1] The yard embraces about fifteen or twenty acres of land and now encloses the ruins of about the same number of buildings—some of them quite imposing. The whole of them is surrounded with a heavy brick wall (except on the water side) twelve feet high, loopholed for musketry. It is guarded by marines who good naturedly admitted me without a pass. Nothing but the decayed ribs of the burned vessels are to be seen, as they are partly submerged in the river. The workshops are having roofs put on and machinery rebuilt, but it will be long ere the yard takes again the important place it held before the outbreak of the war. Portsmouth and Norfolk are goodly cities and may perhaps be ranked in size and population with Middletown and Hartford. Their inhabitants are bitter secessionists—some of whom are very pretty ones.

On Sunday evening (2nd August) the steamer "Escort," somewhat larger than the Harlem [River] boats, came up and took our luggage aboard, and on Monday morning at 8 o'clock, with eight hundred men including eight companies of the 112th N.Y. and two of the 103rd N.Y. as passengers, we started out upon the Atlantic. With such a boat and such a load a storm would have been fatal to us. I forgot to say that, in addition to our other freight, we had 25 cases of new Springfield rifles, which had just come up for the 3rd in place of the poor Enfield we have hitherto used.

Our voyage was a remarkably pleasant one, though the steamer rolled considerably, especially off Cape Hatteras where a breeze sprang up and sent a few waves aboard. Some of the boys got sea-sick and added to the contents of the ocean. I didn't, but slept comfortably on a bed of tents below deck, drawing rations from the haversacks of my friends and living on coffee, hard tack, and

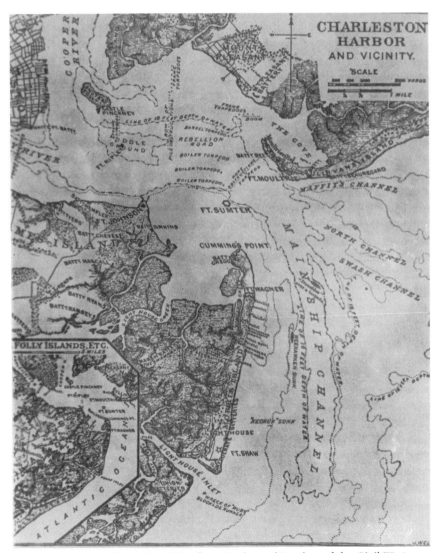

The Charleston Campaign (*Map from* Battles and Leaders of the Civil War)

bacon. We had a new way of making coffee, bye and bye. A cask was filled two thirds full of water, the coffee and sugar dumped in, a pipe reaching to the bottom and connected with the steamer's boiler inserted, steam let in, and the whole cooked in four or five minutes. A couple or three casks of coffee sufficed for all on board.

Early on Wednesday morning a cheer awoke me, and springing up, I saw before me, about eight miles distant, the solid walls of [Fort] Sumter and the spires and housetops of Charleston. Close by were a fleet of vessels, prominent among which were the three Monitors,[2] the frigate Wabash, and a number of ironclads, while from the sand forts on Morrison's Island an occasional puff of smoke and the booming of heavy guns told [us] that the siege was still in progress. No encampments were to be seen, but after we got our orders and taken a pilot aboard and neared the shore, we gradually traced the outlines of the white tents on the background of white sand, which almost appeared to blend with them.

We anchored that night in Stono Inlet[3] and this morning, after traversing a straight [strait] as narrow as a canal for two or three miles, brought up at the dock at last and landed on Folly Island. The first thing that attracted my attention was a palmetto tree, reminding me that I am indeed in the heart of the "South."

Our camp is in the midst of the sand hills on the beach of the Atlantic, whose roaring breakers I hear tumbling in upon the shore as I sit here writing. The boys have already caught a crocodile weighing eleven hundred pounds, and one of them has been so unlucky as to have his leg bit off by a shark. The position is a healthy one. Wells can be dry [dug] anywhere, and sulphur water is uniformly found at a depth of eight or ten feet. It is altogether preferable to our position at Portsmouth, where I was but forty paces from a standing swamp infested with all sorts of vipers. One evening I found a spotted adder more than two feet long in my tent there. I gave the alarm and a dozen of us, deploying as skirmishers outside, arrived with tent pegs, surrounded and dispatched his snakeship as he came out. While there, too, the fatal vapors ensured at least one funeral a day, and sometimes two coffins came by our door in one ambulance, preceeded [sic] by muffled drums and the comrades of the dead, with reversed arms. The order which sent us here was therefore a healthy one. Only the first brigade of our division came. The others remain behind.[4]

I have no time to write more or even to review what has been so hastily scribbled. My health is first rate, weight 157 lbs. Campaigning agrees with me. Fort Wagner will have to succumb soon. We are close up under it.

The 3rd is engaged in doing picket duty. A rebel shell dropped in the midst of one of our companies the other day, but only one man was injured. The rest dropped in the sand so suddenly that the danger passed over them.

As ever, I remain
Yr. Aff. Son
Ed

Folly Island near Charleston, S.C.
August 24, 1863

Dear Bro:

Our mail communication with the North has been interrupted for several weeks in consequence of the operations against Charleston, the government fearing revelation of its plans and strength at this point. I can scarcely write, having a painful felon on one of the fingers of my right hand, but as there has been little fighting done here of late, I suppose it is necessary in order to assure the folk at home that I am still safe and well.

I left the Quartermasters Dept. a couple of weeks ago in disgust and returned to my company. I was offered a [the] position of Quartermaster Sergeant if I would remain but declined, for the Quartermaster is green [and] often imposed upon, and I have no wish to become implicated by endeavoring to keep his accounts. I was asked to act as Brigade Quartermaster Clerk but demured [sic] and then [was] detailed as clerk to the general court martial sitting in [on] the island . . . but [I] couldn't see it and requested to be placed in the ranks where I am at present. While in the Quartermasters I had succeeded in getting two men of the 9th appointed as First Sergeants, [John W.] Knowles of Company C and young [George W.] Rogers of Company H (my old company).

The men of the Third are almost constantly on picket. There are now but about two hundred and twenty . . . in the regiment. No drafted men join us, and there is the prospect of the organization breaking up. The sooner the better, for a greater collection of stupid rascals, officers and men, I have never met with.[5] I attempted to get transferred to another regiment but unsuccessfully. No position in the Third would be honorable or worth retaining. The Colonel [Alford] and Lieut. Col. [Eldridge G. Floyd] have recently got themselves in hot water by trying to make three year men of two year men. About twenty refused to do duty and are now held as prisoners until the matter can be inquired into.

You have probably heard before this of the bombardment of Charleston. The day I joined the company, we changed camp further up the island, cutting away an immense quantity of brush and briar wood to make room for our tents. On the 16th inst., in the afternoon, the whole regiment was ordered to Morrison's Island to support the land batteries, and the next morning we opened with heavy guns on the rebel works.

The first night we bivouaced [sic] on the beach behind sand works, under fire of shells from Fort Johnson.[6] They dropped plentifully around us, but no one was hurt. Next evening we, as we thought we were about to return [to] camp, were ordered forward and advanced to within 400 yards of Fort Wagner and remained there twenty four hours, with shot and shell of almost every caliber howling and screaming and bursting over our heads. We sat quietly under the "splinter proof" and looked on. Poor Sumpter [sic] got an awful peppering by the five hundred pound shots of the monitors and collosal [sic] messengers of the big siege guns of the island. We had narrow escapes by the score, but only one man was wounded. A night attack has been expected, and our pickets were once driven in, and we took position at the parapet to meet Johnny Reb, but he didn't trouble us further.

On the 18th, after dark, we started to return to camp. The tide being up, we had to wade knee deep in water for a couple of miles. We bivouaced [*sic*] within supporting distance of the works and next day about noon got back to our tents, after an absence of three days and nights without rations, tents, or blankets.

The health of the men is not good here. Almost everyone has either a felon or a couple of boils to amuse himself with. The drinking water is bad, and the men bathe too much.

Sumpter is breached in several places, but I think it will be many a day before Charleston falls. No heavy guns have been fired for three or four days.

In haste,
Ed. K. W.

Folly Island, near Charleston, S.C.
August 30, 1863

Dear Wool:

Your letter of the 18th inst, enclosing one from Mary, is just received. The postage stamps were very welcome, for it is impossible to procure them here.

So it seems you are preparing for jolly times at home. Well, I am glad to hear of it. There seems to be no end to my picnic. This changing of spots so often, which you remark upon, according to sound Baptized doctrine an impossible feat for leopards, is yet both pleasant and profitable to that temperament of humanity to which I am assigned. Since I have been out (the first year of my service expired on yesterday) I have visited many cities new to me, [such] as Phil., Baltimore, Washington, Fredericksburg, Norfolk, Portsmouth, Suffolk, etc, besides running like a crazy bedbug, seeking whom I might devour, all over Virginia. I have been over the most terrible battle fields in the country and have seen many of our most formidable forts and earthworks: Newport News, Yorktown, White House, Williamsburg, Suffolk, Fort Monroe, and Charleston. I would not have missed [them] on any account—particularly the bombing of Charleston by our monitors. It is the grandest thing you ever saw. Think of those little cheese boxes, apparently so fragile, hurling their 500 lb. shot with such terrific vim against the crumbling walls of Sumpter and meanwhile riding carelessly at anchor in water seething with foam thrown up by the shots of the rebel guns.

The bombardment has recommenced, but it will doubtless yet be many days before we obtain possession of Charleston. James Island[7] is covered with hostile batteries, and new ones are being erected every day. Both sides exhibit marvelous energy. As for Morrison's Island, we have crept up to Fort Wagner, captured one half of it, and are now amusing ourselves throwing hand grenades[8] into the other part. It must soon fall.

Tomorrow we shall move camp further up the island. Good. The water here is worse than miserable—brackish and unhealthy. The felon on my finger has almost kicked the bucket—killed by remedies. Kept me off duty for two weeks.

As for letter[s] from home I am glad and anxious to hear from you all just as often as you can write without inconveniencing yourselves. But I have no right to expect that you should give so much of your time to me. If you may have written weekly, many of your letters must have miscarried. It was only a couple of days since that I got one from you, Mary, and Abbie, dated July 8. Have any of mine miscarried. . . ?

Doff your cap for me to the Hunter ducks and say, "how d'ye do. . . ." Tell Lilly I can swear to having [not] killed anybody or anything during the first long year of my service except a snake, a lizzard [sic], and a poor chamelion [sic]. Perhaps I am just as content for all that.

Mary's sketch of herself and the Zou-zou in a previous letter was done in the highest style of art. It tickled me wonderfully.

As ever, Yr. aff. Bro
Ed

Black Island near Charleston, S.C.
September 14, 1863

Dear Bro:

Oho, you bandy little specimen of the "Harlem Guard." It seems you and the other buddies are rejoicing at having escaped the draft. Well, perhaps the Fates have not decreed that any of you shall lug rifle and knapsack and canteen and cartridges over the sacred soil of Rebeldom. Rest assured of this, though, if you had been sent, you would have been roped into a set of secrets which, although the faithful records of your amiable brother may have induced you to think yourselves familiar with, would have racked both mind and body. Nothing but actual experience could give you an idea of the character of a soldier's life. So, although I should probably return to the field if discharged, I am as glad as you can be that our benevolent Uncle Samuel has seen fit to hold you in reserve.

I presume that the family are by this time all at home. I have received letters from Jim, Mary, and Abbie, dated Aug 19th, and from Charley and Mary at Cromwell, dated Sept 1st. All appear to be having "high old times." But I can not help thinking how much better it would be for each member of our family if all would make health seeking a habit rather than an impulse. Confinement such as they endure would have made Hercules dyspeptic. Do they expect that riding a couple of weeks through the country will invigorate them for a whole year until [the] experiment can be renewed[?] Bless their simple souls.

"But to return to the subject." You will observe that this is headed "Black Island." On the 31st of Aug the whole regiment was ordered hither on picket duty for ten days. Our wedge tents were left standing in the old camp, and we took with us shelter tents and overcoats. Four big whale boats transported us from the norther[n] side of Folly Island (Morris Island) through a meandering swampy inlet to Black Island, between Folly and James, a low marshy strip of ground three quarters of a mile long, covered with tall salt grass except where two low ridges covered with pine trees rise from the sand. Behind these ridges we found a detail of the 117th N.Y. encamped and relieved them. They had already built splinter proofs to retire to in anticipation of being shelled from James Island, which is only about 1400 yards distant and crowded with heavy earth works and batteries.

Here splinter proofs are prepared something like a potato house. A long rectangular hole is dug in the ground to the depth of six feet. It is roofed with heavy logs running both length wise and across, the whole sloping toward the front or away from the hostile batteries. The roof rests on stout pillars and is protected on top by layers of sand bags and by loose sand to the height of four or five feet. A narrow appeture [sic] is left under the roof in front and a square hole serves as a door to dodge in at. If a shell of any size should strike plump upon such a concern, it would of course knock it into pie. They are chiefly intended as a protection against fragments. You folks at home laugh at the idea of dodging shot and shell; but it is the nicest thing in the world, as you would be convinced had you see[n] our men when in front of Wagner bobbing into the holes whenever the sentry shouted, "Cover Wagner," "Cover Johnston," or "Cover Gregg."[9] Those lively batteries made us hop around like hot peas on a shovel.

My first picket post was in the top of a pine tree fifty feet from the ground. Sticks had been nailed crossways on the trunk at convenient distances to ascend by, and a platform constructed for the sentry. From this point a splendid view is obtained of Sumter, Gregg, Wagner, Johnston, Moultrie,[10] of the rebel works on James Island, and of our own batteries. I have sat in that cover[ed] place by the hour watching the forts as they plumped [pumped] shot and shell into each other, like a disinterested spectator looking at the war. The picture as it looks from on top of the pine tree is like this [sketch deleted]:

I flatter myself that's about as complicated as a "herald" map. The dotted lines show the direction of the fire.

James Island looks as though she could blow us out of the water without any effort, and we expected she would do it on several occasions. As yet, though, we are undisturbed except by an occasional heavy shell from Johnston and a few light weights from the neighborhood of Secessionville.[11]

Our worst picket duty is on the borders of the swamp on the James Island side. There myriads of stout ring-tailed mosquitoes "rush" upon the detail the instant it appears and jab their bills in, chuck up to the head, on the first thrust. Even overcoats are no protection from the torturing rascals, [who] pierce through everything. Sleep is, of course, impossible with such a ravenous hoard [sic] of blood suckers singing and biting and buzzing and p[r]icking and screaming and chewing and poisoning, getting up your sleeves and trouser legs, crawling slyly down your neck or dashing into your ears and down your throat, wearing a fellow's life out with coughing, slapping, pinching, and scratching.

The day following our arrival at Black Island we were set to work to complete the battery of two thirty-two and one one hundred pound rifled guns, with which it was intended to throw "Greek Fire" shells[12] into Charleston. We then threw up an entrenchment six feet high and two hundred yards long, leading from the battery to a bomb proof hospital, which was next constructed. The distance from this point to Charleston is between four and five miles, so that the pieces had to be given the greatest elevation in firing. The work was done under cover of the woods, and when the first shot was fired, I was up the pine tree. The shells fell short, and the battery, proving a failure, was removed. We are now building a large stockade fort on the other end of the island, and the men of the 3rd dig so well that they have been ordered to stay twenty days instead of ten, as at first proposed.

On the night of the first inst. the roar of the Monitors guns and the rapid shots of the Ironsides[13] roused us from sleep. The ironclads had opened on Sumter. The thundering reports were like the explosions of so many magazines. The earth trembled with the shock of the broadsides, and the concussions were distinctly felt in the air. In the morning poor Sumter looked as if it had been on a bender. No fast man with his hat caved in, cravat awry, waist coat wrong buttoned, coat split in the back [and] trouser legs tucked in his boots ever appeared so hopelessly forlorn. Riddled, battered, and mauled, the honey combed walls of this "King of the Harbor" seemed, when the sun shown [sic] brightly upon them, dropping black shadows everywhere across the ruins, hardly worth the labor of possessing. Yet it still remains a bone of contention. The rebels hold it, but it is harmless for offensive purposes—at least in their hands. The number in the garrison is estimated at from one hundred to six hundred men,[14] who communicate with the city by means of a black steamer. Several small boat expeditions have been fitted out against it, but no serious infantry assault has been made. I am ignorant of the cause of delay.

Against Batteries Wagner, Gregg, and Cummings Point[15] our operations were more successful. Our Monitors and land batteries opened on these Forts on the morning of the 5th with terrible earnestness. Columns of sand and salt spray, spiriting thirty feet up, . . . marked unmistakably the force and accuracy of the solid shot, while the shell, glancing neatly on the parapet, burst like thunderbolts over the center of the enclosures. At times the roar was incessant and the clouds of sand so dense that one could almost swear that Wagner had been loosened from the earth and driven into the air.

The rebels[16] were well casemated, or they could not have endured it an instant. Early in the morning of the 7th they endeavored to evacuate, but our infantry advanced both on the water and the land side and captured about one hundred. Our loss was but three killed and five wounded.[17] The loss of the rebels must have been severe for the bomb proofs are said to be pelted down.

Inside the forts, where our shells burst, holes were found big enough to top a couple of hogs heads into. Many rebel dead had been buried in the works; these the remorseless shells had torn from their resting place and scattered in bloody fragments everywhere. It was like a pest house. In some parts the walls had been almost leveled with the ground. The enemy tried their torpedo[18] tricks and attempted to blow up the magazine, but without success. As soon as we had taken possession, Sullivans, Johnstons, and all the neighboring rebels opened but did not deter our men from repairing the works and mounting new guns. All this time the 3rd Reg. was on Black Island.

On the 8th inst. the stubborn monitors poked their way out into the harbor and, deliberately taking their position, . . . commenced with their usual imponderability(?) to fire into Sullivan's Island.[19] In about two hours time there was an explosion, and it was reported that the magazine of Moultrie had been blown up. It is now thought to have been something else. About dark the graybacks began to handle their guns with astonishing activity. The whole of Sullivan's Island, to the right of Sumter, was but one sheet of flame. The cannonading soon after ceased. What the result is we do not know.

September 15. I have just received letters from Jim and Mary at home, dated Sept. 8. Mary's account of her trip is very complete and interesting. Ask her to send me the photographs. Remember me to Abbie.

In haste, Yrs. Truly
Ed

P. S. The "Swamp Angel"[20] in the drawing [deleted] originally contained the 200 pounder which fired Charleston. Unluckily, it burst. The Rebs don't know it, and waste ammunition by the cartload. Quite a joke. We laugh a great deal over their splendid shots at a deserted underbank. A man occasionally shows himself on the works to keep up the delusion.

E

Folly Island, S.C.
Tuesday Even. Nov 18 [17], 1863

Dear Bro:

I have only a few moments before "taps" to tell you of my safe arrival here [following furlough in New York].

The "Arago" left New York at one and a half o'clock on Wednesday the [1]4 instant. She was heavily laden with army stores and had also to tow a schooner to Hilton Head, so that our progress was very slow indeed—averaging only about seven miles an hour. The citizens you saw aboard were mechanics in government employ. They became obstreporous [sic] shortly after leaving the city, not being satisfied with the soldier's rations provided for them, so that Gen. Terry,[21] who was a passenger, fearing a mutinous outbreak, took military command and organized a guard. Consequently I was up all Wednesday night with bayonet in hand, guarding the engineer's room. But the strategical genius of Wightman soon became so apparent that he was made a corporal on the spot and placed in command of a squad, in which capacity his military bearing was so imposing as to overawe the giddy multitude and squelch all signs of disturbance.

We were five and a half days on the route. Reached Port Royal on Sunday evening at sunset. Stayed over night and at ten next morning embarked on the steamer "Escort" for Folly Island where we landed at sunset on Monday, and an hour afterwards found ourselves once more at home. Part of the voyage was rough, and many a Jonah was cast overboard by the unhappy travellers. Luckily, I escaped all symptoms of seasickness. My provisions just lasted the trip out, although I am free to acknowledge that I did "hanker after" the other mince pie which Ell tried to force on me when about leaving the house.

After doubling Hatteras we had real July weather for awhile. Butterflies came aboard, and it was too warm to be comfortable except in the shade. On reaching camp, however, a cold snap set in, equal to anything you have yet had at the North. Last night was almost freezing, and I lay awake listening to the heavy guns at Cummings Point as they hammered away at Sumter.

An infantry assault is shortly to be made (it is said) by the 7th Conn. Vols. with [Colt's] revolving rifles and scaling ladders in boats especially constructed for the purpose. They are to be supported by another regiment. The assault will probably be made by daylight while there are but few rebs in the fort, our gunboats at the same time engaging the enemy's batteries. The 7th (a splendid batallion [sic]) is close to our camp and rehearses its role daily—success to it.

The Island is much more healthy than when I left. The cold drives disease away. The number of men on the sick list is comparatively small. The new location of our camp is much better than the last, and we have at length found clean water.

I have been all day polishing my rifle and getting it in working order. New furloughs are to be given, and a general movement seems as far off as ever. We hear that one Regiment (3rd Infty) is to be separated from the other troops of the division and posted in detachment[s] in various works, as heavy artillery.

Tell Charley I went to Gen Gordon's[22] Hdqs this morning to see [Captain] Cooper, but he had gone to St. Augustine, Fla on leave for his health. They think he will resign and not return here.

I have just been weighed and tip the beam at 169 lbs. Healthy as a brick. Love to all the phellers.

In haste, yrs.
Ed.

Folly Island, S.C.
November 23, 1863

Dear Bro:

I wrote to you on arriving here about the 10th inst, according to promise. Since that time a change has taken place, both in our position and duties. Just a week ago the 3rd Regiment was broken up into detachments. One company went to Gen Vogdes[23] as headquarters guard; six to man the works and guns (they were drilled as heavy artillery at Fort Monroe) at the northern end of Folly Island and there to take charge of four light guns at Pawnee Landing. I am with my company at the latter place. There are two docks here, and it is the headquarters of the Post Quartermaster and Commissary. Our picket duty is done. We have only to drill at the guns and to guard them and the camp. During the past week I have been on guard but twice.

The coldness of the weather here when I wrote to you last was due to the prevalence of north winds. The [rough] surf lasted but three or four days. Since that time it has been very mild and summer-like—just my kind of weather and agrees with me like a charm. I am in remarkably good condition. The health of the regiment is vastly improved. In place of the eighty on the sick list one month ago there are now but nineteen . . .

Six officers and twenty five men of the 3rd, it is reported, are to go North to obtain recruits for the Regiment. I think that their chances of success are slim and that after the expiration of sixty days we shall be consolidated [with another regiment]. The regt. has no lever to work with. It is but little known and that little is not in its favor. I suppose I might get hom[e] with the rest but then doubt the advantages of such a step.

Nothing of moment occurs here, and every day promises more positively winter quarters. The bombardment is slowly kept up, and there are never wanting rumors of general attacks to be made; yet nothing is done. The 7th Connecticut, who volunteered to assault Sumter, have gone away, it is supposed to their old camp.

As to the 3 yr. men of the 9th [New York], Col. Hawkins proposition for a transfer[24] has been submitted to them, and they have decided to remain where they are. I have communicated the result to Col. Hawkins.

Having nothing more to say, I further proceed to say it and subscribe myself

Yr like thunder, by golly,
Ed K. W.

P.S. Wish I were at home on the 26th [Thanksgiving] to chase folks around the chimney.

Yrs by golly, etc
Ed

Folly Island, S.C.
December 2, 1863

Dear Bro:

The first winter months find me "sound and kind, in harness." Folly Island at this season is quite a healthy place. The weather generally is mild and summer like, though for a couple of nights past, following a Northeast storm, ice has formed in the neighborhood. Still, the fact that we are pestered with multitudes of flies, at most [almost] without cessation, speaks favorably for continued warmth.

There is no military news. We are in status quo. My company acts now as both artillery and infantry. We drill on the guns in the morning and in the afternoon shoulder our muskets and nearly march our legs off, maneuvering with the division on the beach, fatty Vogdes commanding. Every alternate night I am on picket. Night before [last] I was nearly frozen stiff at it, having been posted where no fires were allowed. Tonight my turn comes again, but luckily the weather has moderated.

I suppose you passed a merry Thanksgiving at home. My celebration of the day was not so bad either. I made a trip to the northern end of [the] island and feasted at the Quartermaster's on juicy roast beef, mealy potatoes, green peas, bread and butter, coffee, etc, and then smoked a couple of segars, just for all the world as though I were at home. To be sure, I missed the beet joke, the Sambo joke, and the Worth joke, and heard nothing about "gobbling" nor about the Sunday School dinner, etc., yet managed, notwithstanding, to worry things down.

After dinner we went to a slaughter house nearby to see a dozen black butchers kill and dress cattle. The darkies stood on a plank platform, each one with a knife in his mouth to give him a butcher-like air, the whites of two dozen eyes rolling in a manner fearsome to behold. The fun commenced when one end of a rope had been fastened to the horns of an ox and his wooliheaded [sic] executioners had slipped the other through a ring on the platform and made the first heave to lug him forward. The ox ran [the butchers] backward, with a terrible thump, onto their knees. They bit their knives savagely and looked as fierce as the "roaring lion" in scripture. Then the ox swung up his tail like a thunderbolt. The niggers scrambled behind the nearest trees as fast as their legs could carry them and glared at him. Finally, one more venturesome than the rest pulled in the slack, and the animal was considered conquered. But alas, no sooner had his sable enemies congregated to congratulate themselves than he jumped into the air, butted two of them head first into a heap . . . and kicked the third square into the blood tub. Such a yell of broad-mouthed laughter [resulted] as you have never heard the like of—but not a man took the knife from his teeth. That wouldn't have been according to Hoyle.

In the afternoon we returned to Pawnee Landing and listened to a Thanksgiving sermon by an Episcopalian [minister] . . . It was read in the open air, the troops forming in a hollow square. Later we attended the funeral of a corporal who went home with me on furlough. He had been ill for several weeks and ought to have gone into a hospital in New York. When we arrived here, he was too weak to walk from the dock to the camp. I finished off the evening with a game of chess.

There are no signs of a general movement. If an infantry attack is to be made, we shall first have to be largely reinforced. Perhaps the naval authorities are waiting for the Dictator and other monitors. We have reports of a great victory by Grant in the West,[25] but as yet no papers or details. As you may suppose, the troops here are jubilant and regard the battle as the most important of the war—one of the finishing blows. On yesterday all of our vessels displayed their colors in honor of the event, and the batteries everywhere thundered out their salutes.

In haste,
Ed K. W.

Folly Island, S.C.
January 6, 1864

Dear Rod:[26]

Here's a letter to you at last. I should have written long ago had it not happened that the time allowed for such purposes in the Dept. is limited, and I had so many other correspondents to attend to. You'll not be offended when I acknowledge frankly that I rather calculated on your good nature to overlook any seeming negligence while I was hastily forwarding conciliatory messages for more exact correspondents and to testy acquaintences. I don't know what you'll think of me, Rod, when I sheepishly confess that some of them are ladies—a thing to be deplored—an accident—a catastrophe absolutely bedoozling to contemplate. Pray for me.

Affairs (in the neighborhood of Charleston) are at a standstill. All our general officers appear to be straddling the fence or sitting in solemn council, with straws in their mouths, to take a big think, or standing up whistling, with their hands in their pockets; all of which is respectfully intended to convey an idea of "masterly inactivity." To be sure, we throw a shell in the city occasionally, but it isn't expected to hit anybody, and we should be very much alarmed if it were discovered that we had accomplished much in this way. What astonishes us here, is that you folks in the North should continue to imagine that we are going to capture Charleston. We have no such ridiculous aspirations. We are content to live on sand hills, eat salt junk, and drink dirty water. It is true that the Herald startles us sometimes by showing some trifling advantages we have unwittingly gained; but I solemnly assure you, my dear fellow, that we don't intend to do anything energetic or dashing, and that such little episodes are purely accidental.

The Third Regiment, to which I am at present attached (an Albany regiment, bye the bye, composed of the most part of sneak thieves and jail birds— delightful associates) has been divided in three detachments and is now serving as light artillery. My Company is posted at Pawnee Landing where there are four guns, two bronze field pieces (six pounders) and two thirty pound Parrots.[27] We guard these and in addition furnish details for a half a dozen picket posts. Then we have fatigue work, besides drill and the guns, and as an infantry of the line, skirmishe[r]s, and so forth.

We live in comparative comfort. We have none of the heavy marching and cold weather of last winter—nothing to compare with our Fredericksburg experiences, though the water freezes here at times. Northern winds always bother us, but when they do not prevail, we luxuriate as becomes the inhabitants of "the sunny south." All the troops of the island are provided with wedge tents, which by the order of the surgeons are raised on logs about two feet from the ground. Many of them have fireplaces and chimneys. Wightman has one and is at this moment toasting his shins at the blazing wood fire. Our bunks are made of crotches of poles and barrel staves combined.

Doubtless you have long since suspected that I have no news to write. You are sharp, sir, sharp. Let me close. I don't know that I am justified in calling this a letter at all. Remember me to Mrs. Kimball and little Kim and believe me as ever

Yours truly,
Ed K. W. Co. H 3rd Infantry, N. Y. V.
Folly Island, S. C.

Folly Island, S. C.
January 15, 1864

Dear Bro:

I have to acknowledge the receipt of a vast number of letters from various members of the family since my last. As a consequence I am thoroughly posted in regards to your doings at home during the holiday week. . . .

The position of the regiment here is unchanged, though it is rumored that an expedition is about to start soon from Hilton Head to some unknown point. General Gilmore[28] moves his headquarters to that place today. We now suppose that that is where the troops sent from Folly and Morris Island[s] have been concentrated. General Vogdes has gone to New York on a thirty day furlough. He resides in Brooklyn. General Terry (formerly at Suffolk) is left in command. All this looks as if we were not to be disturbed. The prospect of monotonous inactivity is anything but pleasing.

Attempts are being made to re-enlist for three years those men in the Department who have but one year to serve. They are to have $800 to $900 bounty and thirty days furlough. When enough re-enlist to make it an object regiment, regiments are to be sent home en mass[e]. Several have already gone. The proposition is favorably entertained by many of the old members, but there are not enough of them to take the regiment to New York. Furlough, except for re-enlisting men, has been stopped.

The men are still healthy in spite of long continued wet weather and short rations. We are on picket or fatigue duty every day. They alternate. The fatigue is digging—leveling the camp streets (rooting out stumps and so on) and preparing our parade ground. We live on ten hard crackers and two cups of coffee per diem.

Did I tell you I had built a turf fireplace and chimney to my tent? Such is a fact, and it makes the house quite cheery and comfortable.

The Herald has nominated General Grant for the presidency. He would be more useful and less dangerous in the field. What are his politics?

Yours truly,
Ed

General Quincy A. Gillmore *(Photograph courtesy of the Library of Congress)*

Folly Island, S.C.
February 14, 1864

Dear Bro:

My last letter from home was received eight or ten days ago. Mary intimates that a box is about to be forwarded. I am almost sorry to hear it for you know how much trouble there was about the others. We have begun to move here too at last, and there is no telling how long the Regiment will remain on the island. Troops are leaving every day, either for home or (it is said) for Florida.[29]

I have no doubt that you have heard, long before this, more of our movement here than we know ourselves. What the mischief have we been doing? How many of us were killed and wounded in the last fight? Did enough get knocked on the head to make a sensation at home? Is there glory enough to cover all the troops or only a hatful or so for General Gilmore and staff? All we know is that Gilmore has taken an expedition to some point farther south, has landed, and is now advancing into the interior. As near as I can conjecture from the prevalent rumors, he is in the upper part of Florida, moving towards Georgia, as though to aid in concert with Grant.

When this expedition left Hilton Head, a second one started from Stono Inlet across the neighboring islands toward the Charleston and Savannah railroads, as a blind. One of the regiments of our brigade, "the 117th of New York," went with the latter. They landed on Cole's Island, passed over Kiawalst [Kiawah] and Seabrook [Seabrooks] and then crossed to John's Island[30] and proceeded in a northwesterly direction. There were two brigades and two columns. They met the rebs, created a rumpus, burned a bridge, and captured a few prisoners. They were then ordered to retire, as our generals were informed that the enemy had detached 8,000 men to meet them. We are told that the movement as a whole was a success.

Infantry and artillery leave the island almost daily to reinforce Gilmore. It is reported that the 3rd will embark [sic] within ten days. Parts of the 89th and 103rd New York Brigade,[31] companions of the old 9th, have re-enlisted and have been sent home to recruit. They have done a great deal of tough marching and fighting and rank among the very best regiments in the service.

On Thursday night last [February 11], at about midnight, the rebs opened their guns upon us along the whole line. We were brought out under arms, ready to resist an attack, and some of our old lady officers were much alarmed. I was detailed to the battery at Pawney [sic] Landing, where I was assigned a position at the muzzle of a thirty pounder Parrot—where I expected to sponge and ram with awful energy. This proved to be no [such] occasion. At present everything is quiet.

The weather is mostly such as you have at home in June, but there are cold snaps sometimes, the night is severe, and the dews almost as heavy as rain. The health of the men is remarkably good and so forth.

Ed K. W.

P.S. Tell Jim not to direct his letters as hitherto. The address is wrong. Let it simply be Edward K. Wightman, Company H. Third Infantry, N.Y. V. Folly Island, S.C.

Evening—Letters from Mary, Ell, and Jim of February 1st just received.

Folly Island, S.C.
March 8, 1864

Dear Bro:

I have just received letters from home up to February 23rd. The box has not yet arrived but is supposed to be at Hilton Head. . . .

Our detachment is now employed every day in loading and unloading vessels at the wharf. We have no rest even on Sundays. The citizens who have hitherto done this work have been sent to the Head. Today we have been shipping army wagons. General Vogdes has gone to Florida, and Col. Alford of the 3rd is left in command of Folly and Long Islands.[32] Vogdes will return, it is said, in a few days.

We have no late news from Florida. No reinforcements have yet arrived from Fort Monroe. There are two brigades on this island and three regiments only on Morris Island. A slow bombardment is kept up on the city of Charleston, but, of course, no active operations are to be expected in the neighborhood for some time to come. It seems to be the determination of our officers to remain here, if possible, permanently. They may succeed, and may not.

I am interrupted here by the cries of a riotous squad of citizens who, it seems, have been ordered to relieve us. "Z'all right." Bully for us.

I'm in an awful hurry and would not write were it not for mother and the girls, for there is no news. Yes, we have just raised a flagstaff and flag [in camp]. That's about the sum total.

There is an item for Ell, though. You must know that snakes of all kinds abound here. Well, I awoke suddenly three or four nights since and found myself leaning on one elbow and staring through the darkness at the other side of a tent where, underneath the bunk, several animals seemed to be rolling and tumbling in a fierce conflict. Squeaks, bumps, and hisses alternated with wonderful rapidity. There was an occasional sound, too, like the cooing of a dove. I roused the fellow beside me and suggested it was a snake and rat fight. He agreed. We listened breathlessly, not daring to step out on the floor. Once I reached out my hand toward the matchbox, but a rattling of tins on the shelf suggested adders and lizards, and it was jerked back in a very frisky style.

Finally I summoned up pluck to strike a light and discovered—what do you think? Two thundering big tom cats, scrambling around with their ears tucked back and their tails the size of your office stove pipe. We had never suspected there were any cats on the Island and were wonderfully pleased with our visitors. I sat up half an hour to look at them. In the morning they had escaped.

What's the news? Remember me to the fellas and believe me

Yours truly,

Ed K. Wightman

P. S. Ma[r]y offers to exchange the enclosed photograph for another. So may it be. Ask Charlie to send one too if he has any to spare.

Ed

Folly Island, S.C.

March 20, 1864

Dear Bro:

As it seems to be considered necessary that I should employ all the time not actually given to sleep in writing home, I seize an opportunity to relieve the unsupportable anxiety of our family by stating that I am well. If I should not be heard from again in two or three days, there seems at present no reason to suggest that it will be in consequence of any overwhelming misfortune. . . .

The troops here are still inactive. An expedition, comprising 3,000 infantry, left here week before last in gunboats and after sailing over to Johns Island returned and landed somewhere in the rear of Sullivan's Island. It was probably a reconoitering [sic] party. The troops are now back in their camps.

No men have yet been sent to us from Fort Monroe, but considerable bodies of recruits have come down from New York to join the brigade. The 3rd, however, is nowhere. It has no name to build on and will probably in the end exhibit a case of spontaneous combustion. Col. Alford is said to have been appointed Brigadier General by the President and to be awaiting the ratification of the Senate. The regiment now cannot number more than 250 men all told and has a super abundance of commissioned and non commissioned officers. Some of the companies have only half a dozen privates. Company H has thirteen, two unfit for duty. Taken together, it is a disorganized rabble. Of those who remain, many are old men and many young boys. I hope it may soon break up.

A newspsper called the "Palmetto Herald" has been started in the Department. I'll send you the first number.[33]

Yours,
Ed. K. W.

P. S. There's nothing further about our going to Florida.

Folly Island, S.C.
March 27, 1864

My Dear Boy [Fred]:

. . . I received letters from you and Abby, dated the 14th and 9th inst. respectively, and others from Jim, Charley, and Mary. Charley's photograph is very good indeed, and the enclosure of postage stamps came in the nick of time. I am glad, too, to have your summary of army news for lately we have been in the dark here as to the military movements in other parts of the country. Since then, however, papers have arrived to enlighten us. We expect to hear of the terrible fighting [in Virginia] within the next three months and perhaps to do a little on our own account.

For sometime back I have feared that the War Department would scatter our forces so much as to tempt the rebels to concentrate successively at different points and overwhelm us in detail. But I conclude, from what you hear, that the various expeditions sent out during the winter[34] were merely intended to distract the enemy, to deprive his troops of rest, to retard reorganization, and to reconoiter [sic].

It is now time for us to concentrate for the energetic opening of the spring campaign. The promotion of Grant and his appointment to the command of the armies[35] has given great confidence to the soldiers in the Department, and they now look to the end as assured. Rumor rides around among us busily as ever, and everyday we are amused with the repeated issue of fresh orders for the movement of the regiment. Only yesterday we were to be assigned as artillerists to Long Island. Today we are to begin to expect a trip to Mobile. . . .[36]

Our Brigade is to be broken up. The 89th and 103rd New York are to report to Burnside in New York before the middle of next month. Butler[37] is to send reinforcements to Florida instead of here. Foster's Brigade is to return to us. The 117th New York will join Foster, and then the 3rd will be left out in the cold. Suppose all this is true. What then? Why, evidently "the cat's run away without the pudding bag's string,"[38] which is hardly worth mentioning.

It is pleasant to be able to say that we are more at leisure than heretofore. The crazy commander of the detachment [i.e., of the regiment] having leveled down all the sand hills in the neighborhood, now rests from his labors. He does nothing now but walk around and round the camp from sunrise 'til midnight with his hands in his pockets, grinning from ear to ear at every remark he can construe as a compliment on the good appearance of the place. It is a mild form of lunacy, and the poor fellow is perfectly harmless. His name is [Captain John] Fay, and he grew out of the swamps around Morisania [New York].

I am waiting patiently for the regiment to tumble to pieces. About sixty men will be discharged within the next three months. No recruits can be obtained because the organization has no fighting reputation. Those who remain may either be consolidated by special act of Congress or transferred into a Battery.

The weather we have is glorious. "The time of the singing birds has come and the voice of the turtle is heard in the land."[39] The pine trees and palmettoes are putting forth fresh leaves, and a new crop of grass is sprouting up. The nights are still cold—sometimes freezing.

On St. Patrick's Day I went on a spree. Luckily our captain [Fay] is an Irishman. A party of five got a surf boat of a stevador [sic] at the dock and road [sic] up the inlets and around the swampy islands. We had previously procured fish lines at the sutlers and provided ourselves with regular genuine original Jacob fish hooks. Bullets were used for sinkers. None of your fine brooks. We also laid in a good stock of fisherman's grub, consisting of crackers and cheese. We had the foresight, too, to make some oyster knives of iron hoops and took with us a liberal supply of pepper and vinegar. I care nothing about line fishing but shell-fishly (joke) thought only of the oysters which grew in great beds along the shore.

The position for fishing was no sooner taken than it was discovered that we had neither anchor rope, anchor, nor bail. So much for our endeavoring to celebrate an Irishman's birthday. You needn't grin, though, my boy; for you would have given your bandies to be present at the feats which followed. We approached the shore and planted "our gunboats" on an enormous bed of stupendous bivalves. They stood together like a big crowd of fat voters on election day. I grasped my knife and, with that same unerring instinct which guides me in the selection of sweet potatoes and bananas, oysterly raised the fatest [sic] of the group and attacked him with a knife. Jerusalem, what a sockdolager! He looked like Falstaff on the half shell. How hungrily I smiled over that trembling rebel oyster! How I peppered him! How I bathed the poor fellow in vinegar! How I—ah, it takes my breath away to think of it. . . .

Excuse me again, me boy, my pipe's gone out, and the "sodger" is warning me from outside that a snake has just run down our chimney. Here goes for the snake. Remember me to the fellas.

Yours truly,
Ed K. W.

P. S. Tell Jim that Lily's letter was received and acknowledged at this time. I should judge from what I hear that about one half of my notes miscarry. Enclosure in the letter.

Your picture of Uncle Sam's review of the candidates for the presidency was stared at by all the gawkies in the company. They thought it the most tremendous hit they had ever seen. It isn't bad. The poor hams, though, were incapable of making those nice discriminations [of caricature] which your gigantic intellect traced out.

Folly Island, S.C.
April 13, 1864

Dear Bro:

This is probably the last letter from Folly Island. We are under marching orders to proceed to Fortress Monroe, Virginia, and shall start as soon as relieved by colored troops now on their way. All the white regiments except the 103rd New York (a part of which left for New York last Sunday) will be taken from Folly and Morris Islands. So a report says. We may start tomorrow.

The general opinion seems to be that we are to join the Army of the Potomac; but I cannot avoid the impression that we are to advance with the Grand Army up the [Virginia] penninsula [sic]. Anyway, we are going to help strike at Richmond. The men are in high spirits at the prospect. The leadership of McClellan on the penninsula [sic] (where it is suspected he is to take command)[40] is in concert with Grant in northern Virginia [and] will, it is believed, make our Grand Army now concentrating here irresistible, and the fall of Richmond certain.

I cannot tell how glad I am to return again to active service. The avoidance of the second summer in Folly Island is in itself a great point (our camp here is in splended condition. The parade ground level, covered with grass, the streets padded, a [flag]staff erected, trees set out with fences and flower beds in front, and everything in apple pie order). Perhaps we take our shelter tends [sic] and leave without reluctance.

In great haste.

Ed K. W.

[P. S.] Direct letters to Company H, 3rd N.Y. V., Fort Monroe, Va., until otherwise instructed. Letters of April 5th received. No box.

6

BERMUDA HUNDRED AND
COLD HARBOR

[Late in April 1864 the Tenth Corps of Quincy Gillmore, conceding defeat at Charleston, sailed north to try to win the war in another, more promising theater of operations. At Fort Monroe, Virginia, the corps, plus "Baldy" Smith's Eighteenth Corps and Brigadier General August V. Kautz's division of cavalry, set out, in Edward's words, "to try our luck against Richmond." The young soldier again had high hopes of writing his family from an occupied Confederate capital—this time under the command of Ben Butler, the most notorious political general in American history. Edward knew the army leader was considered a shrewd, even a brilliant, politician, but a military tyro (the West Point-educated Smith later termed him "as helpless as a child on the field of battle and as visionary as an opium eater in council"). At least, service under Butler promised not to be dull.

The spring campaign was devised not by Butler but by the new Commanding General of the Army, Lieutenant General Ulysses S. Grant, fresh from a string of brilliant victories in the western theater. Grant would travel with the larger Union army in Virginia, the Army of the Potomac, now under the immediate command of Major General George Gordon Meade, Joe Hooker's successor. While Meade operated against Lee's troops above Richmond, Butler's Army of the James would try to enter the capital by the back door, from the southeast. That door seemed wide open, for local garrison troops were few, and reinforcements toward the south and west would require several days to reach the city.

On May 4, Butler started upriver from Fort Monroe via his army's namesake river. His move came as a rude surprise to the enemy, thanks to simultaneous feints such as that which the Third New York made up the Virginia peninsula along the York River. Soon, however, the army's advance bogged down. Butler's lieutenants halted to dig earthworks inside Bermuda Hundred, six miles below Richmond. Then General Kautz detached his troopers from the army and led them on two inconsequential raids. And then Gillmore and Smith failed to coordinate operations against the railroad that connected the capital to its supply hub at Petersburg. On May 9 the Third New York, its feinting movements ended, participated in one of these flawed offensives; Edward recorded its bloody outcome.

On the twelfth, following several days of hard marching and harder fighting, Butler's infantry and artillery started north against Richmond—only to learn that their dawdling had allowed numerous reinforcements to occupy defenses along the west bank of the James, a few miles below the capital. A surprise assault on the sixteenth by these troops, under General P. G. T. Beauregard, took the Federals by storm. After some resistance, Butler's army trudged back to Bermuda Hundred, where Beauregard "bottled" them up after failing to crack their works.

Then came Cold Harbor, where Grant's errant tactics cost seven thousand Federal casualties—many of them in Smith's composite command—in less than ten minutes of fighting. Only a return to Bermuda Hundred by Smith's men for a movement against vital and vulnerable Petersburg—a product of Grant's never-say-quit attitude—offered the hope that this long run of Union misfortune would finally end.]

Camp at Gloucester Point, Va.
April 24, 1864

Dear Bro:

The mail leaves at six and a half A.M. tomorrow. Therefore, although afflicted with a violent stomach ache, I took time spasmodically by the forelock and prepared an epistle for your enlightenment.

The stomach ache, I regret to say, is a consequence of reckless dissipation. We were confined to a salt diet so long on Folly Island that some of the men were attacked with scurvy. I escaped that, but my constitution became possessed of a deep seated hankering after flesh pots generally, a disease [in] which the symptoms are not ameliorated by the experiences of five days on shipboard. At sunrise this morning (before breakfast) I was detailed on fatigue at the docks. After a couple hours hard work, I came across some big oranges. Six fat fellow[s] were since successfully disposed of. A hot dried apple pie, manufactured by intelligent contraband, quickly followed. The next item was a huge tin pailful of bread and milk. Strengthened by these supplies, I returned to camp in time for dinner, which consisted of coffee, hardtack, and fried bacon (pretty confounded fat). This . . . was scarcely on route when a tentmate came in with some hot molasses, cakes, and cookies. Need I add that my adherence to Jeffersonian principles enabled me to partake of these delicacies? I have sent an agent to a country house for some eggs. If the stomach ache leaves me before he returns, I shall be intensely gratified.

You may have heard already that the Department of the South[1] has been abolitionized. Gilmore [sic] and the white troops have come north, leaving but a few Germans behind. The detachment of the 3rd at the Pawnee Landing was relieved by the 53rd [54th] Mass. (colored), about dusk on the evening of the 18th inst. In the midst of a pouring rain we struck our tents, made over our neat camp, with all its comforts, to the sable hero[e]s, and picked up our heavy knapsacks to try our luck against Richmond.

We arrived at the dock well drenched and, the steamer not being ready to take us aboard, passed the night in a large blacksmith's shop. The tools made a comfortable though rather a ropy bed. Early next morning we embarked on the old steamer Neptune for Hilton Head. A strong wind was blowing, and the sea was so rough that many pilgrimages were made to the side of the boat. Strings with chunks of pork attached were freely handed around as gifts but were rarely acceptable.

General William Farrar Smith *(Photograph Courtesy of the National Archives)*

We reached Port Royal in the afternoon and were at once transferred to the propeller[-driven steamboat] "Thames," a new vessel of English make captured while endeavoring to run the blockade. The men were stowed undercover between the decks and when sleeping lay crowded together in two double rows the entire length of the boat; thus the knobs [in the enclosed drawing—here deleted] represent heads and the verticle lines feet. Imagine yourself to be running the gauntlet down the long alley with feet kicking from both sides, and you will have a picture of the fellow's experience every night when he retires. At night, too, the men made a perfect pandemonium of the place with their hideous imitations of the bea[s]ts of the field and the fowls of the air. During the daytime they gambled without intermission.

We left Port Royal at noon on the 20th inst. The voyage to Fort Monroe was completed without accident on the morning of the 23rd. We did not land but were ordered to this place[2] and came without delay. Twenty one regiments landed here on the same day.

Last night we pitched our shelter tents and now are prepared for a campaign. I have cast away one of my blankets and kept only a change of clothing. Even my watch has been prepared for field service. With a hatchet and a file I manufactured a nicely fitting tin plate to insert in place of the crystal, so that the watch now has a hunting case. The tin came from an old milk can.

No one knows how large a force is to be amassed here, but it is supposed [to be] about 50,000. Baldy Smith[3] is at Yorktown, but McClellan may yet assume complete command. His arrival here would be greeted with immense enthusiasm and would establish perfect confidence in the success of the movements—an important consideration with [the] government. We shall probably be organized, inspected, received, and drilled here in division movements before seriously advancing. Our new brigade consists of the 89th, the 3rd, the 142nd, the 117th N.Y. V., and the 40th Mass. Vol[s]. Colonel Alford commands the brigade, General Turner the 3rd Division.[4] Every man is to be provided with two pairs of shoes. We are to be drilled eight hours a day.

Why are we not at the Yorktown side of the river? I do not know. The rebel guerillas are within three miles of us. They sneak up to the lines [and] pick off our wood choppers, while full regiments are sent on picket, and for three days at a time.

Dress parade is near. Take care of yourself.

Yours in haste,
Ed K. W.

West Point, Va.
May 1, 1864

Dear Bro:

I wrote to you in arriving at Gloucester Point, opposite Yorktown. We remained there until yesterday, drilling three hours per day as skirmishers; for it was rumored that the 3rd Division was to be used as the advance guard of the corps. Gloucester Point is fortified with a large fort and other strong earth works. You may remember that the oysters of this neighborhood are famous. Your correspondent has not forgotten it. The correspondent and two tentmates disposed of two gallons of raw and stewed in two successive days. The hard ground, green grass, blossoming trees, and budding flowers and, above all, the pure clean water of Virginia, has [sic] transformed us into new men and made us better soldiers by fifty per cent. . . .

Night before last we suddenly received orders to cook four days rations and be ready to move at a moment's notice. On Saturday morning [April 30] we were "mustered" at 6 A.M. and shortly after struck tents and moved toward the landing. We were made to turn in all our woolen blankets and dress coats and to throw away everything but a simple changes [sic] of underclothes, an over-coat, and rubber blankets. Sixty rounds of cartridges were issued per man. I have no rubber blanket and can draw none at present but shall manage to wag along without.

Late on Saturday afternoon the whole brigade was shipped on four transports. We lay at anchor all night in the stream [the York River] and at sunrise on Sunday morning started under the escorts of two gun boats. The landing was effected at the dock at West Point[5] at ten and a half A.M. in the midst of fifteen torpedoes which Johnny Reb had carefully prepared for us. Fifty three of these interesting trifles are scattered around in the vicinity, some buried in the earth and others part[ly] submerged in the water. A couple of our lieutenants have found four of them, which are now at the Colonel's tents, undergoing the inspection of the curious. They are conical shaped, weigh about twenty pounds, and contain fifteen pounds of gun powder each. They were discovered through the agency of Union contraband.

We may remain here a couple of days but may instead advance toward White House as soon as practicable. There appear to be no rebs near at present, though it is said that two regiments of their cavalry retreated just previous to our arrival.

I have scrawled this hastily by candlelight to get it away in the letter bag early tomorrow morning.

> In haste, yours truly,
> Ed K. W., First Brigade
> 3rd Division, 10th A. C.
> Fortress Monroe, Va.

P.S. I have sent home a box of books by Express and [an] explanatory letter by mail. Enclosed is the Express receipt.

> Ed

> West Point, Va.
> Sunday, May 1st[6]

Arrived at the dock about noon from Gloucester Point, marched northward a mile and a half, and encamped in shelter tents behind the earth works thrown up during McClellan's [1862] operations on the penninsula [sic].

Monday, May 2. Early this morning, while drilling as skirmishers, the Regiment was ordered back to camp, provided with one day's rations and sixty rounds of cartridges, and sent out on a reconnaissance; knapsacks were left behind and tents remained standing. We advanced ten miles beyond the outpost, in the direction of White House. Within seven miles of King William's Courthouse we halted and returned. The road over which we marched was hard and level and lined on either side by dense woods which cast their cool shade upon us nearly all the way. Many of the trees were in blossom, and the scenery throughout appeared wonderfully fresh when contrasted with the scanty vegetation of Folly Island. It is already so warm here in the middle of the day that the heat is oppressive. We miss the cool breeze of the sea.

A number of neat farm houses were passed on the route, and the fields generally show the presence of farm laborers. Col. Hill of the rebel army[7] owns the largest of these places—unluckily, when about five miles from camp a thunderstorm overtook us, so that, as a climax to our opening march of the season (20 miles), we were thoroughly drenched with rain and were plastered with mud to the knees. In this lamentable condition we reached the front steps of our dog houses shortly after dark. The tents were already soaked and leaking, and for an hour the men could only amuse themselves by laughing at each other's misery and by hooting across the company streets whenever the Boreas [i.e., north winds] carried away a new shanty. Finally, however, the storm passed and those who had dry clothes got into them. I had half a suit in reserve and dried the rest by toasting myself before a roaring fire. Made some hot coffee and got into bed shortly after midnight.

Tuesday, May 3. Roused before daybreak and ordered to dry clothes and prepare arms and equipment for inspection at 10 A.M., when we were reviewed by Col. Henry of the 40th Mass., commanding the Brigade.[8] (Alford, still at Gloucester Point, [temporarily] commands the Division). It is now reported that the movement of our Brigade is only a feint and that the main expedition goes up the James River. At 4 P.M. took knapsack, tent, and one day's rations and went on outpost duty. Up all night looking for Johnny Reb.

Wednesday, May 4. On picket all day at a contraband hut in the woods—hut built of logs plastered with clay, chimney ditto. Nigs all gone. No fire allowed. At 4 P.M. we were relieved from picket and returned to camp. Scarcely had we finished our supper of hard tack and coffee, however, when an orderly galloped up, bringing instructions for us to strike tents immediately and embark on the steamers at the dock. Our feint is successful. The enemy are reported near in force. Ten minutes sufficed to put us in motion, but we were not ready to start down the River until next morning.

Thursday, May 5. Left West Point just before sunrise. The rebs had followed us, and they fired with two field pieces at the last transport and at the gunboats, and we steamed down the river past Gloucester Point and Yorktown to Newport News, where we put in for coal. No coal was to be had, so we returned to Fortress Monroe for a supply. There we learned that our destination was Harri-

son's Landing on the James River, whither the troops from the neighborhood
of Yorktown had already gone. Twenty seven transports went up last night.
Hampton Roads is alive with steamers and sailing vessels of all sorts and sizes.
Left Fortress Monroe at dusk, sailed a few miles up the river, and anchored till
daylight for fear of torpedoes.

Friday, May 6. Sailed by Harrison's Landing and stopped at City Point[9] at
ten and a half A.M. The river at this place was crowded with steamers and
gunboats. New York itself could not have equaled the display. Most of the
troops were already ashore.

We landed and advanced about six miles towards Petersburg. Our course lay
on the south side of the James River, the 10th Army Corps having the inner
road and the 18th marching on the flank. As the heat of the sun increased the

General Benjamin F. Butler *(Photograph courtesy of the Library of Congress)*

men began to cast away their clothing until finally the way became lined and paved with blankets, overcoats, shoes, boots, cups, pans, plates, and even knapsacks and haversacks. Property valued at thousands of dollars was thus recklessly thrown away. I have not seen such sacrifices made even in haste in disorderly retreat. When we were ready to pitch camp, I returned to the road and picked up an axe to cut poles for the tent, a good rubber blanket, and a new woolen one to sleep on.

There being a couple of hours to spare before dark, I started out to a day's washing, but I had hardly got the clothes into soak when a man came to tell me that I had been detailed for picket and was wanted in camp. The picket is mounted with knapsacks, packs, shelter tents in the flaps. The clothes were hastily jammed in accordingly, a hot supper left behind, a letter from home hastily snatched up, and, thus prepared, Wightman took up his march to the banks of the James. . . .

Saturday, May 7. Returned to camp at 4 A.M. and struck tents to advance. Advanced a mile and stopped. Rebs reported in front in force. We are digging rifle pits. The Division, "now commanded by Brig. Gen. Turner," lies encamped in shelter tents in line of battle. It is reported that Col. Spears [Spear][10] has taken Petersburg (eight miles from us) with 10,000 cavalry, and they sent for infantry reinforcements. Baldy Smith, Lop Eye[11] Butler, Gilmore, six monitors and several gunboats are with us.

Camp near Petersburg, Va.
May 11, 1864

"Z'all right." You have a diary of events up to Saturday, the 7th inst. On that day, after my letter had been mailed, a detachment of Union troops was sent out to break up the Petersburg and Richmond Railroad, in order to cut off Lee's reinforcements and supplies. The movement was successful, but we were sturdily resisted and lost between 400 and 500 men in killed and wounded. The rebel loss is unknown but was probably equal to our own. At one time there seemed to be promise of a general engagement. Our Brigade was formed in line of battle and awaiting the order to advance when the enemy retired.[12]

On Sunday nothing occurred to disturb our serenity; but on Monday morning we were turned out at three o'clock, provided with one day's rations of hard tack and raw pork and, encumbered only with haversacks and canteens, started off upon a new raid. At first it was supposed to be an independent affair; but we soon discovered that two entire army corps were in motion. The 18th was to threaten Petersburg on the south and east while the 10th pushed its way, under Gilmore's direction, around the southern shore of the James River until it completely severed the rebel communications with Richmond.

Our division, the 2nd, commanded by Gen. Turner, struck [the] Richmond and Petersburg Railroad about 10:00 A.M. at Chester's Station, distance thirteen miles from the rebel capital and nine miles from Petersburg. The other two divisions, under Ames[13] and Terry, were on our flanks. Field artillery was at once posted on commanding eminences, and the infantry [ar]ranged in line of battle. The 3rd was stationed on a little hill parallel with the road. While these dispositions were being made and pickets thrown out, the pioneers and engineers set about burning the depot and tearing up the track. Huge bonfires were made of the ties upon which the iron rails were heated and warped. We then started down the track toward Petersburg, discharging [rifles] as we went. For miles along the route we pulled down the fences and, piling the wood over the rails, set fire to it. We seized upon rails and poles for levers and, working in unison, the multitude heaved up 200 feet of iron rails and wooden ties together and forced the unwieldy masses over the side of the road and down the steep embankment. Sometimes the track was merely hoisted, flop[ped] over, and left to be used by Johnny Reb with the ties up.

To this point the only resistance we had experienced was a sharp fire from rebel skirmishers, who retreated before us firing. At four miles from Petersburg we came upon the battlefield of Saturday, strewn with dead rebels and broken [fire]arms. A little further on we met with the enemy's earth works. They were at once assaulted.[14] Ames' Division was engaged all the afternoon. For a long time we were held in reserve, listening to the rapid rolling firing of musketry and the roar of field artillery. But at length the order came for the Brigade to advance, and we marched up the turnpike,[15] almost smothered in a cloud of dry dust and steaming with perspiration from the heat of the sun. Men suffering from sunstroke were lying in the ditch while others bathed their temples with water. The wounded were borne hurridly [sic] by on stretchers and walked painfully along, resting on the shoulders of comrades. Some were fearfully mangled, but all quieted us with a "go in, boys" or "sock it to em, my hardies."

The Brigade was brought into line in a plowed field bordered by pine woods, each batallion [sic] being formed in column on its center division, with orders to deploy in line after passing through the wood in front. We were then to charge over a broad field upon a fort defended by half a dozen guns. While the preceding brigade was working its way onward, we entered the wood and lay down to avoid the percussion of shells which howled over us, exploding against the trees. In a field on our left, where the rebs had rashly charged us, their dead were lying three deep. Our ambulance men and drummers[16] and surgeons now began to assist in bringing off and attending to our wounded.

At this point, serious as the condition of things appeared, a ludicrous incident brought forth a loud and long peal of laughter. A dozen or fifteen contrabands (officers' servants) had enscounced [sic] themselves in the bushes a few yards to the left, thinking they were out of range of the enemy's guns. There they lay flat on their faces, as quiet as mice, one directly behind another. Suddenly a rebel messenger [i.e., a shell] came rushing along, screeching like ten thousand banshees, close to the ears of the deluded darkies. Every man of them popped up like a "jack-in-the-box" and, grabbing off his cap, raced away as if trying to keep ahead of the ball. It was about the tallest time I ever saw made by bipeds. The whites of their eyes protruded awfully, and the wool of their fellow citizens was almost straightened out with fright.

Night came and the firing ceased; swallowing the last of our raw pork, we threw ourselves down with our arms beside us, without overcoat or blanket or tent or fire, and slept. Fifteen miles of marching, together with the railroad work and the watching, had made us drowsy. At midnight, Johnny Reb fiercely assaulted our lines; a continuous heavy rattling of musketry, gradually drawing near through the darkness, wakened us and brought us to our feet. Two regiments in front had revolving rifles and used them so effectively that the secesh took a big think and went back. The 22nd South Carolinian [sic] Infantry, lately from James Island, was the special recipient of Union favors and was very roughly used indeed. The cheers of our men announced the result, but there was no more sleep for us; we were drenched with dew and chilled to the marrow of our bones.

Daylight [on May 10] came, and with it a report that Lee was in Richmond and was sending down troops to attack us in the rear.[17] At about 9 o'clock, therefore, Gilmore withdrew his men and formed a new line of battle across the railroad, a position which was maintained until afternoon, when all returned to camp, no enemy having shown himself. Our brigade acted as rear guard and did not reach home until sunset.

Once out of the dust and heat of the road we cast off our military harness and rushed for the brook. A good refreshing wash made new men of us. We sat down in the doorway of our dark houses, drank smoking hot coffee, crunched hard tack, took a bedoozling smoke and chatted and laughed for an hour over the incidents of our raid—then enveloped ourselves comfortably in our overcoats and lay down to pleasant dreams.

As I write this, Spears is marching by our camp with 8,000 cavalry. Reports say that he has come up from North Carolina, destroying the railroad by the way.[18] "E Pluribus Unum," so that [the] capture of Petersburg is then superfluous to a fancy job, and the war will end in Richmond.

I know nothing positive about the situation of affairs at present but presume the ideas [sic] is to capture the two railroads which furnish Lee supplies, at Lynchburg and Petersburg.[19] Lee will then be forced to fall back, with a column on each flank and Grant [and Meade] in the rear. He may throw his whole force upon us here in order to break through into the Carolinas or upon Lynchburg to join the army of the southwest. . . .[20]

Ed. K. W.

P. S. The 18th Corps are playing away with their siege guns. Our loss in the late railroad raid has not transpired. It was probably not heavy.

There are hundreds of acres in this part of the country plowed and planted but no male laborers visible.

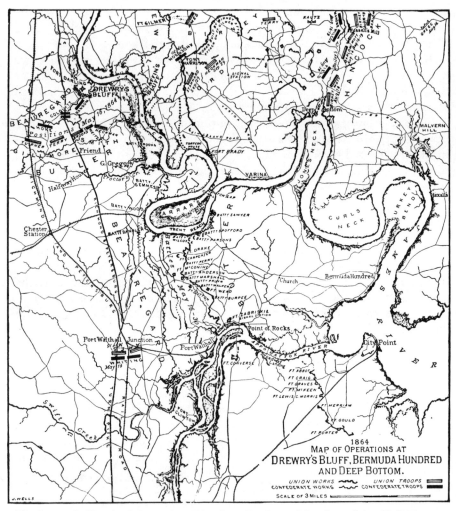

The Bermuda Hundred Campaign (*Map from* Battles and Leaders of the Civil War)

Camp near Petersburg. Va.
Tuesday, May 17, 1864

Home again safe and well without a scratch and in first rate spirits, after five days of almost continual fighting of the roughest exposure.

On Tuesday last [actually, Thursday, May 12] before daybreak, in common with the whole army, we left camp and moved toward Richmond. We had no breakfast and took with us neither tents, knapsacks, nor overcoats. I had no rubber blanket, even. Nothing but a thin blouse as a protection against inclement weather and the heavy night dews. A heavy thunder shower drenched us at the start, and for two nights and three days following the rain kept pouring down upon us as we fought our way onward, skirmishing through the dripping underbrush, fording streams and wading through.

Our brigade had the advance, and we had no sooner left Butler's main line of earthworks than the 3rd was deployed as skirmishers and pushed forward. The first rebs we met were three calvary venditties [vedettes], posted in the road. They shouted, "Halt," and fired.[21] Simultaneously, my neighbor on the right and I dropped on one knee, and a charge of buckshot whizzed over us. I saw nothing, but he, being in the road, got a full view and snapped a couple of [percussion] caps at them. Half a mile further we came upon their skirmishers and [came] under [a] rattling fire of musketry and shells. But we wheeled up a couple of pieces of field artillery, a couple of batallions [sic] swept by the flank in line, and Johnny Reb scadaddled [sic]. Our skirmishers then assembled and deployed in a new direction, taking up a defensive position. Let me make a rough drawing of it [deleted] for you.

I have already told you of the incapacity of our officers. In the present state of affairs they were merely an incumbrance [sic]. Their labors were limited to scaling themselves behind trees and shouting, "Go in, boys, give it to em!" Suddenly the whole brigade of rebels came yelling up in the direction of one four and one [on the enclosed drawing], threatening to annihilate us, for we had only about one hundred men at the fences. The captain commanding the line, AA, having been shot through the coat tail, ordered his men to fall back over the open field on the reserve. His men were so exasperated at his cowardice that one of them fired at him.

I was behind a zig zag fence and, of course, became exposed at once to infiltrating fire and one from the rear. We were ordered to fall back to the position BB under cover of the woods and did so at a double quick but in good order, although many a stout fellow dropped by the way. There we halted to take [a] breath. The reserve advanced and delivered a volley at the yelling rebs and, seeing a company of the 89th [New York] advancing toward the position AA, we sprang over the fence in front and charged over the field again, admidst [sic] a storm of bullets, to our old position.

For five or ten minutes we . . . pegged away with might and main; but then the 89th gave way and exposed us again to a terrific crossfire. Good golly! How the lead whistled through our hair! It was the heaviest musketry fire I ever was under. Had we been massed instead of being deployed, we must have fallen to a man. As it was, the tumbling appeared to be too frequent to be a pleasant feature.

Again we rallied in the woods and this time to some purpose. Below [in another sketch—deleted] is the position. This time we were supported by a second line of skirmishers and by several batallions [sic] formed in line of battle. We saw the preparations of the rebs and knew the receptions that was [sic] [a]waiting us. Our Lt. Col. [Floyd], with remarkable stupidity, halted us at FF on an open ground and not thirty paces from the edge of the woods, and there we remained for three or four minutes as though brought up and respectfully submitted as a sacrifice. The next instance [*sic*], bending low, we rushed for the wood and were saluted with a thundrous [*sic*] crash of rifles. Strangely enough, scarcely a man was hit. We threw ourselves flat upon our faces, yelled out a defiance and then made our muskets talk as fluently as country gossips.

A creek and swamp were found in front of us, and the undergrowth was so thick that secesh stood within twenty paces of us and fired. Seeing nothing, we aimed only at flash and sound. Alternately, Johnny Reb yelled and we replied. As time passed we regarded the fire as [no] more than if it had been harmless, though the balls shot by like hailstones. My tentmate, Sgt.[Benjamin D.] Todd, and I, reclining on our left elbows, fired for two hours without shifting our position. Todd had lost his rammer in the previous engagement, and so mine had to serve us both. During all this time a jolly little bird sat perched in a tree over our heads, hidden in a cloud of smoke but chirping away as though he were singing for dear life. At dark the 89th New York relieved us. When about to retire I picked the enclosed flower to send to the girls as a momento of the "bedoozling" occasion.

While the rebs were thus amused in front, two brigades of Union troops trotted down on their flanks and captured the turnpike, preparatory to a further advance. This was where the laugh came in. Johnny Reb fell back during the night. The 3rd Regiment retired a little and, heartily fatigued with the labors of the day, flopped down in the mud and, with the rain still falling upon them, slept. All day long our clothes had been saturated and our muskets dripping.

At about two o'clock in the morning [of May 13] most of us awoke, chilled and chattering, [and] with the permission of the general commanding built little fires to toast ourselves by. The rain continued. In the afternoon the army moved up the turnpike, directing its course between Fort Darling[22] and Richmond. Night found the 3rd Regiment posted as pickets and reserve in the woods in front of the heavy line of rebel earthworks—the rain still falling and the hostile firing being incessant. No sleep [for] the second night. Saturday morning [the 14th] smiled favorably upon us. During the darkness the enemy's flank had been turned, and their strong [outer] works were now necessarily abandoned. They were at once occupied, and lines of battle pushed on to assault other entrenchments.

The First Brigade was in the front line and under our artillery fire all day. The 3rd Regiment during the forenoon lay upon their faces, under cover of the wood opposite a rebel fort, as support to our skirmishers, losing a man occasionally as the grape and cannister [*sic*] dropped among us. In the afternoon we were sent out to skirmish ourselves and drove the rebs from our front into their breastworks, afterwards picking off their gunners. We approached over open ground to within three hundred yards of them, cheering until we were hoarse, and got in return a rattling volley which made us bob our noses into the ground in a terrible hurry.

After dark we were relieved and went back to an old secesh encampment—

probably the winter quarters of General Clingham's [Thomas L. Clingman's] brigade—at least so I might infer from the enclosed paper, picked up there. The place resembles the school book pictures of the first Virginia settlement, with its log houses and so forth. We were quartered under little shelters constructed by rebs out of pine shingles. It still rained.

On Sunday we rested, the firing ceased and quiet reigned. On Monday morning [the 16th] before daylight, the rebs opened on us. They had received reinforcements from their capital[23] and had commenced an assault under cover of a fog, which enabled them to advance within a few paces of our line undiscovered and at the same time prevented us from sending in our batteries. The Third arose, rubbed their eyes, buckled on their belts, seized their muskets and layed [sic] down in front of their houses to await the attack; for the skirmishers belonging to the 6th [Connecticut] command were already scadaddling [sic] in.

The first thunder was a solid twelve pound shot which struck one of the men on the top of the head, covering several of us with a shower of sand. Showers of grape and cannister [sic] quickly followed, and the number of stragglers increased. Gen. Turner came up and ordered us to the front, and to the front we went, sweeping in line around the old log houses and bearing down at a double quick upon the works from which the rebs had just driven our troops. They consisted of a log barrier in front of pine woods. The rebs met us with a volley that laid some low. The rest ducked, cheered, and rushed on so rapidly that Johnny could hardly wait to receive our fire before he cut sticks and fled. Reaching the entrenchments, we hurrahed until we were hoarse. Other regiments followed and took positions on our right.

Ten minutes later a new assault was made by the enemy in overwhelming force. The line to the right of us was pierced, and the rebel colors planted there.[24] On the left our troops gave way, panic stricken, and whole regiments sped away over the field in retreat. Both our flanks were thus exposed, and infiltrating fire came plunging in upon us. The Lt. Col., "Floyd," commanding us, ordered us to retire, but the men only stood still and cheered and shouted to the broken troops on our left to return and protect the flank. They paused, reformed, and came back shouting. Floyd dropped, shot through the leg, and was carried away. A determined fire to the front drove the enemy back, and a few volunteer skirmishe[r]s followed them into the woods as an alarm guard. Meanwhile, the rebs advanced on the right and cut off our retreat. This was the position [shown in the enclosed sketch—deleted].

The brigade was suddenly faced to the rear and ordered to fall back on the run. I was in the woods when the start was made but with a little extra speed managed to regain my place in the ranks. The rebs saw us leave and let fly at us with a will. Their shots told fearfully. Among the rest, Sgt. Todd, my tentmate, "a member of the old 9th," fell, pierced through the head. This I have just heard from one who saw him. He was a good man and a sturdy soldier.

From one line of field works to another we retired, fighting all the way, the men dropping at every step. General Turner was present, arranging the retreat with wonderful coolness. Everything was done in perfect order. The rebs did not pursue. Our regiment remained in the rear as skirmishers until dark, when we returned to camp with[in] those works which Butler promised to hold against all of Lee's army.[25]

Of the general result of the expedition I can say nothing for I know nothing. I think our lapses were not severe, but that little artillery could be used. The enemy must have suffered more than we, for we were the attacking party. Our men have lost nothing in spirit, but are as full of fight as ever. The works here are [sic] immensely strengthened during our absence.

The Third took out two hundred and fifty men, of whom sixty three were killed and wounded.[26] The men, for raw troops, behaved with great gallantry. General Turner said the Third was "worth its weight in gold . . ."

In haste, yours truly,
Ed. K. W.

P.S. Have heard of Grant's successes.[27] Been feeding on raw meat for nearly a week. There are but seven men and three sergeants left in H Company fit for duty.

Camp at Bermuda Hundreds, Va.[28]
Monday, May 23, 1864

Dear Bro:

After a lapse of several days we have come again into possession of our tents and knapsacks. Writing materials are at hand, and the mailbag is once more accessible.

I have already told you of the advance to within eight miles of Richmond, of the skirmish at Proctor's Creek, of the battle at Palmer's Creek [Drewry's Bluff], and of our retreat to the old position at Bermuda Hundred. The rebels followed us slowly in force but were checked as soon as they drew near to the rifle pits in front of our position. At present we occupy a triangular space, flanked by the James and by the Appomatox [sic] River[s] and protected by strong earthworks in front. We have gunboats in both rivers. The entrenchments, high and thick, built of red clay, are of very formidable character. The woods have been cut away in front to give free play to our batteries, which frown on the rebs from every point of the line. Along the three miles of parapet it is said to be difficult to find a distance of 30 yards between two guns. In addition, there are redoubts and, of course, rifle pits and so forth in front. The gunboats cannot play directly across, because the banks are so high, but they are useful to shell the enemy's camps and to prevent the erection of hostile batteries on the neighboring eminences and bluffs. In case of defeat (extremely improbable) we can fall back to the landing under cover of the gunboats and cross [the Appomattox] on three pontoon bridges already laid. We have an abundance of troops to man the works, and our position is regarded as almost impregnable. Johnny Reb has conceived a great respect for it. He had quite a lively confab with the Union's artillery the other evening and went away like as unto one who has seen the point.

Johnny assaulted our rifle pits in force last Thursday[29] and captured them easily. I was on guard in camp and heard the row. The musketry fire, broken by occasional splurges of light artillery, rolled around steadily from left to right. We were under arms at once, of course, as we have been every day and night since our return. On Friday afternoon the 13th Indiana was sent out to recover the lost ground but was received by a thundering volley from the whole rebel brigade and almost annihilated. The 97th Pennsylvania and 9th Maine Regiments then advanced in turn, supported by artillery, and were very roughly handled. But the rifle pits on our right and center were thus retaken. On Friday night the 3rd was ordered out to help strengthen the works and shoveled until long after daybreak. . . .[30]

At 10 o'clock on Saturday [Friday] night Johnny Grayback attempted a big thing by moonlight, coming up in the most chippery style towards our breast works with infantry, artillery, and cavalry.[31] Well, sir, it would have done you good to have seen us sock it to him. Jeru-salem! How our batteries crashed and roared and rattled out their crossfire of solid shot and shell and whirling grape, drowning alike the hearty cheers of our men and the yells of the [Southern] chivalry. The chivalry went back to look into the cost of the joke and have not troubled us since. One of their caisons [sic] was blown up, but they are dubious as to whether that was where the laugh came in. One of their big generals (Walker) was wounded and captured.

From this you will see that we are under arms almost constantly and liable to be attacked at any moment. Of late we have bivoucked [sic] for five days at a time without tents, overcoats, or blankets, and on half rations, returning to camp only to wash and obtain a change of clothing. Still, there can scarcely be said to be a sick list. The men are in remarkably good health and spirits.

The worst of this experience . . . seems now, however, to be over for a time. Last night the regiment[s] of our brigade moved their camps into the woods back of the entrenchments, so that hereafter we may sleep in our tents. We are posted on the center and right of the line. . . . Since last night we have moved our tents twice. An order has just come to move again. So we go. So long.

Ed K. W.

P. S. Rebel force in front estimated at 30,000 to 50,000. Butler at 25,000 to 30,000.[32] We are pretty well posted as to Grant's movements. The papers come regularly. The danger seems to be that the army [Army of the Potomac] will dash its brains out against the wall of Richmond.

Camp at Bermuda Hundred, Va.
May 26, 1864

Dear Bro:

There is no news of importance from this point, no fighting to speak of since my last. Indeed, our works are so strong that it is doubtful whether anything less than the whole of Lee's army will ever again venture to move against them. Still, we are very busy with improvements. Twelve hours a day, when not detailed for picket, each regiment works with pick and shovel, building batteries and forts and throwing up along the line huge entrenchments of red clay. The labor is exhausting, for the ground is almost as hard as slate, and no time is allowed us to wash and to mend.

We have a splendid corps of engineer officers. The works are admirable, and we have perfect confidence in their strength and in our ability to hold them. The extra fatigue, however, tells on some of the men. Today only 120 of the men (non-commissioned officers included) are reporting for duty in the whole regiment. Your correspondent is pleased to be able to add that he counts [as] one. The rebs are within rifle shot distance of the entrenchments, and their sharp shooters, when so disposed, amuse themselves by picking off the laborers—but this is not often.

Today, being on camp guard, I have a chance to write a few words. The hurrying up of the fortifications is accounted for by a report that Gilmore, with his (our) corps, is to return south as soon as they can be completed and the safety of the 18th Corps assured in this position. Butler has issued a special order announcing . . . the latest successes of Grant. Lee is in full retreat and so forth.[33]

We got a good joke on a reb the other night. Lately there has been but little picket firing, by mutual consent. As a consequence the picket men of the two armies sometimes mingle together, going for water to the same spring, exchanging greetings, and so on. The night of the 24th was dark. A relief [force] composed of the men of the 169th [New York] went out, and when they had been halted at the outposts were astonished to hear a strange voice continue, "Front, Right Dress!" A mistaken rebel lieutenant was trying to command Union soldiers, supposing them to be his own guard. Our fellows politely invited the crestfallen "ham" to wait and see our officers give orders. He did so.

At present we average only half a night's rest, being regularly turned out under arms at 3 o'clock A.M. Last night a rattling fire of musketry awakened us about 12, and quite a squad of rebel bullets were deployed over our tents. But nothing followed and we went to sleep again.

The newspapers come to camp two days after they are published, so that we manage to keep pretty well posted. The rebel loss in their last night attack is now estimated at between 500 and 600 in killed and wounded, and ours trifling. In haste,

Yours truly,
Ed K. W.

White House, Va.
May 31, 1864

Dear Bro:

We have just changed base again, as you can see. On Thursday evening last [May 26] we suddenly struck tents and moved camp about a mile back from the entrenchments at Bermuda Hundred. On Saturday at sunset, in common with the rest of our division and the 18th Army Corps,[34] we packed up and crossed the Appomatox [sic] River on a pontoon bridge and marched to City Point.

As usual it rained like the mischief. On the bridge the water was in some places ankle deep. The clay mud on the roads ditto. Our path lay through dense pine woods over a new cut road, thick set with stumps. The night was one of those cases of "darkness invisible" which Milton talks about. We had no lanterns, and the men slipped and stumbled and splashed and staggered along under the heavy load of knapsack, haversack, tents and equipment, finding their way only by placing their hands on the knapsacks of those who preceeded [sic] them.

At 11 P.M. we halted and bivouaced [sic] in a wheat field. On Sunday we were up before daylight [and] embarked during the forenoon on the steamer Varina [Varuna] for White House. We remained in the stream at anchor until Monday morning, before starting. After spending two days and two night[s] aboard, enjoying a pleasant deck passage (for the James and the York are pretty rivers), we landed here this (Tuesday) morning.

Another change has been made in the place of the 3rd Regiment. It is now [temporarily] assigned to the 3rd Brigade, 3rd Division, 18th Army Corps. Letters will be directed accordingly. Gen. Gilmore is with the 1st and 3rd Division of the 10th Corps [and] remains, it is said, at Bermuda Hundred. Baldy Smith and Ames are our new commanders.[35]

Col. Alford disgraced himself by remaining out of the battle at Palmers' Creek and leaving his brigade to be maneuvered by Gen. Turner. It is now reported that he has offered his resignation. Our senior captain (John H. Fay, of Morisania, formerly of the Baby 7th of N.Y.[36]) was so badly frightened during our raid against Petersburg [May 7–8] that he pretended to be sunstruck while walking through a shady pine forest in the morning just after sunrise. The doctor saw nothing the matter with him, but Fay knew there was hard fighting ahead and tendered his resignation. The upshot of it all was he was dismissed from the service in disgrace. The next officers [sic] in rank is Capt. [Alexander A.] Mann (a notorious coward), who at present commands the batallion [sic]. When sent out a few days since to skirmish with the rebs, he mysteriously disappeared from the men of his company and though they remained out for several hours could not be found until they were relieved or about to return. The third in rank, Capt. [James H.] Wicks, was fired on by his men for running away from Proctor's Creek.

The rest are pretty much cut of a piece. Lt. Hose [John W. Hoes] of H Company, when rebs are near, generally turns the brass wreath of his felt hat (a good mark [for the enemy]) to the rear and then, enscouncing [sic] himself behind a stump or tree, shouts, "give it to 'em, boys," and so forth. The hat is a perfect weather cock. I always watch it, as it is an index of danger near. But all this is as contemptible as it is ridiculous. The men despise their officers thoroughly and purposely insult them almost daily. It is hoped that we may soon be consolidated with another regiment.

It is reported today that Grant has broken Lee's center and is making [haste] into Richmond with the retreating rebs. We cannot believe it. . . .[37] I have just returned from a jolly swim in the muddy Pamunkey River, the first of the season. The river swarms with transports and barges. Many of the troops were landed at West Point and marched up on the other side of the river. We have an abundance of shovels and picks along. Precise destination unknown. Orders: "three days rations, 60 rounds of cartridges, and be ready to move at a moment's notice." Hancock[38] is said to be only seven miles distant, and it is supposed that we are to work on his left. White House is to be the base of supplies for Grant.

Mary's photograph received and acknowledged long ago. It is very good. Just found a splendid magnolia [clipping], hard to get in the letter. In haste

Ed K. W.

White House, Va.
Thursday, June 1st [2nd], 1864

Dear Bro:

You see that we are still at White House Landing; but as the other troops of our Corps, the 18th, have advanced and have been fighting today I thought I would write. The wounded are just now returning in ambulances. All day long the heavy guns in the front have been growling like angry bears. At six and a half P.M. the fire has not slackened. We don't know whether it comes from Burnside or Gilmore.[39] Rumor says that Gilmore, finding the enemy's rifle pits were manned only by the citizens of Richmond, that all of Beauregard's forces had gone to reinforce Lee, boldly pushed forward and captured a large number of the recruits together with a few field guns and then rush[ed] on to the attack of Fort Darling. The heavy firing today is accounted for on the supposition that the commander of the James' fleet is rattling away at the fort.

Grant, it is said, has [had] another terrific battle, punished Lee badly, and taken up a new position within four miles of Richmond. Perhaps it is true, perhaps not.[40] Four hundred wagons are on the other side of the Pamunkey at this point, [a]waiting the completion of a bridge. Our men are working on it like beavers. The wagons are loaded with supplies and forwarded on at once to Grant. Our brigade will act as escorts. We will probably start tomorrow. The train was attacked a couple of days ago by 900 secesh cavalry. They were driven back with heavy loss; defeated by our cavalry dismounted.[41]

[Major General] Fitzhugh Lee with 9,000 cavalry was reported to be cut-off from his friends in Richmond and to be mediating [sic] a raid on the few troops here. Accordingly we were called up last night after tatoo [sic] and made to dig rifle pits around our camps and down to the banks of the river. With the river in our rear and with the position of our gunboats, we hope[d] to be able to hold the position and turn the tables on him, but he did not appear. Reinforcements, black and white, have been pouring in all day. They will relieve us.

Alford is relieved of the command of the brigade and has gone to Fortress Monroe, and I do not expect him to return. Old Gunpowder Fairchilds of the 89th taunted him to his face with being a "sneak, rascal," and so forth.

Squads of grayback prisoners have been a common sight that we are tired of looking at. They appear as tough and wirey [sic] as ever but rather bewildered and by no means so confident [as before]. Some of them expect that the fall of their capital will close the war. Good!

The Regiment has gone out on picket. I am on camp guard and remain. An old member of Company B of the 9th has been here this afternoon—says he is employed as a citizen in the "Construction Corps" for $2 a day and rations—is coming again tonight to bring me four loaves of "soft tack." Bully for him.

As there is nothing in particular to say and as I have already said it, will adjourn. Enclosed are some wild violets and other flowers for the girls from Bermuda Hundred. As ever in haste

Yours truly,
Ed. K. W.

P. S. The railroad to Hanover Junction[42] is to be rebuilt immediately. The men are already at work, and the locomotive is ready. New docks, too, are being built. The steamer Connecticut is here as a hospital boat. The agents of the Sanitary Commission[43] are as plenty as blackberries and have mountains of good things for the wounded. There is plenty of female nurses and so forth. They have the [a] steamer of their own on the river and are as energetic as Grant himself.

[P.] P. S. My collection of photographs is a grand thing. I wish I had the whole family complete.

Camp in the woods at Cole's [sic] Harbor
Tuesday, June 7, 1864

Dear Bro:

My last letter should have been dated June 2nd. On Friday last, the day after it was written, we struck tents, as usual in the midst of a rain storm, and started toward the front as an escort to the wagons of the 9th Army Corps. The escort comprised our entire brigade.

The captain commanding the 3rd [Mann] was so laggard in his motions that before he had reached the position assigned to him, a band of guerillas swooped down, killed a teamster and drove away from 15 to 20 horses. On coming up to the place, the captain, instead of sending out fresh men, ordered the rear guard to be deployed as skirmishers on the flank—a piece of unheard of stupidity. I speak rather feelingly in regard to this matter, because I was one of the guard itself, having already been on duty 36 hours and was now called upon to tramp with knapsacks through wet clover, pine woods, and over numerous hills and across ravines, for the remainder of the day. We were on guard, altogether, from [for] four successive days without being relieved.

On Saturday evening we reached the 9th Corps and left the wagons. As we pushed on to join the 18th, evidence of recent fighting became plenty—dead horses and mules by the roadside added their tribute to the odors wafted from the fragrant magnolias. Ambulances, creaking beneath their load of wounded who, bathed in bloody bandages, were crowded into them, dragged their slow lengths for miles. The bushes, right and left, had been slashed by shot and shell, and stout trees had fallen before the same resistless forces. At about 9

P.M. we halted, stacked arms and, with knapsacks for pillows and rubber blankets for covering, slept in defiance of the pelting storm.

Next morning [June 5] we went into the woods as reserves for the other regiments of the brigade, which occupied the rifle pits. The rebs shelled us with shrapnel all the forenoon but were finally silenced by one of our batteries. At night, an attack being expected, we went to the rifle pits, formed a second line of battle behind the works, and slept in our places in the ranks, with bayonets fixed and muskets beside us. At midnight the 3rd relieved some troops in the advanced rifle pits. We were in turn relieved last night (Monday) and for the first time in four days had a place assigned to us for a camp.

We have now become so used to sleeping any where and any way that we care little about the protection of a shelter tent. The holding of the rifle pits just now is not a very dangerous business; for they are strongly built and comparatively safe. Still, several of our men, owing partly to their own carelessness, were wounded. As I write, the rebs (confound them!) are shelling us again. The pickets skirmish incessantly. When we came up, we were supposed to occupy the front of the center, with Burnside's Corps behind us. But Grant has been shifting his men, one division at a time, from the center to the left, from right to center, until we are now said to hold the extreme right.[44] No charging is being made here. The rebs have taken a very strong position. We are fortified in front and apparently on the defensive, awaiting the action of the left flank, on the Chickahominy [River].

We now have to carry five days rations habitually—pack it in our knapsacks. This adds considerably to the weight of our trap[ping]s. Grant's siege train is ordered up, and some of the guns have already arrived. It may be that Lee will attack us again. If he does, we look for an assault on the right flank or a battle in the Swamp.

Your letter of May 24th is received, together with one from the girls of about the same date. No time to answer in detail. Shells are ripping around me at a terrible rate.

Yours truly,
Ed K. W.

P. S. We shall probably be in the pits again tonight. Much noise but little danger.

[P.] P. S. You will see that my time for writing is limited. We are not allowed to take off our belts or leave our stacks [of rifles] while in front of the pits. As nearly as I can judge, we are seven miles from Richmond on a direct line between White House and Mechanicsville.

Rifle pits at Cole's Harbor, Va.
June 11, 1864

Dear Bro:

Nothing of importance has happened in the immediate neighborhood since I last wrote. We live in the rifle pits. Shelter tents have come to be regarded as somewhat of history and tradition. The rebels are within easy rifle range of us, and the bullets whistle over us day and night as we sit behind the works. Since my last, one of our captains and several of the men have been hit.

Alford has offered his resignation and Baldy Smith refuses to accept it. I hope he may be kicked out of the service. His Adjutant General, a Lt. [Frank M.] Weaver, after sneaking [out of] a fight, resigned and managed to get away. Weaver was one of the model officers of the 3rd.

We have heard of the capture of Fort Darling with 40 guns and 8,000 prisoners, at the cost of 11,000 in killed and wounded; but I cannot believe it.[45]

The works in our neighborhood have been very much strengthened and several new batteries erected. . . . Here we have a perfect puzzle of earthworks; if Johnny Reb ever gets into this labyrinth, he'll wish he had never been born. At every step he will find himself entrapped in a new pit under [a] withering crossfire. All these entrenchments, too, are heavily manned. Grant's headquarters are about a mile and a half distant, and I don't know whether we are on the extreme right or not—neither do any of our officers. Our knowledge of affairs is very limited. . . .

We are comparatively quiet at this point. There is no charging on either side. Lee may attempt a terrific assault, as he did upon McClellan,[46] but unless he does, the siege of Richmond has virtually commenced. Grant is tightening the cord gradually but surely. If Lee butts his head against us here, he must knock his brains out.

In haste,
Ed K. W.

P. S. The cook has just come with the dinner and says that the 5th and 6th Army Corps [of the Army of the Potomac] have passed down towards Bottoms Bridge [on the Chickahominy] and that the 18th is to follow.

7
PETERSBURG

[Once again a gleaming triumph eluded the Army of the James, as Baldy Smith failed to capture Petersburg during his surprise attack of 15 June 1864. Three subsequent days of fighting south and east of the Cockade City, during which Lee's and Meade's armies reached the scene, ended in stalemate. Accordingly, both sides settled down to what promised to be a lengthy siege, replete with hardship and tragedy. In their rifle pits outside Petersburg, Edward (now a sergeant) and his cohorts endured days of sweltering heat, impenetrable dust, sniper fire, and shelling. More than once he became a target for sharpshooters and cannoneers, but each time came away with life, limb, and morale intact.

Late July brought the bungled offensive at the Crater Mine, where Edward's old commander, Ambrose E. Burnside, lost his career and many of his Ninth Corps troops their lives. Held in the rear as a supporting force, the Tenth Corps looked on helplessly as the fiasco unfolded. Edward vividly recorded the scene, as well as the other unsuccessful drives against Petersburg that followed throughout the summer. As autumn came in, he penned even more graphic accounts of the battles above the James River—Forts Harrison and Gilmer (September 29), and Second Fair Oaks (October 27).

During lulls in combat, he also wrote of more mundane subjects: the fraternization between enemy pickets, among whom the "greatest good feeling prevails"; the steady depletion of the Third New York (the regiment contained barely 130 men by early October); and the coming elections, which might decide the fate of the Union. Though sometimes believing Abraham Lincoln "criminally weak and undecided," Edward was never in doubt as to his course at the polls. When his regiment cast ballots in the field in advance of the election, he voted to sustain the President and the war effort.]

General Ulysses S. Grant *(Photograph courtesy of the National Archives)*

One and a half miles from
Petersburg, Va.
Thursday, June 16th, 1864

My dear boy,

For the past few days we have been on just the jolliest picnic you ever saw. Such Union charging and hurraying as there was yesterday and such rebel skadaddling [*sic*], it would have made you crazy to witness.

This morning I am sitting under the shade of a tree within the fire [first] line of works with the good city of Petersburg in plain view before me. General[s] Grant, Hancock, and Baldy Smith are on the same hill, and I have had a good view of all of them. Hancock and Smith are in tiptop spirits. Grant looks care worn but expresses surprise and gratification at the success of our advance. "I started last night," Baldy Smith remarked to him with a laugh, "but didn't expect to top the hills."[1]

On Sunday morning, (the 12th), the 1st [Second] Corps were withdrawn from the works at Cole's [sic] Harbor and marched down to White House, arriving at sunset, a 14 miles [sic] knapsack march. Other corps left at the same time, and the position was evacuated. The 18th embarked at midnight. On Tuesday morning we landed at Bermuda Hundred and on Tuesday night slept on one of our old camping grounds.

On Wednesday morning at two o'clock we formed a line and during the forenoon crossed the Appomatox [sic] on a pontoon bridge, to move against Petersburg. Meanwhile the other corps had come across the penninsula [sic] by land, and the 2nd and 9th were to act in concert with us. Our column first met the enemy in force in rifle pits two miles from [northeast of] the city. They were gallantly charged by the colored troops in the advance, driven out, and a piece of artillery captured.[2] We then pushed on and formed two lines of battle in the woods in front of a formidable line of entrenchments occupying high ground and strengthened by two forts defended by artillery. Here we lay until late in the day under the heavy fire of solid shot and shell.

In the afternoon I was thrown forward with others in the second line of skirmishers. We had nothing to do but to sit behind stumps and await developments, as a support to the first line. Our knapsacks had been left behind with a guard; but we had scarcely left them when the poor fellow was killed by a solid shot.

I had taken my Testament, with the family photographs, along to make sure of them, and now amuse[d] myself by watching the conduct of you fellows under fire. When a solid shot came teeming through the underbrush, I fixed my eye on Charles. With all the impertability [sic] of a philosopher he seemed to take it as a pleasant illustration of "the velocity of forces." A shell came shrieking by. Mary apparently had hard work to keep her sober face. She seemed bursting with repressed giggles. Bullets whistled crossways over the top of the stump. . . . Jim, alone, appeared to be bewildered by the confusion of sound, but all did very well indeed for recruits for the first time under fire.

At sunset I was arranging my haversack to "take tea" when the order was suddenly given to advance. [Sergeant] Rogers had gone back into the woods with our canteens for water, leaving his musket in my care. I waited a moment, irresolute [about] what to do, but [in] a moment decided. Handing the extra rifle to a man who seemed disinclined to start, I sent up my war cry and sprang forward. In front and from the right and left the rebs poured in a torrent of grape shot and shells while the rifle[s] . . . pumped an accompaniment. I saw our lieutenant [Hoes] seated behind a stump which parted a howling stream of grape. He had one eye looking each way, and both stuck out like [a] lobster's.

With yells that might have raised the dead, we rushed like a whirlwind over the broad plowed field, thickset with big stumps, and breasted the hill. Those stumps saved me from many charges of grape. Three minutes later we were

The Assault on Petersburg, 15 June 1864 *(Engraving courtesy of Historical Times, Inc.)*

inside the rebel works, taking prisoners and behaving like wild men. Secesh made tracks at a fearful rate, and we pumped him as he ran. Company G of the 3rd captured a rebel battery [and] flag, and there were taken in all 16 pieces of artillery.[3]

Finding an opportunity to resume my supper, I was hastily draining hocake [*sic*] from a gray back's haversack when General Smith rode up, and one of the boys proposed three cheers for "Old Baldy Smith." The mouthful of hocake [*sic*] by no means prevented me from cheering him. He took off his hat and smiled from ear to ear, but remonstrated by waving his hand gently as does an orchestra leader when he means "pianissimo."

Our officers, as usual, were nowhere [to be seen] and the men commanded themselves. The majority of the officers, pale as ghosts, came [in] after the fight was done.

Immediate measures were taken to secure the position, which commands the city. We can knock it down in half an hour. . . . One of the forts is behind a deep ravine and is elaborately built. We all wonder at its weak defense. Last night the 3rd slept in the gardens of a house within the works, on beds of peas surrounded by roses plucked for the girls, which I enclose.

Our brigade comprised the 3rd, 117th, 142nd, and the 148th New York, the 97th Penn., and the 4th New Hampshire.[4] This morning at about 8 o'clock the 148th charged the rebel skirmishers, distance about 200 yards, and with the help of a few guns drove them in splendid style. Another movement is about to be made, and today we expect to enter the city. I forgot to mention that as a preliminary to our assault, the railroad communication with Richmond was destroyed.[5]

With Grant on the south and west [east] side of his capital, what is Jeff [Davis] to do? Perhaps we will force Lee onto the Penninsula [sic] and end the war at Yorktown. The rebs are despondent and surrender themselves willingly, some of them joyously. We hear that the citizens of Petersburg have all been pressed into the service. . . .

In haste,
Ed

Bermuda Hundred, Va.
Saturday, June 18, 1864

Dear Bro:

As you see, we are back again in[side] Bermuda Hundred. In my last note to you, it was intimated to you that the new advance movement was to be attempted with very good chances of success. Unfortunately our reinforcements came so late that large masses of rebel troops had time to get down from Richmond, and in consequence we have met with a very heavy resistance. I had supposed that the 9th Corps was at the front with the 18th and the 2nd; but it seems that it did not arrive until 5 P.M. on Friday afternoon.[6]

Just at sunset [on Thursday, the 16th] the 2nd Corps commenced an assault on the left, our batteries, which were almost crowded along the brows of the hills, opening with a stunning crash at the same time. The 3rd was at first posted as support of [Lieutenant Robert M. Hall's] Battery D, 1st U.S. Artillery; but as the battle increased in fierceness on the left, our brigade was moved off in that direction and formed in a column with brigades front, either to charge or to support a large number of guns which had been playing away upon the rebel front with terrific violence. In this position, although lying down behind the brow of a hill, several men were wounded.

The full moon was already up, and in the open ground it was almost as light as day; but the artillery and small arms rolled out their volleys so rapidly and incessantly that heavy smoke soon enveloped us like a thick fog, hiding everything from view. A counterattack from the rebels had been expected, and the vigorous fighting probably resulted from the meeting of the two strong tides.

In a couple of hours the brunt of the contest was over. We had forced the enemy from their entrenchments on the left and driven them back about 500 paces. At 9 P.M. our division formed and marched into the woods [and] took its position in line of battle about 100 paces in the rear of the 2nd Corps, which now stood fighting behind the captured rebel works. After lying on our arms for an hour, one half of the regiment was sent to the rear for entrenching tools. Your servant lugged back two pick axes. By the time he returned skirmishers had been thrown forward. We now took muskets and shovels and, passing the 2nd Corps in company with a couple of other regiments, commenced throwing up a flanking entrenchment in front of the first line and at right angles to it.

All this, you know, took place in the woods. Each company sent one man as a scout forty paces forward. From our company I was detailed. I had scarcely reached my post when I heard heavy groans in the distance and, pushing cautiously on, soon found a poor fellow who had been shot through the body, lying under a tree and praying for death to release him from his torture. While I was pouring water down his throat from my canteen, one of our nervous skirmishers saw me and, knowing that I was ahead of the line, let drive with the intention of killing a reb. It was a very poor shot. We soon had a stretcher ready, and the wounded man was carefully placed upon it and carried away.

Nothing unusual occurred for a couple of hours. Then one of the pickets on my left went in toward the regiment and a couple more hastily followed, snapping dry twigs and tearing dry bushes as they went. At last, to cap the climax, one of them discharged his piece. Seeing no cause for alarm, I had remained where I was. Anticipating a panic, with "fixins," I threw myself flat upon the ground just in time to avoid a scathing volley of rifle balls from the muskets of the gallant [regiment], their third, who were thus endeavoring to murder their own pickets. To make matters worse all the rest of the rebs within 300 yards, being thus stirred up, plugged away from the opposite direction. The only thing wanting to complete the fix was the opening of the 2nd Corps on my left flank.

Luckily, they remained quiet. So did I as long as my patience lasted . . . (about three minutes) when, boiling with rage, I marched back to the regiment, yelling at them as soon as I came in sight and rating them in distinct and decided tones as "simpletons" and "confounded yoguls [yokels]," and so forth. They ceased firing but expressed great surprise at seeing me alive and unhurt. Poor innocent harmless creatures.

Half an hour later we were ordered to fill up the trench just dug and to fall back behind the main works. This was at 2 A.M. [June 17]. We did so and slept until daylight. At daylight the rebs opened upon us, under fire of musketry of [at] a distance of about 100 yards, [and] in the rear of the first line of the works we had to throw up a second line. Well, sir, you should have seen us throw dirt. Roots and stumps were cut through and out with the shovels as easily as though they had been twigs. In half an hour we had banked up earth and logs breast high.

During the forenoon our division was relieved and took post on a hill near one of the recently captured forts. At 8 P.M. the entire 18th Corps was relieved by the 6th, which had come up during the afternoon, and took up its line of march for Bermuda Hundred, crossing the Appomatox by pontoon for the third time. We were on the road until 3 o'clock this morning, when we reached our old camping ground. Our position near Petersburg was two and a quarter miles from the city by measurement, and not one and a half miles as I first wrote to you.

As we retired our ears were greeted with the bellowing of artillery and the roll of musketry as the rebels commenced their attack. After daylight this morning the same deadly sounds were heard. It is reported that the enemy had made seven desperate assaults upon the position and were fearfully slaughtered. Poor fellows. We have artillery enough there to blow the entire Confederacy into the air, and before we left, our army had been so strongly entrenched that their position was next to impregnable. It is rumored that the courier from Lee to Beauregard was intercepted between Richmond and Petersburg with instructions to retake those works, if every man was sacrificed in the attempt. . . .

Grant's army is all south of the James. Lee must keep his eyes peeled.

Ed K. W.

Rifle Pit at Bermuda Hundred, Va.
Saturday, June 25th, 1864

Dear Bro:

The day after my last note to you was written we broke up camp and moved to the works in front, where the Third Division relieved a division of the 6th Army Corps which in turn started to rejoin its corps at Petersburg. After lying for a couple of days behind the entrenchments, a detail of 50 men was called for, for pickets in front. It chanced to be my turn, and I came out with the others.

We are in little holes behind the barriers of logs and clay hastily thrown up. The pit I am in accomodates [sic] two men. Eight or ten yar[d]s further on is a line of "videttes" [sic] who are posted two in a pit. A thickly wooded ravine is before us and behind is such an impenetrable mass of brush and stumps, so well commanded by the enemy's guns, that our capture would be certain should they attack us in force.

At some points the rebs are within twenty yards of us, and as [if] by mutual consent picket firing has ceased, [and] we expose ourselves without fear of consequences, walking about in plain view of each other. A reb amused himself and us yesterday by plaintively singing "No One to Love." One of our men, laying aside his rifle, would walk out boldly half-way to the enemy's line, leave a little bag of coffee on a stump, and return. Johnny Reb would then issue forth, take the coffee and substitute in its place a big plug of tobacco, which was speedily secured for the service of the Union. Other "vanities" were exchanged in the same way, but at last rebel officers forbade further intercourse.

Still, the greatest good feeling prevails between the men of the hostile pickets. Yesterday, someone in authority determined to make a demonstration. Rebs and Yanks were ballygogging around with hands in their pockets and staring at each other. All at once the rebs started for cover, but not before they had called out warningly, "Take care, Yanks, we're going to shell ye." To this our boys replied by flopping into pits, leaving but one eye exposed and crying with equal friendship, "Lay low, Rebs!" The artillery fire opened on the right, intermingled with rapid volleys of musketry, and worked gradually around to us. In our immediate neighborhood shells were dropped in profusion, spiced with a few rifle balls; but no advance was made and no one was hit. In an hour everything was quiet again, and we all came forth whistling and laughing as before, to cook our supper. The rebs did likewise. It had been nothing more than a passing shower.

Some of the Hundred Daymen were here from the West,[7] and our "southern brethren" can't endure them; for they are green soldiers and, beside[s] being nervous, some of them are a trifle too anxious to try their skill with a rifle. As a consequence, they keep both themselves and the rebs in hot water all the time they are on picket.

Our detachment now has been out three days without being relieved. To make matters worse the regiment has gone with the rest of the division, nobody knows where, under Baldy Smith.[8] They have taken our rations along, and rumor says that they may be gone a week. I wish them success, of course, but want to have it understood that I can eat my own grub. A very small force has been left in this point, but then the rebs have only one division in front of us, and our works, defended as they are by artillery, are perfectly safe. We think a great battle imminent; for both parties seem to be concentrating all their available forces.

I see the Herald gives us no credit for capturing the fort on the hill near Petersburg [on June 15], yet it was our brigade which did it. It was not captured by a line of battle, but by the triple line of skirmishers. The Third Regiment was in the second line of skirmishers and in the charge passed the first line and entered the fort first, capturing the rebel flag, the artillery officer commanding, and turning the guns on the retreating enemy. Our men, you know, have been drilled as artillerists. I was over the works and passed the guns before the rebels ceased firing on our men; but neither then nor for ten minutes after did I see Birney's Brigade[9] there. However, "z'all right" [and] will make no difference 200 years hence.

The heat has been almost suffocating. What arrangements have you made for the 4th [of July]? Wish you all a jolly time. Wish Grant and I might celebrate it by taking Richmond.

Goodbye, I am out as a vidette [*sic*] in five minutes. Love to all. . . . In haste

Yours truly,
Ed K. W.

P. S. 6 P.M. Everything is quiet today. . . . We hear that Grant is entrenching in front of Petersburg and that our regiment is there. There is heavy firing in that direction every day.

Ed K. W.

Entrenchments near Petersburg, Va.
Tuesday, June 29th [28th], 1864

Dear Bro:

Letters received from home from Jim, Charley, Mary, and Ell, dated the 21st inst., remind me that I ought perhaps to write again—not because there is anything important to communicate, but to tell you of several changes and to assure you that in our position "all is well."

My last note was written while on picket at Bermuda Hundred. We remained there five nights and six days, constantly on the alert and almost without sleep or rest. In the position we last moved from, the hostile videttes [sic] were not more than ten feet apart. Consequently, though each man during the night had four hours nominally allotted to him to sleep, the snapping of twigs or the delivery of an order in the rebel works frequently caused us to spring up from our doze and grasp our arms.

One day we were shelled and so forth, but with that exception scarcely a shot was fired, and an excellent understanding seemed to be established between the Yankees and the Secesh. In spite of the efforts of the officers to prevent communications, one reb went so far as to send us a note, enclosed in a hocake [sic], suggesting that in case firing were resumed, both parties should elevate their pieces so as not to injure anyone. Deserters come into us every night. One night, after assuring them that in case of surrender they would not be conscripted for the Union Army, fifty of them promised to come over; but the report was brought that the 3rd was to be relieved, and Johnny, being distrustful of new troops, remained. There is a great dissatisfaction between the rank and file of Lee's army. They wrote to us that they were convinced that "we privates could finish this war" and protested that they were heartily tired of it.

Our picket line was about the only protection for Butler's strong works. To be sure, we heard a terrific din of drums along the line when "tatoo" [sic] sounded in the evening, but we well knew it to be a sham and that with the exception of a few Hundred Daymen, no one was there but the drummers. A strong force of artillery remained, however, equal to several thousand men. We were kept so long at the front simply because there were no tried troops to relieve us. Yesterday afternoon a relief was raised somewhere, and we were ordered to rejoin the brigade, which is once again the First Brigade, Second Division, 10th A. C. We crossed the Appomatox for the fifth time and found the regiment in the second line of entrenchments and about the right center of the line.

We are under a shell and sharpshooter's fire; but advance by digging, gradually and yet surely. We are in front of and to the left of the forts captured in the first charge. One point of grass line is said to be within a musket['s] range of the city, which, however, like Fredericksburg, is strongly defended by the batteries on the other side of the river. Grant is said to be still working around to the left. Both parties are gathering and massing all their troops and all their artillery. The talk is of digging and shelling the enemy out of his position. It is believed that the 4th of July will find us in possession of Petersburg, which the rebel prisoners pronounce equivalent to the capture of Richmond and the desolation of Lee's army. . . .

Yours truly,
Ed K. W.

The Petersburg Campaign (*Map from* Battles and Leaders of the Civil War)

Camp near Petersburg, Va.
July 9, 1864

Dear Bro:

We have been quite quiet of late. Even the picket firing has generally ceased, and we are bothered only occasionally by the enemy's batteries. It is . . . dangerous to show ones head above the works anywhere, but there are comparatively few chance shots flying, and the danger is therefore correspondingly diminished.

Rogers and I and [Sergeant George E.] Avent had a lively time two or three days ago, while calling on a friend of the 9th Army Corps. His position is about two miles to the left of us, and to reach him we had to pass along a second line of works which were rather low and imperfect in construction. Every time we leaped over a curtain or traverse, the rifle balls of the sharpshooters sung in our ears like canary birds. We are so used to that kind of fun now, though, that the closest shots only provoke a laugh.

Our brigade is now on duty in front of the forts captured in the first assault at Petersburg. The Third Regiment, when at the front, is in the first line of works, packed between two mortar batteries, with a nest of light and heavy rifle batteries on the other side of us. Of course, we shell the rebs and the rebs shell us almost constantly. Two old houses nearby are fairly riddled by solid shot and shell and bullets, and their chimneys have been battered down. We keep in the trenches, watch the explosions, and generally avoid injury from them, although the shells often burst over head on the parapet, raining down showers of small fragments and balls and covering us with clay and dust.

On the 30th of June we were ordered out into the rifle pits, formed in line of battle on the right of Barton's Brigade,[10] with fixed bayonets, and held ready for an assault of the rebel works about sixty yards distant. The principle [sic] advance was to have been made by Burnside's Corps, on our left. But the rebel position and troops were found to be too strong, and as his [the enemy's] reinforcements rapidly came up, the design was abandoned, and we retired to our old place. We were severely shelled but had, I believe, only two men wounded.

It is the custom now for one half of the brigade to rest as a reserve in the rear, while the other half is on duty. The regiments remained [sic] at the front forty eight hours at a time, during which they are up night and day. The front rank watches one half the night, the rear rank the other. In addition to this, a large picket force is sent out to the rifle pits ahead, which in its turn privides [sic] videttes [sic].

Last night, just before we were about to be relieved, the rebs created an alarm by advancing their skirmish line and opening upon us with their mortar and field batteries. We had all taken off our belts and were rapacious in devouring a supper made palatable by a ration of dried apples, stewed, presented by the Sanitary Commission. But in an instant every man was up, musket in hand, watching the line of flame which he saw just along the top of the enemy's works, two hundred and fifty yards distant. At this point a mortar shell, seemingly from the sky, dropped plump into the trench and exploded, carrying away the head of one of our men, shattering the arm of another, and dashing off the knapsack of a third. It fell close to Knowles, and his escape was almost miraculous.

Back here in camp, five hundred yards from the first line, we come to rest two days at a time. The place is held to be less dangerous than the other, being a small spot behind a hill; but, unluckily, it is just behind a battery also, and in consequence a kind of place of deposit for spent missles [sic]. The last time we were here a man was shot through the body with a solid ball.

We now number about one hundred privates [present] for duty. Our officers, frightened at the now serious aspect of affairs and thinking that consolidation would help them out of the service, have formally applied for consolidation with the 142nd New York Volunteers. Col. [N. Martin] Curtis is in the same brigade.

Grant is placing guns and mortars for a terrific bombardment—a hundred pounder and fifteen inch guns. Look out for breakers.

The Fourth here was hot, quiet, and stupid [i.e., boring]. We have heard of the sinking of the Alabama[11] and of Ewell's Raid.[12] Hope the latter will frighten the North into sending us reinforcements. Hundreds fall here every week. Stretchers are plenty.

A letter [came] from Mary dated the 5th inst., enclosing a copy of the 4th's resolution. Bully.

In haste,
Ed

Trenches near Petersburg, Va.
July 17th, 1864

Dear Bro:

. . .We hear today that the enemy has been driven from the neighborhood of Washington with the loss of 8,000 men, ten wagon trains, and a battery, and that Sherman has waxed Johnson [Johnston] so at Atlanta[13] that the poor fellow begins to doubt whether he really has Sherman "where he wants him." May the report prove to be at least half true.

As to movements here, I can give you but little light. The troops in the neighborhood are comparatively few in number, though enough to hold the position. The 6th Corps is one from our left,[14] and the Second Corps, leaving behind only a strong picket line, has vacated its position;[15] for several days past [it] has been very busy leveling the works in our rear. What does this mean? The colored troops who formed the third line of battle in our rear have left for parts unknown.[16] Within a few days Grant is supposed to have been making important movements—in what direction no one knows. At one time rumors were rife that the position was about to be evacuated. Now the opinion is different.

With regard to the Third Regiment I have to state that it is again in the 10th Army Corps, under the command of Baldy Smith.[17] We are still at the front, spending alternately two days in the front line of works, when pickets are thrown out covering the regimental front, and two days in the second line of works, about 100 yards further back. While in the first line we are constantly under the heavy fire of musketry and artillery, and our losses are considerable. The number of privates for duty is now reduced to 107. We have two or three wounded every day. The rebs have now acquired a splendid range of our breast works and are sending over their mortar shells in threes. They lessen materially the chance of a successful dodging. We are today resting in the second line. The last time we were here three men were hit by a rifle shell, and within twelve feet of me. Still, we are doing well. Our batteries can fire their shots to the rebels and do splendid execution.

Narrow escapes are so common as to have ceased to cause remarks. By the bye, I had one two days ago. I happened to be sitting on the ground with my back to a rebel battery when a shout caused me to turn my head. I saw an eight inch solid shot, half spent, bouncing along, aiming to take me between the shoulders. A side jump of three paces, performed with startling agility, carried me clear of it and provoked a laugh that ran a quarter of the mile along the line. All right! A joke's a joke.

About the same time, Knowles was slammed against the parapet by the explosion of a shell, remaining otherwise uninjured. Rogers had a heavy piece of shell driven through a bombproof where he was sitting, and [it] lodged beside him. A lieutenant had the roof of a bombproof fall upon him and was drawn forth laughing and uninjured. Another, close by us, seeing a shell drop in his battery, caught it up while the fuze was burning and threw it over the escarpment to burst outside. Such incidents are of hourly occurrence and [help] to keep up a gentle excitement. . . .

My health is very good, though heavy marching agrees better with me than lying still. But my duties are lighter than they have been heretofore; for a sergeantcy [*sic*] having again been offered me about two weeks ago in H Company, I have accepted it.

Jim complains of the heat. One day's frying of his brains here would make him rejoice to substitute the trifling inconvenience of a northern summer.

Everything promises well. We hope to finish the war this fall. Today, Sunday, firing has ceased, and we are as quiet as citizens.

Truly your affectionate brother,
Ed K. W.

Camp near Petersburg, Va.
Sunday, July 21 [24], 1864

Dear Bro:

For the first time in a month I am able to write you from a veritable camp not under the enemy's fire. I am under a shelter tent, too. We came from the front line last night and henceforth, we are told, shall rest here eight days out of [every] twelve. It looks almost like a paradise in prospect.[18] Tonight, however, the left wing of the regiment, including Company H, returns to the trenches for two days and nights. Afterwards, a rest. The two wings go out with other troops, alternately.

Just before we left last evening, a rebel came from their lines in broad daylight, waving in his hand a newspaper as though desiring to exchange. But when near our works he suddenly took [to] the double quick and dodged in. After he had safely crossed the line, I saw him quietly smoking his pipe and heard him laughingly observe that he "reckoned it was better to exchange himself than newspapers."

During the past week I have had what you would call a couple of pretty narrow escapes. On Monday night, while out in charge of our regimental picket line, a rebel sharpshooter drew bead on my scrubby head and cut a groove in my left ear with his rifle ball. As I was facing towards him, you can judge how close a shave it was. "Bombproof Jack" [Lieutenant Hoes], who was sitting near by, dryly remarked "that I must have heard that pretty plain."

Next day we were relieved and returned to the first line of works. In the afternoon we were sitting . . . eating our dinner, when my worthy colleague and tentmate, Sgt. Avent, suddenly shouted, "here she comes!" and cast himself against the parapet. At the same instance [sic], down comes a 45 pound mortar shell "chuck" into the trench, within four feet of him and six of me. I had only time to draw up my feet when it exploded with a terrific crash. The whole thing was so sudden there was no time to get excited and, as a glance revealed, the fact [was] that the general plastering with mud was the only damage the men had sustained, and I enjoyed a hearty laugh. . . . I should mention, though, that poor Avent had his thigh lamed by the weight of the "sacred soil" thrown against it. Luckily, a recent rain had so softened the clay that the shell buried itself by the force of its fall.

We are concentrating [on] putting in new batteries, and the rebel guns at this point are now well under our control. There is little news of general importance. According to an official report . . . Grant has now 90,000 men for duty, including Butler's troops.[19] The spirit of the army is unchanged, notwithstanding the ridiculous reports the enemy circulates of desertion towards Norfolk and so forth, though it must be acknowledged that its ardor is a trifle dampened by the backwardness of the North in providing reinforcements of men and means. This is [not] a time to pause; the case is in our hands now and only wants summing up. Our motto should be that emphatic though vulgar one of the rank and file, "sock it to em."

We have heard of the evacuation of Atlanta by Johnston and of the successes of Smith and Hunter.[20] There is a rumor here that Burnside has a part of the rebel troops undermined opposite the 9th Corps and that the explosion is to be the signal for a general assault. We shall see. Every day things grow more quiet.

In haste,
Ed K. W.

Camp at Bermuda Hundred, Va.
August 1, 1864

Dear Bro[ther Charles]:

I have received letters from you and Mary up to July 25th. I write at the first opportunity to prevent unnecessary anxiety. Fred is supposed to be out-of-town, and I accordingly address you.

When I last wrote home, we were constructing a camp. On the evening of the 29th of July at 9 o'clock P.M., after three days of rest, we suddenly got orders to pack up and move to the front. We were told that Burnside was about to blow up one of the enemy's forts which he had undermined and that a general assault would follow. We were on the road all night long, gradually moving through masses of the other troops to the left, where we were to act as support to the 9th Corps.

I believed the signal for the attack was to be given at 3 o'clock A.M., but the ball didn't open until [almost] 5 o'clock. I had thrown myself down for a doze and [was] suddenly awakened by a dull smothering sound of the explosion, and by the jarring of the earth. Simultaneously, a mountain of clay was forced into the air in front of us, and our artillery opened with a terrific crash, which drowned out all other sounds. We sprang upon our feet and eagerly strained our eyes and listened for the well known signs of an infantry assault. They were not long wanting. A loud cheer, and then the trifling pauses between the rapid shots of the gunners were followed by a heavy rattle of musketry. The rebel shells began to plunge among us, squads of prisoners were let in, the wounded borne in on stretchers. The battle had fairly commenced.

Another cheer, heard faintly through the crackling din of the rifle guns! The first line is captured. Another still, and the second line is ours. "Forward the Third," shouted the Colonel [Curtis] commanding our brigade, and out we go, nothing loath to take a hand in the charge of the third and last line.[21]

Alas, before we had reached our position, the tide of battle had turned. The rebel general [Brigadier General William Mahone], suddenly massing his troops, had thrown them forward with the determination of recovering the ground he had lost. The colored troops, seeing half a dozen lines advancing against them, had become panic-stricken [and] dropped their arms and fled without dealing a blow, embarrassing the white troops around and behind them and in the end ensu[r]ing for us a defeat.

Our regiment was on its way to the scene of action through a deep trench, the sides of which rose seven or eight feet high on either side. These were brought to a halt by the terror-stricken darkies, who came surging over with a force which seemed almost irresistible. They insisted that the rebels were close on their heels and would gobble us all up—that their strength was twice our own. They yelled and groaned in despair, and when we barred their progress to leap and scramble up the sides of the trench, they did their prettiest to jump out of our empty barrel. You might form an idea of the performance of some of the poor nigs on the extraordinary occasion.

Knowing that our services would at this moment be valuable in front, and being unable to force the darkies to return (for their brigadier [General Edward Ferrero] had scrambled past the entrenchments, grabbing and clutching like a cat on a fence on a windy day), we hoisted up our color bearer and then, helping each other up, rushed over the parapet with a great volley of musket balls and, trotting down a little hill, formed under cover of the N & P [Norfolk & Petersburg] Railroad. Two hundred yards further brought us to where the brigade was formed for the charge. We had already taken our position and were waiting for the command when the order was countermanded, and we retreated under a heavy fire into the trenches, having lost two lieutenants [wounded] and half a dozen men [killed and wounded].

All day long we lay in the trenches under the broiling rays of the southern sun. Many a poor fellow fell of sunstroke—my tentmate, Sgt. Avent, among the number. In common with others, I panted like an overheated dog; but Avent had to be taken to the rear, and I took him.

At sunset, when completely exhausted, we were relieved by fresh troops, and after running the gauntlet of the rebel fire, we reached the rear and stacked arms. When called up to report to the Brigade Commander, I found myself to be the last and only remaining man of the Company H, an honor due to good luck and a good constitution. On going into the fight we had but four privates, two sergeants (Rogers, an acting sgt. major), and a lieutenant. The lieutenant and acting first sergeant pegged out, two privates were wounded and the others had scadaddled [sic], leaving me in command of the company, comprising only Edward K. W., formerly of the 9th [Infantry] of New York.

We had no sooner stacked arms than we dropped upon the ground and slept. A couple of hours later the order was given to fall in, and in the hurry of the movement I marched off without my knapsack, unwittingly abandoning overcoat, tent, rubber blanket, clothing, photographs, needlebook—everything prized by a soldier, [especially] my jolly old knapsack. For two years I have lugged it through mud and sand and water, over mountains and through ravines and valleys. It was like parting with an old friend.

At night we returned to our old position; but at 3 o'clock next morning we were roused up to march to City Point, where we're to embark for the defense of Washington. We started, but on the route the order was countermanded, and we were brought to Bermuda Hundred, to join the rest of the 10th Corps under General Birney, so we are now again the First Brigade, Second Division, 10th A. C. The day was so excessively hot that the men staggered along and, though it was dark, we crossed the Appomatox on a pontoon. The jolly sun seemed to have taken a contract for splitting heads and, by George, I believe mine was included. However, I survived and am as well and lively as a lark.

At present we are waiting for orders, perhaps for Washington. The 19th Corps[22] has already gone. Grant may have gained an advantage in the last battle, but his losses were severe in killed and wounded and prisoners.

In haste,
Ed K. W.

Bermuda Hundred, Va.
August 28, 1864

Dear Bro:

There has been so much fighting in this neighborhood of late, in which my corps and division were engaged, that it seems necessary that I should write a few words home, though far from being in the vein of writing. For a week past I have been almost broken down in consequence of the hardships of the campaign, the exposure and labor of which showed themselves in aching joints, rheumatism, and fever. I have struggled on, however, doing my duty with only a break of four days. Still it is doubtful whether at this moment I could lug my knapsack five miles without dropping hopelessly exhausted by the way. Under the circumstances, thinking rest more needful than medicine, I have left the ranks for a while and set to work writing up regimental returns for the adjutant. This I can do with a clear conscience, for the men of the brigade are exposed to no real danger, they having been retained here in the works and having nothing more to do than picket duty. I am picking up gradually and hope soon to be able to resume my place in the Company. There are other men in much worse condition and with small chance of immediate relief. We have now but four commissioned officers left for duty. The Third, of course, has taken no part in the late fighting and has suffered no loss.[23]

I have received letters from you and from Charley and Mary and one from the latter enclosing another photograph, for which I am greatly obliged. I am sorry to hear Charley speak so discouragingly of the [army's] prospects. We do not think Grant's campaign a failure. We care nothing for Richmond except as a stronghold which shields Lee's army. We seek to destroy the army, not the city, and . . . we will do it if properly backed by the people at home. It matters little whether they are weakened or scattered here, at Atlanta, or in the Shenandoah [Valley]. Our work is to destroy and subdue all traitors appearing in arms against the Republic. . . . As for extravagance and corruption [in Washington], history should have taught him [Charles] that they are inseparable from war and, more particularly, from civil war. I think the main weakness of the administration has been the failure to establish and enforce taxes comprehensive enough to serve as a sound basis of finance; and the indecision (cowardice) which did not dare to make just drafts of men to recruit and increase the strength of our armies.

At all events, whatever the weaknesses of the administration may be, I am satisfied this is no time to carp at things which, compared with the success and re-establishment of the Republic, are insignificant. At such [a] crisis a division and discord in the North would be fatal. . . . Rebel agents are working in this way to annihilate our strength. Shall we let our hair be shorn, to be content with the poor privilege of pulling down our temples of liberty on our own heads or on our enemy's?

In haste as ever,
Edward K. Wightman

Trenches in front of Petersburg, Va.
Tuesday, August 30th, 1864

Dear Bro:

. . . As you see, we are again at the Petersburg front. We marched up last Saturday, but not to an old position. Our brigade now rests on the Appomatox River. The rebs are able to open a terrible shell fire on us whenever they please, and they please too often for our convenience. Things are so arranged that we spend 48 hours in the trenches and then are relieved and face back into a ravine for 48 hours.

I am in much better health than when I wrote last and constantly improving. Just in the nick of time I received the appointment of acting Ordnance Sgt. for the regiment. This exempts me from fatigue, camp guard, and picket duty, and gives me a fine chance to rest. The march from Bermuda Hundred, together with a couple of long walks, has walked the rheumatism out of my joints and again they are comparatively supple. Our hospital has a good stock of medicine, and our rations are good.

Sometime ago I informed you that the officers of the Third had applied for a consolidation with the 142nd New York and still later that five of our lieutenants had tendered their resignations. The consolidation movement was disapproved by the War Department. The resignations were refused to be accepted, and "Lopeye" [Butler] went so far as to dishonorably dismiss the lieutenants from the service, make them forfeit six months pay and allowances, and order them to set to work as citizens in the trenches. They are at present in the provost guard house, and their departure has left us but two officers for the ten companies, viz. "senior captain commander, and the acting adjutant." The first sergeants will probably be promoted at once to fill the vacancies.

General Turner, commanding our division, it is reported, died of fever yesterday afternoon at Fort Monroe.[24] He was the coolest officer I have ever seen under fire and as a commander has the entire confidence of his men. General Foster succeeds him. One of General Birney's aides is said to have gone over to the enemy last night.

In our immediate brigade front nothing important has happened since our arrival. There is little liklihood [sic] of an assault here by either party. The River gives great strength to our position. . . . The position is far preferable to the one we had when last here and would be comfortable (speaking after the manner of soldiers) were it not for the occasional hot shell fire.

Yesterday I took a holiday and started off with my tentmate, Avent, to visit his brother, who is an executive officer (an ensign) on board the steamer Commodore Barney, lying near the pontoon in the Appomatox. We took dinner and tea (bully for us) and returned recuperated. The Barney is a ferry boat and carries [a] very heavy battery, including one 100 [pounder] Parrott. Everything aboard was in the nicest order. The cigar and watermelon department was met with the ungratified approbation of the court "if she knows herself."

(Grant's army, as they say, is too much exhausted to advance except by maneuvering or by regular approaches [i.e., siege warfare].) The prospect seems to be that we shall have to reorganize and reinforce behind the works during the winter. The term of many of the troops [will] expire during the next two months, and they must be replaced. The draft must now be enforced without trifling. It is a matter of vital importance. The soldiers are dissatisfied and disheartened at seeing so little effort being made at home to support them.

The flowers enclosed are for Abby. They were taken from the banks of the Appomatox, just behind the entrenchments. They grow on a vine with leaves resembling that of a bean.

In haste,
Edward K. W.

Trenches near Petersburg, Va.
September 17, 1864

Dear Bro:

. . . The regiment is in the same position as when I last wrote to you, viz., that is, close to the Appomatox. We are on duty for three days and nights in the trenches and then retire for an equal length of time in a ravine about 500 paces to the rear of the entrenchments. The enemy's artillery opens on us occasionally, and the sharpshooters are at work almost incessantly. Casualties, however, are very rare.

Rumors have been plenty of late of an expected attack on the Weldon Railroad,[25] but Grant has been so largely reconciled that Lee will have to fight both skillfully and desperately to gain any advantage. Night and day we are laboring on the works and constructing bombproofs. Recruits and convalescents are reported to be arriving in City Point at the rate of between [sic] 3,000, 4,000, and 5,000 per day. They are sent at once to the left [flank].

The Tenth [Corps line] now extends from the Appomatox beyond where Burnside's headquarters used to be[26]—a very long line. Grant is engineering so that his right may be held by the smallest possible number of men. His new railroad from City Point to [the] Weldon Road is now complete[27] and adds vastly to the transportation of supplies while it provides means of rapidly reinforcing any part of the front, in case of attack.

Fever caused by the exposure to the malaria of the swamps multiplies, but measures have been taken to guard against them [sic]. Quinine is now issued in regular rations to the men as a preventive. My own health is completely reestablished, and I am in better condition for campaigning than have been for many weeks. (Hello, there goes a 30 pound Parrott, the signal for a heavy cannonade.)

A stringent order from Division Headquarters has returned almost all detail[ed] men to their places in the ranks. In consequence, I am now acting both as ordnance sergeant and as first sergeant of H Company. You will remember that I wrote to you of the dismissal of several of our officers by General Butler and of the order to fill their places. I was offered a first lieutenancy but declined until told that Knowles, Rogers, and my tentmate Avent had accepted similar propositions. Then I assented; but I found that a miscalculation of numbers had been made, and it was finally decided to give the preference to Albanians [i.e., residents of Albany] and senior sgts. In ignorance all but one of them came to me to make out their applications. I was then offered a 2nd lieutenancy but refused it. The wisdom of the choice was suddenly proved by the fact that the newly appointed officers were incapable of making out their own company muster rolls. That labor devolved upon Avent and Wightman, who have been saddled with a great deal of writing for two weeks past.

Love to everybody. In haste.

As ever,
Ed

Deep Bottom, Va. in the trenches
October 4, 1864

Dear Bro:[28]

We have made an exhausting march and two terrific charges on the enemy works, losing the Regimental colors and more than half of the men engaged; yet I am perfectly well and sound.

Late in the afternoon of the 28th of Sept. the 10th Corps left the Petersburg front and during the night crossed the Appomatox and James Rivers on pontoon bridges, to Deep Bottom. The distance was about twenty miles, and the march with knapsacks was so severe that hundreds of men halted and straggled on the way. When we stopped on the East [north] side of the James, early in the morning of the 29th, only forty men and two commissioned officers of the 3rd Regiment were present. One of the officers was Capt. Wicks, [regimental] Comdr., and one [was a] newly appointed second Lieutenant. The Adjutant [Lieutenant Dwight Beebe] had fallen from his horse when drunk a few days before and was in the hospital.

Heartily tired, we threw ourselves upon the muddy ground and were allowed one hour, by the watch, for sleep. The men were then aroused and told that twenty five minutes remained in which to cook coffee and eat their breakfast. In half an hour the 2nd Division was advancing against the enemy to[ward] the Newmarket Road, which leads to Richmond.

When we reached the turnpike (where the 2nd Corps was recently repulsed)[29] the works had been carried by colored troops, and the slaughtered negroes lay piled in heaps in front of them.[30] Our Brigade was in advance of the Division, and the column at once proceeded up the road by the flank. We were marched several miles and were resting when Gen. Grant and staff came in. The men sprang to their feet and cheered till they fairly caused the old fellow, cigar and all, to fall from his saddle.

The route was resumed, and a couple of minutes later a couple of rifle balls whizzed by, announcing that we had come upon the enemy. The crash of artillery followed instantly from two heavy guns in front, and the shells tore through our ranks with awful effect. Our officers were in fault. Skirmishers had been thrown out only twenty paces beyond the head of the column.

We were hurridly [sic] deployed in line of battle across the road and ordered to charge. But, meantime, many of our men had fallen. I was stationed as a file closer behind the line to the left of the colors and close to them. Two successive shells burst amongst the heads of the color guard, killing four and wounding as many more. On the left, the enemy's shots, hurled with fearsome accuracy and rapidity, were equally fatal. The color sergt. dropped, and one of his guard caught up the flag. We were ordered to move to the right. Terror stricken by the howling of the fatal shells, the men had scattered and sough[t] shelter behind the trees; for we were in the midst of a dense wood. I threw myself beind a log to avoid a passing shell and flopped into a nest of yellow jackets. Of course, they stung like blazes and brought me up again in a jiffy.

Finding that the left wing had become separated from the right, taking the officers with it, and learning no one ranking myself [was] disposed to command, I brought out the color bearer and tried to rally our dozen remaining men around him. My tentmate, Sergt. Avent, had already gone to the rear, wounded in the foot. Rogers and Knowles now joined us, and one of Foster's staff, riding up, ordered us to charge. The general followed and repeated the order. "But we have not men enough to protect the colors," we remonstrated, "the enemy skirmish line may capture them." "Go on, I'll take the risk," he replied, and the next instant we were rushing forward, calling upon the 3rd to rally as we went.

In company with the 169th N.Y., we rushed out of the woods and up a hill in front, the rebels retiring. Moving gradually to the left, we came upon Capt. Wicks, his lieutenants, and half a score of men. The whole division was now halted and formed a line on a road running parallel with the new rebel position.[31] The accompanying sketch [deleted] will give some idea of the works about to be assaulted.

When everything was ready, the 3rd Regiment, posted between the 117th and the 112th New York, was formed to number ten files (twenty men). Gen. Foster, who was dismounted and lead [sic] the command in person, gave the command, and the long line moved steadily to the front, over the protecting banks of the road and through the thin belt of pines that covered the space between it and the first ravine. Johnny's shells began at once to drop among us, right and left.

With a trifling loss, we reached the first ravine and descended its steep slope, over fallen trees and through thickset underbrush. We crossed the marshy ground below and slowly toiled up the opposite ascent. A burst of artillery from the right and front met us as we kept on over the level ground beyond. At the double quick we plunged into the second ravine, the battery on the right now infiltrating the line, and shot and shell ploughing through the ranks as we leaped and stumbled onward. Here a shell burst among our legs, there amongst a crowd of heads. Cheers and cries of agony and horror strangely mingled. Still the line toiled on, panting but resolute, up the second ascent and, hurrying over the level land, slid, rolled, and tumbled into the third ravine, the din and fury of the enemy's fire increasing every moment and disasters multiplying at every step. Death fairly reveled in that third ravine. Shells hissed and exploded in our ears incessantly, and crushed heads and mangled bodies thickly strewed our pathway.

Again we struggled through fallen trees and tangled brush, sinking knee deep in mud and water. A man walking on the same log with me had both legs carried away by a single shot, and groaned awfully as he fell. We drowned his cries by hoarsely shouting, "forward."

The top of the ravine was reached, and for a moment we paused to recover breath and gather strength for the last grand effort. Hundreds of men had already fallen, exhausted, by the way. Of the 3rd Regiment, only two sergeants, one private, the color bearer, and myself remained grouped around the colors. All the others had been killed, wounded, or lost in the ranks of other regiments.

Suddenly the order, "Forward," rang out in clear tones from our leader. The answering cheer from thousands of brazen throats seemed to shake the earth. A moment more and we were running through the cornfield under the [most] murderous, pitiless storm of musketry, shrapnel, and grape and cannister [sic] that I ever conceived [of]. The ripping, howling, and screaming of the missles [*sic*], mingled with the shouts of the attacking party, the yells of the rebels, [and] the groans of the wounded, were horrible beyoud [*sic*] description. The leaves of corn, cut by the flying shot, floated before our eyes continually and fell to the earth in showers. Many a poor fellow beside me was struck the second time before he reached the ground with his first wound.

We had passed a little log house and were within forty paces of the abbatis [*sic*] of the fort when a whirlwind [of riflefire] seemed to rush across our front. The line disappeared as though an earthquake had swallowed it. The fatal hissing increased in volume a hundred fold. Perfectly bewildered, those who remained standing, halted. The ground was covered with our slain, and we had come thus far with fixed bayonets and without firing a shot. Everyone recoiled and Foster, who was still with us, ordered a retreat.

The rebels stood in crowds upon their parapet of the fort, shouting at us in derision. I tried to bring down one of them, but my rifle missed fire. I never was so angry in my life.[32] As I turned, a heavy piece of shell flattened my canteen, nearly knocking me off my legs but doing no other injury. The canteen saved my left hip joint. Tired and riled as I was, I would not have double quicked a step to save a thousand lives.

On looking around for our colors, I thought I recognized them and their bearer twenty paces ahead and, satisfied that they were safe, did not hasten to overtake them. Nothing now remained to be done but to get off the wounded. I found two of our wounded sergeants, one shot through the body and unable to walk. While getting him into a blanket, Rogers came up and together we lugged him from the field, the rebs pegging away at us till the last. On reaching the road from which we started, we found Knowles, who like Rogers and myself is unharmed, the Captain, lieutenant, and one or two others, and then for the first time learned that the colors were missing and had probably been captured. That has stuck in my crop ever since.

Out of the forty men with which we started, twenty nine (more than half) had been killed and wounded. We remained on the road until dark and were then withdrawn to the present position, which we had fortified and sincerely hope that the Rebels will attack. We are told that Grant ordered the assault merely to stir up the Rebs and make them send troops to their left. He did stir them up, by thunder. Still, if we can gain a victory elsewhere by being licked here, Johnny may lick us every day in this week if he can. While we were fighting, the 1st Division of our Corps went to within one mile and a half of Richmond, and Grant's line advanced on the left. We hear now that he occupies Petersburg.[33]

The 3rd Regiment now numbers (after the fight is over and when stragglers have been returned by the provost guard) one hundred and thirty men. They are divided into two companies which form, respectively, the right and left wings. A dozen non commissioned officers have been reduced for cowardice.

Enclosed are sprigs of sugar cane tops and seed from . . . near Petersburg, Va.

The sugar cane so nearly resembles brome [broom] corn in appearance that you would not know the difference unless told. In the field I saw it grow to the height of seven to 12 feet.

No news from home. Mails irregular. We are about to get six months pay.

In haste,
Ed K. W.

Camp near Deep Bottom, Va.[34]
October 26, 1864

Dear Bro:

. . .The weather here is decidedly cold, but we now have woolen blankets and overcoats and are prepared for it. The 1st and 3rd Division[s] have already put up dry log shanties for winter quarters, and today we are to prepare a permanent camp—perhaps for the winter. Men are moving their quarters while I write, and the strokes of the axe and the crash of falling trees resound in all directions.

My health is first rate and my duties considerably lighter than they have been. I have been partially relieved as regular clerk and first sergeant and appointed acting Sgt. Major. This exempts me from all details and from lugging a musket. Active operations may or may not be done for the season in this quarter. The rebs are now well entrenched, and so are we. Neither could carry the other's works without vastly superior numbers. We may sally forth occasionally to keep our hands in, but it is the general impression that unless Grant attempts a grand row on the left to close up Lee's communications before winter sets in, nothing more will be done here. Still, we may be transferred to the South, leaving only men enough here to hold the lines.

As to the [coming Presidential] election, I have already forwarded to Jim my vote to support the administration. I have no very great respect for either of the presidential candidates as individuals. Abe is sadly in want of a new set of brains and is criminally weak and undecided. McClellan, on the other hand, ambitiously thrusts his private interests in advance of the interests of the country and lays himself open to the accusation of being a demagogue. His position is too equivocal and his acceptance of the [Democratic Party] nomination too cautiously worded to be satisfactory.[35] If he has not independence enough to express his views openly before election, he would equally be a puppet in the hands of others afterwards. But the platforms both seem to me, as exponent[s] of views of the great parties, to be contemptible; but as the main question seems to be whether we shall continue the war until the rebellion is subdued (for the rebels have repeatedly, until we are tired of hearing it, said that they will never make peace till independence is acknowledged), I vote in the affirmative, believing that the integrity of the Union can be restored only by force of arms and that such a course is necessary in order to vindicate the honor and establish the power of the Republic.

Having voted as a citizen, I am equally ready to return to the field as a soldier. As you say, we gave Johnny a pretty severe thrashing on the 7th inst.[36] Our brigade was in the second line of battle, behind the 7th [Connecticut], but when the rebs fell back, our line, passing the other, followed up a full mile beyond our works. On the 14th we reconoitered [sic] in force[37] but, although under fire, there were no casualties in our regiment. Remember me to the fellers, particularly to little Ned[38] and believe me as ever

Yours truly,
Ed K. W.

Headquarters, 3rd N.Y. Vols.
near Deep Bottom, Va.
October 29, 1864

Dear Bro:

My last letter had scarcely been mailed when we got orders to strike tents and be ready to move. Before daylight on the morning of the 27th, we piled our knapsacks and, marching up to the right of the line, passed out of the works and advanced about two miles beyond. There we formed in line and halted.

A skirmish line was pushed forward and fighting commenced at once. Our Adjutant, Lt. Beady [Beebe], soon came in mortally wounded. Capt. Wicks, commanding the regiment, was then sent out to maneuver the skirmishers on our brigade front but had not been long away when he was brought back, shot through the left breast. Two wounded, belonging to H Company, quickly followed. We had but a single line of battle and had come out only with the intention of stirring up Johnny and of causing a diversion.

At about 4 o'clock P.M. our brigade massed under cover of the woods and charged in the hopes of grabbing the rebel skirmishers; for we learned that they had weakened their front opposite in order to strengthen their right. The rebs were not to be caught. They withdrew their skirmishers in[to] the earth works and, as we burrowed on the way through the almost impenetrable underbrush, poured into our struggling ranks a terrific shower of case shot and grape and cannister [sic] spiced with balls of musketry. At no time could we see more than fifteen feet ahead, but on we plunged toward our unseen enemy, yelling and occasionally firing in return. Taking it for granted that the rebs were behind the big trees, our fellows were directed to aim to the left side of their trunks, breast high. When we got into such a position that we were infiltrated by artillery from both the right and the left, the order was given to halt and lie down, which we did.

After remaining there for half an hour listening to the shrieking and howling of missles [sic] overhead and losing about one tenth of our men, we retired by order without having had a glimpse of the enemy, though we were close up under some of his guns. The Third had 77 men engaged and lost thirteen in killed and wounded and missing. I was not touched. Neither was Knowles. At night we slept in the mud and rain and on the afternoon of the 28th returned to camp. Meanwhile, the 18th Corps had made a raid toward Richmond and lost a brigade in prisoners. They returned before we came in.[39]

One of Charley's Sunday School teachers, a member of the Sixth Connecticut Vols. named Stuyvesant, was with me when the order to move arrived. He is a headquarters clerk and looks like a healthy boy.

Ask mother and the girls if they have time to knit me a pair of those one fingered mittens and send them by mail. It is growing cold very fast.

> Camp, Third Regiment, N.Y. V.
> near Laurel Hill, Va.
> November 4, 1864

Dear Pater Familias [Jim]:

Take my congratulations regardless of expense. Happy to hear of the little [baby]—seems to be a regular "double ender." Precocious boy—reason to be very proud indeed of such a nephew. Hope he will prove a bigger gun than a Rodman. Give him my compliments and let some of the women kiss him on my account. . . .[40]

Heaven knows I should be glad enough to get turkey with the "old folks at home" on Thanksgiving Day [November 24] and to skate with the young folks on Christmas, but as General Grant's motto, like that of the ancient orator, seems to be "action, action, action," my chances appear very slim indeed. Since the engagement of the 27th, we have lain quietly in camp with nothing but the ordinary picket and fatigue duty and an abundance of regimental writing to amuse us. The opportunity has been improved by the men by erecting log shanties. Knowles, 1st Sgt. of C Company, and I now tent together and have very comfortable quarters. Our shelter tents are raised on four layers of pine logs, halved, and the floor is boarded, and one room is kept comfortably warm by a stove. The "stove" consists of a camp kettle and a sauce pan riveted together and inverted thus [in an enclosed sketch—deleted]. The bottom is knocked out of the kettle in order to open communication between the two, and a hole cut in the bottom of the pan to admit the fuel. A flattened tin plate serves as a cover, and a pipe, constructed of tin preserve cans joined artistically together and inserted in the side of the mess pan, completes the whole. We have a brick hearth, too. The machine works like a charm. Bully for us!

Capt. Wicks, who was wounded on the 27th, died on the 31st at Fort Monroe. Our Adjutant, Lt. Beady [Beebe], is believed to be still living.[41] Another of the old officers, 2nd Lt. Whipple, has been dismissed from the service for absence without leave and disobedience of orders.[42] I have been recently appointed as the Sgt. Major of the Regiment, to rank from November 1st.

Whether we shall remain here during the winter is yet a matter of doubt. A number of the troops, including the 112th New York of our brigade, left here night before last for parts unknown. They embarked on transports on the

James and go perhaps north, perhaps south. Are you going to have a second rebellion in the North when election day comes? It looks stormy there.[43]

Don't think that the southern negroes will hesitate to fight for their masters if called upon. They have been taught to obey in their ignorance and can easily be made the tools of their masters. Already the "yankee niggers" are as hateful to the black southerners as are the Yankees to their white masters. If the threat of Jefferson Davis[44] is carried out, the spring will open [for] us with a brutal, horrible phase of the war.

In haste,
Ed. K. W.

P. S. By thunder! I have just found a letter in my portfolio dated October 29th that I supposed to be sent by mail a week ago. Well, I must be growing old fast. You will find it enclosed.

Edward K. Wightman

[P. P. S.] Winter is almost upon us. We had a hailstorm yesterday. The woods are almost impassable.

Camp, 3rd Infantry, N.Y. Vols.
near Richmond, Va.
November 28, 1864

Dear Bro:

. . . I am glad to hear that you are well but sorry to hear that you didn't have a grand time Thanksgiving. On that day your worthy relative feasted on roast chicken and cranberry sauce, bread and butter, and mince pies (plums in 'em), oysters, raisins, and trifles enough to fill in the chinks after the heavy packing had been completed. All this, too, was due to private enterprise. The turkeys and so forth from the North did not arrive until the 25th, but when they did come, there was an abundance—one pound and a half of turkey, goose, or chicken to every man, besides cakes, pies, eggs, apples, dried fruit, and so forth.[45] Today Knowles received a box from home containing a leg of fresh pork, stuffed and roasted, fresh beef ditto, balony [sic] sausages, head cheese, mince pies, apples—phew, we have been living like fighting cocks. Poor soldiers!

There is nothing doing here—that is, no fighting. We are corduroying the roads and perfecting our quarters. Rumor says there may be another grand movement within fifteen days, but there is no immediate sign of it. The Dutch Gap Canal will not probably be finished for several weeks yet.[46] I am inclined to think that our action will depend somewhat on Sherman's movements and to [on] the countermovements of the rebels.[47]

Desertions of conscript[s] and bounty seekers from this part of our lines have become so frequent that an order has been issued from division headquarters offering twenty day furloughs to those who will arrest or shoot deserters. One of them was shot near our camp on Friday by order of the general court martial.[48] The regiment was present at the execution; I preferred to be excused.

The army appears to be reorganizing.[49] The Third Regiment is now the smallest in the 10th Corps, mustering but 302 officers and men on paper and showing only 128 muskets for active duty. Capt. George W. Warren of C Company now commands us. He is a good officer.

The mittens mother knit came through safe by mail. They fit like gloves and cover my wrists almost halfway to the elbows. . . . I am very thankful to Lady Clara for them. Jim's obscure joke about the [recent election] fight I have not been able to laugh at yet, but I am studying it pretty hard and expect I shall split myself when I see the point. His enclosure of postage stamps is herewith acknowledged.

. . . . In a word to all the folks and all the babies, remember your truly humble and highly contemptible brother.

Ed K. W.

P. S. It has rained steadily for the past week, and we are nearly smothered in mud. Previous to this in the vicinity, it was extremely cold. It is now warm and pleasant again.

Ed

[P. P. S.] Ask Mary to send a darning needle in her next letter. They cannot be procured here.

8
FORT FISHER

[Throughout November 1864 it is doubtful that anyone in the Third New York gave much thought to Fort Fisher, North Carolina, its fifty cannon, its twelve hundred-man garrison under Colonel William Lamb, or the hundreds of other Confederates who held the line between the fort and nearby Wilmington. By early December, that earthwork between the Atlantic Ocean and the Cape Fear River had taken on great importance to the Third as well as to many other regiments in the Second Division of the newly-formed Twenty-fourth Corps and the Third Division of the all-black Twenty-fifth Corps. For in that month General Grant decreed that a sixty-five hundred-man contingent from the two commands must capture the fort, closing the last Confederate seaport and staunching a flow of blockade-runners' goods worth an estimated seventy million dollars per year.

As Edward recorded, the ocean-borne journey to Wilmington was notable for terrible weather and for the failure of the land troops (led in person by Ben Butler, against Grant's wishes) to coordinate operations with an allied flotilla of sixty gunboats, monitors, and sloops of war under Rear Admiral David Dixon Porter. As the sergeant noted ruefully: "probably a more mismanaged expedition never left our ports." As a result of the poor planning and equally poor execution, Butler's Christmas Day attack went awry. Admiral Porter failed to level the earthwork with naval ordnance alone, a scheme to detonate an explosives-laden "powder boat" near the fort proved a fiasco, and a heavy surf menaced Butler's landing. Finally, the politician-general, believing exaggerated reports of Fisher's invincibility, called off the offensive after a few hundred men had reached shore. Still aboard ship when this decision was made, Edward feared for the safety of the luckless troops, who spent a long night under the guns of the fort. By the morning of December 26, when these men were gotten off safely, Butler was en route to Virginia, leaving the navy and many of his transports behind.

Edward was disgusted with his commander's performance; Grant was livid.

217

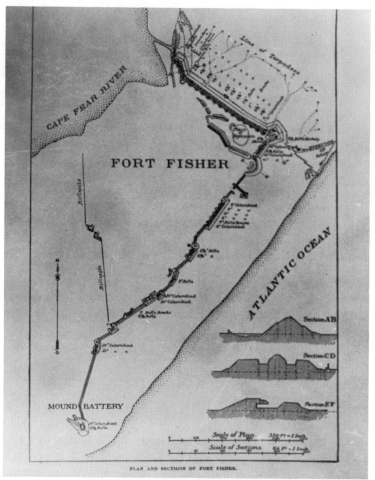

Fort Fisher, North Carolina (*Map from* Battles and Leaders of the Civil War)

On January 8 he relieved Butler from his post and packed him off to his home in Massachusetts. A few days earlier, he had sent the Third New York, all other regiments that had participated in the aborted campaign, plus fifteen-hundred reinforcements, back to Wilmington. The new expeditionary leader was Major General Alfred H. Terry of Connecticut, a soldier who possessed the tenacity and cool judgment that Ben Butler lacked.

Terry's determination to succeed where his predecessor had failed resulted in a well-planned assault on the fort's land and sea faces on January 15. This offensive, following an effective bombardment by Porter's fleet, precipitated some of the most desperate close-quarters fighting of the war. By nightfall the Stars and Stripes had replaced the Stars and Bars on Fort Fisher's parapet. Atop that parapet, however, also lay the body of Sergeant Major Wightman, his face toward the enemy, a minié ball in his right breast.]

Tuesday night, December 6, 1864
Near Richmond, Va.

We are off again in a hurry. The transports and 23 days rations. Three weeks of rough campaigning promised and plenty of hard knocks. "Savannah" is the word. The whole division goes. How many more, I do not know. We start early in the morning.

In great haste,
Ed K. W.

On board the Steamer Transport
Weybosset, Hampton Roads, Va.
December 11, 1864

Dear Bro:

We left camp the day following that on which my last note was written at about 5 o'clock P.M., in light marching order, with overcoats, shelter tents, rubber blankets, and one change of clothing. We crossed the James River on the pontoon [bridge] at Jones' Neck, marched over the Point of Rocks on the Appomatox [sic], which was reached about one o'clock A.M., and bivouaced [sic] there until daylight. We were then brought back to Bermuda Hundred landing on the James and embarked, a very complicated piece of strategy.

Next morning we were at Fortress Monroe, and there we remained, awaiting orders, with the twenty days rations aboard. Our destination is unknown. It is variously grasped as being Savannah, Charleston, Wilmington, Mobile, and Texas. A man from on shore this moment brings the news, said to have been received from telegraph from New York, that Sherman has taken and occupied Savannah, "so may it be."[1] There are two divisions embarked in the Roads, one white and one black.[2]

There are quite a fleet of gunboats and several monitors, which it is said will accompany us, the "[New] Ironsides" also. So we are probably to force a landing somewhere. The strength of the Third Regiment is 130 men and officers.

Letters received from Mary and Jim enclosing needle[s], for which I am much obliged.

There is talk of a march of 160 miles inland after we get ashore, and the order was to take with us only men capable of enduring exceptional fatigue. Now you know quite as well where we are going as any man in the fleet. Old Butler is here and perhaps will command the expedition—in order to insure its failure.

In haste for the mail.

Ed K. W.

P. S. December 12. The above was too late for the mail yesterday. We are still at

Fortress Monroe with no prospect of an immediate start. The weather is very cold. This morning my hair froze stiff while walking. The men suffer for want of sufficient clothing, especially those who sleep on deck.

Ed

On board the Transport Weybosset
near Wilmington, N.C.
December 16, 1864

Dear Bro:

I wrote to you hurriedly from Fortress Monroe saying we broke up camp on the 7th inst. and embarked at Bermuda Hundred on the 8th for some unknown point, supposed to be Savannah. Before daylight on the morning of the 13th, after taking aboard provisions and water for twenty days, the fleet, consisting of twenty ocean steamers under the direction of Commodore Porter and bearing about 10,000 [sic] troops under command of Major General Butler, left Hampton Roads and sailed up the Potomac River almost to Acquia Creek. This movement was merely a blind for the rebs on the left bank. At sunset on the 14th we put about and on the morning of the 15th woke and found ourselves anchored in the mouth of the Chesapeake Bay. Thence after a short delay we put to sea, doubled Cape Hatteras and this afternoon, having been eight days on transports, are lying off the North Carolina coast, about to enter the Mason [borough] Inlet, which will land us within eight miles of Wilmington.

Thus far, the weather, though rainy at first, has favored our enterprise. The passage around the Cape was not rough for the season, and the men suffered only from close quarters and seasickness. Five hundred soldiers are crowded on the Weybosset. Part are on the decks, part between, and part of them are half smothered in the lower hold, where they remain day and night making their bed on the coal. Coffee is made for them twice a day by steam, a caskful at a time. This, together with raw pork and hardtack, constitutes their rations. In the early part of the voyage, however, we had some codfish, which the boys called "Lincoln trout," and a few rations of dried herring, which they have christened, "Lincoln's sardines."

The appearance of the fleet at night when the vessels sail abreast and each steamer displays three lights, red, white, and blue, is magnificent. In the cabin where I was so fortunate to be quartered, the evenings were enlivened by music and dancing. We have a violin, good singers, and contrabands without number, whose performances in the Terpsichorean line would make you laugh yourself into an apoplexy. At present we rest here at tranquil water, the men fishing over the sides of the steamer and although out of sight of land pull[ing] in fine sea bass as fast as they wish.

We are a little ignorant of the end arrived at by the expedition. It hardly seems probable that we will be expected to capture Wilmington or to advance very far inland with the small force assigned. As we have brought a large number of entrenching tools, the general opinion is that we are to feel the strength of the enemy, take everything which can be taken, and then select a position and fortify it.[3] No gun boats came with us, but it is supposed that they will either precede us or follow us from Fort Monroe. We shall probably land tomorrow morning.

Until some port is reached we are, of course, shut off from all news. My last letter from home was Mary's of December 10th, promising a Christmas box. I am very much obliged but would rather you did not try to send it. You will see from this note how unsettled we are and how uncertain our movements. We may turn up in China next, for all I know to the contrary. As for my getting home [by] Christmas, or at any other specified time, it is entirely out of the question. Even if it were possible to get a furlough now, I doubt whether I should wish to leave the field before the 29th of August next, when the term of my enlistment expires. Then, if I live so long, I hope to see home once more, and if the war is done, to settle down and enjoy a peaceful life of a respectable citizen. As ever, yours truly,

Your affectionate brother,
Ed K. W.

On board the Transport Weybosset
at Beaufort, N.C.
December 22, 1864

Dear Bro:

The enclosed letter, written nearly a week ago, has lain quietly in my pocketbook because I have had no opportunity of sending it by mail.

Day after day we have been tossed drearily on the waves off the bleak coast, out of sight of land, living on raw pork and hardtack and crowded almost without breathing room into the filthy old transport, last used to convey paroled prisoners north from Savannah. This completes the fifteenth day aboard. The lower decks and hold are so confined that it is wonderful how the men have thus far escaped pestilence. Had our soldiers been so roughly treated by the rebels, there would have been no end to cries of "shame" and the accusation of "barbarity" from the enlightened press. Probably a more mismanaged expedition never left our ports. As yet nothing has been accomplished beyond testing uselessly the endurance of the troops, and this long two weeks of seasickness and suffering has undoubtedly harrassed and worn them [down] more than six weeks of active campaigning could have done.

We arrived off Wilmington long before the gunboats were ready, and then it was found that the enemy's works were so strong that it would be inexcusable folly to attempt to carry them by assault. On the 17th inst. General[s] Ames and Weitzel[4] reconoitered [sic] in a tug and found the rebel entrenchments extending four miles along the coast and protected by an abundance of artillery. Our Brigadier, Curtis, then visited us and communicated this information and said it was proposed to land [Colonel Louis] Bell's Brigade six miles above Fort Fisher, where they were to entrench. A barge ladened with gunpowder, iron, and other missles [sic] was to be sent in and exploded under the walls of Fort Fisher (which is close to the sea), and simultaneously the boats were to open (throwing seven tons of iron per minute) and five brigades, including ours, were to land and assault the Fort—a wild and, I believe, an impracticable scheme. This was the program for the 18th, but meantime the ironclads had to be sent for from Fort Monroe.[5] Rough weather set in, the fleet of transports scattered, coal and water gave out, and finally we are at Beaufort, N.C., taking in fresh supplies.

Last night was the roughest we have experienced at sea. The vessel rolled terribly. Everything movable was dashed and slammed around in the most confused manner. The officers rushed across the cabin like locomotives off the track. One shut the door of his stateroom on his coat tails and then pitched forward and tore those tails clean off. The poor darkies dove around, butting their hard heads through the panels and howling like demons with pain; Wightman laughed till he was blue in the face. Tis all fun, me boy.

Just now all are well, and we are safe in still waters, but no one is permitted to land, and tomorrow we start again for Wilmington. The brunt of the work is now to be assigned to the ironclads.

We have heard of Sherman's and Thomas' success[6] and learned that the 5th Corps, together with a division of the 2nd, has captured Weldon and is advancing this way.[7] Success to it and to us. We find no mail here from home, and it is said that whatever we write here will be detained for some days.

Poor rations have reduced my weight until I am thin as a rail, but otherwise I am well. I expect a First Lieutenant's commission in the next mail but probably shall not be mustered out [of the noncommissioned ranks] until the end of this month, perhaps later. . . .

We expect no winter quarters. Hope to have the Union fixed up as "good as new" next summer.

In haste,
Ed K. W.

P. S. Merry Christmas and Happy New Year.

On board Transport Weybosset
off Fort Fisher, near Wilmington,
N.C., December 23 [26], 1864

Dear Bro:

We left Beaufort, N.C., on the afternoon of the 24th inst. in company with the other transports, well supplied with water and fuel, and reached our old ground near Wilmington about 5 o'clock P.M. on the 25th inst. We learned that the gunboats (including monitors and the Ironsides, said to be fifty in number) had already been pegging away twenty four hours at the rebel works and had succeeded in quieting several of the minor batteries.

At sunrise on Christmas morning, everything was quiet. The sky was cloudy but the sea tranquil and disturbed only by a gentle swell. There was no wind blowing, and the beach was only three miles distant. Everything seemed to favor our enterprise, and the troops, who had been eighteen days embarked (long enough to visit Europe and return), were eager to land. Some idea of the position may be had from this sketch [deleted].

Fort Fisher was the main point of attack. The iron clads were formed in line within easy range of it, while the first class wooden sloops-of-war, etc., were drawn up in a second line in rear of them. The landing was to be effected on the neck of land to the right [the northeast angle] of the fort. This neck, or rather penninsula [*sic*], is a sand bar about three quarters of a mile wide and covered with pine trees on the side opposite the Atlantic Beach. Along its whole extent, at unequal distances, the rebels have thrown up works and built batteries. Fort Fisher, I believe, is an old U.S. fort and very elaborately constructed with bomb proof casements.[8]

Early in the forenoon our artillery opened. Light draught gunboats ran in between the transports and the shore and shelled the bar in front of us, and the old steamer Brooklyn, following in their wake, formed a terrific broadside whenever the rebel guns replied. Meanwhile, the ironclads and their consorts thundered away at Fort Fisher with such stunning violence that the ocean fairly trembled.

I can imagine nothing like the bellowing of our fifteen inch guns. The belching of a volcano with accompanying explosions may suggest a corresponding idea. The din was deafening. Above the fort the countless flash[es] and puffs of smoke from bursting shells spoke for the accuracy of our guns while occasion-

The Bombardment of Fort Fisher (*Engraving from* Battles and Leaders of the Civil War)

ally columns of sand heaved high in the air suggested that possibly the case-ments were not so safe and cozy after all. "I'd rather Johnny'd be where them eggs is breaking than me," was the sententious remark of a philosophic who stood with his hands in his pockets on the deck of [the] Weybosset. His comrades rolled the quids in their mouths and responded in chorus, with quiet earnestness, "Them's my sentiments."

By 2 o'clock the batteries on the bar had been silenced, our consort of gunboats had worked in and taken positions near the shore, and five hundred men, Brg. Gen. Curtis commanding our brigade, were making for the beach in yawl boats, arranged in line of battle. We watched them anxiously. Before they touched shore, the men were over the sides of the boats waist deep in water and were actually deploying at skirmishing and advancing at a double quick ere they had reached dry land. A rousing cheer—a stentorian Christmas cheer—went up from the whole fleet.

Forward the first line ran with their heels toward us and their front to the enemy while, more rapidly than I can write, a solid line of battle formed close behind and followed on. A moment later a white flag fluttered from the sand hill, and one hundred fifty "gray backs" surrendered themselves and a piece of field artillery.[9] Jack Knowles and I, seated on the pilot house, shook hands on the strength of it. "Now for our Christmas dinner," said my worthy comrade cheerily, "I guess we can afford to feast on sour bacon and hard tack in honor of that performance," and so we did, watching lynx-eyed the moving panorama on shore, pointing out probable points of attack with our forks, calling atten-tion to gallant charges by gestering [sic] eloquently with crackers, and making all sorts of odd noises by trying to chuckle while masticating.

The skirmish line soon came to a halt and laid down, and the main body of troops, their flank being thus protected, double quickened [sic] to the left along the edge of the water toward Fort Fisher. Small boats were now rapidly launched and sent in with reinforcements. Our turn came in due course. Just as eight bells struck (four o'clock P.M.) the last boat left our ship, containing, among others, Wightman. But we had not traversed half the distance to the shore when we met one of the boats returning, bearing an order from Gen. Butler for us to pull back. Capt. Warren, commanding the 3rd, and the Adju-tant were with us and, although very much surprised, obeyed. For some un-known reason all the troops had been ordered to re-embark without loss of time. Perhaps it was partly that the wind had changed to the northeast and the surf was boiling.

The command came too late. Many boats were swamped and dashed in pieces on the sands. A part only succeeded in getting away, and the remainder, including two thirds of our regiment, were left to defend themselves as best they might during the night.

From some of the men who came back we learned that our fellows pushed up close under the walls of Fort Fisher—so close that its defenders fired at them with rifles from the embrassures [sic]. Fortunately, the garrison was confined to the casemates by the terrific shelling of the gunboats. One of the aides on Gen. Curtis' staff approached so easily that he was able to make a sudden dash, capture a rebel flag, mount a rebel horse, and escape unharmed with his trophies.[10]

The enemy are said to have 1,000 men at Fort Fisher. Two hundred fifty more, because they could not be accomodated [sic] with safe quarters inside, fell into our hands. Our losses throughout have been trifling.

Now for the rough side of the picture. There are still a large number of our men on shore—probably over one thousand. The one day's rations they took with them are exhausted. The water has been so rough today that no boats could land to bring them off or take provisions to them. The sky is overcast and threatening, and the surf runs so high that nothing but life boats can live in it. The Rebs may overwhelm our boys and gobble them up before they can be rescued.

As I write (8 o'clock P.M.) the gunboats are blazing away in the fog to frighten the enemy off. All the small boats have been ordered to approach the beach, and it is reported that hausers [sic] have been passed ashore, by means of which life boats are to bring off the troops under cover of the darkness through the breakers. Many may be drowned, and even if successful, all the poor fellows will be drenched. The aspects of Butler's military reputation are certainly not much improved by this bungle.

We have received no mail since leaving Fort Monroe, and there is no opportunity to send this at present.

December 28, 1864

At daylight on the morning of the 27th we were all on deck, looking anxiously toward shore. All night long rain had been falling heavily, and the surf tumbling at such a rate that its roar would have drowned the sounds of an engagement with musketry. Our little band, still safe, were drinking coffee and warming themselves by the fires on shore. Under cover of the darkness they had thrown up two strong lines of entrenchments parallel to each other just above [the] high water mark; one to protect them from the enemy and the other to save them from the friendly gunboats in case the latter should fire grape and cannister [sic]. As the men were not provided with shovels, a great deal of the work was done with oar blades, pieces of board, tin plates, etc. The ruins of about thirty small boats littered the beach, so that fuel was plenty.

New attempts were now made to reach the men and bring them off, and with success. As the Weybosset was short of hands, I took an oar and worked with the navy for awhile. The boys had a lively time getting off, but they made a joke of the whole thing. As soon as a boat came to them, five or six men grasped it on each side and turned its prow to the sea. Then throwing aboard their bundles, muskets, and equipments, they waded out until breast deep in the water, where a final shove was given and all climbed in. Very often the boats swamped, but the boys came up laughing to renew their attempt.

Early in the afternoon the last man had embarked, only two of our men and one rebel prisoner having been drowned in the operation. Thoroughly drenched, they reached their respective steamers, where hot coffee had been kept for them all night; but there was no chance to dry their clothes, and they had no change with them, so they shivered and made the best of the position. Finally, the gunboats fired a parting salute, and the transports weighed anchor and started on their return to Deep Bottom. The Monitors had already left.[11]

The work of the expedition was done—perhaps. Was it done? I don't know, but I do know that curses enough have been heaped on Butler's head to sink him in the deepest hole of the bottomless pit. . . . Everybody is disgusted. Officers and men express [the belief] that the fort was ours and that no one but Butler prevented them from taking it. The men were close up to the embrassures [sic], and all the rebel guns were silenced[12] when the retreat was ordered. The officers raved and the men swore, but back they had to come.

The rebel flag which I spoke of was picked up at the foot of the rampart, where it had fallen by a shot from our gunboats. The flag was torn up by the Third Reg. for relics, and I enclose a piece to you for preservation.

It is now supposed that the movement was a feint to assist in the capture of Charleston.[13] But even so, there could have been no harm in capturing the fort and bagging a few more prisoners. It is now said that the garrison now numbers 3,000, but all except half a regiment were boys and raw troops. The prisoners we took average about seventeen years of age, officers included, and call themselves "The Seventeen-year-olds." They said the troops opposed to us were chiefly the "Senior" and "Junior" Reserves of North Carolina.

But I must stop for I have other work to do. This will be dropped in the mail at Fort Monroe, which we shall reach at 4 o'clock P.M. on the way to our old camp near Richmond.

Your bro,
E. K. W.

Camp near Richmond, Va.
January 1, 1865

Dear Bro:

On Friday afternoon [December 30] we reached Deep Bottom, landed, and marched back to our old camping ground near Chapin's [Chaffin's] Farm. We had been twenty three days on the water.

On reaching our old position, we found not a log of our houses remaining. Everything had been taken away by the troops in the neighborhood [for firewood]. Nothing was left but the muddy ground which, after exhausting performance during the last three weeks, seemed poor pickings. The weather was very cold, a cutting wind was blowing, our knapsacks had been sent to Bermuda Hundred, and we [were] altogether in a miserable plight. To make matters worse, a driving rain rushed in a heavy snow storm which continued without intermission throughout the next day.

Knowles and I got up a shelter tent as soon as possible and tried to imagine ourselves as comfortable, though wet and freezing. Fresh meat and crackers were soon issued, and we were so ravenous as to eat the former raw, not having patience to wait for it to broil on the coals.

Today it is clear and cold. The ground is covered with snow. We have to get our stove up and our knapsacks back and are ourselves again. A squad of men have just been detailed to build a new camp, and in a day or two we should be settled again. Tell Mary she can forward that box "double quick," as she pleases. Direct to E. K. W., Sgt. Major, Third Infantry, New York Volunteers, Fort Monroe, Va.

We found a big mail [a]waiting us here, two letters from Mary dated December 12 and 19. I am well and "chirp as a cricket." Happy New Year to all.

Ed

P.S. Tell Jim to send more stamps.

On board Steamship "Atlantic"
near Fort Fisher, N.C.
January 12, 1865

Dear Bro:

Just previous to leaving camp at Chapins Farm, Va., I sent a hasty note to inform you of our intended departure. We struck tents on the 3rd inst., marched to Bermuda Hundred, and embarked there on the steamer "Thomas Colyer" for Fort Monroe. On arriving at the Fort, our whole Brigade was transferred to the steamship "Atlantic" for transportation to North Carolina. Our accomodations [sic] are much better this time than on the first trip, as we have more room and better ventilation. My quarters are in the after cabin. The men are able to get their pork half boiled.

We left Hampton Roads on the morning of the sixth and, after the roughest passage (this is the seventh) I have experienced round Cape Hatteras, arrived off Beaufort on the morning of the eighth. Since then we have been delayed by various causes until now, the evening of the twelfth. On Sunday night [the 8th] we were treated to a heavy thunder shower accompanied by so much wind that we were forced to put to sea.

Our second attempt, it is rumored, is to be made in a different direction from the first. Although Gens. Ames and Curtis[14] are both with us, no one knows anything positive; but it is believed that the troops, to the number of 15,000 [sic] will be landed tomorrow morning at Gainsboro Inlet, to march direct to the City of Wilmington.[15] I am ignorant as to who commands the expedition. It is said that Gen. Hancock has a division of his new corps here and will lead us.[16]

Sleeping under cover does not agree with me. I caught a severe cold the first night I bunked in the cabin. I am now getting the upper hand of it and think that a good ducking, coupled with a little exposure, would completely cure me.

No mails have been received since leaving Chapin's Farm, and some days must elapse before we can hear from home. It may be a long time, too, before I shall have the opportunity to write again, although I will do [so] as soon as possible after we strike.

Yours truly,

Ed

[P. S.] Direct letters as before.

On board the steamship "Atlantic"

Near Fort Fisher, N.C.

January 12, 1865

Dear Father, Mother, Fred, Abbie, Jim, Lillie, Chas, Mary, Ell, and the babies:

Your Christmas family letter dropped into camp on New Years Day like a five hundred pound Parrot [sic] shell and administered such a shock of homesickness and hunger that I came near being annihilated. What had I, a free going, half starved soldier to do with your savory turkey, and mealy sweet potatoes and lucious [sic] plum pudding and hot mince pies and foaming lager? Ah, my friends, thus was it with the Captain in ancient times, when afar off he gazed woefully at the smoking ruins of the beloved city of his birth, burned by a barbarous enemy. Now, "veni" "sed" "vidi," though, without the rest? Well, well, if we all do see another Christmas, maybe it will be a jolly one.

I am glad to hear that you had such a pleasant time. Our family is very fortunate, indeed, to have preserved thus far its circle unbroken and to be able to meet and enjoy quietly an occasional holiday. You will readily believe, without much assurance from me, that I long to rejoin you and resume my place in your midst. Let us hope that the year 1865 will restore peace in the country and to all Americans the rights and privileges of respectable citizens.

As ever your Affectionate son, brother, and uncle,

Ed K. W.

Fort Fisher, N.C.

January 16, 1865

Stillman K. Wightman

195 Broadway

N.Y.C.

Dear Sir:

One of the most terrible battles of the war has just been terminated in our favor, but not without removing suddenly from among us our beloved "comrade" Edward K. Wightman, whose long association with us has deepened [our] every sentiment into the warmth of earnest attachment. In him our Country has lost a true soldier, always faithful in the discharge of his duties and unflinching in the hour of danger; your family an affectionate son and brother; and we a worthy example, and an associate, who had endeared himself to us by his many virtues and by the open frankness of his character. He died while

The Northwest Salient of Fort Fisher, Where Edward Wightman Was Killed, 15 January 1865 *(Photograph courtesy of the Library of Congress)*

gallantly charging at the head of our regiment and was among the "first" to enter the fort.[17]

He was buried this morning and the grave marked so that it can be found at any time if needed. He was hit on the right side and expired immediately.

I have a few things, found in his knapsack, which I have taken charge of. I shall send them on to you at the earliest opportunity, [and] any further particular you wish to hear of you can learn from [me].

With much sorrow for your untimely loss,

Your Obdt. Servt.
1st Sergt. John W. Knowles
Co C, 3rd Infty N.Y. Vols.
Fort Fisher, N.C.
Via Fort Monroe, Va.

EPILOGUE
A Father's Journey

[Stillman Wightman was devastated by the news of his son's death. Yet he managed to throw off his grief and to undertake a sixteen-hundred-mile trip to recover Edward's body and return it home for burial. The ordeal was intensified by his poor health and the difficulties and uncertainties of travelling through a country unsettled by war. Through it all, his religious faith and sense of paternal duty kept him going—enabling him to demonstrate the same fidelity, resolve, and endurance that his son had exhibited through two and a half years of war.]

It was on Thursday morning, the 19th of January, 1865, [that] we found it announced in the Herald of that date that "Sergeant Major Whiteman 3d N.Y. V. was killed" in the battle. Our house was immediately enveloped in sad mourning.

I went down to my office and made inquiries, and soon came to the conclusion, after prayerful deliberation, that it was my duty to go to Fort Fisher. It was a great undertaking for me at that season of the year, and especially as I was not at the time in very good health, and I had not for many years been subject to so great exposure. I returned to my house and held a consultation with my family and told them what I had thought of doing. They did not discourage me but left the matter to my own sense of duty.

I accordingly resolved to go; and at seven o'clock on the evening of the same day I started in the cars at Jersey City, and after riding through a cold, sleepless night I arrived in Washington, D.C., at six o'clock the next morning. My object in going to Washington was to procure a pass to and from Fort Fisher. I was informed that it was difficult to procure such a pass; and so, in order to be more certain of success, I first waited on Gideon Welles, Secretary of the Navy, an old friend of mine,[1] who gave me a letter of introduction to the Secretary of War [Edwin M. Stanton], which proved all sufficient in insuring me a pass. I forthwith presented the note to the War Department and immediately obtained

230

the pass; and at three o'clock in the afternoon of Friday, the 20th [of] January, was on board a steamer lying at a wharf in the Potomac, and soon afterwards was sailing down the River in her for Fortress Monroe. . . .

Fort Monroe is a very strong fortification and may be regarded as almost impregnable. There I was unavoidably detained for want of a transport, until Tuesday following; during which time it was very cold and stormed almost incessantly. Having learned unexpectedly that there was a Capt Warren of Albany, belonging to the 3d Regiment N.Yk. Volunteers, who was then at the Chesapeake Hospital at Hampton, I lost no time in procuring a pass from the Provost Marshall [sic] and walked a distance of about three miles on Sunday, in the face of a rain and a strong wind, to the Hospital, where, after some difficulty, I found him confined to his bed by sickness. I also saw Lieut. [Edwin A.] Behan, belonging to the same Regiment, who had been wounded in the neck at the battle of Fort Fisher and was under treatment in the same room with Capt Warren. They gave me the first reliable information I had been able to obtain respecting Edward.

"I regret to inform you," said the Captain to me, "that your son Edward was killed, being in the front ranks that commenced the attack in the storming of Fort Fisher. I had known him well for a long time. Edward was not rash, but was a bold man, and never flinched from danger. He was very correct and circumspect in all his habits and deportment. I never saw him drink any spirits. He was strictly temperate, and never used profane language. He was very social, kind, and affable, and was held in great esteem by the men of the Regiment. Whenever engaged in battle, he was firm, cool, and collected, and understanding his duty, he never failed to discharge it with promptitude and bravery. perhaps," said the Captain, "the best description I can give of him is that I considered him a model soldier."

Lieut. Behan was present and attested to the truth of what the Capt had said to me. "Edward and myself," he remarked, "were at the head of the Regiment and among the first to attack the Fort at the commencement of the battle. I," said he, "had got upon the parapet, and Edward was mounting the slope in front, and just upon the point of reaching the same parapet, near me, not far from the north west end of the Fort, when he was shot, as I think, in the left breast by a minie ball from a rifle, and fell while shouting to the Regiment to press bravely on to the charge. Some friend ran immediately and brought a cup of water and placed it to his lips; but his eyes were closed, and he never opened them afterwards."

The sad reality now came over me, that Edward was no more a living man in this World; and I left the Hospital with a heavy heart and returned to the Fortress. My aim then was to speed my journey as rapidly as possible; and I spent Monday in unceasing but fruitless efforts to accomplish my purpose. Besides, I was obliged to stay nights at a miserable dining saloon, sleeping a short and broken rest on a sofa, taking irregular meals, and being very uncomfortable from exposure to the storm and want of suitable fires. . . .

At length, on Tuesday morning, I learned that the Transport Ellen S. Terry had arrived from New York the previous night, bound for Newbern, N.C., and was lying nearby at anchor in Hampton Roads; and as I knew her Captain, I resolved I would take passage on board of her. After much trouble, I finally found her master, Capt Chapin; and having procured a pass from the Provost Marshall and paid for my transportation, I was taken on board of the vessel.

I found she had several horses and sixty head of cattle on her second or under deck that were to be taken to Newbern. Two of the cattle had died in the passage from New York and had been thrown overboard, and another had just died in the harbor; and the stench that came through the hatches was at times almost suffocating. Nevertheless my courage was not abated, but I resolved to continue on board and share my chances with the passengers and crew.

About eleven o'clock in the forenoon of Tuesday, the 24th January, the storm cleared away and the Transport steamed out of the harbor, past the Rip Raps;[2] and by meridian [noon] we were ploughing old ocean with a stiff breeze and a heavy roll of the boat. . . .

At length we saw Cape Hatteras on our starboard and the light house standing upon the Point; and, having sailed Tuesday and Tuesday night, we entered Hatteras Inlet about ten o'clock Wednesday forenoon, the 25th Jany. There the vessel had the ill luck to get aground upon a bar and remained aground until six o'clock in the evening when, by the assistance of a steamship, she was got off and proceeded immediately on her way through Pamlico Sound and up Neuse River to Newbern, N.C., where we arrived about nine o'clock in the morning of Thursday the 26th Jany, just one half an hour too late for me to take the cars there that day for Morehead City, opposite Beaufort, N.C.

Newbern must have been at the commencement of the War a desirable place for business and for the residence of gentlemen of leisure. Before the War probably some ten or twelve thousand inhabitants were residents there; but since our army took possession, most of the inhabitants have abandoned their homes, and many of the buildings are occupied by our officers and troops for war purposes. Having leisure, I spent Thursday in rambling through the town. Aside of officers, soldiers, horsemen, and heavy baggage wagons, each drawn by a team of six mules, I saw very few persons in the streets except Negroes, who were very numerous. Although it was a severe[ly] cold day, I was surprised to find the tree tops filled with robins and other birds, chirping from limb to limb as if it were midsummer. I returned at night to the Ellen, satisfied from observation that the place was ruined for the time being.

On Friday morning at 9½ o'clock I took the cars at the depot for Morehead City. The cars proceeded on southerly over a thin, sandy, level soil tinctured occasionally with iron and extensively covered with pine forests, until we arrived at Morehead City. Now and then I could see three or four negro huts by the wayside, and there were three or four military stations on the route and a Fort about five miles north of Morehead City; but on the whole road, a distance of forty miles, I did not discover a single dwelling house. I was told the land was worth ten shillings per acre.

It was a very cold day and, having suffered severely with cold feet and frosty air while riding in the cars, I alighted with great pleasure on the wharf at Morehead City, opposite Beaufort, N.C., at 11½ o'clock on the same day, Friday the 27th January, in the forenoon, and immediately went to the Quartermaster's office for information. There I was pleased to find E. R. Middlebrook, a brother of the First Baptist Church, New York City, who kindly proffered me every assistance in his power. He was chief clerk in the department, and he and Capt [Daniel D.] Wheeler, the Quartermaster, insisted on my dining with them, to which I reluctantly assented; and after a full repast, resumed the prosecution of my business. Brother Middlebrook furnished me with a good pine coffin, ready made, for Edward, which I got put on board the Transport Montauk, then lying near the wharf, and went on board of her myself about five o'clock in the afternoon on my way to Fort Fisher. She was taking in supplies for the army nearly all the following night.

On Saturday morning at 9½ o'clock, the 28th of January, the Transport Montauk, Capt Greenman, started for Fort Fisher. We had a moderately rough time during the day and ensuing night and arrived at Fort Fisher about 7 o'clock on Sunday morning, the 29th January, and anchored within the bar near the southern extremity of Federal Point, just easterly of where Cape Fear River empties into the ocean. Here we had a fine view of the river, which is about a mile in width, and of the Point, and Fort Buchanan, Fort Lamb,[3] and Fort Fisher, and the headquarters of the army, further north on the east bank of the river.

The sun was shining bright and clear, but the wind was cold and piercing. I fell well nigh worn out with want of rest, fatigue, and exposure; but my anxiety was so great to learn further particulars of Edward's fate that, at about 9 o'clock on Sunday morning, the Capt at my request landed me on shore; and I proceeded immediately on foot toward Fort Fisher, the north eastern extremity of which was about two miles from the place of my landing. The whole distance was but a continuation of loose, deep sand or muddy salt marsh, which was covered, much of it, with water by every flowing tide.

Everything was new and strange to me. Fort Buchanan was on the Point, an earth work perhaps 50 feet in height, somewhat in the shape of a cone. Fort Lamb was situated about three quarters of a mile easterly on the shore of the sea, being another earth work of conical form, of much greater magnitude, rising perhaps 70 feet from its base. Upon both these forts were heavy ordinance [sic]. And then, near Fort Buchanan, were the offices of the Commissariat, the Quartermaster, and the Captain of the Port; and interspersed between Fort Buchanan and Fort Fisher were encampments of some of our troops. . . .

There was an explosion of a magazine in the Fort on Monday the 16th

January, and many had been killed or buried in the ruins.[4] Whether Edward's body had been buried at all, or had been covered in the ruins, or whether I should ever be able to find or identify his remains, was to me a matter of entire uncertainty; especially as I was told it was a custom, where many were killed, to bury the bodies in trenches, sometimes three or four deep, and when buried in separate graves there were comparatively but few instances where the name of the deceased was to be found, indicating his identity.

These doubts and difficulties and my well nigh exhausted condition all had a strong tendency to almost dishearten me, until the pressure of my feelings began to find vent in tears. At first I thought I would sit down and rest, but I was in the midst of a salt marsh, and that was impracticable. Next, I sought for some spot where I might be partially shielded from the cold, cutting wind; but there was not any place any where near me to afford the least relief. It was at this time that my heart broke forth in prayer to God, to strengthen and nerve my mind and body and enable me to perform what I had undertaken, if it could be consistent with His holy will. Almost at the same instant, the promises of God came into my thoughts with great force and energy. . . .

Meanwhile, I had reached the more immediate region of the battleground of Fort Fisher, which was strown [sic] with shells, broken and unbroken, with balls, shot and shrapnell [sic], and diverse other missils [sic] and implements of death. Torpedoes, broken cannon, and fragments [of] wheels and carriages, and other evidences of destructive warfare, arrested my vision in various directions; while the massive earthworks before me and on the right, rising to an elevation of about 25 feet, with traverses or mounds of earth on the parapet rising perhaps 20 feet still higher, and the whole extending from the north to south more than half a mile and then from south to west almost a like distance until nearly reaching Fort Lamb, lay just before me and on my right in fearful grandeur.

All the front of the Fort not bordering on the sea had a ditch at its base, filled with water from the tide, and also a strong stockade outside the ditch, built of the bodies of small pine trees placed in juxtaposition, about 12 feet in height, with sharpened points at the top and holes cut through in near the ground for the use of sharpshooters. The Fort in front and rear rose almost perpendicular from its base. It embraced about 70 acres of land and to the eyes of a civilian would seem absolutely impregnable.

I passed through a gateway cut in the stockade at the north extremity of the Fort and, crossing a small ridge, turned to the right and came immediately upon a plain of sand that stretched southward to the sea and northward perhaps two or more miles to a pine forest and westward, with salt marsh, to the banks of Cape Fear River. I was now in front of the northwest end of the Fort and within about 250 feet of the stockade. Here the fierce, cold wind made a rushing sweep, raising at times clouds of dust.

With the exception of a single soldier strolling near me, I was alone. I inquired of him if there were any graves in that region, of soldiers killed in the battle of the 15th of January. He replied there were and that some of them lay at a short distance from me on a slightly elevated knoll of sand in front of the Fort. Thither I repaired alone immediately, where I saw perhaps thirty graves, the most of which were left without any indication of the name or identity of the person buried. Extending my vision northward, I saw several other places where there were many graves at convenient distances but most of them without any identification.

I began to feel alarmed lest, after all my long, wearisome journey and constant anxiety and hopeful anticipations, it might be my sad lot to fail in the accomplishment of my purpose; and yet I could not delay a moment in my eager efforts. I commenced with the nearest grave to the Fort, about 250 feet northerly of the stockade. It had no indications of identity. The next grave had a small, narrow pine board erected at the head of it. I turned my back to the wind, to keep off the flying dust, and, leaning over the grave and looking through my spectacles, read the following words, legibly written with a small lamp-black brush upon the board:—"Sergt Major 3d N.Y. V.—E. K. Wightman."!!!

O, how my heart leaped with joy! No tongue nor pen can describe my feelings. Within perhaps three or four hundred feet of the spot in the parapet where Edward was killed, with the evidence before me, I could not hesitate in the belief that his body was buried there and that I was standing beside his grave, which gave me unspeakable satisfaction. All his life came up before me, and how beloved he was by his parents and brothers and sisters, and what an interest we had felt and manifested in his welfare and happiness—and there I stood alone and mourned and wept. . . .

At length, I started for headquarters, distant about a mile northerly from the Fort. I passed large numbers of rifle pits and breastworks that had been hastily dug and thrown up by our forces in their approaches to attack Fort Fisher; and soon came to camps of soldiers and finally, first, to the headquarters of General Ames and then, just beyond, to the headquarters of General Terry, which were situated on the sandy soil, somewhat elevated above and a few rods easterly of the easterly side of Cape Fear River.

My first object was to get an introduction to General Terry. I went to his headquarters and found he was absent but would return soon. Meanwhile I had a conversation with his chief clerk, and he became interested in my behalf. After a time General Terry came in, and at my request I was introduced to him. He shook hands and treated me in a gentlemanly manner. But I felt that I must enlist his sympathy. "General," said I, "were you not formerly a practicing lawyer in New Haven, Connt, and a clerk of Court?" "I was," said he. "Well," I continued, "I am a practicing lawyer in New York City; but I once resided, near five years, in New Haven, while I was at Yale College and studying law, and I subsequently practiced law in Connecticut until I removed to New York City in 1843."

"Is this," said the General, "Stillman K. Wightman?" I replied, "It is." "Give

General Alfred H. Terry (*Engraving from* Battles and Leaders of the Civil War)

us your hand," said he. "How are you. I have, a long time, known you well by reputation. Anything that I can do for you, shall be done with the greatest pleasure." Whereupon orders were forthwith given to me, directed to General Ames, to afford me all the facility in his power in the removal of the body of my son, and to the [Assistant] Chief Quartermaster, Capt [Samuel T.] Lamb, to furnish me with every facility for the removal of the body by government transport.

With these orders I proceeded to the headquarters of General Ames, presented my authority, and made known my wishes. He treated me very kindly and sent for the Surgeon general, Dr. Washburn, and other officers, who soon appeared, and thereupon we held a conversation. I first made a brief statement when and where I had been informed Edward was killed, and that I believed I had found his grave; and spoke of my desire to procure his remains and take them home with me.

Surgeon Washburn enquired if I had a lead coffin. I replied no, it was simply made of pine, and was all I could obtain at Morehead City. "I think," said he, "it is too late for you now to take up the body [due to imminent decomposition] and carry it away with only a pine coffin; and my advice to you would be to abandon the idea for the present. At some future time, you might perhaps send a lead coffin, eight or ten months hence, and obtain the remains of your son."

A chaplain of a regiment was there, and he approved of the Surgeon's views, as did others present. I felt that it was an important moment with me; and if I could not get their approval, I would probably fail in the whole object of my journey. Thoughts whirled through my mind with great rapidity, during which time not a word was spoken by anyone.

At length I broke silence and, addressing myself to General Ames, "General," said I, "a long and tedious journey from New York City I have just performed to this place, to obtain the body of my son. . . . This is an object eminently worthy of my utmost efforts, and I must say, without intending to give offence, that if it not be counter to God's will I will never leave Federal Point without taking the body of Edward with me."

Here another pause ensued. "Well," said the General, "I will cheerfully aid you all I can; but we are as yet in a very unsettled condition." Others present proffered their services. "It is possible," said Surgeon Washburn, "if the body were deposited in the coffin and the residue of the space filled with salt and rosin, you might be able to carry the remains north in tolerable safety at this season of the year." Having arrived at this favorable point, I did not deem it advisable to press the matter further for that day; and so I bade them good afternoon.

The night was approaching and I was three miles from the Point, and was obliged to be there about sunset or I might fail to get them to send me a boat from the Montauk, where I was forced to go and stay nights, as there was neither food nor lodging of any kind for me on shore. So I commenced and waded through quicksands and salt marsh to the Point, where in about half an hour afterwards they sent me a boat and took me on board the Montauk. . . .

On Monday morning, the 30th January, I again went ashore at the Point and saw Capt Lamb, the Quartermaster, and gained his sympathies in my behalf, with his promise to aid me all in his power. The wind blew severe from the north or north-east and was accompanied with some rain, and it was uncomfortably stormy and cold. But I drew my overclothing around me and started again on a pilgrimage to headquarters, not forgetting to stop at Edward's grave on my way.

Having arrived at General Terry's headquarters, I obtained an interview with Doctor Barnes, a physician [Surgeon Norman S. Barnes, Medical Director of Terry's Corps], and inquired if he knew where I might obtain salt or rosin.

General Terry remarked that he could furnish me with plenty of salt; and Doctor Barnes said there was no rosin to be found there, but he expected to go to Smithville, across Cape Fear River, the next day, and if he could find any rosin, he would bring some over on his return. With these assurances I found myself obliged to be content for the day. I saw that the business must take time for its accomplishment; and too much haste might defeat my purpose.

So I spent the rest of the day in roaming through the camps among the soldiers, and in examining critically the rifle pits and breast works and Fort Fisher and Forts Lamb and Buchanan, and in holding sundry conversations with officers and soldiers. During the day I found an officer who told me that he had three bodies taken up last June at Newbern, N.C., that had been buried three months. That he procured tent-cloths and covered the cloths with hot pitch, and wound them around the bodies, and put hot pitch on the inside of the coffins, and deposited the bodies in the coffins, and sent them to Brooklyn, New York, where they were buried in Greenwood Cemetery; and no fault was found, or complaints made; and he kindly offered me his assistance if I should need it. I then went to General Ames' headquarters and saw Surgeon Washburn and reported the facts to him; and he thought the plan a better one than he had suggested the day before.

Finally, after a day of anxious care, I returned to the Point and went on board the Montauk. At supper we had at the table Capt [Andrew] Ainsworth, the harbor master, and also the Capt of the small steamer Howard, which was accustomed to run from the Point up the River to a wharf abreast of General Terry's headquarters and was engaged in other harbor service. I inquired of them, as I did of many others, for information [about] where I might obtain pitch or rosin or tent-cloth. No one could tell me where I could obtain either of the articles. The soldiers needed all their tent-cloths; and as for pitch or rosin, they did not know where they could be found.

The next morning, Tuesday the 31st January, I went ashore again at the Point and waded through sand and salt marsh until I reached Fort Lamb; and from there to the north easterly extremity of Fort Fisher I made [a] thorough search throughout the whole rear of the Fort for pitch and rosin, inquiring of every person I saw if they knew of any such articles; to which I received the uniform answer, that they had no knowledge respecting it. Finally, observing a rising knoll of sand lying in the rear near the tide water of the River, I repaired thither and with the fragment of a pick-axe I went to work, picking at a slight mound of sand; when, to my astonishment, I found a whole barrel of rosin there, buried in the sand! I was affected even to tears, and thanked the Lord and took courage.

I then sought for and found a large sand-bag and, emptying out the sand, I commenced filling it with large lumps of rosin; and, having obtained from 25 to 30 pounds, and seeing a large four-wheel wagon drawn by a team of six mules just passing me, I begged the privilege of depositing the bag of rosin in the wagon—which was freely granted, and the rosin was thus carried to a point within half a mile of headquarters. There I took the load upon my back and carried it through deep sand to the headquarters of General Ames, and left it in charge of a soldier for the ensuing night.

The same day I had the coffin sent ashore and saw Capt Lamb, and by his orders the coffin was forwarded and left in charge of another soldier near the same headquarters. I got a permit and obtained a sufficient quantity of boards to make a box to inclose the coffin, and had the coffin and boards left in front of Capt Gordon's tent [Captain Daniel D. T. Gordon, Assistant Quartermaster of Terry's corps], who promised the next morning to detail a carpenter and have the box made, and in the meantime to have the coffin and boards properly guarded and not taken away. It was now near nightfall, and I was greatly fatigued. . . .

It seemed to me I could not walk back to the Point in season to get on board the Montauk; and so, after a moment's reflection, I moved slowly toward an officer standing near General Ames' headquarters. I had conversed with him the day before, and he had known Edward and felt an interest in my success. Addressing myself to him in a half mournful, half jovial tone, I said, "Pity the sorrows of a poor old man, whose trembling limbs have borne him to your door! I am quite fatigued," said I, "and yet I must be at Federal Point by sunset, or perhaps lose my night's rest on board the Montauk."

Turning round to an orderly, he said, "Orderly, take your horse and another, and go with this gentleman to the Point." And in less than five minutes, I was on horseback, with the orderly by my side, and away we galloped to the Point, where the orderly took my horse and returned, and I went aboard the Montauk for the night.

I went ashore at the Point early on Wednesday morning, the 1st of February, and again waded, as usual, through sand and salt marsh in the face of a keen, cold wind, until I arrived at the spot where I had before found the barrel of rosin; and now commenced making [a] search for pitch. I critically examined every place where I thought there was any probability of success. Finally, I betook myself to the edge of the tide from Cape Fear River, which was beginning to ebb; and there, after a short search, I discovered what I judged to be a barrel of pitch, embedded in the sand under the water. This unexpected good fortune enlivened my hopes and gave me a fresh impulse, and encouraged me to persevere.

I then proceeded immediately to General Ames' headquarters and told him of my labors the day before, and that it was necessary for me to procure assistance in endeavoring to obtain the pitch and more rosin than I had been able to carry through the deep sand on my back. He very kindly reproved me for not asking for assistance instead of carrying the rosin myself; and ordered a detail of men and a team forthwith to be at my disposal. In a few minutes I was provided with a heavy four-wheel wagon, drawn by six mules, with a driver and three men; and on we moved to the places where were the rosin and pitch. We gathered a further quantity of rosin, and then went for the pitch.

The tide had receded, and in digging around what I supposed was a barrel we found it was only three barrel staves, which, however, had pitch on the inside about two inches thick. This, we concluded, would not be sufficient, so, while one of the men was severing the pitch from the staves, we strolled over south-ard [sic], beyond the barrel of rosin, into the central part of the rear of the Fort, and there found a barrelhead covered with pitch from 4 to 6 inches thick, embedded in the sand; which was all and more than I needed. I felt extremely elevated in this sudden and unexpected discovery. We carried it with the rest of the pitch and the rosin to the wagon, and went and deposited the whole at General Ames' headquarters.

I next repaired to Capt Gordon's tent, to see what progress had been made in finishing the box, and found the lumber had not been touched by a carpenter. The coffin was there, but the boards had been removed some distance to a pile of joists. I sought out Capt Gordon and respectfully remonstrated. He went with me immediately to the only joiner there was there and ordered him to leave all other jobs and make me the box. The carpenter obeyed, and I stood by him and helped him, every way I could, for about five hours, when, it being near nightfall, and seeing that the work was about done, I walked from head-quarters to the Point, very much fatigued, and again went aboard the Montauk, and slept sweetly through the night.

Thursday morning, the 2d February, I again went ashore at the Point, and walked as usual to headquarters. It was cold and the wind blew very hard from the northwest. I called upon General Ames and told him the progress I had made, and now all I wanted was a tent-cloth. He said I would have to go to General Terry for that. I immediately repaired to General Terry's headquarters and told him what I needed; and by his direction I was furnished with an order on the physician at the hospital, a mile above, to deliver to me a tent-cloth to wrap the body in, and a detail of men and a team to take up and remove the body. He also ordered me a horse, to be at my disposal during the day.

So I mounted the horse and galloped away, through clouds of dust and sand, to the hospital, and saw the physician, who politely informed me that he could not furnish a team nor a detail of men; but he would send a tent-cloth to General Ames' headquarters, where the rest of my materials were deposited. He gave me an order on an officer at General Ames' headquarters for a team and detail of men. Consequently I had to ride back to those quarters; and there the officer gave me an order for a team and detail of men on another officer, three quarters of a mile above the hospital.

I found the box and coffin, rosin and pitch, and subsequently the tent-cloth, all deposited together at General Ames' headquarters. I then galloped off in the eye of the keen wind, with my mouth, eyes, and ears filled with dust and sand, to the station above the hospital, and presented my order to the officer. He ordered up a team and a detail of four men, besides a driver.

Thus equipped, we moved forward and, arriving at General Ames' head-quarters, we loaded in the coffin box, and tent-cloth, and rosin, and pitch, and started for Edward's grave. On the way I conversed freely with one of the men, a Lieutenant, who was the most intelligent and did the most important part of the work. He said his father was an undertaker.

Having arrived at the grave, we selected a spot about five feet below the top of the knoll, just west of where Edward was buried; and then, while they were digging a hollow place and lining it with large stones and procuring pine wood for a fire, I rode around in the rear of the Fort, and there I found an old iron pot, partially broken, and a bit of an old iron sauce pan, which we carried to the place; and, putting fuel upon the stones and starting a fire and fixing the pot thereon, we threw in a plenty of pitch, with a little rosin, and when it was boiling hot, we put it on with an old brush and swab and covered the inside and top board of the coffin, so that it appeared to be air tight. We pitched the inside and top of the box in the same manner—always filling the cracks and seams of box and coffin. We then covered one side of the tent-cloth with pitch, so that it appeared water tight.

We then repaired to the grave, and the men began to dig. By this time, including straggling soldiers, there were about twenty standing around the grave. I stood at the foot, anxiously watching every particle of sand that was removed. When they had dug down about four feet, they came to his body. They carefully removed the sand.

He was lying partly on his back and partly on his right side, with his face inclining toward the East. He was buried in his military dress, just as he appeared when he was shot on the parapet. The collar, or rather cape, of his coat had been drawn up and each end of it folded over his face. When they came to move aside the collar, or cape, revealing his countenance, I was sadly struck with the sight. His face was white and very much swollen; his eyes had evidently been in some way injured, his chin dropped down very low, and his upper teeth were very prominent. However, his forehead and eyebrows and hair and ears were very natural, his hands were unmistakable, and his limbs— all were evidently his remains. In addition to this, he had on his left shoulder the badge of Sergt. Major.

I saw the holes made by the ball that was the cause of his death. It had passed through the muscles of his right arm, about equidistant between the shoulder and elbow, and entered his right breast, perhaps five inches below the collar bone. He had evidently been shot while fighting with his sword [or rifle] in his right hand, by a minie ball from the rifle of a sharpshooter. He was shot while on the southeast verge of the top of the first mound at the northeast [northwest] extremity of the Fort, at about five o'clock in the afternoon. His legs gave way under him, and he dropped down where he was shot. He had marched with his Regiment across the bridge about four o'clock in the afternoon, when they climbed up around and on the top of the mound and fought there, often hand to hand with the enemy, until he was killed. He was the fifth man that first entered the Fort. . . .

I still stood at the foot of the grave and looking at everything critically, wishing to satisfy myself entirely that it was, beyond a doubt, the body of Edward. Observing a manifest disposition to proceed in the removal, I requested the men to delay a short time, as it was my desire to become first fully convinced of his identity.

"And ye can have no doubt about that," said a rough son of Erin, "for sure now he greatly resembles ye."

On some other occasion, such an Irish bull might have provoked a smile in me; but it passed unheeded. . . .

I stood in silence, looking at his remains. His whole life rushed upon my memory; his affection for father and mother and brothers and sisters and relations, his finished education, his judgment and intelligence, and the hopes he entertained, in common with all of us, that when he had honorably served out the term of his enlistment for three years he would return to his welcome home and quietly resume his wonted avocations in civil life; gazing upon his lifeless remains before me, the wreck of all this and our fond anticipations, and feeling that I, his father, was standing there alone, a stranger in a strange land, far away from my family, with no one present heartily to sympathize with me in the loss, my emotions overcame me and for a brief time my cheeks were wet with tears. No one can conceive of the agony of my trials on that occasion.

I gave the men directions to remove him from the grave and place him in the coffin. This was soon done. They spread out the tent-cloth, with the pitch on the outside, and laid his body in the cloth, upon his back; and, stretching his legs, and folding his arms over his body, and winding the cloth around him, deposited the body in the coffin, which proved to be just the right length and size for his remains. I then requested them to nail down the top of the coffin and pitch the seams on the outside with hot pitch, and then deposit the coffin in the box prepared to receive it, and nail down the top and pitch the outside seams in the same manner. Meanwhile I mounted my horse (for I could not bear to hear the driving of a nail) and rode rapidly to Fort Lamb, and there obtained from an officer an order or permit to have the body deposited in a bomb-proof, under guard, until it should be transferred to a transport.

On my return to the grave, I found the work was completed; and we went immediately and examined some of the bomb-proofs and came to the conclusion not to deposit the box there, as it was large and very heavy and would take from four to six men to carry it; and I determined to send it to and deposit it in a building on and near the head of the wharf of Cape Fear River, abreast of General Terry's headquarters—where it was accordingly carried and deposited, and remained under guard during the ensuing night.

The sun was near setting. I rode to headquarters, and General Terry's brother [Captain Adrian Terry, Chief of Staff of the corps] directed an orderly to go with me, and we rode with great speed to the Point, where the orderly took my horse and returned to headquarters, and I went on board the Montauk. I sat down at the table, almost completely exhausted, but after supper felt revived. Perhaps it had been to me the most painful day that I had ever experienced. As I was very weary, I soon betook myself to my berth and slept soundly through the night.

Friday morning, the 3d February, I again went ashore at the Point, and first visited the headquarters of Capt Lamb, the Quartermaster, and was told that he was at the headquarters of General Terry. I then had to wade through the sand and marsh to General Terry's headquarters, and was there informed that Capt Lamb had gone to the Point. I found the box in the building on the wharf, under guard.

Soon afterwards I had a long, pleasant interview with General Terry in his private room, by special invitation. I told him I must see Capt Lamb and that it was my wish to return to New York at the earliest possible moment. He ordered me a horse and that an orderly should go with me to the Point to see Capt Lamb; and in a short time I was galloping, with an orderly by my side, back to the Point, where we soon arrived. Capt Lamb was not there, and I had to wait for him a long time; and so I sent the orderly back to headquarters but kept my horse for further use.

When Capt Lamb came, I told him the body was ready for transportation and inquired of him if there was any vessel there, bound for the Port of New York. He replied, no; but the Transport North Point was lying at anchor near the Montauk, and she would sail for Fortress Monroe that afternoon or early the next morning. I told him where the box was. He said the Howard would soon go from the Point up the River to the wharf, and if I were there, the box could be put on board and carried by the Howard and put on board the North Point.

While we were talking, the Howard came sailing around the Point up the River, on her way to the wharf. Seeing that this was possibly the only chance in my power for expedition, I mounted my horse and ran him as fast as I could make him run, until I reached General Terry's headquarters. Meanwhile the boat had arrived at the wharf and was lying there. I gave up my horse, and went immediately to the wharf and had the box put on board the Howard; and shortly afterwards we were sailing down to the Point. On our right, over on the west side of the River, lay Admiral Porter's flagship, two or three Monitors, and about twenty gun boats, quietly in the stream. We passed the Point, and soon came to the North Point, where the box was put on board. . . .

At noon, the 4th February, we sailed out of the harbor, past Fort Fisher, across the bar, and then were detained two hours, awaiting dispatches from headquarters. On their arrival we put to sea, and I bade farewell to Fort Fisher. Our transport had no cargo on board, and having no side wheels, we were liable at any time to become the sport of the waves. However, we sailed very well through the night; and the forenoon of Sunday, the 5th February, was extremely pleasant and refreshing.

For two hours I sat upon a hatch and chatted with passengers. The sea was quite smooth, the sun was warm, the sky clear, and the air was bland. About 2 o'clock in the afternoon we changed our course and began to steer in a more northerly direction. Presently clouds began to gather in the east and northeast, and the wind grew strong from the northwest, which continued to increase until it blew a heavy gale. The waves ran very high, the vessel rolled and plunged and tumbled. The air became very keen and cold, and there were no places on board for comfort or accommodation. The Captain (Capt Kerwan) was sick with neuralgia, and two of his crew were confined with fevers.

Night came on, the most uncomfortable I ever witnessed. Down to this time I had not been sea-sick during my journey. I stayed up till 10 o'clock at night in the Pilot House and then went to my berth in the rear cabin. It was impossible to walk the deck or take a step anywhere without holding on to something. I went to my berth, a nasty, filthy place unfit for a human being to sleep in, small in dimensions and full of confined air peculiar to forecastles in sea vessels. The vessel was tossing at a terrible rate, and I very soon became seasick. I did not regret it, for I knew it would do me good. After I had got near exhausted, I fell over on my back and went to sleep. During the night the North Point rolled tremendously. On one occasion the Captain was thrown out of his berth prostrate upon the floor.

We arrived at Fortress Monroe and anchored in Hampton Roads about 9 o'clock in the morning of Monday, the 6th February. I immediately went on shore and, after much trouble and delay, went out in a steam tug and got the body from the North Point and had it brought and deposited at the head of the wharf. I then started and went to the Chesapeake Hospital to see Lieut. Behan. I found him and Capt Warren as before. Lieut Behan said he was not positive whether Edward was shot in his right or left breast, but he knew it was one or the other. That was all I wanted to know from him.

I returned to Fortress Monroe and, having procured an order of transportation from the Provost Marshal, I succeeded, at 5 o'clock in the afternoon, in getting the box and myself on board the steamer Alida, which soon set sail up the Chesapeake Bay for Baltimore. The vessel was crowded with civilians and soldiers, some of whom were sick, having but just left the hospital. I sat up all night, sleeping about two hours in an arm chair. During the night two soldiers died of sheer exhaustion. One of them fell down on the deck and died in five minutes after calling in vain for some kind of spirits to revive him. He had not a friend on board.

We arrived at the wharf in Baltimore at 7 o'clock on Tuesday morning, the 7th February. At 9 o'clock I had got the body transferred and put on board the cars, when we started in the New York train for New York [City]. There came up a storm of snow, which caused some delay, and I did not reach the depot in New York until about 8 o'clock in the evening, where I left the body in charge of the baggage master for the night. I arrived at home about 9 o'clock in the evening, having travelled about sixteen hundred miles in less than three weeks, and in better health than when I first started on my journey.

On Wednesday morning, the 8th February, the body was brought to our house, No 65 East 14th Street. The box was found to be air tight. The funeral

Edward Wightman's Grave *(Photograph courtesy of Mrs. Edith Wightman Kreitler)*

was attended at our house on Friday, the 10th February, at 3 o'clock in the afternoon. Relatives and numerous friends were present, and the services were solemn and appropriate. Saturday morning, about half past 7 o'clock, the body was taken to the depot at 27th Street. There we had it put on board a car, and myself and three sons, Frederick, James, and Charles, proceeded with it in the cars to Middletown, Connt., where we arrived at about 2 o'clock in the afternoon.

We had previously written to friends in Middletown and Cromwell of our wish to bury the body that day in Cromwell. We found several warm hearted friends waiting for us at the depot, and a carriage and hearse and all things in readiness. From there we went to Cromwell and to the cemetery, where we had the body buried in our family burying ground. Edward's remains were deposited beside the grave of his little sister [Clarissa], who died at about two and a half years of age and was buried in 1832. The funeral services at Edward's grave were appropriately performed by Revd Stephen Topliff, the only surviving brother of Mary Butler, deceased, widow of James Butler, deceased, the brother of my wife.

Before I left the grave, I went back and took a long, last lingering look at the box, containing the remains of a son that was near and dear to me. Many friends attended the burial and services at his grave. "And there," said I, "his body lies, and I trust will be permitted to lie, in peace till the morning of the resurrection."

I came away feeling that all my care and toil was nothing, compared with the satisfaction of knowing that his remains had been taken up from a grave in an enemy's land and had been safely transported to the land of his birth and peacefully buried in our family cemetery. . . .

New York 4th March 1865
Stillman K. Wightman

NOTES

Prologue

1. Actually, at this time the Ninth New York was en route from Fredericksburg to Brooks Station, Virginia, and from there to Washington, D.C. The Zouaves would lay over in the capital from September 5 to 18, prior to participating in the Antietam campaign. Frederick H. Dyer, comp., *A Compendium of the War of the Rebellion* (Des Moines, Iowa, 1909), 1409.

2. The Ninth had already seen hard campaigning and won a name as a fighting regiment. Organized in New York City during the first weeks of the war, it had been recruited from among members of a national guard unit, the "Old Company of New York Zouaves." Under Colonel Rush C. Hawkins it was sworn into federal service on 4 May 1861. In June the regiment was sent to Newport News, Virginia, and it saw its first active service two months later as part of an army-navy expedition against the North Carolina coast. On August 28 the Ninth helped seize Fort Clark, near Hatteras Inlet, cutting off a sea channel through which Confederate supplies had been transported inland. In February 1862 the regiment accompanied Major General Ambrose E. Burnside against enemy works on Roanoke Island, north of Hatteras Inlet, participating in an offensive that overwhelmed a force under Brigadier General Henry A. Wise. Later Hawkins's Zouaves saw action near Elizabeth City and South Mills, before being transferred to garrison duty at Norfolk and then back to Newport News. One of its companies, however, remained in North Carolina to help occupy Plymouth. By the first week in August 1862 the veterans of Burnside's Carolina campaign had grouped around Fredericksburg, ready to join the Army of the Potomac in opposing Lee's invasion of Maryland. Ibid., 1408–9; Matthew J. Graham, *The Ninth Regiment New York Volunteers (Hawkins' Zouaves): Being a History of the Regiment and Veteran Association from 1860 to 1900* (New York, 1900), 40–280; Rush C. Hawkins, "Early Coast Operations in North Carolina," *Battles and Leaders of the Civil War*, 4 vols. (New York, 1887–88), 1:632–59; John G. Barrett, *The Civil War in North Carolina* (Chapel Hill, N.C., 1963), 37, 46–61, 92–111.

Chapter 1. Antietam

1. Unless otherwise noted, all letters so addressed were sent to Fred Wightman and, through him, to the rest of the family.

2. The trip from Manhattan to Staten Island, thence to New Jersey, was made by way of two streams with Dutch names, the Kill Van Kull (which separated Staten Island from Bayonne) and the Arthur Kill (between the Island and South Amboy).

3. "Zou-zou" was, in the popular jargon of the time, a member of a Zouave outfit, Union or Confederate. The typical Zouave was one whose dress, drill, and deportment were based on those

of the Algerian light infantry of the 1850s—even to copying the Africans' habit of shaving their heads (note Edward's many references to the "scrubby heads" in his regiment). At the outset of the war, a tuneful ditty had publicized the Zouave motif: "My love is a Zu-Zu, so gallant and bold, / He's rough, and he's handsome, scarce / Nineteen years old." Mark M. Boatner III, *The Civil War Dictionary* (New York, 1959), 954.

4. This was twenty-two-year-old Private Terance Brady, who had enlisted in Company I of the Ninth on the day that Edward joined Company B. He was to transfer to K Company in October 1862 and seven months later would follow Edward into the Third New York Infantry. Matthew J. Graham, *The Ninth Regiment New York Volunteers (Hawkins' Zouaves): Being a History of the Regiment and Veteran Association from 1860 to 1900* (New York, 1900), 629.

5. The Tenth Massachusetts and the "14th Brooklyn" (Eighty-fourth New York Volunteers) were moving to Washington to rest and recruit. Both regiments had participated in Major General John Pope's Second Bull Run campaign as part of his Army of Virginia; now they were about to join the Army of the Potomac. The Thirty-seventh New York also took part in Pope's campaign, and was heading for a stint of garrison duty in the capital. Frederick H. Dyer, comp., *A Compendium of the War of the Rebellion* (Des Moines, Iowa, 1909), 1251, 1417, 1438.

6. A folding writing-desk was one of numerous unwieldly and impractical contraptions that added weight to the baggage of soldiers yet to make their first march with knapsack, weapons, and other accoutrements. Many models of this "apparatus" sold well among raw troops in 1861–62. For more on such devices, see Frederic Shriver Klein, "The Civil War Was a Pitchman's Paradise," *Civil War Times Illustrated* 2 (June 1963): 30–33.

7. This was a soldier's retreat, the "Cooper Shop Volunteer Refreshment Saloon," located at Otsego Street near Washington Avenue in Philadelphia's Southwark section. It provided food, rest, medical care, and toilet facilities for Union troops, many thousands of whom traveled to Washington, D.C., from the north and west by train through the City of Brotherly Love. The facility, capable of accommodating over one thousand troops daily, had been founded early in the conflict by a local philanthropist, Anna Maria Ross (c. 1811–63); it was maintained by private funds. For further details, see James Moore, *History of the Cooper Shop Volunteer Refreshment Saloon* (Philadelphia, 1866).

8. This was a regiment on occupation duty within Baltimore and also in garrison in Washington, D.C. Composed predominately of German-Americans, its official title was the Third Battalion, New York Heavy Artillery. Dyer, *Compendium*, 1383.

9. Much like the Cooper Refreshment Saloon, this soldier's rest had been established in June 1861 to provide for the health and comfort of state volunteers and their families, and to care for other troops passing through the city to the capital. The facility was administered by the Baltimore Relief Association, S. F. Streeter, Chairman. Up to this point, the Relief Association had fed and cared for over 126,000 soldiers at a cost of $18,600.78. *War of the Rebellion: A Compilation of the Official Records of the Union and Confederate Armies*, 4 series, 70 vols. in 128 (Washington, D.C., 1880–1901), series 3, vol. 2, 683–84.

10. The quote is from Milton's *Paradise Lost*, bk 1, line 302: "Thick as autumnal leaves that strow the / Brooks / in Vallombrosa. . . ."

11. The "Monitors" were the 127th New York Volunteers, a New York City regiment mustered in on 8 September 1862. At the time it was heading for Washington and points south, ready for field duty. Charles Wightman's friend was the thirty-three-year-old commander of Company B of the regiment. Frederick Phisterer, comp., *New York in the War of the Rebellion, 1861 to 1865*, 5 vols. (Albany, 1890), 4:3516.

12. Aquia (not "Acquia") Creek was one of two major Federal supply bases on the Potomac River. It lay thirty-eight miles south of Washington. The landing at Aquia Creek, on a neck of land along the south shore of the river, is known today as Youbedam Landing. The Federals had established the site in the spring of 1863, constructing a military railroad from it to their forward base at Fredericksburg via the Richmond, Fredericksburg & Potomac. Harold F. Round, "Federal Supply Bases on the Potomac," *Civil War Times Illustrated* 5 (November 1966): 20–26.

NOTES   249

13. These were three prominent anti-slavery advocates, two clergymen and authors, and one editor. George B. Cheever (1807–90) was a Massachusetts Congregationalist reformer, author of *God Versus Slavery* (1857) and *The Guilt of Slavery and the Crime of Slave-Holding* (1860): Allen Johnson and Dumas Malone, eds., *Dictionary of American Biography*, 20 vols. (New York, 1929– 36), 4:48–49. Editor of the *New York Tribune*, Horace Greeley (1811–72) was also a Whig political activist and in 1872 a Presidential candidate on the Democratic ticket: Ibid. 7:528–34. And Henry Ward Beecher of New York (1813–87), brother of the famous abolitionist, Harriet Beecher Stowe, was a Congregationalist preacher, orator, and author of political and religious articles: Ibid. 2:129– 35.

14. The Twenty-ninth Ohio was another of those regiments defeated under Pope at Second Bull Run. It, too, was en route to join the Army of the Potomac in Maryland. Dyer, *Compendium*, 1510.

15. *Webster's Third New International Dictionary of the English Language, Unabridged* (Springfield, Mass., 1981), defines this term as: (1) Something that ends or settles a matter; a decisive blow or answer; and (2) Something outstanding or exceptional.

16. Edward paraphrases Part 1, Act 2, Scene 4 of Shakespeare's *Henry IV*, in which Falstaff tells the prince: "Why, thou knowest I am as valiant as Hercules; But beware instinct; the lion will not touch the true prince."

17. This is incorrect; on September 13, McClellan made his headquarters in Frederick, about eighteen miles north of Poolesville. *Official Records*, 1, 19, pt. 1, 26.

18. Again Edward is misinformed. On the fourteenth, Burnside's corps moved to Middletown, Maryland, and from there to South Mountain via Turner's Gap. Ibid., I, 19, pt. 1, 417.

19. About noon on September 13, McClellan was presented with a military godsend: an authentic copy of Lee's September 9 orders to his troop commanders, detailing his dispositions for the coming days. These included his dispatching of part of his army, under Major General Stonewall Jackson, to capture the Union garrison at Harpers Ferry, west of South Mountain. Not till the next morning, however, did the ever-cautious "Little Mac" move westward toward the South Mountain passes—and by then Lee had learned the fate of his errant directive. Accordingly, he sent troops under Major Generals James Longstreet and Daniel Harvey Hill to Turner's Gap, just in time to block passage by Burnside's First and Ninth Corps. At the same time, Confederate Major General Lafayette McLaws turned east from the Harpers Ferry area to oppose a Union force under Major General William B. Franklin, heading for Harpers Ferry via Crampton's Gap, five miles below Turner's, ensuring Harpers Ferry's capture. See James V. Murfin, *The Gleam of Bayonets: The Battle of Antietam and the Maryland Campaign of 1862* (South Brunswick, N.J., 1965), 159–85.

20. Major General Irvin McDowell (1818–85), though subordinate to Pope, received much blame and derision for Second Bull Run. For unfathomable reasons, many of his troops believed they had lost the campaign through his treasonous collusion with the enemy. Widespread publicity was given to a deathbed accusation of that sort from the colonel of the First Michigan Cavalry, who was mortally wounded at Second Bull Run: E. S. Williams, ed., "Col. Thornton Broadhead's [Brodhead's] Last Letter," *Michigan Historical Collections* 9 (1886): 209. A luckier but no more talented field leader, Major General Henry Wager Halleck (1815–72), a studious West Pointer of little charm and suspect acuity, would nevertheless retain a high place in the War Department till war's end. Currently the army's General in Chief, he would finish out the conflict as its Chief of Staff. Johnson and Malone, eds., *Dictionary of American Biography*, 8:150–51.

21. Edward would soon find this rumor to be untrue. Lieutenant Colonel Edgar A. Kimball (ca. 1823–63) was a hard-fighting, hard-drinking native of New Hampshire who had entered the war as major of the Ninth New York. A one-time newspaper editor, a veteran of the Mexican War (winning honors at Contreras and Churubusco), he had been a customs employee and a militia officer in New York City at the outbreak of the conflict. At Antietam he had displayed pluck and agressiveness but, despite furnishing a target for numerous Confederate marksmen, had escaped unscathed. Graham, *Ninth Regiment New York Volunteers*, 39–40, 417–18.

22. No serious fighting took place on the night of September 18, as Lee began his withdrawal to

Virginia via Boteler's Ford on the Potomac. McClellan might have menaced, or at least complicated, the retreat (twenty-four thousand of his troops had seen little or no action on the seventeenth, and twelve thousand reinforcements had reached him since), but he allowed his opponent to depart Maryland without further molestation. E. B. Long, *The Civil War Day by Day: An Almanac, 1861–1865* (Garden City, N.Y., 1971), 268.

23. At South Mountain, with Burnside temporarily in command of McClellan's right wing, Major General Jesse L. Reno, a thirty-nine-year-old West Point graduate and Mexican War veteran, had immediate command of the Ninth Corps. Near Turner's Gap he was shot dead by enemy fire while examining his troops' skirmish line, shortly before sunset on September 14. Jacob D. Cox, "Forcing Fox's Gap and Turner's Gap," *Battles and Leaders of the Civil War*, 4 vols. (New York, 1887–88), 2:589.

24. The Ninth's casualty total at Antietam was 235: 45 killed, 176 wounded, and 14 missing. This, the heaviest loss in the Ninth Corps, represented sixty-five percent of the regiment's effective strength. *Official Records*, 1, 19, pt. 1, 197.

25. The commander of the brigade was a driven and dedicated man, both as a soldier and as a collector of incunabula. Born in September 1831 in Pomfret, Vermont, Rush Hawkins received no formal education but at age twenty began a law career in New York City—six years after lying about his age to serve in the Mexican War. In June 1860 he helped establish the militia company known as the "New York Zouaves," the foundation of the Ninth Volunteers. He led the latter to immediate fame under Burnside in North Carolina and held brigade and divisional command prior to Antietam (a battle he missed, having gone on leave). Imperious and argumentative, he feuded with many superiors, which may have played a role in his muster-out in May 1863. Later he was named a brevet brigadier general of volunteers but never retook the field. After the war he made a fortune in investments and real estate, and until his death in an automobile accident in New York in October 1920 he was a state legislator, a patron of the fine arts, and an avid collector of early specimens of printing. At the time of his death his collection, later placed on permanent display in Providence, Rhode Island, was considered the finest outside the British Museum. Johnson and Malone, *Dictionary of American Biography*, 8:415–16; Graham, *Ninth Regiment New York Volunteers*, 23–24.

26. About 7 A.M. on September 17 McClellan had ordered Burnside to attack across Antietam Creek against Lee's right flank. For reasons never fully explained, the corps commander for six hours made only piecemeal efforts to cross at and near a span afterward known as Burnside's Bridge. This enabled Lee to shift troops northward to oppose other Union drives. Not until about 3 P.M. did the Ninth Corps surge across the stream and capture high ground southeast of the village of Sharpsburg, causing the enemy flank to waver. Once on the far bank, the Ninth New York was opposed by infantry sheltered by a wall at the head of a ravine. Undaunted, Lieutenant Colonel Kimball led his men through a cornfield, a meadow, and a strip of plowed land toward a Rebel battery. The regiment swarmed over the guns and battled their crews hand-to-hand. The artillerymen broke and fled, were cut down, or surrendered. Unfortunately, minutes later Confederate reinforcements arrived from Harpers Ferry to shore up Lee's right and halt the offensive. *Official Records*, 1, 19, pt. 1, 420, 450–51; Graham, *Ninth Regiment New York Volunteers*, 281–307; Murfin, *Gleam of Bayonets*, 267–90.

27. A private in Company G of the Ninth also observed piled enemy bodies during the Antietam campaign. His reaction was thoughtful and sensitive: "All around lay the Confederate dead—undersized men mostly, from the coast district of North Carolina, with sallow, hatchet faces, and clad in "butternut"—a color running all the way from a deep, coffee brown up to the whitish brown of ordinary dust. As I looked down on the poor, pinched faces, worn with marching and scant fare, all enmity died out. There was no 'secession' in those rigid forms, nor in those fixed eyes staring blankly at the sky. Clearly it was not 'their war'. . . ." David L. Thompson, "In the Ranks to the Antietam," *Battles and Leaders*, 2:558.

28. This rumor also proved false. Major General Samuel P. Heintzelman, a fifty-seven-year-old West Pointer, had led McClellan's Third Corps on the Virginia peninsula and had also fought under

Pope. Now his corps was stationed in the Washington defenses, and he was destined to remain there for several months as commander of the capital's military district. Boatner, *Civil War Dictionary*, 189, 392.

29. The promotion was temporary, for an interim commander was needed to replace Brigadier General Isaac P. Rodman, mortally wounded at Antietam. Hawkins did not have the rank required in a permanent commander: "The command of a division is, under ordinary circumstances, that of a major-general, but the scarcity of officers just then, due principally to the exceptionally large number killed and wounded during the battle of the 17th, made it necessary to assign the surviving officers to a much larger command than their grade would entitle them to under ordinary conditions": Graham, *Ninth Regiment New York Volunteers*, 338.

30. Rather than crossing the Potomac with aggressive speed, McClellan led his army south with a lethargy bordering on indifference. Not until October 26 did the Army of the Potomac end its idleness with a crossing in force, an operation completed on November 1. Six days later, Abraham Lincoln relieved "Little Mac" in favor of Burnside. Long, *Civil War Day by Day*, 281, 283, 285.

31. The Sibley was a tall, wide tent designed by an old Regular who had become a Confederate general, Henry Hopkins Sibley. Military texts described it as conical in shape and capable of accommodating twelve soldiers in comfort. Field troops described the dwelling in other ways: "Sibley tents—those cumbersome . . . caravansaries, in which eighteen men lie upon the ground with their feet toward the center." H. L. Scott, *Military Dictionary: Comprising Technical Definitions* . . . (New York, 1861), 142; Thompson, "In the Ranks to the Antietam," *Battles and Leaders*, 2:556.

32. Another military dictionary defines tattoo as "the evening sound of drum or trumpet, after which the roll is called, and all soldiers not on leave of absence should be in their quarters." Thomas Wilhelm, *A Military Dictionary and Gazetteer, Comprising Ancient and Modern Military Technical Terms* . . . (Philadelphia, 1881), 574.

33. This was Captain James R. Whiting, Jr., of Company K, who left the regiment on September 30. Edward later refers to his drinking to excess, though in later years another member of the Ninth recalled that "his loss was much regretted by nearly every one. . . . He had always shown himself to be a good officer." Graham, *Ninth Regiment New York Volunteers*, 339, 630.

34. Thaddeus Sobieski Constantine Lowe, a self-taught scientist from New Hampshire, had become a practitioner of the fledgling art of aeronautics in 1854, at age twenty-two. By the time of the war he had established a reputation in the North as a balloonist. Aborting a long planned balloon trip across the Atlantic, he offered his services to the Union in 1861. Backed by some War Department appropriations, "Professor" Lowe was soon making ascents along the upper Potomac, reconnoitering Rebel positions and providing aerial direction of artillery fire. In the spring of 1862 he gave similar support to McClellan's army on the peninsula, using a number of ballons, including his most famous, "Intrepid." Stricken with malaria at the end of the Richmond campaign, the aeronaut had been convalescing until recently, when he resumed command of his balloon corps. Johnson and Malone, *Dictionary of American Biography*, 11:452–53.

35. On September 24 fourteen Northern governors had met in Pennsylvania to pool their dissatisfaction over Lincoln's war policies and his stance on slavery. In the end, however, the governors passed resolutions approving emancipation and generally supporting, rather than condemning, the Administration. William B. Hesseltine, *Lincoln and the War Governors* (New York, 1948), 253–59.

36. Chaplain Thomas W. Conway of the Ninth New York had resigned on September 4, after serving sixteen months. Apparently he was never replaced. Graham, *Ninth Regiment New York Volunteers*, 568.

37. The regimental historian explained the reason behind the separate instruction for newcomers: "The newly arrived recruits were regularly assigned to the various companies and they began to receive instructions in their duties and practice in the drill and manual as was usual, but Kimball would not at first permit them to parade in the ranks with the other men upon occasions of ceremony. . . . He explained to them that it would be out of place to permit new and untried men to

parade with, and at once become part of, such a regiment, and that he wished to give them the opportunity to study the command to which they had been assigned. He informed them that they must consider themselves very fortunate in getting into the best regiment in the service and in sharing the honor that regiment had already gained. . . . There is not the slightest doubt that the incident had a very beneficial and elevating effect on both veteran and recruit." Ibid., 334–37.

Chapter 2. Pleasant Valley and Loudoun County

1. The soldier was Silliman J. Hubbell, a twenty-year-old private in Company B, wounded at Antietam. He would become a close friend and tent-mate of Edward. Matthew J. Graham, *The Ninth Regiment New York Volunteers (Hawkins' Zouaves): Being a History of the Regiment and Veteran Association from 1860 to 1900* (New York, 1900), 580.

2. At this point, Edward was still seeking a commission; hence the reference is to tactics manuals. A would-be officer had to demonstrate a thorough knowledge of military science before one of the examining boards established by federal regulation in July 1861. These boards, by weeding out incompetents, raised the quality of the officer coprs and eliminated the abuses that may have led to the Union disaster at First Bull Run. See Fred A. Shannon, *The Organization and Administration of the Union Army*, 2 vols. (Cleveland, 1928), 1:185–87.

3. The nature of Hawkins's arrest is unknown. Given his ready temper and sensitive pride, it may have developed from an unwilliness to relinquish command of his division, when on October 4 George W. Getty superseded him. Getty, a Regular artilleryman with no experience in infantry command, had been jumped from lieutenant colonel to brigadier general of volunteers only two weeks before. Under the circumstances, Hawkins may have felt slighted as well as overslaughed, and thus resentful. Mark M. Boatner III, *The Civil War Dictionary* (New York, 1959), 329–30; Frederick H. Dyer, comp., *A Compendium of the War of the Rebellion* (Des Moines, Iowa., 1909), 316.

4. Pioneers were construction and fatigue troops "detailed from the different companies of a regiment and formed under a non-commissioned officer, furnished with saws, felling axes, spades, mattocks, pickaxes, and bill-hooks." H. L. Scott, *Military Dictionary: Comprising Technical Definitions . . .* (New York, 1861), 463.

5. Apparently Fred's letter included a request that Edward be allowed to put his medical training to use as a hospital steward or as an assistant to the regimental surgeon, Major George H. Humphreys. Fred Wightman was a prewar professional acquaintance of Colonel Hawkins.

6. This was the bible of infantry tactics for both sides. It was compiled prior to the war by an officer who became a lieutenant general in the Confederacy: William J. Hardee, *Rifle and Light Infantry Tactics . . .*, 2 vols. (Philadelphia, 1855, 1861).

7. Noted the regiment's historian: "Ever since the opening of the [Antietam] campaign on September 7th, all the knapsacks belonging to the regiment, together with the company property, had lain piled together under the trees of Meridian Hill [within the Washington defenses], covered with tarpulins, unguarded and at the mercy of those 'whom it might concern.' Consequently neither officers nor men had opportunity to change underclothing. Each man's wardrobe consisted of just what he stood in. The only article of extra raiment provided was for the feet. . . ." Such deprivation did not cease till the campaign concluded, when the Quartermaster's Department forwarded the knapsacks to Pleasant Valley. On October 9 they reached the regiment, bringing joy to their owners—till an inspection revealed that many of them had been rifled by persons unknown. Graham, *Ninth Regiment New York Volunteers*, 354–57.

8. In mid-October, Burnside was given command of the troops in and near Harpers Ferry, the Second and Twelfth Corps. General Willcox commanded the Ninth Corps from that time until January 1863. *War of the Rebellion: A Compilation of the Official Records of the Union and Confederate Armies*, 4 series, 70 vols. in 128 (Washington, D.C., 1880–1901), series 1, vol. 19, pt. 2, 420; Dyer, *Compendium*, 313.

9. Drafting did not take place in New York in November 1862. The President's July call for 334,835 volunteers had been followed by a War Department order for 300,000 militiamen to accept federal service for nine months. By November a militia draft was scheduled, to make up any shortages in the latter call. Since more than 430,000 volunteers had enlisted by then, however, Lincoln postponed the militia draft. Eugene Converse Murdock, *Patriotism Limited, 1862–1865: The Civil War Draft and the Bounty System* (Kent, Ohio, 1967), 6; C. Joseph Bernardo and Eugene H. Bacon, *American Military Policy: Its Developments Since 1775* (Harrisburg, Pa., 1961), 197–98.

10. Laudanum was tincture of opium, a general medication for the relief of pain such as caused by battle wounds.

11. John Brown of Kansas (1800–59), had been captured and hanged after leading twenty-one followers in an assault on the U.S. arsenal at Harpers Ferry in October 1859, in prelude to a slave insurrection in the South. Stephen B. Oates, *To Purge This Land With Blood: A Biography of John Brown* (New York, 1970), 274–302.

12. Major General Edwin Vose Sumner (1797–1863) was Massachusetts-born and West Point-educated. An Indian wars and Mexican War veteran, he commanded the Second Corps, Army of the Potomac. He had seen hard fighting under McClellan on the peninsula and at Antietam. On 7 October 1862 his poor health and the severe compaigning he had experienced forced him to resign his command temporarily. Major General Darius N. Couch succeeded him. Allen Johnson and Dumas Malone, eds. *Dictionary of American Biography,* 20 vols. (New York, 1928–36), 18:214; *Official Records,* 1, 19, pt. 2, 400, 483–84.

13. These were references to New York City fire departments, many of them known by their station numbers or the nicknames of their engines. In the Civil War era, big city volunteer fire fighting was a well-regarded avocation; it attracted many adventuresome young men for social and political reasons as well as for the municipal good. See the early chapters of Paul Ditzel, *Fire Engines, Fire Fighters: The Men, Equipment, and Machines, from Colonial Days to the Present* (New York, 1976); and Charles Haywood, *General Alarm: A Dramatic Account of Fires and Fire-fighting in America* (New York, 1967).

14. Two army-navy coastal expeditions—one large, the other of limited scope—had recently taken place. The larger, begun in July by Admiral David G. Farragut, had resulted in the capture of several points along the Gulf Coast of Texas, including Galveston, Corpus Christi, and Sabine City. The second had moved up Florida's St. Johns River to St. Johns Bluff, destroying hundreds of enemy small craft and shelling towns thought to be harboring Rebel troops. Boatner, *Civil War Dictionary,* 275–76, 322; Virgil Carrington Jones, *The Civil War at Sea,* 3 vols. (New York, 1960–62), 2:289–91.

15. Skirmishers were detached infantry—usually two companies per regiment—deployed several hundred yards in advance of a main body moving against the enemy. They would make first contact, draw the enemy's fire, and ascertain his strength and position, then fall back on the main force with warning of imminent conflict. Hardee, *Rifle and Light Infantry Tactics,* 1:171–75; Silas Casey, *Infantry Tactics, for the Instruction, Exercise, and Manoeuvers of the Soldier . . .,* 3 vols. (New York, 1862), 1:6–11; 2:3–4.

16. Member of the Military Academy Class of 1846, Brigadier General Samuel D. Sturgis (1822–89) had become on September 3 commander of the Second Division, Ninth Corps. An old-line cavalryman, he was a veteran of the Mexican conflict and a frontier scout and Indian fighter. Before joining the Army of the Potomac, he had been a staff officer in the West and a garrison commander in Washington. Johnson and Malone, *Dictionary of American Biography,* 18:182–83.

17. At this point in the war a Union private received thirteen dollars per month. The rate would rie to sixteen dollars monthly after June 1864. Soldiers were supposed to be paid at bimonthly intervals, though in practice four months and even longer passed before many field troops were compensated. Shannon, *Organization and Administration of the Union Army,* 1:244–45; Bell I. Wiley, *The Life of Billy Yank: The Common Soldier of the Union* (Indianapolis, 1952), 49.

18. This sound heralded a skirmish between some of McClellan's troops and Confederate infan-

try and cavalry near Philomont, Virginia, and Snicker's Gap in the Blue Ridge Mountains, both a few miles northeast of Edward's position. The Union First Division, Second Corps, drove Rebel horsemen away from the gap, then employed cannon to prevent enemy foot troops from retaking it. *Official Records*, 1, 19, pt. 2, 137, 531–32.

19. Edward's last glimpse of Little Mac came shortly before the army leader's relief. On the seventh, at army headquarters, Rectortown, Virginia, an emissary of the War Department brought McClellan an order from Lincoln, penned on the fifth, removing him in favor of Burnside. McClellan was directed to return home and await further orders—which never came. Ibid., 1, 19, pt. 2, 545, 557; Richard B. Irwin, "The Removal of McClellan," *Battles and Leaders of the Civil War*, 4 vols. (New York, 1887–88), 3:102–4.

20. Born in Germany in 1824, Franz Sigel had fled his native land following the unsuccessful revolution of 1848. Before the Civil War, he taught school in New York and St. Louis and served in the militia. He helped recruit German-Americans for the Union, and by March 1862 had gained the rank of major general of volunteers. Under Pope he led the First Corps, Army of Virginia, and under McClellan the Eleventh Corps, Army of the Potomac. When Little Mac crossed the Potomac into Virginia late in October, he picked up Sigel's detached corps near Thoroughfare Gap in the Bull Run Mountains. On November 4, skirmishing took place between McClellan's advance and Lee's outposts near Thoroughfare Gap and Ashby's Gap in the Blue Ridge, but neither Sigel's nor Sumner's troops were heavily involved. Johnson and Malone, *Dictionary of American Biography*, 7:153–54; *Official Records*, 1, 19, pt. 2, 542–45.

21. Manassas Gap is a wide defile through the Blue Ridge, about eleven miles west of Rectortown and some twenty-two miles northwest of Warrenton, where McClellan had planned to mass his army. Through this gap, in July 1861, Confederates from the Shenandoah Valley had ridden the railroad to Manassas Junction, in time to turn the tide at First Bull Run. See William C. Davis, *Battle at Bull Run: A History of the First Major Campaign of the Civil War* (Garden City, N.Y., 1977), 29, 132, 136–40.

22. Confederate horsemen under Major General J. E. B. Stuart had moved toward Orleans, about fourteen miles southwest of Manassas Gap, to ascertain if the whole of the Army of the Potomac was moving through the mountains and, if so, whether it seemed vulnerable to a strike. The Federal advance, which the Ninth New York accompanied, bore down on Stuart just as he moved north. Upon observing the movement, Stuart withdrew in haste. Subsequently, Lee found no opportunity to smite the Union army on its long, circuitous swing toward Falmouth and Fredericksburg. *Official Records*, 1, 19, pt. 2, 693–96, 711.

23. This was probably the wife of Lieutenant Colonel Thomas Marshall, commander of Stuart's Seventh Virginia Cavalry. The colonel was the grandson of the famous jurist, John Marshall. Mrs. Marshall did not become a widow, however, until November 12, 1864. Robert K. Krick, *Lee's Colonels: A Biographical Register of the Field Officers of the Army of Northern Virginia* (Dayton, Ohio, 1979), 243.

24. By November 9, Lee had noted Burnside's halt at Rectortown and his efforts to concentrate along the line of the Manassas Gap Railroad. He again sent Stuart's cavalry to return intelligence on the Federal positions and intentions. On the morning of the tenth, Stuart moved up to the southernmost position of the Army of the Potomac, struck Burnside's advance, and pushed part of it toward the hamlet of Amissville, perhaps seventeen miles northwest of Warrenton Junction. On this occasion Stuart led one brigade of horsemen, plus two infantry regiments (not the entire corps of James Longstreet). He killed or wounded several Federals, but neither he nor Lee reported cutting off a supply train. *Official Records*, 1, 19, pt. 2, 706–7.

25. These were rifled, muzzle-loading cannon, varying from three-inch to ten-inch and firing shells weighing from ten to 250 pounds. Named for their designer, Robert Parker Parrott (1804–77), a West Point alumnus and superintendent of a foundry in upper New York State, the cannon featured a wrought-iron band around its breech, to make the barrel strong enough to withstand the pressures exerted by its projectiles. Maximum range of the twenty-pounder Parrott was thirty-five hundred yards; effective range was a maximum of twenty-five hundred yards. Warren Ripley, *Artillery and Ammunition of the Civil War* (New York, 1970), 109–26.

26. This was the Fifth New York Zouaves, a regiment raised in May 1861 by Colonel Abram Duryee, a wealthy Manhattan merchant and militia officer. It took its name not from the colonel, but from Lieutenant Colonel Hiram Duryea, under whom it had won fame during the Peninsula campaign. It was never brigaded, however, with the Ninth New York. Boatner, *Civil War Dictionary*, 252, 593–94; Dyer, *Compendium*, 1406–7.

Chapter 3. Falmouth and Fredericksburg

1. The General was "a term for the roll of the drum which calls the troops together" for drill or march. To "beat the General" was a phrase drived from a French drillmaster's order: *"Battre la Generale."* Thomas Wilhelm, *A Military Dictionary and Gazetteer, Comprising Ancient and Modern Military Technical Terms* . . . (Philadelphia, 1881), 188.

2. Although the Third Division of the Ninth Corps (to which the Ninth New York belonged) did not participate in the Second Bull Run campaign, the First and Second Divisions of the Corps, under General Reno, did. Attached to the First Division was Lieutenant Samuel N. Benjamin's Battery E, Second United States Artillery. During the last week in August it fought in the Warrenton vicinity, though it saw most of its service farther north, along the Manassas Gap Railroad. See *War of the Rebellion: A Compilation of the Official Records of the Union and Confederate Armies*, 4 series, 70 vols. in 128 (Washington, D.C., 1880–1901), series 1, vol. 12, pt. 2, 279–80.

3. The Ninth New York's historian recalled how the battery disposed of the Rebel opposition: "In a few minutes he [Benjamin] arrived, and securing a position on a promontory, concealed by a patch of low shrubs, the pieces were loaded, carefully sighted and elevated and the whole battery discharged almost simultaneously. The result was astounding to all beholders. A [Confederate] caisson was exploded, several men and horses killed or wounded, and the battery totally disabled. Benjamin had made a historic shot, and from that time on to Falmouth, the center column was permitted to march in peace." Matthew J. Graham, *The Ninth Regiment New York Volunteers (Hawkins' Zouaves): Being a History of the Regiment and Veteran Association from 1860 to 1900* (New York, 1900), 365–66.

4. The December trimonthly return for the Army of the Potomac showed that Burnside's main army (six infantry corps, with cavalry and artillery attached) totalled 114,612 "present for duty, equipped." Against these, Lee had approximately 58,500 troops of all arms, available for duty. *Official Records*, 1, 21, 1121; "The Opposing Forces at Fredericksburg," *Battles and Leaders of the Civil War*, 4 vols. (New York, 1887–88), 3 : 146–47.

5. Company F had been left in Plymouth, North Carolina, on garrison duty, in the spring of 1862. On 23 September 1862, Company K had been detached from the regiment for similar duty at Harpers Ferry, atop adjacent Bolivar (not Loudoun) Heights. In early November, it took part in an extended reconnaissance of the Shenandoah Valley. And on October 31, Company G had been detailed as Burnside's headquarters guard. Graham, *Ninth Regiment New York Volunteers*, 340, 360–61, 395.

6. Shortly after assuming command, Burnside had reorganized the Army of the Potomac. At that time he elevated General Sumner to command the Second and Ninth Corps, the "Right Grand Division" of the army. The Ninth New York remained in the latter corps. *Official Records*, 1, 19, pt. 2, 584.

7. Port Royal lay along the Rappahannock, about eighteen miles below Fredericksburg. A division of Confederate infantry was stationed there during the December campaign to prevent a Union crossing—a crossing Burnside elected not to make. Even so, a small engagement took place there on the fourth. J. H. Moore, "With Jackson at Hamilton's Crossing," *Battles and Leaders*, 3 : 141; E. B. Long, *The Civil War Day by Day: An Almanac, 1861–1865* (Garden City, N.Y., 1971), 293.

8. Actually, the Eighth Connecticut was in the Second Brigade, Third Division, Ninth Corps, commanded by Colonel (later Brigadier General) Edward Harland. *Official Records*, 1, 21, 53.

9. Burnside's engineers laid several pontoon bridges across the Rappahannock to Fredericksburg. The uppermost, directly opposite the enemy-held city, was begun before dawn on December

11, but by sunup, when the Second Corps was supposed to cross, the span had not been completed. Rebel sharpshooters in Fredericksburg had cut down so many engineers that the bridge-building had been halted. Burnside resorted to shelling the place, but failed to flush out the snipers. Almost in desperation, detachments of the Seventh Michigan and Eighty-ninth New York were rowed across the stream in pontoons, covered by riflemen on the Falmouth side. The troops made a successful landing and, aided by two Massachusetts regiments, gouged the Rebels from their hiding places in street-to-street fighting. This enabled the building to resume and the army to cross. See H. G. O. Weymouth, "The Crossing of the Rappahannock by the 19th Massachusetts," *Battles and Leaders,* 3 : 121; and Wesley Brainerd, "The Pontoniers at Fredericksburg," Ibid., 3 : 121–22.

10. A note by Edward's mother, appended to this letter, reads: "These falls were from sheer fatigue, as he afterwards told me."

11. It appears that the unit involved was actually Captain Charles A. Phillips's Fifth Massachusetts Battery, composed of six three-inch ordnance rifles. Benjamin's battery was a part of the bank of artillery atop Stafford Heights. *Official Records,* 1, 21, 181, 185, 311, 344, 404.

12. This reference is erroneous. Infantrymen and other Civil War soldiers not familiar with artillery operations often spoke of facing grape or grapeshot in battle, but they meant case shot, such as shrapnel and canister. Some years before the war, grapeshot had been discontinued for field artillery use. Warren Ripley, *Artillery and Ammunition of the Civil War* (New York, 1970), 264–65.

13. At Fredericksburg on December 13, the Ninth New York lost one killed, eight wounded, and six missing: *Official Records,* 1, 21, 133. For the battle reports of Colonel Hawkins and Lieutenant Colonel Kimball, see Ibid., 1, 21, 335–36, 344–45.

14. Since their marriage in 1857, Fred and Abigail Wightman had lived on 129th Street, in New York's Harlem. From there Fred commuted to his law office in Manhattan via stagecoach, horse car, and/or the Harlem steamboat.

15. At Fredericksburg one regiment in the Ninth Corps, the Eleventh New Hampshire, had suffered 195 casualties; another, the Seventh Rhode Island, lost 158 men; a third, the Twelfth Rhode Island, lost 108. The heaviest loss of any regiment during the campaign (11–15 December 1862) was 243 casualties, shared by the 142nd Pennsylvania, of the First Corps, and the Seventh New York Volunteers, Second Corps. *Official Records,* 1, 21, 129, 132, 139.

16. Lowe's "Eagle" was fed from two large gas generators drawn by horses. She made daily ascents from many locations; on December 13 she went aloft from the Lacy house near Falmouth, headquarters of General Sumner. For a memoir by one of Sumner's staff, who went up in the balloon on the thirteenth, see William W. Teall, "Ringside Seat at Fredericksburg," *Civil War Times Illustrated* 4 (May 1965), 27.

17. This rumor proved false. The Ninth Corps was not transferred to that part of northern Virginia. Nor was the Seventh Corps at Alexandria at this time; it was spread across the Norfolk-Suffolk-Portsmouth-Yorktown region. Edward may have been referring to the Eleventh Corps, then headquartered at Stafford Court House, and previously stationed in the Alexandria area. *Official Records,* 1, 21, 962; Mark M. Boatner III, *The Civil War Dictionary* (New York, 1959), 191.

18. The regimental history dates Company F's return as January 26. The same date is listed as marking the return of Company G from duty as Burnside's bodyguard. Graham, *Ninth Regiment New York Volunteers,* 395.

19. The guns had been presented to Company K late in 1861, when it was doing duty at Newport News, in the Department of Virginia. At that time the department was commanded by a brigadier general of Regulars, John E. Wool (1789–1869). This veteran of the War of 1812 was, after the then-Commanding General, Winfield Scott, the oldest general officer in the Union. Frederick H. Dyer, comp., *A Compendium of the War of the Rebellion* (Des Moines, Iowa, 1909), 330; Allen Johnson and Dumas Malone, eds., *Dictionary of American Biography,* 20 vols. (New York, 1928–36), 20 : 513–14.

20. Though frequently absent from the army, Jardine did well in battle. At Antietam, his brigade leader accorded him "great praise" for his service. His regiment's 103 casualties shows that it was heavily involved in the fighting. Such activity helped Jardine win the brevet of brigadier general of

volunteers in 1865. *Official Records*, 1, 19, pt. 1, 197, 451–52; Boatner, *Civil War Dictionary*, 435.

21. Elmer Ephraim Ellsworth and his U.S. Zouave Cadets of Chicago visited New York City in mid-July 1860 during a tour of Northern cities, displaying the dress and drill that helped spawn the Zouave craze. Ruth Painter Randall, *Colonel Elmer Ellsworth: A Biography of Lincoln's Friend and First Hero of the Civil War* (Boston, 1960), 186–88.

22. A New Jersey veteran of the Army of the Potomac made a similar (though slightly more charitable) observation in a post-war memoir: "In a company of one hundred enlisted men, only about one third of the number prove themselves physically able and possessing sufficient courage to endure the hardships and face the dangers of active campaigning; the rest, soon after going into the field, drift back to the hospitals and finally out of the service." Benjamin Borton, *On the Parallels . . . A Story of the Rappahannock* (Woodstown, N.J., 1903), 134.

23. Major Generals Joseph Hooker (1814–79) and William B. Franklin (1832–1903), along with General Sumner, commanded the major components of the Army of the Potomac at this time. Hooker led the "Center Grand Division," embracing the Third and Fifth Corps, while Franklin commanded the First and Sixth Corps, the "Left Grand Division" of the army. As of January 1863, Franz Sigel commanded the "Grand Reserve Division," the Eleventh and Twelfth Corps. *Official Records*, 1, 19, pt. 2, 583; Ibid., 1, 21, 962, 986; Johnson and Malone, *Dictionary of American Biography*, 6:601–2; Ibid., 9:196–98.

24. As the Ninth New York's historian noted, the regiment was spared a part in the inglorious "Mud March": "The movement had not progressed far enough to involve the division to which the Ninth belonged . . . and consequently it did not break camp." Graham, *Ninth Regiment New York Volunteers*, 395.

25. Edward puts a wry twist to the Latin adage, *sic transit gloria mundi* ("thus passes away the glory of the world"). During the Mud March the glory of the Army of the Potomac's world sank out of sight.

26. One day before Edward wrote, "Fighting Joe" Hooker had assumed command of the army and General Sumner, having lost respect for Burnside and unwilling to serve under his successor, had asked to be relieved of his command. The sixty-six-year-old Sumner, his health ruined, died two months later while en route to assume a new post in the western theater. *Official Records*, 1, 21, 1005, 1010; Johnson and Malone, *Dictionary of American Biography*, 18:214–15.

27. Major General Daniel Edgar Sickles (1825–1914), a former attorney and Congressman, had organized New York's "Excelsior Brigade." He now led the Second Division, Third Corps. Impetuous, headstrong, of undisputed courage, he would rise to corps command little more than a week after Edward wrote. Ibid., 17:150–51.

28. The "Second Fire Zouaves" was the nickname of the Seventy-third New York Infantry, which had been recruited among Manhattan fire departments. Despite Edward's statement, the Seventy-third never merged with another regiment. Dyer, *Compendium*, 1433.

29. Fred Wightman's grasp of military geography was weak. Confederate General Braxton Bragg (1817–76), commander of the Army of Tennessee, had been defeated at Stones River in late December and early January by Major General William S. Rosecrans's Army of the Cumberland. Afterward the Confederates drifted south from the Murfreesboro vicinity toward Shelbyville but remained in their namesake state until the following autumn. Long, *Civil War Day by Day*, 302–3, 307–8, 370–71, 407.

30. Lee did not move south of Fredericksburg; he held his position beyond the city throughout the Mud March. For Confederate efforts to deal with the ill-fated offensive, see *Official Records*, 1, 21, 1101, 1103, 1108, 1111.

Chapter 4. Newport News and Suffolk

1. Major General John A. Dix, a sixty-five-year-old New Yorker, War of 1812 veteran (as a teenaged ensign), prewar Senator, railroad magnate, and Secretary of the Treasury, commanded the Department of Virginia. From his headquarters at Fort Monroe, he also led the Seventh Corps.

Allen Johnson and Dumas Malone, eds., *Dictionary of American Biography*, 20 vols. (New York, 1928–36), 5:325–26; Raphael P. Thian, *Notes Illustrating the Military Geography of the United States, 1813–1880* (Washington, D.C., 1881), 101.

2. Fort Monroe, one fortress in Confederate territory that remained in Union hands throughout the war, was a lage masonry structure built in 1819–23 at Point Comfort, on the west side of the entrance to Chesapeake Bay. Before the war it had served as the site of the army's Coast Artillery School. At this point it was the administrative seat of the Department of Virginia (later the Department of Virginia and North Carolina). Francis Paul Prucha, *A Guide to the Military Posts of the United States, 1789–1895* (Madison, Wis., 1964), 92.

3. Gushed the Ninth New York's historian: "It is doubtful if during the entire term of the regiment's service a better example of the result of intelligent, well directed labor could be shown. Nearly all the mechanical trades were well represented in the regiment, plenty of skill and ability, supplemented with an abundance of energy—the latter a native possession of these young soldiers. The work progressed rapidly and the old stables were very soon transformed into respectable looking and comfortable quarters." Matthew J. Graham, *The Ninth Regiment New York Volunteers (Hawkins' Zouaves): Being a History of the Regiment and Veteran Association from 1860 to 1900* (New York, 1900), 398.

4. The *Cumberland* was a twenty-four-gun sloop that had been stationed in Hampton Roads on the morning of 8 March 1862 when the prototype ironclad, *Virginia* (formerly the *USS Merrimack*), entered the stream to give battle. In brief time, *Cumberland* was rammed and sunk. One day later, the *Monitor* came up to battle *Virginia* on more equal terms. William C. Davis, *Duel Between the First Ironclads* (Garden City, N.Y., 1975), 76–95.

5. The monitor constructed immediately after that which fought the *Virginia* was the *Passaic*, commissioned on 25 November 1862. By the summer of 1863 she was a member of the South Atlantic Blockading Squadron, off Charleston harbor. Robert MacBride, *Civil War Ironclads: The Dawn of Naval Armor* (Philadelphia, 1962), 23.

6. Major Jardine had begun the conflict in the Seventh Regiment, New York Militia. In May 1861, at age thirty-one, he was commissioned captain of Company K of the Ninth New York Volunteers, which he had recruited. On 14 February 1862 he was promoted to major of the regiment, six days after fighting valiantly on Roanoke Island, and on April 19 he was wounded at South Mills. He would be mustered out of the Ninth upon the expiration of its service term in May 1863, after which he would become lieutenant colonel of the Seventeenth New York Infantry. He was to close out the war as an officer in the Veteran Reserve Corps. Mark M. Boatner III, *The Civil War Dictionary* (New York, 1959), 435; Graham, *Ninth Regiment New York Volunteers*, 39, 567; Rush C. Hawkins, "Early Coast Operations in North Carolina," *Battles and Leaders of the Civil War*, 4 vols. (New York, 1887–88), 1:644.

7. When Burnside lost his army after Fredericksburg, he did not at once return to the Ninth Corps, which was led by Brigadier General Orlando B. Willcox (Edward habitually misspelled his name), former commander of its First Division. General Getty, who had succeeded Colonel Hawkins in charge of the Third Division in October 1862, remained in command of that unit. In February 1863 this Mexican War and Indian wars veteran also became military governor of Newport News and vicinity. Johnson and Malone, *Dictionary of American Biography*, 7:230–31; Ibid., 20:243.

8. Rope Ferry, Connecticut, was Fred Wightman's favorite summer vacation spot. It was the name of a village and a ferry crossing near an inundated bar between Black River and Niantic Bay, about ten miles east of the mouth of the Connecticut River. This information is taken from his manuscript, "Rope Ferry," in the possession of Mrs. Edith Wightman Kreitler, Radnor, Pennsylvania.

9. Babcock, a college classmate of Edward, was second-in-command of the Twenty-seventh New Jersey Infantry. He identified himself as such on a pass headed "Camp Burnside, Va., Feb. 20, 1863—Provost Marshal," which Edward enclosed in a February 21 letter to Fred.

10. This was Lieutenant James Gilliss's Battery A, Fifth United States Artillery, one of two

batteries attached to Getty's division. It employed six 12-pounder "Napoleon" smoothbores. *War of the Rebellion: A Compilation of the Official Records of the Union and Confederate Armies*, 4 series, 70 vols. in 128 (Washington, D.C., 1880–1901), series 1. vol. 21, 182, 928.

11. This was another of Edward's college mates, Gilbert H. McKibbin of New York City. At this time he was a captain in the 51st New York Infantry as well as an assistant adjutant general. As a staff officer, he had served conspicuously in the Antietam campaign, and he would finish out the conflict as a brevet brigadier. Ibid., I, 19, pt. 1, 449; P. J. Mosenthal and C. F. Horne, *The City College: Memories of Sixty Years* (New York, 1907), 375–76.

12. Gilbert McKibbin's superior was Colonel Edward Ferrero, formerly commander of the Fifty-first New York. From early February 1863 until about the time this letter was written, Ferrero had led a division in the Ninth Corps as a brigadier general of volunteers. The appointment had expired when the U.S. Senate failed to confirm it, hence Edward's reference to him as "acting Brig. Gen." Johnson and Malone, *Dictionary of American Biography*, 6 : 338–39.

13. The references to "school" and "posish" refer to Charles Wightman's career as a teacher in the New York public schools, from 1855 to 1859. Not till 1867 would he enter the ministry.

14. Kimball was murdered at about 2 A.M. on April 12, while heading to or returning from General Getty's headquarters. Edward's account of the incident seems to be accurate save for the probablity that the lieutenant colonel was afoot when slain. One version of the crime is that Kimball blocked the path of Corcoran, a brigade commander in the Seventh Corps, and of a dozen or so companions—army officers and civilians. After some "words of altercation, a shot rang out, and Kimball fell and instantly expired. The bullet from Corcoran's pistol had passed through his neck, severing one of the carotid arteries, and causing death almost instantly." Corcoran later claimed that he was suspicious of the identity of the man accosting him, that he (Corcoran) had identified himself but that the stranger had shouted, "I do not care a damn who you are!" and had attempted to restrain the general bodily. Other testimony held that the lieutenant colonel was drunk and abusive, not an unlikely condition. Graham, *Ninth Regiment New York Volunteers*, 411–13.

15. Tempers ran high among the men of the Ninth New York for several days after their commander's murder, and General Getty had to work hard to avert a clash between Kimball's and Corcoran's men (the latter comprising the 155th, 164th, 170th, and 182nd New York Volunteers). No charges were filed against Corcoran, and he was never arrested. Eight months later he, too, died in an unusual incident, when his horse fell and rolled over him. Boatner, *Civil War Dictionary*, 175–76.

16. This action was nothing more than skirmishing, brought on when one of Peck's brigades regained a foothold on the Somerton road, south of Suffolk. That locale, where the Union picket line had been stationed, was seized by Longstreet's advance guard, under Major General George E. Pickett, the previous day. Even after Peck's success, Longstreet enclosed Suffolk on the north, west, and south, from the Nansemond River to Dismal Swamp. *Official Records*, 1, 18, 275.

17. There was no Captain Guthrie in the Ninth New York, nor was any member of the regiment killed during the Suffolk campaign. Ibid., 1, 18, 286.

18. Battery Montgomery lay at the southeastern corner of the Suffolk defenses, just west of the Dismal Swamp Canal. Fort Nansemond, which Colonel Hawkins commanded and where the bulk of the Ninth New York was stationed, sat at the northwestern corner, guarding the Petersburg & Norfolk railroad and roads running south from Suffolk. After shifting position, Captain Morris (working a battery of twenty-pounder guns, not thirty-pounders) was given "great credit" by General Getty for silencing a brace of enemy batteries opposite him. He enjoyed similar success at two other points in the works, Battery Stevens and Battery Kimball, the latter named for the Ninth's late commander. Ibid., 1, 18, 277, 280, 303, 305 , 307, 317, 672.

19. It appears that Hawkins was seeking government permission for all the members of the Ninth—including those, like Edward, who had enlisted after the regiment took the field—to be discharged in New York City in May. Graham, *Ninth Regiment New York Volunteers*, 430–31.

20. Private Langbein, who had enlisted at fifteen as a drummer boy in Company B, won honors

at South Mills, 19 April 1862, where he "voluntarily and under a heavy fire went to the aid of a wounded officer, procured medical assistance for him, and aided in carrying him to a place of safety." For this act he was later (January 1895) awarded a Medal of Honor. *The Medal of Honor of the United States Army* (Washington, D.C., 1948), 108.

21. The regimental historian placed the number of those mustered out at 539, with 264 others remaining in Virginia to complete their enlistments. Graham, *Ninth Regiment New York Volunteers,* 432, 440.

22. Although each recruit had enlisted for a stated term dating from the day of his muster-in, everyone in the Ninth had been assured that they would go home together before the "recruits" were transferred to another regiment (one of their choosing) to complete their stints. When this proved not to be the case, the recruits "were grievously disappointed. They had looked forward with pleasurable anticipation to the time when they would march up Broadway with the regiment, participate with it in whatever reception was accorded it, share in its honors and claim their proportion of the glory it had won. These hopes were now all dashed to the ground and the men felt very bitter on account of what they believed to be unjust treatment." Ibid., 434.

23. On 30 April 1863 three days before the siege of Suffolk was lifted, General Dix appealed to the Ninth to remain on duty past its departure time. He feared to weaken his garrison by so much as a regiment at that critical time. When Colonel Hawkins and his men insisted on their right to go home, Dix informed General-in-Chief Halleck that "the Ninth Regiment New York Volunteers is, I find, determined to leave on Sunday [May 3]. It is one of the best regiments I have and I cannot afford to lose it at this moment." But lose it he did; not even an appeal by General Peck had any effect. The latter subsequently called the regiment's departure on the third "an unfortunate termination of a hitherto brilliant career of service." *Official Records,* 1, 18, 279, 671.

24. The historian of the Ninth elaborated: "A report gained currency, and was also believed, that it had been decided to form the [longer-term] recruits into a light battery to be commanded by Captain Morris, of Company K, of the old regiment. There appears to have been some little foundation for this report as the men to the number of one hundred and thirty were marched to a point between Suffolk and Portsmouth, where they were established in camp and a preliminary organization was begun under somebody's orders. . . . This battery organization, however, was abandoned in a few days. It is doubtful if there was any serious intention on the part of the authorities to complete it." Graham, *Ninth Regiment New York Volunteers,* 436–37.

25. This assault was an unsuccessful attempt to capture rifle pits across the river from Fort Nansemond. From there the enemy had kept up a harassing fire on the garrison for several days. The plucky New Yorkers lost thirteen dead and thirty-one wounded in the effort. Ibid., 424–27; *Official Records,* 1, 18, 299.

26. This was a percussion musket (actually Model 1842) about 150,000 of which were available from 1861 to 1865. Produced by the U.S. arsenal at Springfield, Massachusetts, the weapon was outdated by the time of the war but nevertheless made up the bulk of Confederate armament in the early phases of the conflict. Boatner, *Civil War Dictionary,* 860.

27. The Rebels had begun to withdraw from Suffolk late on May 3, but General Peck's troops did not learn the fact for several hours. Two columns of infantry then set out in pursuit via southward leading roads. By 6 A.M. on the fourth, the Union advance was skirmishing with Longstreet's rear echelon; in this action Colonel Ringold of the 103rd New York was killed. Despite the pressure, Longstreet made good his retreat along the line of the Blackwater River and thence northward to rejoin the Army of Northern Virginia. *Official Records,* 1, 18, 278, 289–90, 305–7, 1029, 1032, 1034.

28. Here Edward enclosed a sketch of a member of the Third New York, wearing a knee-length coat with brass shoulder scales, and a tall, black felt hat with an upturned brim. It was the latter, a bit of dress-parade finery, that Edward disliked. He had a lot of company among the men of other regiments affecting this headgear. One called the tall hat "rediculous [sic]." Another wrote his parents that "my new hat looks as near like the pictures that you see of the pilgrim fathers landing on plymouth, tall, stiff, and turned up on one side. . . . I dont wear it any more than I am obliged

to." Bell I. Wiley, *The Life of Billy Yank: The Common Soldier of the Union* (Indianapolis, 1952), 59.

29. This was the recently inaugurated Governor of New York, Horatio Seymour. Edward suspected that his failure to secure a commission was owing to political moves by the governor. A Democrat, Seymour supported the war but was a firm believer in state's rights and a zealous guardian of party patronage. Many accused him of bestowing military rank primarily on those of Democratic persuasion. William B. Hesseltine, *Lincoln and the War Governors* (New York, 1948), 229–30, 282–86.

30. This was probably the work of General Dix, who had planned to place the remaining members of the Ninth New York into the ranks of the Third. The Third, one of the earliest regiments to enter the service, had been in the field since May 1861 without receiving adequate compensation for personnel depletions. On 21 May 1863, the original members had been mustered out, and the remnant would have to be augmented if the Third was to survive as a cohesive unit. As the outfit had been stationed in Dix's bailiwick for most of its term of service, he probably felt a compelling desire to sustain its organizational integrity. Recently he had referred to the Third as the "flower of [my] command." Frederick H. Dyer, comp., *A Compendium of the War of the Rebellion* (Des Moines, Iowa, 1909), 1406; *Official Records*, 1, 18, 387.

31. On May 29, Major Jardine had received authority from Albany to recruit a new Ninth New York, with himself as colonel and William G. Barnett, former commander of the old Company B, as executive officer. Because of circumstances beyond anyone's control, the outfit was never reorganized; in October the men Jardine had recruited were transferred to an existing regiment, the Seventeenth New York. Jardine served as this outfit's lieutenant colonel but resigned due to disability on 10 May 1864. Barnett was forced to accept his old grade of captain, and while part of the Seventeenth he was killed on 16 March 1865, at the battle of Averasborough, North Carolina. Frederick Phisterer, comp., *New York in the War of the Rebellion, 1861–1865*, 5 vols. (Albany, 1912), 3:1843, 1936, 1938.

32. The Third New York's unremarkable, undistinguished record of field campaigning might seem to bear out Edward's unflattering opinion of the regiment. Organized at Albany shortly after the Fort Sumter crisis, the outfit had been mustered into service for two years on 14 May 1861. Seventeen days later it was sent to Fort Monroe, then Baltimore, a part of Dix's Middle Department. Then it moved to Newport News and Suffolk, both within the Department of Virginia, Dix's new post, where it became a charter member of the Seventh Corps. Along the Virginia peninsula it saw action in one battle, with almost disastrous results. On 10 June 1861, it blundered into another Union regiment in a neck of woods and came close to being decimated by artillery fire. For the next two years it was relegated primarily to the arduous, frustrating, and somewhat inglorious duty of garrison service. Dyer, *Compendium*, 1406; *Official Records*, 1, 18, 288, 385.

33. By now Edward had become proficient at staff and support duties. At the close of the Ninth New York's service, he had headed its commissary department; writing after the war, the historian of the regiment praised his managerial ability in that capacity. Graham, *Ninth Regiment New York Volunteers*, 436–37.

34. This was a detachment of Colonel Joseph Roberts's Third Pennsylvania Heavy Artillery, a regiment that garrisoned Fort Monroe and adjacent Camp Hamilton, as well as Suffolk. *Official Records*, 1, 18, 272, 288, 735; Ibid., 1, 27, pt. 3, 453.

35. This is incorrect: Edward's new regiment was not a part of the Ninth Corps, nor was Getty's division. Upon its transfer to Newport News, Getty had become commander of the Second Division, Seventh Corps, and the Third New York a part of his First Brigade. Ibid., 1, 27, pt. 3, 452.

36. Edward is referring to Lee's invasion of Pennsylvania, which followed his decisive defeat of the Army of the Potomac at Chancellorsville in May. Lee's advance element, a brigade of cavalry, had crossed into the Keystone State as early as June 15. The offensive was to culminate in the decisive battle at Gettysburg, July 1–3. Militiamen and "emergency troops" were called out to defend Pennsylvania until the Federal army, dogging Lee's heels, could overtake him. For details on

the prelude and planning of the invasion, see Edwin B. Coddington, *The Gettysburg Campaign: A Study in Command* (New York, 1968), 3–25; and Wilbur S. Nye, *Here Come the Rebels!* (Baton Rouge, La., 1965), 3–20, 38–59, 66–90, 124–36.

37. This is a sarcastic reference to the defeatist stance seemingly adopted by the editor of the *New York Tribune*, whose newspaper often appeared a platform for his views on how the war should be prosecuted. A mercurial observer of the conflict, Horace Greeley had recently wallowed in pessimism, telling his readers that if Lee's invasion was successful and Grant's siege of Vicksburg faltered, the war to save the Union was virtually lost. Glyndon G. Van Deusen, *Horace Greeley, Nineteenth-Century Crusader* (Philadelphia, 1953), 296–98.

38. In April 1862 McClellan's advance on Richmond had been halted by the Confederate garrison at Yorktown, under General Joseph E. Johnston. Though outnumbering his foe, Little Mac dug in for a heavy siege. As befitted the army of a general skilled in military engineering, McClellan's men constructed durable, high quality earthworks. George B. McClellan, "The Peninsular Campaign," *Battles and Leaders of the Civil War*, 4 vols. (New York, 1887–88), 2:167–72.

39. No battery commanded by a "Lieut. Phillip" was a part of Getty's division at this time. Edward probably referred to Battery A, First Pennsylvania Artillery, commanded by Captain John G. Simpson, or to Lieutenant Gilliss's A, Fifth United States. *Official Records*, 1, 27, pt. 3, 453.

40. White House, on the Pamunkey River about twenty-one miles northeast of Richmond, took its name from the nearby home of Confederate Brigadier General William Henry Fitzhugh ("Rooney") Lee, son of the commander of the Army of Northern Virginia. Douglas Southall Freeman, *R. E. Lee: A Biography*, 4 vols. (New York, 1934), 4:386.

41. On June 27, some 1,050 troopers from Pennsylvania, Illinois, and Massachusetts regiments had raided Hanover Junction, northeast of Richmond, along the line of communications between the Rebel capital and Lee's army in Pennsylvania. They destroyed trackage and rolling stock, captured over one thousand prisoners (including Rooney Lee, convalescing in the area following wounding in battle), and confiscated seven hundred horses and mules. *Official Records*, 1, 27, pt. 2, 793–99; Robert Bingham, "We Saved General Lee's Communications With Richmond," *Civil War Times Illustrated* 5 (December 1966): 22–25.

42. Prior to his movement against Richmond, General Dix reported his force at White House as 18,730 strong. This included Getty's division; the Second Division, Fourth Corps, under Brigadier General George H. Gordon; Henry D. Terry's and Robert S. Foster's brigades of the Seventh Corps; and "some other troops," including three infantry regiments under Colonel Robert M. West. *Official Records*, 1, 27, pt. 2, 820.

43. This rumor was false. At this juncture, Hooker was bowing out and his successor, Meade, had too much to do, to spare troops for service below the James River. The Army of the Potomac was concentrating for a drive northward, not toward the south. The War Department had ruled out Richmond as its objective, compelling it to move against the Army of Northern Virginia. Coddington, *Gettysburg Campaign*, 83–84.

44. In conjunction with Meade's confrontation with Lee, the War Department on June 14 had ordered General Dix to "threaten Richmond by seizing and destroying their [the Confederates'] railroad bridges over the South and North Anna Rivers, and do[ing] them all the damage possible. If you cannot accomplish this, you can at least occupy a large force of the enemy." When his cavalry failed to destroy every bridge in the Hanover Junction vicinity, Dix sent foot soldiers to do the job. He chose Getty's command, comprising the brigades of Brigadier General Edward Harland and Colonels Samuel M. Alford and Michael T. Donohoe, plus the batteries of Simpson and Gilliss. Temporarily attached to Getty's division was Foster's brigade, a separate demi-brigade of two regiments, a Massachusetts battery, and Dix's recently returned cavalry, the whole numbering ten thousand men. On the evening of 30 June 1863, it was ferried to the north side of the Pamunkey. Four days later it reached the vicinity of its major objective, the Richmond, Fredericksburg & Potomac Railroad bridge across the South Anna River. *Official Records*, 1, 27, pt. 2, 820–22, 837–54; 1, 27, pt. 3, 452–53.

45. Major General Erasmus Darwin Keyes (1810–95), a Massachusetts-born veteran of artillery service, a former West Point instructor, and a prewar secretary to Lieutenant General Winfield Scott, led the Fourth Corps, another part of the Department of Virginia. When Getty moved against the South Anna bridge, Keyes, with three brigades of infantry and some horsemen, made a cooperative demonstration down the main road from White House toward Bottom's Bridge, on the Chickahominy River, directly east of Richmond. He had been instructed to hold a position there until Getty had accomplished his mission. Keyes made contact with the Confederates near Bottom's Bridge on the evening of July 1 but the next morning retreated from the much smaller enemy force. Ibid., 1, 27, pt. 2, 821–37, 854–57; Dyer, *Compendium*, 298; Boatner, *Civil War Dictionary*, 41–42; Johnson and Malone, *Dictionary of American Biography*, 10:365–66; George H. Gordon, *A War Diary of Events in the War of the Great Rebellion, 1863–1865* (Boston, 1882), 122–28.

46. The Enfield was an English-made rifle, adopted by the British Army in 1855. Large quantities were imported by both Union and Confederacy, smaller numbers being manufactured under contract in America. It featured a bore diameter of .577 of an inch, fired minié ball-like ammunition, was very accurate at eight hundred yards and fairly accurate for an additional three hundred. Boatner, *Civil War Dictionary*, 266.

47. The Confederates at the South Anna bridge did have an impressive array of artillery, much of it mounted on flatcars. But an unwillingness to expose his own artillery by drawing fire stopped Getty from engaging in a cannon duel. General Foster found that the enemy's guns commanded the surrounding terrain and enfiladed all the roads. Moreover, the defending force was reported to be almost equal in size to the Federals and well dug-in. *Official Records*, 1, 27, pt. 2, 837–42, 854.

48. So much of this fruit was found along their route that the men in Getty's column remembered the offensive of July 1–7 as the "Blackberry Raid." See Sheldon B. Thorpe, *The History of the Fifteenth Connecticut Volunteers in the War for the Defense of the Union, 1861–1865* (New Haven, 1893), 51; J. A. Mowris, *A History of the One hundred and Seventeenth Regiment, N. Y. Volunteers* . . . (Hartford, Conn., 1866), 73; William L. Hyde, *History of the One Hundred and Twelfth Regiment N. Y. Volunteers* (Fredonia, N.Y., 1866), 38; B. F. Blakeslee, *History of the Sixteenth Connecticut Volunteers* (Hartford, Conn., 1875), 39.

49. King William Court House was eight miles due north of White House, between the Mattapony and Pamunkey Rivers. It adjoined the main road to West Point, a major communications line above the Virginia peninsula.

50. Edward was correct about the extent of action at the South Anna bridge, although he misidentified one of the regiments engaged. The fighting was borne strictly by Getty's attached demi-brigade, under Colonel David W. Wardrop of the Ninety-ninth New York. It consisted of Wardrop's regiment and the 118th New York, Lieutenant Colonel Oliver Keese, Jr. Wardrop sent two companies of Keese's outfit against the rail span and, when they ground to a halt in long-range skirmishing, added another company of the regiment, plus one from his own. Some of Dix's cavalry, supported by the Massachusetts battery, also came under fire, but were not actively engaged. Wardrop's casualty total was two killed, ten wounded, and four missing. *Official Records*, 1, 27, pt. 2, 842–54.

51. A corduroy bridge was one whose floor had been shored up by branches or the split trunks of small trees, laid side by side. A similar process improved traction on muddy or otherwise impassable roads. Boatner, *Civil War Dictionary*, 176.

52. More commonly known as Big Bethel, this site, eight miles above Hampton, Virginia, saw the first land battle in the eastern theater of the war. This was familiar ground to the Third New York: here it was, in June 1861, that the regiment came under friendly fire from artillery, receiving an almost tragic introduction to combat. Joseph B. Carr, "Operations of 1861 About Fort Monroe," *Battles and Leaders*, 2:144–52.

53. Edward was far off base with these figures, if his departmental commander is to be believed. Dix estimated that fewer than twenty thousand Confederates (including home guards, plus veterans outside the city proper) defended Richmond on 1 July 1863. He placed his own command at

sixteen thousand: ten thousand in Getty's column, the rest under Keyes. *Official Records*, 1, 27, pt. 2, 821, 823.

54. Edward is referring to the New York City draft riots of July 1863. On Saturday, the eleventh, a U.S. marshal began to draw the names of enrolled residents who would be conscripted into the army. Public anger and resentment resulted; when the drafting resumed on Monday, mobs of dissenters ransacked government offices, then private dwellings. Soon a crowd fifty thousand strong, egged on by anti-draft and anti-black spokesmen, was sweeping parts of the city. The rioters burned a Negro orphanage and church, attacked the offices of the *Tribune*, set fires, looted homes and stores, caused over one hundred deaths, and inflicted $1.5 million in damage. Not till city, state, and federal troops restored order did the rampage end late on July 13. For details, see Adrian Cook, *The Armies of the Streets: The New York City Draft Riots of 1863* (Lexington, Ky., 1974); and James McCague, *The Second Rebellion: The Story of the New York City Draft Riots of 1863* (New York, 1968).

55. On July 18, General Dix established in Manhattan the headquarters of his Department of the East. His recent effort against Richmond had convinced the War Office that he lacked the drive required of a field leader. However, Dix's administrative talent and his knack for civil-military positions recommended him for the task of ensuring that no repeat performance of the draft riots occurred in the city. He did his job so well that he remained in New York till July 1865. Thian, *Military Geography of the United States*, 61.

56. Edward's hope of gaining a commission under Major Jardine died during the draft riots. In New York City when the disorder broke out, Jardine offered his services to the government. He was given a howitzer detachment, which he trundled into the riot-torn parts of the city, seeking to disperse part of the mob. Instead, he was shot and badly wounded by a rioter. Left for dead, he crawled to safety, and finally escaped through the aid of other members of the mob who had served in Hawkins's Zouaves. Jardine's long recuperation prevented him from completing the organization of his new version of the Ninth New York. Cook, *Armies of the Streets*, 153–54; McCague, *Second Rebellion*, 147–50; *Official Records*, 1, 27, pt. 2, 891.

57. A three-term mayor of New York, Fernando Wood (1812–81) was the leader of the Democratic faction that met at Mozart Hall. A staunch opponent of the Lincoln administration, he had come out for peace by conciliation in late 1860. He was highly popular, especially among the working class, which had furnished large numbers to the riots. By his vocal dissent against minority rights and federal conscription, he had (in the eyes of many observers) provided encouragement and support to the mob. Johnson and Malone, *Dictionary of American Biography*, 20 : 456–57.

58. After the battle of Gettysburg, the War Department heeded calls by New York officials and editors to detach troops from the army to protect the city against the rioters. On July 15, General Meade sent a couple of Regular units to New York—too few to weaken the army, as Edward feared. *Official Records*, 1, 27, pt. 2, 918.

Chapter 5. Charleston

1. The Gosport Navy Yard, outside Norfolk, was gutted by order of Captain Charles S. McCauley, its commandant, to keep its ships and facilities out of Rebel hands. Five vessels were burned to the waterline, four others (including the *Merrimack*, later the Confederate ironclad *Virginia*) were sunk after burning, another vessel was abandoned, and three ships sailed away to safe territory. The action destroyed about one-fourth of the Federal war fleet and cost the government one of its largest bases. E. B. Long, *The Civil War Day by Day: An Almanac, 1861–1865* (Garden City, N.Y., 1971), 63.

2. Many more than four monitors were on station at Charleston by this time. The entire *Passaic* class of turreted ironclads, save one—*Passaic, Montauk, Patapsco, Weehauken, Catskill, Lehigh, Nantucket, Sangamon,* and *Nahant*—were there, as were other, newer monitors. P. G. T. Beauregard, "The Defense of Charleston," *Battles and Leaders of the Civil War*, 4 vols. (New

York, 1887–88), 4 : 10; John Ericsson, "The Early Monitors," Ibid., 4 : 30; Robert MacBride, *Civil War Ironclads: The Dawn of Naval Armor* (Philadelphia, 1962), 23.

3. Stono Inlet is the body of water that links the meandering Stono River and the Atlantic Ocean, some ten miles southwest of Charleston.

4. This was true: only Alford's brigade left Getty for South Carolina. The latter's Second and Third Brigades went with him to man the defenses of Portsmouth, Virginia. Many of these regiments later moved to garrison Norfolk, Newport News, Yorktown, and points in North Carolina. They would be united with Alford's troops at the opening of the 1864 campaign in Virginia, as members of the Army of the James. Frederick H. Dyer, comp., *A Compendium of the War of the Rebellion* (Des Moines, Iowa, 1909), 116–17, 176–77, 229, 332–33.

5. Officers in a better position to judge than Edward had a much higher opinion of the Third New York. General Peck's predecessor at Suffolk, Major General Joseph K. F. Mansfield, observed that, though the regiment had seen little fighting, it was highly experienced and well-drilled. Late in 1862, General Dix pleaded with Washington to retain the services of the Third, which he felt among the best troops at Suffolk. The very month Edward joined the regiment, Dix termed it "one of the finest regiments in service." *War of the Rebellion: A Compilation of the Official Records of the Union and Confederate Armies*, 4 series, 70 vols. in 128 (Washington, D.C., 1880–1901), series 1, vol. 18, 385, 389, 691.

6. Fort Johnson was a harbor battery on an island about two and a quarter miles southeast of Charleston, due west of (and about a mile and a half from) Fort Sumter. There and on adjacent Shell Point the Confederates had erected a battery of heavy ordnance, including a ten-inch Columbiad, a 6.4-inch Brooke rifle, and three ten-inch mortars. In April 1861, before built up to such strength, Fort Johnson held the signal gun that started the bombardment of Fort Sumter. Beauregard, "The Defense of Charleston," *Battles and Leaders*, 4 : 15; Quincy A. Gillmore, "The Army Before Charleston in 1863," Ibid., 4 : 53; Stephen D. Lee, "The First Step in the War," Ibid., 1 : 76.

7. James Island, a large land mass on the south shore of Charleston harbor directly below the city, contained several Confederate batteries, including Fort Johnson. With its neighbors to the east and southeast, Morris and Folly Islands, it constituted the main arena of operations of the siege forces. According to General P. G. T. Beauregard, who directed the defense of Charleston, James Island posed the most threatening avenue of advance available to his enemy. Beauregard, "The Defense of Charleston," Ibid., 4 : 4–5, 14.

8. Civil War-era hand grenades were often artillery shells (especially six-pound spherical case shot) fitted with percussion caps. They were most frequently used against troops attacking fortifications, particularly those massed in the ditches of the fort. Their employment in war (in various forms) dated to the fourteenth century. Thomas Wilhelm, *A Military Dictionary and Gazetteer, Comprising Ancient and Modern Military Technical Terms* . . . (Philadelphia, 1881), 201.

9. Fort Gregg was a Confederate battery at the northern tip of Morris Island, just above Fort (or Battery) Wagner.

10. Constructed in 1798, Fort Moultrie sat on Sullivan's Island at the northeastern side of the entrance to Charleston harbor. It had been the original post of Major Robert Anderson before he moved his garrison to neighboring Fort Sumter, which four months later drew the war's opening shots. Francis Paul Prucha, *A Guide to the Military Posts of the United States, 1789–1895* (Madison, Wis., 1964), 93; Abner Doubleday, "From Moultrie to Sumter," *Battles and Leaders*, 1 : 40–49; E. Milby Burton, *The Siege of Charleston, 1861–1865* (Columbia, S.C., 1970), 9–12.

11. "Secessionville" identified a former Rebel battery seated on a narrow peninsula adjacent to Lighthouse Inlet, which separates Folly and Morris Islands. Before the war it encompassed a cluster of summer homes maintained by planters from James Island. In the summer of 1862 it was the scene of bitter fighting during an unsuccessful Union effort to capture Charleston from the south. Ibid., 98–112.

12. "Greek Fire" was a variant of a type of inflammable ammunition first used during the Middle Ages, most notably by Byzantine Greeks at the Siege of Constantinople. Shells fired with a fluid composition known as "Short's Solidified Greek Fire" (probably a solution of phosphorus in

bisulphide of carbon) were hurled into Charleston beginning in late August 1863. A terror weapon directed against a civilian population as well as an enemy army, the ammunition provoked Confederate outrage and spawned atrocity stories. The Rebels, however, also planned to manufacture the shells. See *Official Records*, 1, 35, pt. 1, 595–97; Wilhelm, *Military Dictionary and Gazetteer*, 201; and Burton, *Siege of Charleston*, 254–55, 260.

13. This refers to the *New Ironsides*, an iron-clad frigate mounting fourteen eleven-inch guns, one of the most formidable warships in the U.S. Navy. As the flagship of Rear Admiral Samuel F. Du Pont, she had accompanied an armada of ironclads during the first attack on Charleston, 7 April 1863. Now Du Pont was gone, having resigned under a cloud stemming from the failure of that assault, but the ship was still a part of the Charleston fleet under Rear Admiral John A. B. Dahlgren. Beauregard, "The Defense of Charleston," *Battles and Leaders*, 4:10–11; Burton, *Siege of Charleston*, 135–45.

14. Fort Sumter was held by seven companies of the First South Carolina Artillery, under Colonel Alfred Rhett, some 350 strong. All told, General Beauregard commanded over fifty-eight hundred troops at Charleston. Beauregard, "The Defense of Charleston," *Battles and Leaders*, 4:10, 14.

15. Cummings Point, then the site of Fort Gregg, is a neck of land stretching into Charleston harbor directly below Fort Sumter. On 6 September 1863 when Fort Wagner was evacuated, the Point was abandoned as well, along with seven heavy cannon. Gillmore, "The Army Before Charleston in 1863," Ibid., 4:64.

16. "The rebels" numbered about nine hundred infantrymen under Colonel Lawrence M. Keitt. Only four hundred of them were able to do duty by the time Beauregard approved the battery's evacuation, thanks to Gillmore's forty-two-hour-long barrage against the garrison. *Official Records*, 1, 28, pt. 1, 26–27, 88–90; Burton, *Siege of Charleston*, 178–79; Gillmore, "The Army Before Charleston in 1863," *Battles and Leaders*, 4:63–64.

17. This light casualty figure obscures the great losses Gillmore had absorbed during his assaults of July 10 and 18. Lacking the ordnance support supplied in September, the attack of the tenth cost 399 casualties out of two and a half regiments engaged, including one brigadier and three colonels killed or mortally wounded. Of 5,264 attackers on July 18, 1,515 became casualties. *Official Records*, 1, 28, pt. 1, 12–16; Gillmore, "The Army Before Charleston in 1863," *Battles and Leaders*, 4:57–60; Burton, *Siege of Charleston*, 154–68.

18. In Civil War parlance, a "torpedo" was a land or sea mine. Torpedoes strewn about Fort Wagner on and after 10 July 1863 consisted of fifty-six ten-inch shells buried in the sand in front of the works. They were activated when an unsuspecting Yankee crushed a copper cap, setting off primer material that in turn ignited a fuze connected to a powder charge. The mines caused several casualties during siege operations in August and September as well as during the July attacks. See Milton F. Perry, *Infernal Machines: The Story of Confederate Submarine and Mine Warfare* (Baton Rouge, La., 1965), 37–38, 54, 58–60.

19. Sullivan's Island is on the northern side of Charleston harbor, overlooking Fort Moultrie and about a mile northeast of Fort Sumter. It was the site of "Battery Beauregard," which its namesake had erected there in 1861 to protect the eastward approaches to Charleston. Beauregard, "The Defense of Charleston," *Battles and Leaders*, 4:2.

20. After the failure of his July assaults on Fort Wagner, Gillmore concentrated on Fort Sumter, whose long-range guns had damaged his attack columns. From August 17 to 21 his cannon blasted away at the historic fortification, which he soon termed a "shapeless and harmless mass of ruins." On the twenty-second, he selected a new target, Charleston itself. To reach the city he used an eight-inch Parrott rifle mounted on a marshy part of Morris Island. This battery, which became known as the "Swamp Angel," hurled two hundred-pound shells into Charleston at a range of almost four miles. Defective ammunition caused the rifle to burst during its thirty-sixth discharge, throwing it forward upon the parapet of the work. As one of Gillmore's aides noted: "The gun as it appeared on the parapet seemed to the Confederates as if in position for firing, and a large amount of ammunition was needlessly expended upon it." To replace the Swamp Angel, Gillmore ordered a

four-gun battery erected on nearby Black Island, work in which Edward participated. Burton, *Siege of Charleston*, 177, 186, 255–56; William S. Stryker, "The 'Swamp Angel'," *Battles and Leaders*, 4:72–74.

21. A prewar attorney from Connecticut, Brigadier General Alfred Howe Terry had become one of the ablest nonprofessional soldiers in the Union ranks. The thirty-seven-year-old Yale alumnus had risen from field officer in the Second Connecticut Volunteers to divisional command in the Tenth Corps. He had distinguished himself in numerous actions in South Carolina, including the attacks on Port Royal, Secessionville, and Fort Wagner. His present command encompassed all forces on Morris Island. At present, like Edward, he was returning from a furlough in the North. Allen Johnson and Dumas Malone, eds., *Dictionary of American Biography*, 20 vols. (New York, 1928–36), 18:378–79.

22. Another New England attorney with an Ivy League background, Brigadier General George Henry Gordon (1823–86), a graduate of both West Point and Harvard Law School, commanded Union forces on the southern end of Folly Island. Ibid., 7:421–22.

23. Meanwhile, leading the troops on the North End of Folly Island was Brigadier General Israel Vogdes, a forty-seven-year-old Pennsylvanian who had graduated in the West Point Class of 1837. A former artilleryman, veteran of frontier and Florida Indian wars, Vogdes had been a Confederate prisoner for ten months in 1861–62. Ezra J. Warner, *Generals in Blue: Lives of the Union Commanders* (Baton Rouge, La., 1964), 529–30.

24. Apparently Hawkins, as Major Jardine, hoped to reenter the war with a command built from the men of his old regiment. The refusal of the erstwhile Ninth New Yorkers to leave the Third New York for his proposed outfit may have foiled Hawkins's plans. Perhaps also because of the tarnish given his career by the Ninth's refusal to extend its period of service, he never returned to the field. Mark M. Boatner III, *The Civil War Dictionary* (New York, 1959), 387.

25. At Lookout Mountain, Tennessee, on November 24, and on the following day at adjacent Missionary Ridge, Grant's armies outside Chattanooga had beaten the life out of Braxton Bragg's Confederates. By the twenty-seventh, a series of rear-guard actions put the finishing touches to Bragg's retreat into Georgia. Bruce Catton, *Never Call Retreat* (Garden City, N.Y., 1965), 259–65.

26. This was Edward's old school chum, Rodney Kimball. He had recently resigned his captaincy in the Forty-fourth New York Volunteers to return to his old position as a professor in Albany's New York State Normal School. P. J. Mosenthal and C. F. Horne, *The City College: Memories of Sixty Years* (New York, 1907), 376–77.

27. A "bronze" (brass) smoothbore cannon, firing shells weighing six pounds, was one of the standard artillery pieces of the Civil War. It was a gun—that is, a field piece with no barrel chamber to concentrate its powder charge and whose projectiles described a relatively flat trajectory. The thirty-two-pounders Edward mentions were either howitzers (which had a powder chamber, and whose shells featured a more arcing trajectory) or, if indeed Parrott rifles, were thirty-pounders. Warren Ripley, *Artillery and Ammunition of the Civil War* (New York, 1970), 17, 45–55, 109.

28. Major General Quincy Adams Gillmore (another general whose name Edward consistently misspelled) was a thirty-eight-year-old native of Ohio. Trained as an engineer at West Point, he was considered one of the most learned members of that profession. Since late 1862, however, he had been a field general, first in the West, then (from June of 1863) as commander of the Department of the South. Never overly talented in this role, he had grown ever less aggressive and energetic since his disastrous attacks on Fort Wagner in July. To his regret, he did accompany for a time the expedition that Edward alludes to here, which resulted in another Union debacle, this at Olustee, Florida. Johnson and Malone, *Dictionary of American Biography*, 7:295–96.

29. The troops were bound for Florida, thanks to Gillmore's doing. A month before, Abraham Lincoln had approved the general's plan to aid Florida Unionists in establishing a loyal state government. Gillmore had suggested an expedition into hitherto inaccessible parts of the state to cut off enemy supplies and recruit regiments of freed slaves, as well as to occupy permanently territory of strategic importance. On 4 February 1864 he ordered three brigades from his department, under Brigadier General Truman Seymour, to proceed to Jacksonville, Admiral Dahlgren's

FROM ANTIETAM TO FORT FISHER

gunboat fleet providing support for the landing. The Federals reached the Florida coast three days later. Moving inland, they met such little opposition that a confident Gillmore turned the entire command over to Seymour and returned to Jacksonville. The next ten days saw skirmishing between the invaders and fifty-two hundred Rebels under Brigadier General Joseph Finegan, followed by a battle near Olustee and Ocean Pond. There, on February 20, part of Finegan's force routed two of Seymour's regiments, flanked the Federal right, and inflicted heavy losses. At dark Seymour withdrew, having suffered over seven hundred killed and 1,152 wounded. A few days later, Gillmore withdrew the division from the state, dashing Lincoln's hopes of wartime reconstruction. John E. Johns, *Florida During the Civil War* (Gainesville, Fla., 1963), 190–99.

30. Kiawah and Cole's Islands are situated off the southern end of Folly Island and are separated by Stono Inlet, approximately ten miles southwest of Charleston. John's Island, west of both, lies across the Kiawah River from the latter's namesake island. Seabrooks Island is located in the midst of the northern tier of James Island, across the Ashley River from Charleston.

31. These regiments, once part of Hawkins's brigade, were now grouped with the Third and 117th New York under Colonel Alford. They comprised one of three brigades (including one of black troops) on the north end of Folly Island, General Vogdes commanding. "The Opposing Land Forces at Charleston," *Battles and Leaders*, 4:75.

32. Lying within a stream-crossed section of James Island, Long Island is about a mile and a quarter southeast of Secessionville and two and a half miles southwest of Lighthouse Inlet.

33. A copy of this soldier-printed newspaper is in the possession of Edward Wightman's descendants. Dated 3 March 1864, it is primarily devoted to accounts of Olustee.

34. These "various expeditions" presumably included the cavalry raid of Brigadier General William W. Averell against Confederate-held railroads in southwestern Virginia, 8–21 December 1863; the Meridian, Mississippi, expedition of Major General William T. Sherman, also directed at rail lines, in February 1864; the battle of Olustee; and the raid of Brigadier General H. Judson Kilpatrick and Colonel Ulric Dahlgren (son of Admiral Dahlgren) on Richmond, which came to grief in the first days of March. Long, *Civil War Day by Day*, 445, 460–71, 474–89.

35. Late in 1863 Abraham Lincoln had decided to name Ulysses Grant, his most successful field commander, General-in-Chief of the Union armies. On 29 February 1864 Lincoln approved the congressional act reviving the grade of lieutenant general; the third star went to Grant a week later at a ceremony in Washington. The next day, Grant paid his first visit to the Virginia headquarters of the Army of the Potomac. He would travel with that command during the spring campaign, mapping strategy for it and the other Union forces, while George Meade handled the army's tactical operations. In the West, Sherman would take Grant's former command, the Military Division of the Mississippi. Ulysses S. Grant, "Preparing for the Campaigns of '64," *Battles and Leaders*, 4:97–117.

36. As part of his grand strategy, Grant had wanted the army of Major General N. P. Banks to mass at New Orleans for an expedition against Mobile, one of the last open Confederate ports. Banks's earlier decision to move into Louisiana's Red River country, however, had taken him in the wrong direction. Still, Union ships had reconnoitered Mobile Bay late in January, and in February and March additional probings took place. Both sides considered it a matter of time before a full-scale offensive occurred there. Long, *Civil War Day by Day*, 456, 464–65.

37. The most notorious political general in American history, Benjamin Franklin Butler (1818–93) had risen from Massachusetts legislator to brigadier of militia to major general of volunteers in only a few years' time. Shrewd, sometimes duplicitous, of seemingly flexible principles, he was not a brilliant field leader but was an able and tireless military administrator. He had acquired fame early in the war by seizing secessionist Baltimore and by capturing Rebel forts along Hatteras Inlet, North Carolina. On 1 May 1862 his troops, supported by the fleet of Admiral Farragut, occupied New Orleans. During seven months as military governor of the Confederacy's largest city, Butler had made a stormy, controversial record and came to be regarded in Southern eyes as a war criminal. For further details on his life and career, see *Autobiography and Personal Reminiscences of Major-General Benj. F. Butler: Butler's Book* (Boston, 1892); Jessie Ames Marshall, comp., *Private*

and Official Correspondence of Gen. Benjamin F. Butler During the Period of the Civil War, 5 vols. (Norwood, Mass., 1917); and Richard S. West, Jr., *Lincoln's Scapegoat General: A Life of Benjamin F. Butler, 1818–1893* (Boston, 1965).

38. The plethora of conflicting, groundless rumors seemed to Edward utter nonsense. Thus, his paraphrase of a popular nursery rhyme: "Sing, sing! What Shall I sing? / The cat's run away with the pudding-bag / String."

39. Another paraphrase, this of a biblical passage (Song of Sol. 2:11–12): "For, lo! the winter is past, the rain is over and gone; the flowers appear on the earth; the time of the singing of birds is come, and the voice of the turtle is heard in our land."

40. Here was another baseless rumor that proved false. McClellan was out of the war for good. However, rumors that he would return to uniform were occasionally coined by officers who thought the army's morale in need of a boost. Bruce Catton, *Glory Road: The Bloody Route from Fredericksburg to Gettysburg* (Garden City, N.Y., 1952), 287–88.

Chapter 6. Bermuda Hundred and Cold Harbor

1. This department, originally comprising South Carolina, Georgia, and Florida, had been commanded by Gillmore from the summer of 1863 to 25 April 1864. Upon the transfer of Gillmore and his Tenth Corps to Virginia, the department passed to Brigadier General John P. Hatch, then to Major General John Gray Foster. Though white troops still predominated in its new organization, more than fifty regiments of U.S. Colored Troops also served in the department. For its revamped structure, see Frederick H. Dyer, comp., *A Compendium of the War of the Rebellion* (Des Moines, Iowa, 1909), 372–74.

2. Gloucester Point is situated on the north shore of the York River, directly across the water from Yorktown and some eighteen miles northwest of Fort Monroe.

3. William Farrar Smith (1824–1903) was an 1845 graduate of the Military Academy, where his prematurely thinning hair (which never developed into complete baldness) earned him the nickname, "Baldy." One of the most talented military engineers in the army, he had the respect and affection of his troops. He also possessed a chronic inability to get along with his peers and superiors, a quality exacerbated by his egotism and biting wit. Edward G. Longacre, " 'A Perfect Ishmaelite': General 'Baldy' Smith," *Civil War Times Illustrated* 15 (December 1976): 10–20.

4. As of the first week in May, Brigadier General John Wesley Turner (1833–99), a New York-born West Pointer and a former artillerist and staff officer, commanded the Third Division, Tenth Corps. His First Brigade, Colonel Alford's, was constituted as Edward reported. Turner's command also included a brigade under Colonel William B. Barton, and three batteries. *War of the Rebellion: A Compilation of the Official Records of the Union and Confederate Armies*, 4 series, 70 vols. in 128. (Washington, D.C., 1880–1901), series 1, vol. 36, pt. 1, 117; Allen Johnson and Dumas Malone, eds., *Dictionary of American Biography*, 20 vols. (New York, 1928–36), 19:67.

5. West Point was a village at the head of the York River, on the tip of a peninsula formed by the York's tributaries, the Pamunkey and Mattapony Rivers. In this area, the Third New York's brigade feigned construction of additional wharfage and made threatening movements westward. These came to the attention of local Rebels, who brought word to Richmond that Butler was planning a movement against the capital from points north and east, not along the line of the James. *Official Records*, 1, 36, pt. 2, 327, 349; "Notes on the May [1864] Campaign on the James River," *United States Service Magazine* 3 (1864): 22–28.

6. This letter, written over a week's time, contained what Edward, in a cover note dated May 7, called "awkward jottings . . . scrawled during little scraps of time and [which] could not be sent before. They will at least show how busy we are and perhaps what it is intended we shall do."

7. This was probably the residence of Major James Christian Hill, of the Forty-sixth Virginia Infantry, later a businessman and state legislator. Robert K. Krick, *Lee's Colonels: A Biographical Register of the Field Officers of the Army of Northern Virginia* (Dayton, Ohio, 1979), 175.

8. At this point, supposedly, Alford was unable to command due to illness. From what Edward says of him later, the colonel had a habit of going on sick leave when active operations were imminent. His replacement, Colonel Guy V. Henry (1839–99) was an able leader of both foot soldiers and mounted troops. A West Pointer (Class of May 1861), he had risen steadily from second lieutenant in the Regular Artillery to brigade leader of volunteers, a post he held through most of the 1864 campaign. By war's end he accumulated four brevets and a Medal of Honor. In the postwar army he held several commands during the Indian wars and led a division in Cuba in 1898. *National Cyclopaedia of American Biography*, 60 vols. to date (New York and Clifton, N.J., 1898–   ), 9:27–28.

9. City Point is a northeastern suburb of Petersburg near the confluence of the James and Appomattox Rivers. Prior to the 1864 campaign it was chiefly notable as the site of prisoner-of-war exchanges. Before the spring was out, Grant would locate his headquarters there. *Official Records*, 1, 40, pt. 2, 49, 86–87.

10. This is a reference to Colonel Samuel P. ("Old Spuds") Spear, a prewar Regular, the former commander of the Eleventh Pennsylvania Cavalry, and now in charge of a brigade in the Cavalry Division of the Army of the James. He had led Dix's horsemen during the previous summer's operations near Hanover Junction and Richmond. Rumors of his taking Petersburg on the present occasion were false, although beginning on May 5 he had taken part in the first of two back-to-back expeditions against the railroads around Petersburg and Richmond, by which Confederate reinforcements might come up from the Deep South to oppose Butler. For details on Spear, see *History of the Eleventh Pennsylvania Volunteer Cavalry* (Pittsburgh, 1910), 165; for information on the raid, see August V. Kautz, "First Attempts to Capture Petersburg," *Battles and Leaders of the Civil War*, 4 vols. (New York, 1887–88), 4:533–34.

11. Ben Butler may have been the war's ugliest general. He was fat, with gangly legs, a bald head, a seedy mustache, a pudgy, ravaged face, and bulging eyes—which left him looking like a dissipated toad. Perhaps his most notable feature was a droopy-lidded eye, which reinforced his look of sleepy deviousness.

12. On May 4–5, most of Butler's main army had landed at Bermuda Hundred and City Point; other elements were dropped off at strategic points along the James. Because of feints such as Colonel Henry's and the celerity of the army's movement from Fort Monroe, local Confederates were taken by surprise. Landing virtually unopposed southeast of Richmond, the Federals began to fortify on both sides of the James, while preparing to move against the railroad between Richmond and Petersburg. A properly conducted operation would sever Lee's lifeline and further hamper Confederate reinforcements coming up from the south. On the sixth, however, a push toward the railroad accomplished little, Butler's column being stymied by a scratch force of defenders, later supported by troops from the Richmond defenses. On the seventh, Butler tried again, with a larger force. Some of Baldy Smith's men tore up track near Port Walthall Junction, three miles southwest of Bermuda Hundred neck, then clashed with the local troops. Despite enjoying superior numbers, the Federals again retreated to Bermuda Hundred, after suffering only three hundred casualties. *Official Records*, 1, 36, pt. 2, 34, 73–75, 125, 132–33, 136–38, 154–55.

13. Brigadier General Adelbert Ames (1835–1933) commanded Gillmore's Third Division. A month after graduating from West Point, he had won a Medal of Honor at First Bull Run, 21 July 1861, as a subaltern in a Regular battery. Following the Peninsula campaign he transferred to the infantry and took command of the Twentieth Maine Volunteers and molded it into one of the finest regiments in the Army of the Potomac. He had been a brigadier since May 1863 and had been in the Tenth Corps since August, rising to division command early in 1864. Ezra J. Warner, *Generals in Blue: Lives of the Union Commanders* (Baton Rouge, La., 1964), 5–6.

14. This action, on May 9, occurred in the vicinity of Chester Station, four miles above Port Walthall, and extended south to Swift Creek, which crossed the railroad two and a half miles south of the latter depot. Confederates falling back from Chester Station used hit-and-run tactics till reaching works thrown up on either side of the creek. Gillmore and Smith launched unsuccessful drives against these defenses, as Edward describes, before pronouncing them too formidable to

carry. When they suggested new tactics to Butler (who had remained behind to supervise the strengthening of the Bermuda Hundred defenses), the politician-general castigated them for their failure to push on to Petersburg. Both West Pointers took offense, and thereafter their relations with Butler were not cordial. *Official Records*, 1, 36, pt. 2, 34–36, 45–46, 49–50, 58–59, 66–67, 69–71, 75–76, 80, 96–97, 99–100, 106–7, 126–27, 133–34, 137–39, 147–49, 155–56; 1, 51, pt. 1, 1231–34, 1238–41, 1259–60.

15. This was the Richmond-Petersburg Turnpike, the main route between the cities. Coming up from the south, it crossed the line of the Richmond & Petersburg Railroad just above Port Walthall Junction, thereafter paralleling the rail line on its eastern side.

16. During any battle, members of regimental bands were often used as stretcher-bearers and surgeons' assistants. Kenneth E. Olson, *Music and Musket: Bands and Bandsmen of the American Civil War* (Westport, Conn., 1981), 183.

17. Lee was not in Richmond, but was fighting Meade far above the capital, at Spotsylvania Court House. Troops moving against the Army of the James were not heading south but were coming up the railroad from North Carolina. On April 23, Gillmore's opponent at Charleston, General P. G. T. Beauregard, had assumed command of the Confederate Department of North Carolina and Southern Virginia. In this capacity he was responsible for repelling Butler's anticipated thrust at Richmond. Suspecting instead a Federal drive on Petersburg, Beauregard had begun to withdraw troops from the Carolinas when, during the first week in May, he learned of the danger to the north. He hastened his men in that direction, and their advance contingent reached the railroad above Petersburg just in time to stifle Butler's initial advance. P. G. T. Beauregard, "The Defense of Drewry's Bluff," *Battles and Leaders*, 4 : 195–96.

18. Spear's troopers were marching past the camp at Bermuda Hundred, to which Butler's infantry had retired following its failure at Swift Creek. The cavalry's appearance marked a one-day rest between raiding missions. Its strength, however, was closer to two thousand than three thousand; it had started the campaign from the Portsmouth vicinity, not in the Carolinas; and it was led by Brigadier General August V. Kautz (1825–95), a German-born Regular, a veteran of service in the West, and a former administrator in the U.S. Cavalry Bureau. See Kautz, "First Attempts to Capture Petersburg," Ibid., 4 : 533; and Johnson and Malone, *Dictionary of American Biography*, 10 : 263–64.

19. Kautz's division was attempting to destroy parts of three railroads, the Petersburg & Weldon, which ran into North Carolina; the Richmond & Danville, which traveled southwestward from the enemy capital; and the Petersburg & Lynchburg (more familiarly known as the Southside Railroad), heading west from Petersburg and crossing the line of the R & D at Burkeville Junction. From May 5 to 10, Kautz struck the Weldon Railroad near the Carolina border and moved up to Bermuda Hundred. On May 12–17, his people wrecked portions of the other lines, cutting the Weldon again on returning to the main army. *Official Records*, 1, 36, pt. 2, 171–91; Kautz, "First Attempts to Capture Petersburg," *Battles and Leaders*, 4 : 533–34; Edward Wall, "Raids in Southeastern Virginia Fifty Year[s] Ago," *Proceedings of the New Jersey Historical Society* 3 (1918): 147–61; Edward G. Longacre, ed., " 'Would to God That War Was Rendered Impossible': Letters of Captain Rowland M. Hall, April–July 1864," *Virginia Magazine of History and Biography* 89 (1981): 448–56.

20. The "army of the southwest" was Joseph E. Johnston's Army of Tennessee, he having replaced Braxton Bragg in December 1863. Lee did implement a plan to join Johnston—but too late, in April 1865, short days before the Army of Northern Virginia surrendered. E. B. Long, *The Civil War Day by Day: An Almanac, 1861–1865* (Garden City, N.Y., 1971), 447, 449, 658, 669.

21. The fighting of May 12 occurred after Butler's army moved up the turnpike toward Richmond, the Tenth Corps on the left and the Eighteenth Corps on the right, reaching almost to the looping James River. The column met enemy skirmishers soon after setting out. The Confederates fell back steadily until reinforced by troops holding rifle pits and other works astride Proctor's Creek, about nine miles below Richmond. On the thirteenth, as Smith sought a way to flank the Rebels in his front, Gillmore sent Terry's division into the enemy rear via Wooldridge Hill, perhaps

half a mile west of the railroad. Terry was halted by a withering fire, but the Confederates evacuated the rifle-pits, retreating to their main defense line south of Richmond. This enabled the Tenth Corps to occupy the Proctor's Creek works, and the Eighteenth Corps to advance as well. *Official Records*, 1, 36, pt. 2, 36–37, 41–42, 50–52, 60, 67, 72, 78, 81, 85–86, 93–94, 97–98, 100, 102–3, 108, 111–15, 127, 129, 131, 134, 137, 139, 141–42, 146, 148, 151, 157, 163–64, 166, 170; 1, 51, pt. 1, 1241.

22. Fort Darling was the principal Confederate battery atop Drewry's Bluff, on the south side of the James and some seven miles south of Richmond. It contained several heavy cannon and a growing force of artillerists and infantrymen. Mark M. Boatner III, *The Civil War Dictionary* (New York, 1959), 292.

23. The Army of the James had dallied too long; its bickering, slow-moving commanders had given Beauregard time to make the works below Richmond formidable if not impregnable. By the morning of May 14, they were held by ten brigades of veterans, most of whom had ridden the still largely intact railroad from the Confederate interior, detouring around broken sections either afoot or in wagons. Many had arrived on the tenth and the eleventh, while the Federals massed at Bermuda Hundred for the push north. Beauregard, "The Defense of Drewry's Bluff," *Battles and Leaders*, 4:196–201; William Farrar Smith, "Butler's Attack on Drewry's Bluff," Ibid., 4:208; *Official Records*, 1, 36, pt. 2, 199–200, 205–10.

24. Butler gave Beauregard the opening he wanted, and the Confederate attack on the foggy dawn of May 16 caught the Army of the James off guard. At the critical moment the attackers cut around Smith's flank along the James River, which for obscure reasons lay virtually unguarded. Slowly, Beauregard rolled up his enemy's line from east to west. Butler eventually ordered a pullback. By evening his command was back at Bermuda Hundred. Beauregard, "The Defense of Drewry's Bluff," *Battles and Leaders*, 4:201–4; Smith, "Butler's Attack on Drewry's Bluff," Ibid., 4:210–12; *Official Records*, 1, 36, pt. 2, 37–40, 42–44, 48–49, 53–54, 62–63, 68, 72–73, 79–80, 83–84, 86, 94–95, 97–98, 100–01, 108–9, 112, 116, 122–23, 128–32, 135–37, 139–40, 142–44, 147–48, 150–53, 157–65, 196–205.

25. Beauregard mounted an energetic pursuit, reaching the western end of the Bermuda Hundred peninsula on the morning of the seventeenth. For the next several days—until the Confederate War Office ordered a large portion of his command to Lee's army—the Rebel leader tried unsuccessfully to breach Butler's lines. Thereafter, realizing that he need not sacrifice his troops, he constructed his own line of works parallel to those of his enemy. This simple expedient enabled even his reduced force to keep Butler inside the peninsula. This General Grant ascertained after sending emissaries to study the situation there. To Grant, Butler's army now resembled the contents of "a bottle strongly corked." Beauregard, "The Defense of Drewry's Bluff," *Battles and Leaders*, 4:204–5; *Official Records*, 1, 36, pt. 1, 20–21.

26. This figure is too high. According to an official count, the regiment lost 58 killed and wounded (plus eight captured or missing) during the whole of the campaign, May 5–31. Ibid., 1, 36, pt. 2, 14.

27. By May 17, when Edward wrote, Grant and Lee were spending relatively quiet hours around Spotsylvania. The outcome of the Union drive above Richmond was much in doubt. After the nineteenth, Grant would shift eastward and southward around Lee's right, as he had done following the equally inconclusive fighting of May 5–6 in the Wilderness. Edward's optimism was probably generated by erroneous dispatches from the War Department, circulated throughout Butler's army, and by newspapermen who magnified Grant's small gains into giant victories. Long, *Civil War Day by Day*, 492–94, 503–6.

28. The term "Bermuda Hundred" (or "Hundreds," as many not familiar with the region spelled it) was probably of British origin. In the seventeenth century a hundred referred to the one-hundred-acre basic grant for a share in the stock of the Virginia Company. Clifford Dowdey, *The Great Plantation: A Profile of Berkeley Hundred and Plantation Virginia from Jamestown to Appomattox* (New York, 1957), 28.

29. Beauregard's attacks on Bermuda Hundred began on the evening of the seventeenth with a decided failure. On the nineteenth, as Edward notes here, the Rebels had better luck. An attack,

after 8 P.M., on the right of the line captured a Tenth Corps picket force. Darkness and a "brisk artillery fire" forced a counterattack by one of Smith's brigades to be postponed at the last minute. *Official Records,* 1, 36, pt. 2, 935–38.

30. The rifle pits that Edward speaks of as captured on the evening of the nineteenth were, in fact, seized the next morning, when Beauregard renewed his pressure on the Tenth Corps line. This caused the advance echelons of both Terry's and Ames's divisions to lose much ground. Ames counterattacked but, as Edward notes, his Ninth Maine, Thirteenth Indiana, and Ninety-seventh Pennsylvania were tossed backward. Terry's command, especially the brigade of Colonel Joshua B. Howell, regained the position after what General Gillmore termed "a severe and sanguinary fight." During the fracas, Brigadier General William S. Walker of Beauregard's command was wounded and captured; he lost a foot to amputation. Ibid., 1, 36, pt. 2, 40, 48; 1, 36, pt. 3, 32–40, 820; 1, 51, pt. 1, 1235, 1237–38; Ezra J. Warner, *Generals in Gray: Lives of the Confederate Commanders* (Baton Rouge, La., 1959), 324.

31. Beauregard did not give up easily. He again tried to crack the Union works on the evening of the twenty-first, this time failing to drive in the picket line, thanks to strengthened defenses and the proximity of the First Connecticut Heavy Artillery. After this, Beauregard settled back, built up his own works, and refrained from heavy assaults except on occasion. *Official Records,* 1, 36, pt. 3, 70–74.

32. Edward's figure for Butler's army seems close to the mark; at this point the Army of the James consisted of some thirty-six thousand effectives. But at this time, also, the authorities in Richmond reinforced Lee at Beauregard's expense. They stripped the latter's force, against his protests, to some fifty-four hundred troops, charged with protecting Petersburg as well as Bermuda Hundred neck. "The Opposing Forces at the Beginning of Grant's Campaign Against Richmond," *Battles and Leaders,* 4:182; Beauregard, "The Defense of Drewry's Bluff," Ibid., 4:205.

33. This may have come in response to a telegram Butler received on the twenty-fourth from Secretary of War Edwin McMasters Stanton, proclaiming that on the previous day "the enemy were driven across the North Anna [River] with severe loss, and our troops are pursuing. Negroes report that Lee is retreating to Richmond. General Grant says everything looks exceedingly favorable to us." In reality, on May 23–24 Lee, dug in south of the river, bitterly contested Meade's crossing and refused to be driven from his position. *Official Records,* 1, 36, pt. 3, 177; Long, *Civil War Day by Day,* 507–9.

34. After learning of Butler's inactivity at Bermuda Hundred, Grant ordered twenty-thousand of his troops to be sent by transports, via the James and York Rivers, to join the Army of the Potomac. On May 26, the troops chosen (only about ten thousand were readied in time for the trip) began to depart the peninsula for White House, on the Pamunkey. *Official Records,* 1, 36, pt. 3, 68, 140–41, 176–78, 234–39, 261–62, 278, 319.

35. The command arrangement in the force drawn from the Army of the James was rather involved. As most of it came from the Eighteenth Corps, Baldy Smith assumed overall command. His field troops were placed under Brigadier Generals William T. H. Brooks and John H. Martindale; between them they led twenty-three regiments of infantry and three batteries. Thirteen infantry regiments from the Second and Third Divisions of the Tenth Corps were also included in the detachment. Parts of this force brought up the rear of the column, not joining the Army of the Potomac till June 4. The Tenth Corps troops were originally commanded by Brigadier General Charles Devens, Jr., but before the operation ended, they came under Adelbert Ames, the only Tenth Corps division leader involved in the movement. Ibid., 1, 36, pt. 1, 179–80; 1, 36, pt. 3, 263, 319, 372, 429–30; "The Opposing Forces at Cold Harbor," *Battles and Leaders,* 4:187.

36. The Seventh New York Militia (or National Guard) had won fame in the conflict's early days. Beloved by the city of New York, whose citizens thronged Broadway to see it off to the war, the nattily attired, precisely drilled outfit became on 25 April 1861 the first regiment to march to the relief of isolated, vulnerable Washington, D.C. For details of its career, see William J. Roehrenbeck, *The Regiment That Saved the Capital* (New York, 1961).

37. Edward was wise not to give credence to this rumor; like so many earlier reports of great

Union field successes, it was groundless. May 31 saw much of Meade's army shift toward Old Cold Harbor, a crossroads site between the Pamunkey and Chickahominy Rivers. But Lee countered with a southward movement that again blocked the road to Richmond, frustrating his enemy and setting the stage for one of the most vicious battles of the war. Martin T. McMahon, "Cold Harbor," *Battles and Leaders*, 4:214–15.

38. Major General Winfield Scott Hancock (1824–86), one of the most formidable soldiers on either side, commanded Meade's Second Corps. A West Pointer, an Indian wars veteran, recipient of honors in the Mexican campaigns, he had won the appellation "The Superb" for his fighting in the Peninsula campaign. He had also served with skill at Antietam, Fredericksburg, Chancellorsville, and Gettysburg. Johnson and Malone, *Dictionary of American Biography*, 8:221–22.

39. Ambrose E. Burnside had been allowed to return to the Army of the Potomac at the head of the Ninth Corps. Stationed north of the Union line at Cold Harbor, on June 2 he absorbed an attack by a Confederate division, probably accounting for the commotion Edward heard. On this day, too, Quincy Gillmore, still at Bermuda Hundred, repulsed some limited assaults by Beauregard, but the distance from there was such that the noise would not have reached Edward's ears. *Official Records*, 1, 36, pt. 2, 500–01, 504, 515–19.

40. Actually, Cold Harbor lay some nine miles northeast of the Rebel capital; moreover, the action of June 2 had been of limited scope and duration. A large-scale Union assault scheduled for that afternoon—a follow-up to the partially successful drive on the first—was postponed till the next morning. McMahon, "Cold Harbor," *Battles and Leaders*, 4:215–17.

41. Edward may be referring to the cavalry clash at Cold Harbor on May 31. Part of Major General Philip H. Sheridan's Cavalry Corps, Army of the Potomac, had occupied the crossroads site in advance of Meade's main body, holding it by fighting dismounted until infantry could relieve it. The Federals repelled several assaults by horsemen under Major General Fitzhugh Lee, Robert E. Lee's nephew. Casualties of this fight included the dead horses whose carcasses lined the road from White House to the battlefield and whose odor greeted Edward on June 4. *Official Records*, 1, 36, pt. 2, 469–70, 867; McMahon, "Cold Harbor," *Battles and Leaders*, 4:214.

42. The reference is obscure. The only railroad serving White House, the Richmond & York River, ran directly west to the Rebel capital. Parts of it had been burned by McClellan during the Peninsula campaign, when he changed his base of operations from the York to the James. This railroad did not stretch to Hanover Junction, where the Richmond, Fredericksburg & Potomac and the Virginia Central intersected. Daniel H. Hill, "McClellan's Change of Base and Malvern Hill," Ibid., 2:383.

43. This was a civilian relief organization that ministered to Union troops in ways that the federal government could not or would not: by promoting army hygiene, caring for the wounded, coordinating programs to transport rations and supplies into the field, and keeping track of inmates of military hospitals. See William Quentin Maxwell, *Lincoln's Fifth Wheel: The Political History of the United States Sanitary Commission* (New York, 1956); and George Worthington Adams, *Doctors in Blue: The Medical History of the Union Army in the Civil War* (New York, 1952), especially 5–9.

44. Actually, by June 7 the positions along the Union line outside Cold Harbor remained much as they had on the most violent day of the battle, the third: Burnside's Ninth Corps farthest north, near Bethesda Church, followed by Major General Gouverneur K. Warren's Fifth Corps, Baldy Smith's contingent of the Army of the James, Major General Horatio G. Wright's Sixth Corps, and Hancock's Second Corps farthest south. Not until the twelfth did Meade change this order, as Warren swung south to lead a march across the Chickahominy River and Smith headed back to the Pamunkey. By then, the combined Federal forces had suffered some 12,700 casualties in a series of assaults against treacherous earthworks ensconced in woods west of Old Cold Harbor. Between June 1 and 12, Smith's command had absorbed 3,019 losses. Only Hancock's corps had suffered more. For the part played by the Army of the James in this butchery, see William Farrar Smith, "The Eighteenth Corps at Cold Harbor," *Battles and Leaders*, 4:221–30; and *Official Records*, 1, 36, pt. 1, 996–1020; 1, 51, pt. 1, 1248–50, 1252–55, 1260–68.

45. Another false rumor. What Edward refers to is probably the June 9 fiasco outside Petersburg by infantry under Gillmore and cavalry under Kautz. Defended by a handful of Regulars and some local militia and reserves, the city seemed easy pickings, but a timid, indecisive Gillmore and a slow-footed Kautz failed to coordinate operations and, after breaching a sector of the works, pulled out in retreat. For Butler, still seething over Gillmore's mistakes during the Bermuda Hundred campaign, this was the final straw: he relieved Edward Wightman's corps commander, replacing him with General Brooks. Kautz, "First Attempts to Capture Petersburg," *Battles and Leaders*, 4:534; Raleigh E. Colston, "Repelling the First Assault on Petersburg," Ibid., 4:535–37; Edward G. Longacre, "The Petersburg Follies," *Civil War Times Illustrated* 18 (January 1980): 4–9, 34–41; *Official Records*, 1, 36, pt. 2, 273–319; 1, 40, pt. 2, 39, 200.

46. About two miles west of Cold Harbor sat an old granary known as Gaines's Mill, a landmark of the battle of 27 June 1862. That clash had marked the end of McClellan's offensive during the Peninsula campaign; afterward, his army marched toward the James River and away from Richmond. Joseph P. Cullen, *The Peninsula Campaign, 1862: McClellan & Lee Struggle for Richmond* (Harrisburg, Pa., 1973), 98–121.

Chapter 7. Petersburg

1. Sobered by the carnage his frontal assaults had produced at Cold Harbor, Grant returned to his strategy of moving down along Lee's right flank—trying to outmaneuver, not outslug, the Confederate commander. On the evening of the twelfth, he gingerly removed his troops from their rifle pits and put them on roads leading south. As part of the maneuver, Smith's command returned to White House, reembarked on transports, and retraced its path to Bermuda Hundred. From there Smith moved not toward Richmond, but toward Grant's new objective, Petersburg. On the morning of the fifteenth, with part of the Army of the Potomac below the Chickahominy, coming south by an overland march to join Smith, the latter crossed the Appomattox River and approached the high ground northeast of the "Cockade City." By nightfall his men had breasted many of those hills and were in possession of part of Petersburg's outer works. *War of the Rebellion: A Compilation of the Official Records of the Union and Confederate Armies*, 4 series, 70 vols. in 128 (Washington, D.C., 1880–1901), series 1, vol. 36, pt. 3, 747–49, 759–67; series 1, vol. 40, pt. 2, 18–19, 47.

2. About four miles above the city, troops under August Kautz (whom Butler had absolved of blame for the fiasco of June 9) and black units under Brigadier General Edward W. Hinks struck Rebel outposts at Baylor's Field. Kautz's men could make little headway against the Confederate infantry and artillery, but the U.S. Colored Troops about 8 A.M. seized a portion of the works, including a twelve-pounder cannon. Afterward the blacks, with Smith's white troops behind them, continued southward, driving other Confederates into the city's main works. Ibid., 1, 40, pt. 1, 705, 720–21, 724–26, 728–30, 736, 738–39, 743.

3. Smith was not ready to make his main attack until 7 P.M., due to marching delays, his ill health (an intestinal condition had flared up this day), his need to reconnoiter in person the enemy's works, and the inability of his artillery to deploy at an earlier hour. The evening assault broke the outer Rebel line about two and a half miles from the city proper, several batteries being captured. But the drive then stalled, thanks to Smith's unwillingness to push onward by darkness. When the advance of Meade's army, the Second Corps, came up in his rear just shy of midnight, Smith used it merely to relieve part of his thinly deployed line. Ibid., 1, 40, pt. 1, 705, 713–15, 717–18; 1, 40, pt. 2, 59–61, 72–76, 83–84; 1, 51, pt. 1, 1246, 1255–56, 1262, 1268–70.

4. With the exception of the 112th New York, which belonged to another brigade, this mirrored the organization of the Third Brigade, Third Division, Eighteenth Corps, at Cold Harbor. Upon the return to Bermuda Hundred, the regiments were shifted about. By June 30, Colonel N. Martin Curtis's First Brigade, Second Division, Tenth Corps, comprised the Third, 112th, 117th, and 142d New York; the Ninety-Seventh Pennsylvania and Fourth New Hampshire had

been placed in the Third Brigade of that same division. The 148th New York had remained in the Eighteenth Corps. "The Opposing Forces at Cold Harbor," *Battles and Leaders of the Civil War,* 4 vols. (New York, 1887–88), 4:187; *Official Records,* 1, 40, pt. 2, 553, 555.

5. When Smith assaulted Petersburg on the fifteenth, General Beauregard stripped the works opposite Bermuda Hundred to defend the city. At daybreak on June 16, Butler found his enemy's lines empty but for a few picket posts, which the Federals gobbled up with little effort. Released from their bottle, the Army of the James pushed westward to the Richmond & Petersburg Railroad, wrecking three miles of it in the hope of keeping Lee away from the lower city. By 2 P.M., however, Lee's advance had sped down from above Richmond, stunning the Federals with hammer-like blows. Butler returned to his peninsula prison. His intentions had been good, but his force inadequate to mutilate the railroad. Ibid., 1, 40, pt. 1, 683–91; 1, 40, pt. 2, 101–11.

6. General Burnside reported arriving outside Petersburg at 10 A.M. on June 16, moving to the far left, within supporting distance of Smith, by 1 P.M. There, during the next three days, the Ninth Corps attacked Beauregard or provided covering fire to other troops on the offensive. On the sixteenth, the Second Corps captured points above and below Smith's position, but lost heavily; most of the Rebel line held. On the seventeenth, Burnside's corps, plus Warren's Fifth Corps, made inroads farther north, until delaying actions negated their gains. The Federals attempted a general assault on June 18 but were frustrated by an inability to coordinate movements and were savaged by Rebel musketry and artillery fire. That evening the badly outmaneuvered Lee finally reached Petersburg in force. Ibid., 1, 40, pt. 1, 306–7, 453, 522–23.

7. These raw troops were Ohio militiamen doing three months' federal duty. On June 19 nine regiments of them had been formed into a division under Brigadier General Orris S. Ferry and assigned to duty as the Third Division, Tenth Corps. Ibid., 1, 40, pt. 1, 213–14, 234, 264; 1, 40, pt. 2, 299, 554.

8. On June 23, Turner's Second Division, Tenth Corps, left Bermuda Hundred, to which it had recently moved, and returned to the lines outside Petersburg. There it relieved a division of the Ninth Corps, which moved farther down the line. As most of Butler's troops around Petersburg were from the Eighteenth Corps, and since Baldy Smith commanded in that sector, it seemed natural that Turner's command again become a part of that corps. Ibid., 1, 40, pt. 1, 696–98.

9. The senior division commander in Hancock's Second Corps, Major General David Bell Birney (1825–64), son of abolitionist leader James G. Birney, was a native of Alabama. He had become notable as the leader of a Pennsylvania infantry regiment, as a brigade chief on the Virginia peninsula, and as a division commander at Fredericksburg, Chancellorsville, and Gettysburg. Given a corps after the latter battle, he lost it when his decimated command was discontinued early in 1864. Although not in the June 15 fighting outside Petersburg, he had led the troops who relieved Smith after dark. This summer he would attain command of the Tenth Corps. Allen Johnson and Dumas Malone, eds., *Dictionary of American Biography,* 20 vols. (New York, 1928–36), 2:290–91; *Official Records,* 1, 40, pt. 1, 303–6.

10. On June 30, part of Curtis's brigade, including the Third New York, was ordered to attack a Rebel salient as soon as Colonel Barton's brigade of the same division assaulted a nearby fortification. Scheduled for 5 P.M., Curtis's attack never took place, owing to Barton's "inexcusable dilatoriness" and "gross carelessness and inattention in moving his column over the parapet in full view of the enemy's line . . . thereby disclosing his movement." The element of surprise lost, General Turner aborted the movement and relieved Barton from duty. Ibid., 1, 40, pt. 1, 697–98, 701, 703–4; 1, 40, pt. 2, 538–39.

11. The most successful commerce raider of the war, the *Alabama,* built for the Confederacy in English shipyards, had been launched in May 1862. Under Captain Raphael Semmes, she roamed the Atlantic, menacing U.S. vessels, some seventy of which she sank, burned, or captured. Challenged off the coast of France on June 19, she had been sunk near Cherbourg by Captain John A. Winslow's U.S.S. *Kearsarge.* John M. Browne, "The Duel Between the 'Alabama' and the 'Kearsarge'," *Battles and Leaders,* 4:615–25.

12. This was an expedition from the Shenandoah Valley to the gates of Washington, D.C., led by

Major General Jubal A. Early (1816–94), one of the most cantankerous and talented infantry commanders in the Army of Northern Virginia. Edward's mention of "Ewell's Raid" was a reference to Early's predecessor in command of Lee's Second Corps, Lieutenant General Richard Stoddert Ewell. To divert Union might from Lee, "Old Jube" led ten thousand infantrymen and attached cavalry northward from Staunton, Virginia, reaching Frederick, Maryland on July 9. Planning to assault the capital's defenses on the twelfth, he skirmished near Fort Stevens, in the Washington suburbs, where Abraham Lincoln, an interested spectator, came under fire. At last deciding he lacked the strength to carry the city, Early withdrew that night, crossed the Potomac, and outdistanced bands of pursuers. For details, see Frank E. Vandiver, *Jubal's Raid: General Early's Famous Attack on Washington in 1864* (New York, 1960).

13. In Georgia, as Grant moved against Lee, Richmond, and Petersburg, Sherman was closing in on the Confederate stronghold of Atlanta. The drive had begun early in May and by now was approaching success. On the day before Edward wrote, Sherman's armies crossed the Chattahoochee River, the last great barrier between them and their objective. Johnston's Army of Tennessee fell back before the invaders, as it had time and again during the past two months. The next day the hierarchy in Richmond, exasperated by Johnston's conservative, defensive, prudent tactics, replaced him with a born gambler, Lieutenant General John Bell Hood. Hood promptly attacked—losing heavily and making Atlanta's capture certain. See Samuel Carter III, *The Siege of Atlanta* (New York, 1973), 175–319.

14. The Sixth Corps, Army of the Potomac, was sent to Washington, at the government's request, to oppose Early. Most of General Wright's command reached the capital at noon on July 11; reports of its arrival helped convince Old Jube to forego an all-out assault. Two days before, an advance division of the Sixth, under Brigadier General James B. Ricketts, had opposed the raiders at the Battle of the Monocacy. Jubal A. Early, "Early's March to Washington in 1864," *Battles and Leaders*, 4:492–99; "The Opposing Forces at the Monocacy, Md.," Ibid., 4:499.

15. Eight days before Edward wrote, the Second Corps had left its rifle pits, moving south to plug the gap made by the Sixth Corps' departure for Washington. Three days later part of the Second moved still farther south, to support a cavalry operation in that sector. When the corps shifted locations, it filled in its old trenches, to deny them to attack-minded Confederates. *Official Records*, 1, 40, pt. 1, 320–21; 1, 40, pt. 3, 100–02, 131–32, 158–60, 186–87, 189, 215, 232, 237, 261, 266, 280–81.

16. Two units of blacks had recently changed positions, both formerly stationed near the Tenth Corps' position northeast of Petersburg. U.S. Colored Troops of the Eighteenth Corps had gone to bolster the Bermuda Hundred lines against an anticipated attack. Meanwhile, Ferrero's division of the Ninth Corps, Army of the Potomac, had been changing locations throughout July, mostly to do fatigue duty in sectors occupied by other corps. At other times during this period, Ferrero's blacks went to the rear to drill for the attack they expected to make when the magazine tunnel under the Rebel lines opposite Burnside was detonated. Ibid., 1, 40, pt. 1, 320, 523–24, 594–95; 1, 40, pt. 3, 182, 223–24, 281, 287, 290–91, 304, 307–8.

17. At this time several command changes took place within Butler's army. On July 18, General Terry relieved General Brooks in command of the Tenth Corps (a post into which David Birney would move, five days later). Also on the eighteenth, General Martindale replaced Baldy Smith at the head of the Eighteenth Corps. Smith lost his position because he had antagonized not only Butler but also Meade (whom he blamed for the butchery at Cold Harbor) and Grant (whom he blamed for not removing Butler and Meade). Grant decided to jettison him in the interests of harmony. Martindale held the command only until the twenty-second, when Major General Edward O. C. Ord took it on a permanent basis. Ibid., 1, 40, pt. 3, 272, 287, 308, 313, 330, 334, 359, 361, 417–18, 577.

18. Writing on this same day, a journalist with the Eighteenth Corps helped account for Edward's euphoria: "For the first time since this corps has been in position in front of the city [Petersburg] an entire day has passed without either our heavy or light guns opening upon the enemy." Presumably, the enemy reciprocated. *New York Herald*, 28 July 1864.

19. Inflated though the figure was, Butler reported a total of just under ninety thousand men, as of June 1864, "present and absent" in his department (which included the Districts of North Carolina and Eastern Virginia, as well as the Army of the James). Meade's figure for the month was a mammoth 200,000 present and absent in the Army of the Potomac. "Present for duty" figures for Butler and Meade, respectively, were 54,218 and 112,478. *Official Records,* 1, 40, pt. 2, 542, 552.

20. At this point, the fight for Atlanta was still raging, and the fall of the "Gate City" was five weeks away. In other theaters, Union Major General Andrew Jackson Smith had led a cavalry column from La Grange, Tennessee, against Nathan Bedford Forrest in northern Mississippi. On the fourteenth, Smith's raiders clashed with the "Wizard of the Saddle" near Tupelo, repulsing waves of Rebel attackers. And late in May, Major General David Hunter had led a Union infantry and cavalry expedition from Strasburg toward Piedmont, Virginia, intermittently fighting a smaller force under Brigadier General William E. Jones. At Piedmont, early in June, Hunter killed Jones and routed his army. Thereafter the Union leader mangled railroads and private property across the upper Shenandoah Valley. On June 11, he entered Lexington and burned Washington College and the Virginia Military Institute. Finally, larger Confederate commands, including Jubal Early's, chased him northward at great speed. By evacuating the Valley, Hunter angered the War Department and was forced to resign his command. E. B. Long, *The Civil War Day by Day: An Almanac, 1861–1865* (Garden City, N.Y., 1971), 509, 511, 514–17, 519–21, 523–26, 528, 534–36, 538–41, 544–45, 562.

21. On the evening of July 29, Turner's division, along with Ord's corps, took up positions in front and rear of Burnside. Ord's men, most of them in the front, guarded the Ninth Corps trenches, freeing their inhabitants for the mine assault. The other supports, including Turner's, were to follow up the attack when the mine blew. The latter occurred at 4:44 A.M. on the thirtieth, and Turner moved forward behind and on the right of Burnside's last division. Soon after starting out, however, Burnside's troops and those who were supposed to support them got tangled up. Turner's progress was so impeded that the division of Adelbert Ames, in his rear, could not move at all. It developed that egress from Burnside's lines could be accomplished only by a long, narrow trench, blocked by an overflow of attackers. Only a few of Turner's people got into the fray; the rest, like the Third New York, watched helplessly as the Ninth Corps troops, black and white, were decimated by a re-formed enemy line and forced to flee from the crater. *Official Records,* 1, 40, pt. 1, 698–713, 716–17, 719; 1, 40, pt. 3, 590–91, 596–97, 620, 632–35, 661, 674–77, 685–87. Burnside's report of the fiasco is in Ibid., 1, 40, pt. 1, 523–30.

22. The Nineteenth Corps, part of Banks's Army of the Gulf, had participated in the ill-starred Red River campaign. Upon its conclusion, the high command ordered the corps east for assignment to a more active theater. Two of its divisions, under Brigadier General William H. Emory, reached Fort Monroe on July 12. Rumor had it that Butler would retain them indefinitely. For a time some of the newcomers were attached to the Tenth Corps; but by the end of the month, when Hunter's retreat opened the Shenandoah Valley to Early and other Confederates, the Nineteenth Corps became part of an army there which also included the Sixth Corps and other troops, all under Philip H. Sheridan. Ibid., 1, 40, pt. 3, 92–93, 206, 379–80, 420, 434, 483–84, 488, 491–92, 494–95, 675, 709–10, 712.

23. The "late fighting" had taken place above the James, from August 13 to 20. Aware of Early's departure for the Shenandoah, Grant surmised that Lee's defenses along Bailey's Creek had been depleted of additional troops sent to Early as supports. Grant mapped an offensive there by Birney's Tenth Corps (minus only the brigade in which the Third New York served), plus the Second Corps and a division of Meade's cavalry. The operation carried Birney toward Chaffin's Bluff and Richmond, while much of the Second Corps assaulted Rebel works near Fussell's Mill, and the cavalry made a dash at the enemy capital. Instead of thinly held lines, the Federals encountered heavy opposition, especially on the Second Corps' front. Days of attack and counterattack ended on the night of the twentieth with a Union withdrawal. Some twenty-nine hundred Federals and one thousand Confederates had become casualties during the week-long offensive. Ibid., 1, 42, pt. 1, 18, 99, 216–21, 677–78.

24. In the third week in August, Edward's division leader fell victim to malaria. Sent to Fort Monroe, he suddenly worsened on the twenty-eighth, and rumors of his death made the rounds. On September 2, however, Turner rallied. After prolonged convalescence, he returned to duty, but as Butler's chief of staff. Robert S. Foster replaced him in command of the Second Division, Tenth Corps. *New York Herald,* 31 August, 4 September 1864; *Official Records,* 1, 42, pt. 3, 670.

25. The Petersburg & Weldon Railroad had been the scene of much fighting in past months, as Grant sought to cut Lee's communication lines. In late June, the lieutenant general sent cavalry (including Kautz) to break it, while a large infantry force pushed westward toward other portions of it. Both operations foundered against heavy opposition. In mid-August, Grant tried again, sending the Fifth Corps and some horsemen to wreck the tracks just below Petersburg. Again stiff resistance prevented complete success. From the twenty-second to the twenty-fourth of August the Second Corps, just back from its movement north of the James, wrecked miles of trackage; on the twenty-fifth, a ferocious assault at Reams's Station crumpled the Federals and sent them scurrying north in panic. The Army of the Potomac held that part of the railroad near Globe Tavern, two miles south of the Petersburg defenses. Ibid., 1, 40, pt. 1, 325–30, 366–67, 388; 1, 42, pt. 1, 219–30, 250–54, 293–94, 428–32, 544–45; Orlando B. Willcox, "Actions on the Weldon Railroad," *Battles and Leaders,* 4:568–73.

26. Burnside's headquarters had been near the Dunn house, inside the old line of Battery Twelve, east of Petersburg. The house stood about one and three-quarters miles south of the Appomattox, quite a stretch for a command as depleted as the Tenth Corps to hold. Burnside's headquarters no longer existed, for Burnside was gone—this time for good. A court of inquiry, meeting at Second Corps headquarters from August 6 to September 9, had found him grossly negligent in planning and conducting the assault at the crater mine. The record of the court is in the *Official Records,* 1, 40, pt. 1, 42–163; the location of Burnside's headquarters is noted in Ibid., 1, 40, pt. 3, 261.

27. This was a military railroad that connected Grant's headquarters at City Point with the Weldon Railroad, enabling rations and materiel to be brought to all sectors of the Union line, in any weather. It was completed on September 12. *New York Times,* 17 September 1864.

28. This letter was sent by someone in Edward's family to the *New York Times,* where it was published as the work of "a gallant non-commissioned officer of the Third New York" on October 23. In a note to his brother Jim, Edward later expressed regret over its appearance: "I have always been cautious about attaching my name to any publication and when I have written [for news-papers at other times in the war] have done so anonymously. . . . The matter was well enough for a family letter but for the public there was too much content and egotism to make it palatable."

29. While the Army of the Potomac moved against Lee below Petersburg on September 29, the Army of the James made another drive above the James toward Richmond. In one column, General Ord led some eight thousand men of his Eighteenth Corps up the Varina Road toward Fort Harrison and other works along the capital's exterior defense perimeter. At the same time, eighteen thousand infantry and cavalry, mainly from the Tenth Corps and all under David Birney, crossed the James eighteen miles downstream from Ord and approached the easternmost part of the line, along an elevated expanse known as New Market Heights. The road taken by Edward's column was not a turnpike, but a small thoroughfare known as the Grover House Road. Richard J. Sommers, *Richmond Redeemed: The Siege at Petersburg* (Garden City, N.Y., 1981), 29–30.

30. Preceding Foster's division was an attached division of the Eighteenth Corps, composed of inexperienced U.S. Colored Troops under Brigadier General Charles J. Paine. They drove enemy pickets across the Kingsland Road, then pressed toward New Market Heights as though eager for more action. Bereft of close support, their advance echelon was cut apart by Rebel marksmen holding strong works. The blacks' vanguard penetrated part of the line before its men were killed, wounded, captured, or forced to flee. As Edward reported, their dead littered the ground for yards around. Ibid., 29–36.

31. By this time, the left wing of Butler's army, under Ord, had captured Fort Harrison, the main work on the western flank of Richmond's outer defenses. Learning of its loss, General Lee

rushed up from Petersburg and organized counterattacks, while also bolstering Fort Gilmer, north of Harrison, the key point along the intermediate defense line. Since Ord's thrust had bogged down after Harrison's fall, partly because of his wounding, the task of taking Gilmer fell to the Tenth Corps, which had surmounted defenses on New Market Heights made untenable by Harrison's capture. With Foster's division in the lead, the column moved gamely against Fort Gilmer from the east, across farm fields. Ibid., 50–79; *Official Records*, 1, 42, pt. 1, 702–3, 708, 712–13, 715, 719–20, 726–27, 760–62, 764–67, 769, 772–75, 780–81, 793–95, 798–801, 805–6, 811–12, 817–20.

32. According to one of Edward's comrades who wrote shortly after the war, it was at this point that he made his conspicuous gesture of defiance in front of Gilmer: The order to retreat "was more than a man of the Lieutenant's [*sic*] mold could stand. He turned deliberately on his heel and walked back slowly to the most advanced position that our forces had occupied!" Finally, after courting death, having made known his feelings toward the enemy, he marched just as slowly to the rear. *New York Independent*, c. 22 January 1865, clipping in the possession of Mrs. Edith Wightman Kreitler, Radnor, Pennsylvania.

33. The day after Fort Harrison fell, Lee launched his counterassaults. The Union troops, now well dug in, fought off each of them and held their ground. That same day, after the enemy had spent its effort, Terry's infantry and Kautz's cavalry made a partially successful effort to extend Butler's gains by pushing up the Darbytown (or Central) Road, Kautz moving to within three miles of Richmond's northeast corner. Renewed Confederate vigor forced both leaders to retire, though not as far as to the starting point of their drive. Finally, the Army of the Potomac, during its movement of September 29, had not captured Petersburg. Meade's Fifth and Ninth Corps (the latter now under Major General John G. Parke), with a division of cavalry, charged across Peebles's farm, capturing Rebel works and trenches and hundreds of prisoners. Fighting in that vicinity continued until October 2. For the Terry-Kautz offensive, see Sommers, *Richmond Redeemed*, 93–94, 100–10, 132; and *Official Records*, 1, 42, pt. 1, 713, 716, 720, 730. For Peebles's Farm, see Ibid., 1, 42, pt. 1, 545–46, 552–55, 558, 561–66, 570–75, 578–88, 601–4, 634; and Sommers, *Richmond Redeemed*, 178–417.

34. Deep Bottom was a run on the north side of the James, near a point where the stream makes a curling loop known as Jones's Neck, perhaps four and a half miles southeast of Richmond. There the Tenth Corps column had landed after crossing the James by pontoon bridge on the night of September 28. Ibid., 13–14, 21–22, 26–30.

35. The Union's most prominent Democrat, George B. McClellan, had been offered the opportunity to oppose Lincoln in the November election. Peace advocates, including those of "Copperhead" stripe, had seized control of his party, and when he accepted the nomination in early September, McClellan had been handed a platform that called the war a failure and sought a negotiated peace. Personally committed to a strong war effort but captivated by political aspirations, he had made awkward attempts to reconcile his views with those of his party's leaders. Johnson and Malone, *Dictionary of American Biography*, 11:583–84; Bruce Catton, *Never Call Retreat* (Garden City, N.Y., 1965), 382–83, 390–91.

36. After fighting outside Richmond, Kautz's division had held a line of entrenchments near the Darbytown Road. On October 7, Lee sent infantry and cavalry to turn his north flank and cave in his front. After losing many men and eight cannon, the cavalry leader had retreated to the Tenth Corps' line, farther south. Pressing their luck, the Confederates hit this line late that morning and were sent reeling by Birney's infantry and artillery. Union losses totalled four hundred, Rebel casualties more than three times as many. *Official Records*, 1, 42, pt. 1, 703–4, 709, 713, 720–21, 730–32, 759, 783–92, 823–24, 826–28, 830–33, 844–48.

37. On October 13 (not on the fourteenth), Terry and Kautz once again advanced up the Darbytown Road. Not simply a reconnaissance, this movement was aimed at new Confederate defenses near the Johnson Farm. A gap reported to be in this line was not found, and heavy opposition compelled the Federals to retreat with a loss of 337. Ibid., 1, 42, pt. 1, 681–82, 685–86, 690–91, 706–7, 714, 717, 722, 725–26, 732–33, 740–41, 749–50, 756–57, 776–78, 781–82.

38. This was the newborn son of Jim and Lillie Wightman and the writer's namesake: Edward Stillman Wightman (1864–93).

39. The year's final spate of fighting above the James had occurred on October 27–28. To aid an offensive by the Army of the Potomac below Petersburg, Butler made a diversionary effort against Lee's northern flank. Part of the Tenth Corps demonstrated up the Charles City and Darbytown Roads, while the Eighteenth Corps, bolstered by one of Kautz's brigades, circled east of Richmond toward the battlefield of Fair Oaks. Suspecting that the Tenth Corps was feinting, Confederates near the capital moved against the force to the east. Despite a successful attack by one of Butler's U.S. C. T. brigades, other Union assaults were repulsed, with severe loss. By late morning on the twenty-eighth, the troops had been recalled to home base; they had suffered over eleven hundred casualties (many in captured) against 450 for their enemy. *Official Records*, 1, 42, pt. 1, 691–93, 695, 697, 704–6, 714–15, 717, 722–23, 734–37, 741–43, 750–51, 762–64, 767–77, 779, 795–97, 802–4, 806–8, 810, 812–19, 821.

40. In another letter to Jim and his wife, Edward expressed his feelings about supplying a name for their firstborn: "When I learned my little nephew was also my namesake, I was almost shocked, for, thought I, instead of having the trail of such a reckless vagabond to follow, the boy might just as easily have had the example and friendship of a model man. But since the damage is done, Ned and I will try to make the best of it. I will try to maintain a respectable name and he shall make it famous. . . ."

41. Lieutenant Dwight Beebe did not die of his wound but was mustered out of the regiment on 28 August 1865. Frederick Phisterer, comp., *New York in the War of the Rebellion, 1861–1865*, 5 vols. (Albany, 1912), 2:1721. Mention of Captain Wicks's death is made in the *Official Records*, 1, 42, pt. 1, 153.

42. This was untrue. Lieutenant Benjamin A. Whipple of Company F received an honorable discharge on the same day as Lieutenant Beebe. Phisterer, *New York in the War of the Rebellion*, 2:1723.

43. Fears were entertained by local and federal authorities that Peace Democrats, Confederate spies, and other anti-Lincoln forces would foment rioting in New York City on election day. Rumors of such troubles, circulated weeks before the polls opened, prompted the War Office to send several of Butler's regiments, but not the Third New York, to maintain peace and order in the metropolis. They did so effectively but unobtrusively: no riots broke out. *Official Records*, 1, 42, pt. 3, 444, 447–48, 470, 481, 488–89, 491, 504, 517.

44. In a November message to his constituents, Jefferson Davis had extended a proposal to receive slaves into the Confederate armies. Though not specifying their use as soldiers, the president called for the outright purchase of forty thousand chattels. After extensive debate in the Confederate Congress, a draft of 300,000 men was enacted, without regard to race. But the measure stopped short of granting emancipation to slaves who donned the gray, a provision that Davis hoped would secure British military aid for the South. Slaves were duly recruited and some were trained, but by war's end none had served in active operations. Johnson and Malone, *Dictionary of American Biography*, 5:129.

45. As Edward said, the army's Thanksgiving goodies arrived a day late, but they were abundant, delicious, and gratefully received. Newspapers reported that the Army of the James was presented with turkeys, geese, chickens, ducks, mince pies, cakes, apples, preserves, and other delicacies, much of them prepared at New York's famous restaurant, Delmonico's. Every man in the Tenth Corps received at least two pounds of poultry. *Philadelphia Inquirer*, 29 November 1864.

46. This was a scheme by the inventive Butler to facilitate passage of Union gunboats up the James River to Richmond. To bypass enemy batteries and other obstructions near Dutch Gap and Trent's Reach, the army leader set hundreds of soldiers, black and white, to digging a canal across a 174-yard-wide stretch of land enclosed inside a hairpin bend in the river. Digging started on 10 August 1864, and the canal—obstructed only by a bulkhead at its northern end—was completed in late December. By then some sixty-seven thousand cubic yards of earth had been excavated. On the thirty-first, a large powder charge blasted apart the bulkhead—only to have most of the earth settle

back in place. *Official Records,* 1, 42, pt. 1, 656–59, 669–73; "General Grant on the Siege of Petersburg," *Battles and Leaders,* 4:575.

47. About the time that Edward wrote, he had probably learned of Sherman's capture of Milledgeville, the capital of Georgia, on November 22. This marked the successful end of the first phase of his March to the Sea. Georgia had proved virtually powerless against him and his "bummers," who foraged far and wide, burning what property they could not carry off. Few organized troops opposed the invaders, for the Army of Tennessee, under Hood, had not pursued. Instead, it had advanced into its namesake state for a confrontation with the Union forces under Major General George H. Thomas, near Nashville. Outside that city in mid-December, the once mighty Confederate command would be thrashed and practically emasculated in battle. Long, *Civil War Day by Day,* 598–603, 610–12; Burke Davis, *Sherman's March* (New York, 1980), 58–68.

48. Several thousand troops were on hand that day to witness the execution of a deserter from the Third Brigade, Second Division, Tenth Corps. One of the witnesses took it rather lightly: "The Ninth Maine, near us, had a shooting match, on the 25th; but the shooting was done in a very methodical manner, resulting in the death of a member of that regiment, who had been sentenced thus by a court-martial." Daniel Eldredge, *The Third New Hampshire and All About It* (Boston, 1893), 561.

49. Edward was correct: a large-scale reorganization took place on December 3, when all white troops in the Army of the James were formed into the new Twenty-fourth Army Corps, and all United States Colored Troops became part of the Twenty-fifth Corps. This marked the first and only time in American military history that a corps organization was devoted exclusively to black troops. *Official Records,* 1, 42, pt. 3, 791, 802, 818; Edward G. Longacre, "Black Troops in the Army of the James," *Military Affairs* 45 (1981): 1.

Chapter 8. Fort Fisher

1. On December 10, Sherman's armies reached Savannah, ending their trek through Georgia. Opposed by ten thousand troops under William J. Hardee, Sherman decided to invest the city. Not till the thirteenth did his people capture Fort McAllister, below the city, dooming its residents. On the twentieth, Hardee evacuated, and next day the invaders marched in, seized 250 heavy cannon and large amounts of materiel, but nabbed few of Hardee's men. Burke Davis, *Sherman's March* (New York, 1980), 98–119.

2. The white troops belonged to Ames's Second Division, Twenty-fourth Corps, the blacks to the Third Division, Twenty-fifth Corps, under Charles J. Paine. The latter command had made the gallant but futile initial assault below New Market Heights, September 29. The aggregate force numbered sixty-five hundred effectives and two batteries. *War of the Rebellion: A Compilation of the Official Records of the Union and Confederate Armies,* 4 series, 70 vols. in 128 (Washington, D.C., 1880–1901), series 1, vol. 42, pt. 1, 966, 972.

3. This was the gist of the order that Grant gave to Butler during the formative stages of the expedition. Butler later claimed he had received authority to use discretion as to assaulting or withdrawing from North Carolina. Grant maintained that no such discretion had been authorized, that if Butler found he was unable to take Fort Fisher by storm, he must lay siege to it. Ibid., 1, 42, pt. 1, 970.

4. Major General Godfrey Weitzel (1835–84), an Ohio native and an 1855 graduate of West Point, was the newly named commander of the Twenty-fifth Corps. Grant had designated him— not Butler—the leader of the expedition. Earlier in the conflict, Weitzel had served as Butler's chief engineer in the Army of the Gulf, becoming the politician-general's protégé. Under Butler's patronage, he had been jumped from first lieutenant to brigadier of volunteers. At that rank he led a brigade, then a division, in the Nineteenth Corps, and in the 1864 campaign he had acquired an Eighteenth Corps division, and finally that corps itself. Again thanks to Butler, Weitzel had received a second star in November 1864. He was an able engineer, as were so many commanders in

the Army of the James, but he sometimes doubted his own abilities in field leadership. His recommendation, during a Christmas Day reconnaissance, that Butler abort his assault against an apparently impregnable Fort Fisher, assured the failure of the December expedition. Allen Johnson and Dumas Malone, eds., *Dictionary of American Biography*, 20 vols. (New York, 1928–36), 19:616–17.

5. It was Butler's contention that Admiral Porter's war fleet had dawdled too long at Beaufort, North Carolina, and that by the time it hove to off Fort Fisher, the element of surprise had been lost and the garrison had been bolstered. Actually, Butler had been so secretive about his plans and so reluctant to cooperate with the Navy that he failed to reach an understanding with Porter as to the time and place of a rendezvous. *Official Records*, 1, 42, pt. 1, 967, 969; John G. Barrett, *The Civil War in North Carolina* (Chapel Hill, N.C., 1963), 266.

6. By now Sherman's investment of Savannah had made news up and down the East coast, as had the story of General Thomas's decisive victory over Hood at Nashville. E. B. Long, *The Civil War Day by Day: An Almanac, 1861–1865* (Garden City, N.Y., 1971), 610–16.

7. From December 7 to 11, Warren's Fifth Corps, plus a Second Corps division and a cavalry division, had destroyed the Weldon Railroad as far south as Hicksford, forty miles below Petersburg. Finally halted by Confederate infantry, the Federals did not continue into North Carolina but returned to the investment lines outside the Cockade City. *Official Records*, 1, 42, pt. 1,. 350–57, 361–62, 369–70, 399–400, 443–47, 459–60, 473, 477, 479, 481–82, 497–502, 507–8, 514, 516–17, 519–24, 526–33, 544, 610–13, 630–34, 638, 649.

8. Fort Fisher was not a prewar fortification; North Carolina troops built it early in the war to protect the entrance to the Cape Fear River and nearby Wilmington. It sprawled near the southern end of Confederate Point (before the war the peninsula had been known as Federal Point), between the Atlantic Ocean on the east and the Cape Fear to the west. Fort Fisher had two sides, a 682-yard-long land face that ran diagonally across the neck of the peninsula, facing northward; and a sea face along the Atlantic shore, nineteen hundred yards long. Each face contained an array of bastions and batteries, mounting an aggregate of forty-seven cannon. Within the fort's 14,500 square feet of floor space were several bombproof traverses, many rising ten feet above the fort's twenty-foot-tall parapets. Outer defenses included ditches, palisades, advance batteries, a torpedo-strewn field fronting the land face, and special auxiliary works. Ibid., 1, 42, pt. 1, 979, 990; 1, 46, pt. 1, 406–9; William Lamb, "The Defense of Fort Fisher," *Battles and Leaders of the Civil War*, 4 vols. (New York, 1887–88), 4:642–43; Barrett, *Civil War in North Carolina*, 265–66.

9. The first contingent of the two thousand-odd Federals to reach shore disembarked at about 2:30 P.M., some two and a half miles above the garrison. About a quarter mile farther on, they came to a detached work called the Flag Pond Battery, which contained one disabled twenty-pounder cannon and about one hundred North Carolina Junior Reserves, who, finding themselves cut off from Colonel William Lamb's garrison, promptly surrendered. But the Union infantry did not make the capture: parties of sailors sent out in boats from Porter's ironclad fleet had the young Rebels in custody before General Ames's first division could reach the battery. *Official Records*, 1, 42, pt. 1, 982–83, 986; Barrett, *Civil War in North Carolina*, 269.

10. The navy's bombardment forced the Rebel garrison from the parapets and into its bombproofs. One shell also cut the fort's main flagstaff, pitching the Rebel colors onto the wall of the land face. Lieutenant William H. Walling of the 142nd New York raced through a gap in the fort's stockade, seized the fallen banner, and brought it off. For his daring, he later received a Medal of Honor. *Official Records*, 1, 42, pt. 1, 850, 968, 976, 984–85; *The Medal of Honor of the United States Army* (Washington, D.C., 1948), 183.

11. Porter's fleet had not beaten a retreat, as had Butler. The admiral pulled back to Beaufort but remained on station until, as he expected, the army returned to finish the job so poorly begun under the former Massachusetts legislator. Barrett, *Civil War in North Carolina*, 270–71.

12. The Rebel gunners held their fire during much of the fighting on Christmas Day, deciding not to reply to Porter's thunderous barrage. This cannonade, however, disabled only a few guns, mostly through damage to their carriages. *Official Records*, 1, 42, pt. 1, 979–80, 1001–8.

13. This was not so: Grant's intention had been to seize the fort itself, and conceivably Wilmington as well, before Confederate reinforcements made these objectives unattainable. Charleston would fall on 18 February 1865 as a result of Sherman's northward foray through the Palmetto State. Ibid., 1, 42, pt. 1, 970; Long, *Civil War Day by Day*, 639–40.

14. During the second Fort Fisher expedition, the newly promoted General Curtis, one of the first officers to enter the enemy works, received four wounds (one, in the face, cost him an eye) as well as a Medal of Honor. This award also went to another brigade leader severely wounded on January 15, Colonel Galusha Pennypacker, of Pennsylvania. *Official Records*, 1, 42, pt. 1, 431; 1, 46, Pt. 1, 398, 400; Johnson and Malone, *Dictionary of American Biography*, 4:618–19; *Medal of Honor*, 184.

15. Some eight thousand Federals had indeed landed near Masonboro (not "Gainsboro") Inlet, almost twenty miles northeast of the fort, on January 14. They were not, however, bound for Wilmington. Not until five weeks after Fort Fisher's surrender—by which time Terry's command had been augmented by part of Major General John M. Schofield's Twenty-third Corps from Nashville—did the Federals move against the now-isolated city. It fell with little resistance on 22 February 1865. Barrett, *Civil War in North Carolina*, 280–84; Long, *Civil War Day by Day*, 641–42.

16. This rumor was false. Currently, Hancock was in the East, organizing a command in the Veteran Reserve Corps. The corps was composed of soldiers who, like he, had been partially disabled by wounds or illness but could still do limited duty. Johnson and Malone, *Dictionary of American Biography*, 8:222.

17. The historian of Edward's old regiment, the Ninth New York, wrote that the sergeant major "led a detachment . . . over the parapet [at the northwestern corner of the land face] in the most gallant manner, driving the defenders successively, step by step, from traverse to traverse, encouraging his men by voice and example and winning the admiration of all who saw him until he fell dead, literally in the ranks of the enemy." Matthew J. Graham, *The Ninth Regiment New York Volunteers (Hawkins' Zouaves): Being a History of the Regiment and Veteran Association from 1860 to 1900* (New York, 1900), 445.

Epilogue

1. Gideon Welles (1802–78), who had helped Lincoln build a strong, modern navy, was a former Connecticut editor and politician. He and Stillman Wightman had served together in the Connecticut legislature in the late 1820s and early 1830s. Allen Johnson and Dumas Malone, eds., *Dictionary of American Biography*, 20 vols. (New York, 1928–36), 19:629.

2. The Rip Raps, an island off Hampton Roads, was the site of Fort Calhoun, a military engineering headquarters. Robert E. Lee had served there in the summer of 1834 as a young lieutenant. Douglas Southall Freeman, *R. E. Lee: A Biography*, 4 vols. (New York, 1934), 1:124–27.

3. "Fort Lamb" was the Mound Battery, a two-gun work on the southern end of Fort Fisher's sea face, hard by the Atlantic shore. Its earthen walls stood sixty feet high and provided a "plunging fire" on the sea channel at that point. William Lamb, "The Defense of Fort Fisher," *Battles and Leaders of the Civil War*, 4 vols. (New York, 1887–88), 4:643.

4. Some 130 soldiers were killed or wounded in the magazine explosion. A board of inquiry, meeting at Fort Fisher five days after the disaster, found that on January 16 "soldiers, sailors, and marines were running about with lights [i.e., torches] in the fort, entering bombproofs with these lights, intoxicated and discharing fire-arms. . . . persons were seen with lights searching for plunder in the main magazine some ten or fifteen minutes previous to the explosion." *War of the Rebellion: A Compilation of the Official Records of the Union and Confederate Armies*, 4 series, 70 vols. in 128 (Washington, D.C., 1880–1901), series 1, vol. 46, pt. 1, 132, 401, 421–22, 425–31.

INDEX

Adair, Pvt. John B., 45
Adelaide, 147
Ainsworth, Capt. Andrew, 238
Alabama, 200, 276
Albany, N.Y., 160, 208, 231, 261, 267
Alexandria, Va., 48, 84, 95, 256
Alford, Camp, 138
Alford, Col. Samuel M., 133–34, 136, 143–44, 151, 164–65, 171–73, 185–86, 189, 262, 265, 268–70
Alida, 244
Ames, Gen. Adelbert, 175–76, 185, 221, 227, 235–40, 270, 273, 278, 282–83
Amissville, Va., 254
Anderson, Maj. Robert, 265
Angell, Maj. Jesse F., 80
Antietam, Battle of, 25, 38–39, 41, 51, 54–55, 97, 118, 249–53, 256, 274
Antietam Campaign, 15, 25, 29, 31, 38–40, 247, 249–50, 252, 259
Antietam Creek, 25, 43, 46, 53, 56–57, 250
Antietam Iron Works, 43
Appomattox River, 16; 182, 184, 192, 195, 198, 205–9, 219, 270, 275, 279
Aquia Creek, 29, 95, 101, 103, 110, 113–14, 220, 248
Arago, 156
Army of Northern Virginia, 14, 260, 262, 271, 277
Army of Tennessee, 257, 271, 277, 282
Army of the Cumberland, 257
Army of the Gulf, 272, 282
Army of the James, 16, 168, 190, 203, 265, 270–74, 276–79, 281–82
Army of the Potomac, 15–16, 71, 75, 95, 103, 110, 127, 167–68, 183, 189, 247–49,

251, 253–55, 261–62, 268, 270, 273–75, 277–81
Army of Virginia, 254
Ashby's Gap, 254
Ashley River, 268
Arthur Kill, 26, 247
Artillery Reserve, 101
Atlanta Campaign, 201, 203, 206, 277–78
Atlantic, 227
Atlantic Ocean, 148, 150, 217, 223, 233, 251, 265, 283–84
Avent, Sgt. George E., 199, 202–4, 207–9
Averasborough, Battle of, 261
Averell, Gen. William W., 268

Babcock, Lt. Col. Edwin S., 119–20, 123, 258
Bailey, Pvt. William H., 62, 79, 82–84, 109–10
Bailey's Creek, 278
Baltimore & Ohio R.R., 34, 67–68
Baltimore Clipper, 42
Baltimore, Md., 28, 32, 117, 152, 244, 248, 261, 268
Baltimore Relief Association, 28, 248
Bands, Regimental, 47, 58, 176, 271
Banks, Gen. Nathaniel P., 268
Barnes, Maj. Norman S., 237–38
Barnett, Lt. George A. C., 40, 42
Barnett, Capt. William G., 40, 96–97, 102, 124, 136, 261
Barry, Pvt. David, 80
Bartholomew, Lt. Thomas L., 65, 96–97, 102
Barton, Col. William B., 200, 269, 276
Baseball, 121

285

Battery A, Fifth U. S. Artillery, 258–59, 262

Battery A, First Pennsylvania Artillery, 262

Battery Beauregard, 266

Battery D, First U. S. Artillery, 194

Battery E, Second U. S. Artillery, 79, 255

Battery Kimball, 259

Battery Montgomery, 127, 259

Battery Stevens, 259

Battery Wagner. *See* Fort Wagner

Baylor's Field, Va., 275

Bayonne, N.J., 247

Beaufort, N.C., 222, 227, 232–33, 283

Beauregard, Gen. P. G. T., 169, 186, 196, 265–66, 271–74, 276

Beebe, Lt. Dwight, 209, 213–14, 281

Beecher, Henry Ward, 30, 249

Behan, Lt. Edwin A., 231, 244

Bell, Col. Louis, 221

Benjamin, Lt. Samuel N., 79, 90, 255–56

Berlin, Md., 68, 70

Bermuda Hundred Campaign, 16, 168–69, 171–84, 270–73, 275

Bermuda Hundred, Va., 16, 168–69, 182, 184–85, 192, 194–95, 198, 205–6, 219–20, 226–27, 270–77

Bethesda Church, Va., 274

Birney, Gen. David B., 197, 205, 207, 276–80

Birney, James G., 276

"Blackberry Raid," 263

Black Island, S.C., 145, 153–56, 267

Black River, 258

Blackwater River, 260

Blockade Runners, 217

Blue Ridge Mountains, 36–37, 55, 71, 254

Bolivar Heights, 67, 255

Boston, Mass., 13

Boteler's Ford, 250

Bottom's Bridge, 189, 263

Brady, Pvt. Terance, 26–28, 56, 61, 65, 248

Bragg, Gen. Braxton, 111, 257, 267, 271

British Museum, 250

Brodhead, Col. Thornton F., 249

Brooke rifles, 265

Brooklyn, 223

Brooklyn, N.Y., 161, 238

Brooks, Gen. William T. H., 273, 275, 277

Brooks Station, Va., 247

Brown, John, 66, 253

Brownsville, Md., 63

Buckmaster, Pvt. Robert M., 62

Bull Run, 95

Bull Run Mountains, 55, 254

"Bummers," 282

Burkeville Junction, Va., 271

Burnside, Gen. Ambrose E., 15, 23, 32–34, 37–38, 40–42, 48–49, 55, 57, 63, 69, 72, 75, 78–79, 81–82, 86, 92, 95–96, 100–101, 103, 106, 111–12, 121–22, 133, 166, 186, 188, 190, 200, 203, 208, 247, 249–52, 254–58, 274, 276, 278–79

Burnside's Bridge, 250

Burton-upon-Trent, 10

Butler, Gen. Benjamin F., 16–17, 166, 168–69, 174–75, 182–84, 198, 203, 207–8, 217–20, 224–26, 268–73, 275–83

Butler, Ellen, 117

Butler, James, 246

Butler, Mary, 246

Camden, N.C., 51, 54, 123

Camden, N.J., 27

Cape Fear River, 217, 233–35, 238–39, 242–43, 283

Cape Hatteras, 149, 157, 220, 227, 232

Carte de visite, 123

Catskill, 264

Cavalry Bureau, U.S., 271

Central Road, 280

Chaffin's Bluff, Va., 278

Chaffin's Farm, Va., 226–27

Chancellorsville, Battle of, 261, 274, 276

Charles City Road, 281

Charleston, S.C., 15, 40, 145, 147, 150–52, 155–56, 161, 163–64, 168, 219, 226, 258, 264–66, 268, 284

Charleston Campaign, 15–16, 145, 150–67, 264–68, 271

Chattahoochee River, 277

Chattanooga, Tenn., 267

Cheever, George B., 30, 249

Cherbourg, France, 276

Chesapeake Bay, 115, 220, 244, 258

Chesapeake Hospital, 231, 244

Chester Station, Va., 175, 270

Chickahominy River, 188–89, 263, 274–75

Childs, Capt. Charles W., 96–97

Churubusco, Battle of, 249

City Point, Va., 174, 184, 205, 208, 270, 279

Clingman, Gen. Thomas L., 181

Coast Artillery School, U.S., 258

Cold Harbor, Battle of, 16, 169, 273–75, 277

Cold Harbor, Va., 16, 192, 274
Cole's Island, S.C., 163, 268
Colored Troops, U.S., 269, 275, 277, 279, 281–82
Colt's Revolving Rifles, 157
Columbiad rifles, 265
Commodore Barney, 207
Confederate Point, N.C., 283
Congress, Confederate, 281
Connecticut, 187
Connecticut River, 66, 258
Constantinople, Siege of, 265
Contreras, Battle of, 249
Conway, Capt. Thomas W., 251
Cooper, Capt. George W., 29, 134, 139, 157, 248
Cooper Shop Volunteer Refreshment Saloon, 27–28, 248
Copperheads, 280
Corcoran, Gen. Michael, 112, 125, 259
Corcoran Legion, 125, 259
Cornell, Corp. George D., 45, 90, 99, 137
Corpus Christi, Tex., 253
Couch, Gen. Darius N., 82, 253
Crampton's Gap, 249
Crater, Battle of the, 16, 18, 190, 203–4, 277–78
Crimean War, 63, 86
Cromwell, Conn., 153, 246
Cumberland, 115, 258
Cummings Point, S.C., 155, 157, 266
Curtis, Col. (later Gen.) N. Martin, 200, 204, 221, 224–25, 227, 275–76, 284
Curtis, Lt. Col. Joseph B., 90

Dahlgren, Adm. John A. B., 266–68
Dahlgren, Col. Ulric, 268
Darbytown Road, 280–81
Darbytown Road, Battles of, 213, 280
Davis, Jefferson, 47, 140, 194, 215, 281
Declaration of Independence, 139
Deep Bottom, 209, 212, 226, 280
Delaware River, 27
Delmonico's Restaurant, 281
Devens, Gen. Charles, Jr., 273
Dews, Lt. Edwin, 96
Dictator, 159
Dismal Swamp, 259
Dismal Swamp Canal, 259
Dix, Gen. John A., 113, 121, 130–31, 135–36, 139, 143, 257–58, 260–64, 270
Donaldson, Lt. John L., 96
Donohoe, Col. Michael T., 262

Douglass, Pvt. Eugene, 101–2, 109
Drafting, 64, 138, 141, 153, 207, 253, 265
Draft Riots, 141–42, 144, 264
Dress parade, 51, 58
Drewry's Bluff, Battle of, 181–83, 186, 272
Dunn house, 279
Du Pont, Adm. Samuel F., 266
Duryea, Col. Hiram, 76, 255
Duryee, Col. Abram, 255
Dutch Gap Canal, 215, 281–82

Eagle (balloon), 95, 256
Early, Gen. Jubal A., 277–78
East, Department of the, 264
Eastern Virginia, District of, 278
Eighteenth Army Corps, 168, 174–75, 177, 184–87, 189, 192, 194–95, 214, 271–73, 275–77, 279, 281–82
Eighth Connecticut Volunteers, 87, 135, 255
Eighty-fourth New York Volunteers, 26, 248
Eighty-ninth New York Volunteers, 38, 40, 83, 87, 97, 115, 118, 141, 163, 165, 171, 179–80, 186, 256
Eleventh Army Corps, 254, 256–57
Eleventh New Hampshire Volunteers, 256
Eleventh Pennsylvania Cavalry, 270
Elizabeth City, N.C., 247
Elk Ridge, 58–59, 61
Ellen S. Terry, 232
Ellsworth, Elmer E., 97, 257
Emergency Troops, 261
Emory, Gen. William H., 278
Enfield rifles, 140, 149, 263
Escort, 148, 157
Ewell, Gen. Richard S., 200, 277
Excelsior Brigade, 257

Fairchild, Col. Harrison S., 40, 56, 87, 186
Falmouth Station, Va., 114
Falmouth, Va., 78, 82–85, 93, 103, 106, 112, 119, 254–56
Farragut, Adm. David G., 253, 268
Fay, Capt. John H., 166, 185
Federal Point N.C., 233, 237–40, 242–43, 283
Ferrero, Col. (later Gen.) Edward, 123, 204, 259, 277
Ferry, Gen. Orris S., 276
Fifteenth New York Engineers, 101
Fifth Army Corps, 189, 222, 254, 274, 276, 279–80, 283

Fifth Massachusetts Battery, 256
Fifth New York Volunteers, 255
Fifty-first New York Volunteers, 124, 259
Fifty-fourth Massachusetts Volunteers, 170
Fifty-seventh New York Volunteers, 121–22
Finegan, Gen. Joseph, 268
First Army Corps, 249, 254, 256–57
First Baptist Church of New York City, 233
First Bull Run Campaign, 252, 254
First Connecticut Heavy Artillery, 273
First Michigan Cavalry, 249
First South Carolina Artillery, 266
Flag Pond Battery, 283
Fleming, Lt. James H., 29, 37–38, 56, 96
Floyd, Lt. Col. Eldridge G., 151, 179, 181
Folan, Pvt. James H., 45, 47
Folly Island, S.C., 145, 150, 152, 154, 157–58, 161–64, 167, 169, 265, 267–68
Forrest, Gen. Nathan B., 278
Fort Buchanan, 233, 238
Fort Calhoun, 284
Fort Clark, 247
Fort Darling, 180, 186, 189, 271
Fort Fisher, 17, 217–18, 221–26, 229–30, 233–35, 238, 240–43, 283–84
Fort Fisher, Battles of, 10, 17, 217–31, 282–84
Fort Gregg, 154–55, 265–66
Fort Hamilton, 124, 261
Fort Huger, 112
Fortieth Massachusetts Volunteers, 171, 173
Fort Johnson, 151, 154, 156, 265
Fort Lamb. See Mound Battery
Fort McAllister, 282
Fort Monroe, 96, 110, 112–13, 115, 124–25, 133–37, 141, 152, 158, 164–65, 167–68, 171–74, 186, 207, 214, 219–22, 225–27, 231, 243–44, 257–58, 261, 269–70, 278
Fort Moultrie, 154, 156, 265–66
Fort Nansemond, 125, 127–30, 259–60
Forts Harrison and Gilmer, Battles of, 16–17, 190, 208–11, 279–80
Fort Stevens, 277
Fort Sumter, 150–52, 154–58, 261, 265–66
Fort Wagner, 141, 146, 150–52, 154–56, 265–67
Forty-fourth New York Volunteers, 91, 101–2, 109, 267

Forty-sixth Virginia Infantry, 269
Foster, Gen. John G., 269
Foster, Gen. Robert S., 17, 139, 166, 207, 209–11, 262–63, 279–80
Fourth Army Corps, 262–63
Fourth New Hampshire Volunteers, 193, 275–76
Fourth Rhode Island Volunteers, 89–90
Franklin, Benjamin, 134
Franklin, Gen. William B., 103–4, 249, 257
Frederick, Md., 25, 32–35, 37, 44, 64–65, 249, 277
Fredericksburg, Battle of, 15, 78, 85–93, 255–56, 258, 274, 276
Fredericksburg, Va., 15, 23–24, 78, 81–83, 86–87, 90–93, 100–104, 107, 139, 152, 160, 198, 247–48, 254–57
Fredericksburg Campaign, 15, 78–111, 256
French, Capt. William H., 121–22
Fussell's Mill, Va., 278

Gaines's Mill, Battle of, 189, 275
Galena, 116
Galveston, Tex., 253
Gardner, Capt. Charles T., 139, 144
"General," The, 79, 255
Georgetown, D.C., 31
Getty, Gen. George W., 78, 112, 118, 130–36, 138–41, 144, 186, 252, 258–59, 261–65
Gettysburg Campaign, 138, 261–62, 264, 274, 276
Gilliss, Lt. James, 121, 258–59, 262
Gillmore, Gen. Quincy A., 15, 145, 161–63, 168–69, 175, 177, 184–85, 266–71, 273–75
Glasser, Lt. Charles W., 96
Globe Tavern, Va., 279
Gloucester Point, Va., 171–73, 269
Gordon, Capt. Daniel D. T., 239–40
Gordon, Gen. George H., 157, 262, 267
Gosport Navy Yard, 148, 264
Governor's Island, N.Y., 143
Graham, Capt. Andrew S., 96–97
Graham, Lt. Matthew J., 96
Granite City, 46
Grant, Gen. Ulysses S., 159, 161, 163, 165, 167–69, 182–86, 188–89, 191–92, 194, 196–98, 200–201, 203, 205–9, 211–12, 214, 217–18, 262, 267–68, 272–73, 275, 277–79, 282, 284
Grapeshot, 91, 142, 256

"Greek Fire," 145, 155, 265–66
Greeley, Horace, 30, 138, 249, 262
Greene, Lt. Joseph A., 96
Green, Lt. David J., 96
Greenwood Cemetery, 238
Grover House Road, 209, 279
Guard mounting, 50
Gulf of Mexico, 253

Hall, Lt. Robert M., 194
Halleck, Gen. Henry W., 33, 129, 249
Hammill, Capt. William H., 96–97
Hampton, Va., 141, 231, 263
Hampton Roads, 115, 124, 174, 219–20,
    227, 232, 244
Hancock, Gen. Winfield S., 186, 191, 227,
    274, 276, 284
Hand grenades, 152, 265
Hanover Junction, Va., 140, 187, 262, 270,
    274
Hardee, Gen. William J., 252, 282
Harland, Col. (later Gen.) Edward, 255,
    262
Harlem Guard Militia, 101, 153
Harlem, N.Y., 94, 256
Harlem River, 116, 148
Harpers Ferry, Va., 34, 37–38, 47, 55, 59,
    63, 66, 68, 81, 94, 249–50, 252–53, 255,
    260
Harrison, Lt. John S., 96
Harrison's Landing, Va., 173–74
Hartford, Conn., 148
Harvard University, 267
Hatch, Gen. John P., 269
Hatteras Inlet, 232, 247, 268
Hawkins, Col. Rush C., 14, 38, 40–42,
    58–59, 69, 96–97, 107, 118, 122, 124–25,
    127–28, 130, 134, 158, 247, 250–52, 256,
    258–60, 267
"Hawkins's Zouaves." See Ninth New
    York Volunteers
Heintzelman, Gen. Samuel P., 39–40, 250
Henry, Col. Guy V., 173, 270
Herbert, Lt. George W., 96
Hero, 116
Hicksford, Va., 283
Hill, Gen. Daniel H., 249
Hill, Maj. James C., 173, 269
Hilton Head Island, S.C., 156, 161, 163,
    170
Hinks, Gen. Edward W., 275
Hoboken, N.J., 114
Hoes, Lt. John W., 185, 192, 202

Home Department, U.S., 13
Hood, Gen. John B., 277, 282–83
Hooker, Gen. Joseph, 79, 103, 106, 110–
    12, 127, 138–39, 168, 257, 262
Horner, Lt. James B., 96
Howard, 238, 243
Howell, Col. Joshua B., 273
Hubbell, Ezra, 102
Hubbell, Pvt. Silliman J., 58, 102–3, 109–
    10, 252
Hudson Bay, 114
Humphreys, Maj. George H., 252
Hunter, Gen. David, 203, 278

Indian Wars, 253, 258, 267, 270, 274
Intrepid (balloon), 251
Israel's Creek, 59

Jackson, Lt. Richard H., 96
Jackson, Gen. Stonewall, 249
Jacksonville, Fla., 267–68
Jacobshon, Lt. Louis, 96
James I (king of England), 10
James Island, S.C., 152, 154, 177, 265, 268
James River, 16, 168, 173–75, 182, 185–86,
    196, 209, 215, 219, 262, 270–75, 278–81
Jardine, Maj. (later Lt. Col.) Edward, 96–
    97, 106, 114, 116–19, 121–24, 134, 136,
    143–44, 256–58, 261, 264, 267
Jersey City, N.J., 230
John's Island, S.C., 163, 165, 268
Johnson's Farm, Va., 280
Johnston, Gen. Joseph E., 201, 203, 262,
    271, 277
Jones, Gen. William E., 278
Jones's Neck, 219, 280
Julius A. Walker, 125

Kautz, Gen. August V., 168–69, 271, 275,
    279–81
Kearsarge, 276
Keese, Lt. Col. Oliver, Jr., 263
Keitt, Col. Lawrence M., 266
Keyes, Gen. Erasmus D., 140, 263–64
Kiawah Island, S.C., 163, 268
Kiawah River, 268
Kill Van Kull, 26, 247
Kilpatrick, Gen. H. Judson, 268
Kimball, Lt. Col. Edgar A., 34, 38, 40, 56,
    58–59, 62–63, 65, 69, 73, 84, 90, 96–98,
    102, 106, 112, 124–25, 128–29, 249–51,
    256, 259

Kimball, Rodney G., 91, 101–2, 109, 160–61, 267
Kingsland Road, 279
King William Court House, Va., 141, 173, 263
Klingsohr, Capt. Victor, 96–97
Knowles, Pvt. (later Sgt.) John W., 128, 151, 200, 202, 208–9, 211, 213–15, 224, 227, 229
Knoxville, Md., 70

Lacy house, 256
La Grange, Tenn., 278
Lamb, Capt. Samuel T., 236–37, 239, 243
Lamb, Col. William, 217, 283
Langbein, Pvt. Julius C., 130, 259–60
Laudanum, 65, 253
Leahy, Capt. Lawrence, 96–97
Lee, Gen. Fitzhugh, 186, 274
Lee, Gen. Robert E., 14–16, 55, 78, 89, 95, 111–12, 138, 140, 168, 177, 184–86, 188–90, 194, 196, 198, 206, 208, 212, 247, 249–50, 254–55, 257, 261–62, 270–81, 284
Lee, Gen. William H. F., 262
Leesburg, Va., 71
Lehigh, 264
Lexington, Va., 278
Libaire, Capt. Adolph, 96–97
Lighthouse Inlet, 265, 268
Lincoln, Abraham, 14, 48, 79, 106–7, 130, 138, 165, 190, 212, 220, 251, 253–54, 264, 267–68, 277, 280, 284
Long Island, N.Y., 11
Long Island, S.C., 164–65, 268
Longstreet, Gen. James, 75, 112, 249, 254, 259–60
Lookout Mountain, Battle of, 159, 267
Loudoun County, Va., 69
Loudoun Heights, 66, 81, 255
Lowe, Thaddeus S. C., 43, 95, 251, 256
Lynchburg, Va., 177

McCauley, Capt. Charles S., 264
McClellan, Gen. George B., 13, 15, 25, 29, 31–33, 35–38, 40, 44–45, 48, 55–56, 63, 67–69, 72, 106, 138, 167, 171–72, 189, 212, 249–51, 253–54, 262, 269, 274–75, 280
McDowell, Gen. Irvin, 33, 249
McKechnie, Lt. Robert, 96
McKibbin, Col. Gilbert H., 123, 259

McLaws, Gen. Lafayette, 249
Mahone, Gen. William, 204
Manassas Gap, 72, 254
Manassas Gap R.R., 254–55
Manassas Junction, Va., 254
Mann, Capt. Alexander A., 185, 187
Mansfield, Gen. Joseph K. F., 265
March to the Sea, 283
Marshall, John, 254
Marshall, Lt. Col. Thomas, 254
Martindale, Gen. John H., 273, 277
Marye's Heights, 78
Maryland Heights, 59, 67
Masonboro Inlet, 220, 227, 284
Mattapony River, 263, 269
Meade, Gen. George G., 144, 168, 190, 262, 264, 268, 271, 273–75, 277–78, 280
Mechanicsville, Va., 188
Medal of Honor, 260, 270, 283–84
Meridian Hill, 252
Meridian, Miss., 268
Mitchell, Maj. R. Charlton, 124
Mobile, Ala., 165, 219, 268
Monitor, 258
Monocacy, Battle of the, 277
Montauk (ironclad), 264
Montauk (transport), 233, 237–40, 242–43
Morehead City, N.C., 232–33, 237
Morisania, N.Y., 166, 185
Morris, Capt. Richard H., 96–97, 127, 129, 132–36, 138, 144, 259–60
Morris Island, S.C., 146, 150–52, 154, 161, 164, 167, 265–67
Mound Battery, 233–34, 238, 242, 284
Mozart Hall, 264
"Mud March," 79, 103–7, 257

Nahant, 264
Nansemond River, 112, 259
Nantucket, 264
Napoleon cannon, 259
"Narrows," The, 114
Nashville, Battle of, 222, 282–83
Nashville, Tenn., 282–84
Neptune, 170
Neuse River, 232
New Bern, N.C., 232, 238
New Haven, Conn., 235
New Ironsides, 155; 219, 222, 266
New Market Heights, 279–80, 282
New Market Road, 209
New Orleans, La., 268
Newport News, Va., 51, 54, 112, 115–16,

118, 124, 144, 152, 173, 247, 256, 258, 261, 265
New York City, 10–11, 14, 24–26, 54, 63, 67, 97, 101, 105, 107, 114, 116–17, 119, 130, 135–37, 143–44, 156, 161, 165–67, 219, 232–33, 235, 237, 243–44, 247–50, 253–54, 256–57, 259–60, 264, 273, 281
New York Free Academy, 12–13
New York Herald, 32, 58, 64, 154, 160–61, 197, 230, 277
New York State Normal School, 267
New York Sunday Mercury, 64
New York Times, 279
New York Tribune, 249, 262, 264
Niantic Bay, 258
Nineteenth Army Corps, 205, 278, 282
Ninety-ninth New York Volunteers, 132–33, 260, 263
Ninety-seventh Pennsylvania Volunteers, 183, 193, 273, 275–76
Ninth Army Corps, 15, 23, 32, 39, 48, 78, 90–92, 95, 100, 110, 112, 116, 121, 123, 133, 187–88, 190, 192, 194, 199–200, 203, 249–50, 252–53, 255–59, 261, 274, 276–78, 280
Ninth Maine Volunteers, 183, 273, 282
Ninth New York Volunteers, 9, 14–15, 23, 25–28, 30, 34, 38–40, 43, 46, 54–56, 58, 63, 67, 71, 73, 76, 78, 87, 89, 92, 96–97, 99, 101, 104–5, 109, 112–13, 115–16, 121–25, 127–30, 133–34, 143, 147, 151, 158, 163, 181, 187, 205, 247, 249–52, 254–56, 258–61, 264, 267, 284
Norfolk, Va., 119, 124–25, 128, 135–36, 148, 152, 203, 247, 256, 264–65
Norfolk & Petersburg R.R., 204
North Anna River, 262, 273
North Carolina, District of, 278
North Carolina and Southern Virginia, Department of, 271
North Carolina Reserves, 226, 283
North Point, 243–44
North River, 26

Ocean Pond, Fla., 268
Ohio militia, 197–98, 276
Old Company of New York Zouaves, 247
Old Point Comfort, 258
Olustee Campaign, 162–65, 267–68
118th New York Volunteers, 141, 263
182nd New York Volunteers, 259
155th New York Volunteers, 259
148th New York Volunteers, 193, 276

142nd New York Volunteers, 171, 193, 200, 207, 275, 283
142nd Pennsylvania Volunteers, 256
117th New York Volunteers, 148, 154, 163, 166, 171, 193, 210, 268, 275
170th New York Volunteers, 259
164th New York Volunteers, 259
169th New York Volunteers, 184, 210
103rd New York Volunteers, 38, 40, 80, 104, 125, 132, 148, 163, 165, 167, 260
112th New York Volunteers, 148, 210, 214, 275
127th New York Volunteers, 29, 134, 248
Ord, Gen. Edward O. C., 277–80
Orleans, Va., 73, 254
Osborne, Pvt. Samuel, 63

Paine, Gen. Charles J., 279, 282
Palmer's Creek, Battle of, 182, 185
Palmetto Herald, 165, 268
Pamlico Sound, 232
Pamunkey River, 140–41, 185–86, 262–63, 269, 273–74
Parisen, Lt. Otto W., 96–97
Parke, Gen. John G., 280
Parrott, Robert P., 254
Parrott rifles, 75, 79, 90, 160, 163, 207–8, 228, 254, 266–67
Passaic, 116, 258, 264
Patapsco, 264
Pawnee Landing, S.C., 158–60, 163, 170
Pay, military, 253
Peck, Gen. John J., 112, 259–60, 265
Peebles's Farm, Va., 280
Peninsula Campaign, 13–15, 138, 172, 250–51, 253, 255, 262, 270, 274–76
Pennypacker, Col. Galusha, 284
Perley, Lt. John K., 96
Petersburg, First Attacks on, 190–97, 199, 275–76
Petersburg, Va., 16, 139, 169, 174–77, 185, 190–92, 194, 196–98, 206, 209, 211, 270–71, 273, 275–77, 279–80, 283
Petersburg & Norfolk R.R., 259
Petersburg & Weldon R.R., 208, 271, 279, 283
Petersburg Campaign, 16–17, 190–215, 275–81
Philadelphia, Pa., 13, 26–28, 117, 152, 248
Philadelphia Inquirer, 37, 42
Phillips, Capt. Charles A., 256
Philomont, Va., 254
Pickett, Gen. George E., 259

Piedmont, Va., 278
Pioneer Corps, 59, 252
Planet, 115
Pleasant Valley, 55, 61, 70, 252
Plymouth, N.C., 247, 255
Point of Rocks, 219
Pomfret, Vt., 250
Poolesville, Md., 31, 249
Pope, Gen. John, 33, 74, 79, 248–49, 251, 254
Porter, Adm. David D., 217–18, 220, 243, 283
Porter, Gen. Fitz John, 40
Port Royal, S.C., 157, 171, 267
Port Royal, Va., 84, 111, 255
Portsmouth, Va., 112, 125, 137–38, 141, 146–48, 150, 152, 256, 260, 265, 271
Port Walthall Junction, Va., 270–71
Post, Capt. George, 101, 109
Post, Dr. Alfred, 101
Powell, Lt. Francis S., 96
Proctor's Creek, Battle of, 179–80, 182, 185, 271
Providence, R.I., 251

Rappahannock River, 73–74, 79, 84–86, 89–90, 92, 100, 102–3, 106, 110, 255–56
Reams's Station, Va., 279
Rectortown, Va., 254
Red River, 268
Reno, Gen. Jesse L., 37, 250, 255
Rhett, Col. Alfred, 266
Richmond, Va., 13, 16, 39–40, 71, 78, 81, 85, 92, 94, 112–13, 139, 141, 167–70, 175, 177–78, 180–83, 185–86, 188–89, 194, 196–98, 206, 209, 211, 214, 226, 251, 262–64, 268–81
Richmond & Danville R.R., 271
Richmond & Petersburg R.R., 175–77, 271, 276
Richmond & York River R.R., 274
Richmond, Fredericksburg & Potomac RR, 89, 248, 262, 274
Richmond-Petersburg Turnpike, 176, 271
Ricketts, Gen. James B., 277
Ringold, Col. Benjamin, 132, 260
Rip Raps, 232, 284
Roanoke, N.C., 51
Roanoke Island, Battle of, 247, 258
Robert Morris, 115
Roberts, Col. Joseph, 137, 261
Rockville, Md., 31–32
Rodman, Gen. Isaac P., 251

Rodriguez, Capt. Joseph, 96–97
Rogers, Pvt. (later Sgt.) George W., 67, 137, 151, 192, 199, 202, 205, 208–9, 211
Rogers, Corp. William J., 45, 56–57, 73, 101, 137
Rope Ferry, Conn., 118, 258
Roseberry, Pvt. Thomas H., 93
Rosecrans, Gen. William S., 257
Ross, Anna Maria, 248

Sabine City, Tex., 253
Saint Augustine, Fla., 157
Saint Johns Bluff, Fla., 253
Saint Johns River, 253
Saint Louis, Mo., 254
Sandy Hook, Md., 59
Sangamon, 264
Sanitary Commission, U.S., 187, 200, 274
Savannah, Ga., 163, 219–21, 282–83
Savannah, Siege of, 222
Schmidt, Sgt. Hugo, 90, 99, 135
Schofield, Gen. John M., 284
Scott, Gen. Winfield, 256, 263
Scottsville, Va., 70
Seabrooks Island, S.C., 163, 268
Secessionville, S.C., 154, 265, 267–68
Second Army Corps, 63, 82, 192, 194–95, 201, 209, 222, 252–56, 274–79, 283
Second Bull Run Campaign, 248–49, 255
Second Connecticut Volunteers, 267
Second Fair Oaks, Battle of, 190, 213–14, 281
Seidlitz powder, 109
Semmes, Capt. Raphael, 276
Seventeenth New York Volunteers, 258, 261
Seventh Army Corps, 95, 141, 256–57, 259, 261–62
Seventh Connecticut Volunteers, 157–58, 213
Seventh Michigan Volunteers, 256
Seventh New York Militia, 185, 258, 273
Seventh New York Volunteers, 256
Seventh Rhode Island Volunteers, 256
Seventh Virginia Cavalry, 254
Seventy-third New York Volunteers, 107, 257
Seymour, Horatio, 135, 261
Seymour, Gen. Truman, 267–68
Shakespeare, William, 148, 249
Sharpsburg, Md., 15, 25, 55, 57–58
Shelbyville, Tenn., 257
Shell Point, S.C., 265

Shenandoah River, 67
Shenandoah Valley, 71–72, 206, 254–55, 276, 278
Sheridan, Gen. Philip H., 274, 278
Sherman, Sgt. George W., 143
Sherman, Gen. William T., 201, 215, 219, 222, 268, 277, 282–84
Shoe and Leather Reporter, 13
Shrapnel, 188, 234
Sibley, Gen. Henry H., 251
Sickles, Gen. Daniel E., 107, 257
Sigel, Gen. Franz, 72, 103, 254, 257
Simpson, Capt. John G., 262
Sixth Army Corps, 189, 195–96, 201, 257, 274, 277–78
Sixth Connecticut Volunteers, 181, 214
Sixth Massachusetts Volunteers, 130
Skirmishing, 68, 253
Smith, Gen. Andrew J., 203, 278
Smith, Pvt. John, 62–63, 86
Smith, Gen. William F., 16, 168–71, 175, 185, 188, 190–93, 197, 201, 269–77
Smithville, N.C., 238
Snicker's Gap, 254
South, Department of the, 169–70, 267, 269
South Amboy, N.J., 26, 247
South Anna River, 262–63
South Atlantic Blockading Squadron, 258
South Mills, N.C., 247, 258, 260
South Mountain, 59, 249–50
South Mountain, Battle of, 37, 44, 51
Southside R.R., 271
Spear, Col. Samuel P., 175, 177, 270–71
Spotsylvania, Battle of, 271–72
Springfield, Mass., 260
Springfield Rifle Musket, 133, 149, 260
Stafford Heights, 89, 256
Stanton, Edwin M., 131, 230, 273
Stapleton, Pvt. Thomas, 123
Staten Island, N.Y., 247
Staunton, Va., 277
Stones River, Battle of, 257
Stono Inlet, 150, 163, 265, 268
Stono River, 265
Stowe, Harriet Beecher, 249
Strasburg, Va., 278
Streeter, S. F., 248
Stuart, Gen. J. E. B., 73, 254
Sturgis, Gen. Samuel D., 69, 80, 253
Suffolk, Siege of, 124–33, 259–60
Suffolk, Va., 112, 122–25, 133–37, 141, 152, 161, 256, 259–61, 265

Sullivan's Island, S.C., 156, 165, 265–66
Sumner, Gen. Edwin V., 67, 72, 81–82, 253–57
Sutlers, 26, 34, 42–43, 46, 93, 96, 114–15, 118, 124
"Swamp Angel," 156, 266
Swift Creek, 270–71
Sylvan Shore, 116

"Tattoo," 41, 251
Tenth Army Corps, 15, 17, 168, 172, 174–75, 185, 190, 198, 201, 205, 208–9, 267, 269–73, 275–82
Tenth Massachusetts Volunteers, 26, 248
Tenth New Hampshire Volunteers, 73, 80, 89
Tents, 40–42, 47, 62, 104, 137, 142–43, 153–54, 161, 167, 214, 251
Terry, Capt. Adrian, 242
Terry, Gen. Alfred H., 157, 161, 175, 218, 235–40, 242–43, 267, 271–73, 277, 280, 284
Terry, Gen. Henry D., 262
Thames, 171
Third Army Corps, 250, 257
Third Battalion, New York Heavy Artillery, 28, 248
Third New York Volunteers, 9, 15–16, 112, 133–37, 140, 143–44, 146, 148–51, 155–58, 160, 162–63, 165–71, 173, 176, 180–83, 185, 187–88, 190, 193–95, 197–201, 206–7, 210–11, 216–19, 224, 226–27, 231, 235, 241, 248, 260–61, 263, 265, 267–69, 272, 275–79, 281
Third Pennsylvania Heavy Artillery, 261
Thirteenth Indiana Volunteers, 183, 273
Thirty-seventh New York Volunteers, 26, 248
Thomas, Gen. George H., 222, 282–83
Thomas Colyer, 227
Thoroughfare Gap, 254
Todd, Sgt. Benjamin D., 180–81
Topliff, Rev. Stephen, 246
Torpedoes, 156, 172, 174, 234, 266, 283
Travis, Pvt. William W., 62
Trent's Reach, 281
Tupelo, Miss., 278
Turner, Gen. John W., 171, 175, 181–82, 185, 207, 269, 276, 278–79
Turner's Gap, 249–50
Twelfth Army Corps, 63, 252, 257
Twelfth Rhode Island Volunteers, 256
Twentieth Maine Volunteers, 270

Twenty-fifth Army Corps, 217, 282
Twenty-fifth New Jersey Volunteers, 89
Twenty-fourth Army Corps, 217, 282
Twenty-ninth Ohio Volunteers, 30–31, 249
Twenty-second Connecticut Volunteers, 139
Twenty-second South Carolina Infantry, 177
Twenty-seventh New Jersey Volunteers, 120, 258
Twenty-third Army Corps, 284

Union, Va., 71
U.S. Zouave Cadets, 257

Varina Road, 279
Varuna, 185
Veteran Reserve Corps, 258, 284
Vicksburg, Siege of, 262
Virginia, 258, 264
Virginia, Department of, 256–58, 261, 263
Virginia and North Carolina, Department of, 258
Virginia Central R.R., 274
Virginia Company, 272
Virginia Military Institute, 278
Vogdes, Gen. Israel, 157, 159, 161, 164, 267–68
Vogt, Lt. Alexander, 96

Wabash, 150
Walker, Gen. William S., 183, 273
Walling, Lt. William H., 225, 283
War Department, U. S., 112, 130, 135, 144, 165, 207, 230, 249, 251, 253–54, 262, 264, 278
Wardrop, Col. David W., 263
War of 1812, 256–57
Warren, Capt. George W., 216, 224, 231, 244
Warren, Gen. Gouverneur K., 274, 276, 283
Warrenton Junction, Va., 78, 254
Warrenton Springs, Va., 80
Warrenton, Va., 72, 74, 254–55
Washington College, 278
Washington, D.C., 25, 28–30, 39–41, 47, 62–64, 95–96, 106, 119, 121, 128, 139, 143, 152, 201, 205–6, 230, 247–48, 251–52, 265, 268, 273, 276–77
Washington, George, 30
Waterloo, Va., 72

Weaver, Lt. Frank M., 189
Webster, Capt. Alma P., 96
Weehauken, 264
Weir, Lt. Robert F., 101
Weitzel, Gen. Godfrey, 221, 282–83
Weldon, N.C., 222
Welles, Gideon, 230, 284
West, Col. Robert M., 262
West Point, N.Y., 66
West Point, Va., 172–73, 186, 263, 269
Wettlaufer, Pvt. John, 45, 52, 58, 61–62, 76, 83–84, 102, 110
Weybosset, 220, 224–25
Wheeler, Capt. Daniel D., 233
Whipple, Lt. Benjamin A., 214, 281
White House, Va., 113, 139–41, 152, 172–73, 185–86, 188, 192, 262–63, 272–75
White, Lt. Charles B., 101
Whiting, Capt. James R., Jr., 42, 47, 251
Whiting, James R., Sr., 47
Wicks, Capt. James H., 185, 209–11, 213–14, 281
Wightman, Abigail H. (sister-in-law), 11, 35, 56, 59–60, 94, 100, 111, 117, 120, 138, 147, 153, 156, 165, 207, 256
Wightman, Charles (brother), 11, 29, 46, 60, 82, 94, 111, 117, 120, 123, 141, 153, 157, 164–65, 192, 197, 203, 206, 214, 246, 248, 259
Wightman, Clarissa (sister), 11, 246
Wightman, Clarissa B. (mother), 10, 46, 60–61, 110, 120, 136, 139, 146, 216, 256
Wightman, Edward (ancestor), 10
Wightman, Edward King, education, 9, 12; character and personality of, 9, 12–13, 15–18, 34, 231, 242, 280; as writer, 9, 12, 18, 24; as soldier, 9–10, 16–18, 231, 280; as humorist, 9, 13; death of, 10, 17, 219, 228–31, 241, 244, 284; birth and ancestry of, 10; family of, 10–11; as caricaturist, 13, 61; as athlete, 13; physical characteristics of, 13, 61, 121, 129, 150, 157; pre-war professions of, 13–14, 94; enlistment of, 13–14, 23–25; war service of, 15–17; on politicians, 17, 44–45, 68, 94–95, 106, 138, 206, 212; in Antietam Campaign, 25, 29, 31–40; march to war, 25–38; on Confederate troops, 25, 37, 63, 132, 186–87, 196–98; on army mascots, 29–30, 53–54, 120; on generals, 32–33, 45, 117, 160, 165, 191–93, 221; on skulkers, 33, 91, 99–100, 111, 137, 257; on foraging and looting,

34, 37, 43–45, 56, 74–76, 83, 97, 99, 114–15, 147; on officers, 34, 40, 47, 87, 97, 137, 151, 163, 166, 179, 185, 187, 189, 192–93, 200, 207–9; on rations, 41–42, 44, 47–48, 50, 52, 59–60, 66, 70, 75–77, 83, 89, 93, 95, 102, 111, 119–21, 142–43, 149–50, 159–60, 169, 172, 215, 220, 224; on discipline, 42, 97–98, 185; on slavery and abolitionism, 44–45, 53, 215; on health and hygiene, 44, 46, 50, 52–53, 119, 143, 150–53, 157–58, 161, 169, 205–6, 208, 227; on chaplains, 46, 55–56; on drill, 48, 50–51, 60, 63; on hospitals, 56–57, 59, 206; on marching, 58–59, 140, 173–77, 185, 187, 209; as unit clerk, 61, 99, 110, 112, 116, 118–19, 121–24, 134, 136–38, 142–43, 151; at Pleasant Valley, 61–70; on camp rumors, 67; on war correspondents, 69; at Loudoun County, 70–78; on Virginians, 72, 76–77, 148; on skirmishing, 73; march to Falmouth, 79–82; on brawling, 79, 99, 147–48; in Fredericksburg Campaign, 79–111; first time under fire, 90; in "Mud March," 103–7; at Newport News, 112–24; at Siege of Suffolk, 125–33; at Fort Monroe and Portsmouth, 133–38, 141–44, 146–49; in expedition toward Richmond, 138–41; in Charleston Campaign, 145, 150–67; furlough in New York City, 156–57; in Bermuda Hundred Campaign, 168–69, 171–84; on black troops, 170, 192, 201, 204, 209, 215; on destroying railroads, 175–76; in Cold Harbor Campaign, 184–89, 192; in first attacks on Petersburg, 190–97, 199; in Petersburg Campaign, 190–215; on fraternizing with Confederates, 196–98; on enemy deserters, 198, 202; promotion to sergeant, 202, 206; in Battle of the Crater, 203–4; in Battles of Forts Harrison and Gilmer, 208–11; promotion to sergeant major, 212, 214; in Battle of Second Fair Oaks, 213–14, 281; on reorganization of the Army of the James, 216, 282; on first Fort Fisher expedition, 217, 219–26; on second Fort Fisher expedition, 227–29; recovery of body of, 230–44; burial of, 245–46

Wightman, Edward S. (nephew), 213–14, 281

Wightman, Ellen A. (sister), 11, 46, 51, 60–61, 77, 105, 107, 120, 142, 147, 157, 163–64, 180, 187–88, 193, 197

Wightman, Frederick B. (brother), 11–12, 35, 51, 60, 77, 82, 107, 120, 136, 141–42, 147, 165, 188, 203, 206, 246–47, 252, 256–58

Wightman, James (brother), 11, 46, 52, 60, 71, 94, 105, 107, 117, 120, 123, 128, 134, 136–38, 141–42, 146–47, 152–53, 156, 163, 165, 167, 192, 197, 214, 216, 219, 227, 246, 279, 281

Wightman, Lillie H. (sister-in-law), 11, 105, 117, 153, 167, 281

Wightman, Mary (sister), 11, 46, 51, 55, 60–61, 77, 94, 105, 107, 111, 120, 123, 134, 136–38, 141–42, 146–47, 152–53, 156, 162–65, 180, 186–88, 192–93, 197, 201, 203, 206, 216, 219, 221, 227

Wightman, Stillman K. (father), 10–11, 17, 46, 60, 71, 102, 120, 146–47, 229–46, 284

Wilderness, Battle of the, 272

Willard, Sgt. Charles L., 139

Willcox, Gen. Orlando B., 63, 102, 118, 122, 252, 258

Williamsburg, Va., 139, 152

Wilmington, N. C., 17, 217–22, 227, 283–84

Winchester, Va., 70–71

Winslow, Capt. John A., 276

Wise, Gen. Henry A., 247

Wood, Fernando, 144, 264

Wool, Gen. John, 96, 256

Wooldridge's Hill, Battle of, 271–72

Wright, Gen. Horatio G., 274, 277

Yale University, 10, 235, 267

York River, 168, 172–73, 185, 269, 273–74

Yorktown, Va., 113, 138–39, 141, 152, 171, 173–74, 194, 256, 262, 265, 269

Youbedam Landing, Va., 248

Zouaves, 14, 26, 247–48, 256